THE
HOFFA WARS

This book is dedicated to Mrs. Nancy Nolte; my parents; Robert N. Davis; Cristine Candela (RFL); the Fund for Investigative Journalism and its executive director, Howard Bray; and the members of the Teamster rebel movement who have been blackballed, beaten, and killed in their pursuit of a more democratic union.

THE HOFFA WARS

Teamsters, Rebels, Politicians, and the Mob

Dan E. Moldea

**PADDINGTON
PRESS LTD**

NEW YORK & LONDON

Library of Congress Cataloging in Publication Data
Moldea, Dan E 1950–
 The Hoffa wars.
 Includes index.
 I. Hoffa, James Riddle 1913–   II. International Brotherhood of Teamsters,
Chauffeurs, Warehousemen, and Helpers of America.   I. Title.
HD6509.H6M64   331.88'11'3883240924   [B]   78–14286
ISBN 0–7092–0514–7
ISBN 0–448–22684–7 (U.S. and Canada only)

Portions of this book originally appeared in *Playboy* Magazine.

Designed by Folio Graphics Company.

IN THE UNITED STATES
PADDINGTON PRESS
Distributed by
GROSSET & DUNLAP

IN THE UNITED KINGDOM
PADDINGTON PRESS

IN CANADA
Distributed by
RANDOM HOUSE OF CANADA LTD.

IN SOUTHERN AFRICA
Distributed by
ERNEST STANTON (PUBLISHERS) (PTY.) LTD.

It is always easy to begin a war, but very difficult to stop one, since its beginning and end are not under the control of the same man. Anyone, even a coward, can commence a war, but it can be brought to an end only with the consent of the victors.

Sallust
Jugurtha LXXXVIII

''Hoffa will always be in trouble. Not in jail necessarily, nor even under indictment—just in trouble. This is a man at war in his heart with orthodox society.''

Eric Sevareid
CBS Radio

Contents

PART TWO

Acknowledgments

This work could not have been completed without the invaluable assistance of my associate, Michael Ewing, who has been active in both the Senate and House efforts to reinvestigate the circumstances surrounding the assassination of President Kennedy. The former staff assistant to Senator Harold Hughes of Iowa was instrumental in the preparation of the chapters concerning the CIA-underworld plots to murder Fidel Castro, the assassination of President Kennedy, and the administration of President Richard Nixon.

Special thanks are extended to: Walter Sheridan, author and U.S. Senate investigator; Ralph Salerno, former supervisor of detectives in New York and expert on organized crime; Arthur Fox, attorney for Ralph Nader's Public Citizen Litigation Group and former executive director of PROD; John Sikorski, former research director of PROD, now a law student at New York University; Blair Griffith, former U.S. attorney in Pittsburgh; Vincent Piersante, chief of the Michigan attorney general's division on organized crime; and Charles Siragusa, former deputy director of the U.S. Bureau of Narcotics.

And deep appreciation is expressed to the following members of the press: syndicated columnist Jack Anderson and his associate, Marc Smolonsky; syndicated columnist Clark Mollenhoff; *Detroit Free Press* reporters Ralph Orr and Jo Thomas (now with *The New York Times*); *New Republic* senior editor Eliot Marshall; *Wall Street Journal* reporter Jon Kwitny; *Akron Beacon Journal* reporter Richard Mc-Bane; *Reporter* (of Akron) publisher William Ellis, Sr.; former *New Brunswick Home-News* (New Jersey) reporter and PROD research director Robert Windrem; *Overdrive* investigative editor Jim Drinkhall (now with the *Wall Street Journal*); NBC executive producers Stanhope Gould (now with ABC) and Gordon Manning; NBC news manager Bobby Reid; NBC field producers Bert Medley and Robert Toombs; NBC news correspondents Robert Hager, Mike Jackson, and Irving R. Levine; and WWJ-TV (Detroit) executive producer Robert Giles.

Grateful acknowledgment is made to the American Broadcasting Companies, Inc., for permission to reprint excerpts of interviews with Jimmy Hoffa from the transcript of the ABC NEWS CLOSE-UP: HOFFA. © 1974 American Broadcasting Companies, Inc. Reprinted by Permission. All Rights Reserved.

Sincere gratitude is also expressed to those whose friendship has been vital to my work: the ''Amazing Grace'' commune, on Twenty-first Street in Washington, D.C., Donn Cory, Timothy Davis, Michael deBlois, Vivian deWitt, David M. Dial, George Farris, Louis Farris, Mr. and Mrs. Robert Grant, Guncher's bartenders, Verlin Jenkins, Diane Jones, James Leonino, Gordon ''Mac'' McKinley, Tom Matuk, Philip Mause, Bob Maxwell, Larry Mueller, Gary Nesbitt, Paul Poulos, Pat Pringle, Rafe Sagalyn, Jim Switzer, Joan Tapper, and Robert Verdisco.

Finally, I would like to thank my literary agent, Philip Spitzer; my attorneys, Michael Allen and Steven A. Martindale of Washington, D.C., and Bernard Roetzel of Akron, Ohio; my writing coach, Nancy Nolte; Judy McCusker; Elliot Linzer; Kati Boland; my patient editor, Mary Heathcote, whose devotion to this project is reflected on every page; and John Marqusee and his guerrilla publishing team at Paddington Press.

The research for this book was done with the help of a series of grants from the Fund for Investigative Journalism, in Washington, D.C.

Introduction

When I began research for this book in October 1974, the problems of the rank-and-file membership of the Teamsters Union weren't completely new to me. I had worked on loading platforms at various trucking companies and had even driven a small truck one summer while I was an undergraduate. During lunchroom discussions it was not uncommon for the older workers to voice their frustrations about whether they'd ever receive their union pensions while others discussed grievances filed against management. I listened to the complaints these men had but never said anything. I figured that after college, I wouldn't have these jobs long enough to worry about pensions and grievances.

Subsequently, while I was driving my truck to Columbus one July morning, the oil drums I was hauling exploded, setting the rest of my cargo, the truck, and the highway on fire. The force of the blast knocked the vehicle off the pavement and onto a grass median strip, which also started to blaze as burning oil spilled to the ground. After the truck stopped skidding I dove from the cab and rolled down an embankment. Forced to pull over, other motorists climbed out of their cars, watching the flames from the truck shoot high into the air and waiting for it to explode as the fire spread near its gas tank.

I was dazed and everything seemed to be in slow motion. But if that truck exploded, I might lose my job. With a bizarre sense of courage and probably a greater proportion of stupidity, I ran back up the hill, grabbed a pair of gloves out of the cab, went around to the back of the truck, and dropped the tailgate. As I jumped back into the cab, no less than eight truckers, who had also stopped their big rigs, were racing toward my truck with their extinguishers. While they covered the gas tank with flame-retardant chemicals, I shifted from low to reverse, driving up and down the hill, braking to allow the flaming cargo to slide off the truck.

After the maneuvers were completed and the truck was a safe distance from the piles of burning debris, a highway patrolman told me that I could easily have been killed. I replied that I probably would've been if not for the truckers who risked their lives to help me. While the patrolman filled out his report, several of us sat down on the side of the hill and I wrote down the names of the eight truckers. I never saw any of them again, but my boss and I spent the next day writing letters to them and their companies, thanking them for their help. In each letter I told them that I would try to pay them back some day.

That debt started being repaid on December 17, 1974, at 3:15 A.M. on a dark, snow-covered street corner. A dissident member of the Teamsters and I had arranged the meeting place three days earlier. Both of us were scared and cold, but he was clenching a warm .38 revolver in his pocket and meant to use it if there was any trouble. That was the last thing I needed more of. At the time I was a struggling graduate student at Kent State University; I had been working on my master's thesis and for a small black newspaper in Akron. The topic I had selected for both my thesis and an eight-part series for my weekly column was the Teamsters Union and its relationship with organized crime. And the rebel leader I was meeting that December morning wanted to help by giving me a black ledger book listing the loans from the union's pension fund, many of which had gone to the underworld.

Although the eight-part series came out, the master's thesis did not. At the end of the 1975 spring quarter, I dropped out of Kent State and began traveling around the country, investigating the Teamsters full time while being educated by the victims of its corruption. I drove from city to city in my old, beat-up, blue Thunderbird with my files, tape recorders, and typewriter jammed in the trunk. Some reformers knew me only by my car; others recognized me by my patched blue jeans, leather coat, and the backpack over my shoulders.

Meanwhile I made a little money, writing an article here and there, consulting for law firms, and occasionally lecturing. In strange towns I slept on couches and floors in the homes of rebel Teamsters, who were desperate for anyone to aid their cause. Leading the life of a guerrilla writer was an incredibly romantic, fantasylike existence except for those long lonely hours of driving, not knowing what lay ahead. On one of those trips to Chicago I received an anonymous telephone call. The caller, claiming to have some information, told me to meet him at a bar in a northern suburb. When I got there, I was jumped and beaten by two men.

On July 30, 1975, while my car was being repaired after being vandalized, Jimmy Hoffa disappeared. Five days later, with two dollars cash and a credit card in my wallet, I flew to Detroit, hoping to be hired by a newspaper or magazine for background consulting work on the case. I had forgotten my driver's license and couldn't rent an automobile at the airport, so I walked outside and stuck out my thumb, hitchhiking north to the restaurant where Hoffa was last seen. When I got there I spotted NBC news correspondent Irving R. Levine and introduced myself. I was hired as the network's Teamster researcher in Detroit.

On August 5, my first full day of work with NBC, I received a call from a man who described himself as a former organizer for a union task force headed by Detroit Teamster leader Rolland McMaster. He added that he had learned about me and my new job from a friend in the rebel movement and wanted to give me some information indirectly related to the Hoffa murder.

A week later, as he had directed, I stood in front of a midwestern airport holding a copy of Walter Sheridan's *The Fall and Rise of Jimmy Hoffa* in my left hand. When his sleek black automobile pulled up in front of me, I looked back at the NBC field producer, who was observing the scene from behind a newspaper. I had a feeling that my life would never be the same after I got into the car. And it hasn't been.

Since then I have faithfully pursued the story of Jimmy Hoffa and the Teamsters. I consider this book part payment on my debt to those eight truckers who saved my life on that hot summer day so long ago.

—Dan E. Moldea

Georgetown
July 30, 1978

PART ONE

1 In Search of Jimmy Hoffa

Jimmy Hoffa's most valuable contribution to the American labor movement came at the moment he stopped breathing on July 30, 1975. The involuntary act occurred in the midst of his dramatic bid to recapture the general presidency of the International Brotherhood of Teamsters, which he had lost during nearly five years in prison. Still popular among reporters with short memories who insisted upon portraying him as a working-class hero, and among rank-and-file admirers who had forgiven him for stealing from them, Hoffa nevertheless had slim chances for a comeback.

Convicted in two separate trials of jury tampering and defrauding the union's pension fund, Hoffa had become an outsider to the Teamsters' high command when he entered Lewisburg Penitentiary in March 1967. His union problems began in less than a month, when he and his successor, Frank Fitzsimmons, disagreed over an appointment. The increasingly bitter war between the two old friends lasted until Hoffa died, and it was to be carried on by Hoffa's supporters even after he was gone.

In 1967 Fitzsimmons suddenly inherited the uncontrollable monster Hoffa had created over the past twenty-five years: an alliance between the union and organized crime. Introduced to the underworld by a lover in the 1930s, by the 1940s Hoffa was asking for and getting muscle from the mob in a war with a rival union. He began using the Teamsters to provide his new allies with a façade of legitimacy, even for the international narcotics traffic, of which Detroit was a major center. In return Hoffa became rich and powerful, and so did the IBT. Wealth and power led to a second alliance, this one with corrupt politicians. The general public and the rank-and-file Teamsters, especially those who drove their own trucks, suffered from the two alliances.

Unable and unwilling to battle the underworld, Fitzsimmons promptly decentralized the autocracy Hoffa had used to build his empire, hoping to insulate himself from direct contact with organized crime. Among the immediate benefactors of Fitzsimmons' policies were local and regional Teamster leaders around the country, who acquired a considerable amount of new power in the two-million-member union. Instead of clamoring for the attention of one man, Hoffa, mobsters merely had to call their area Teamster representatives for a favor. Teamster bosses who cooperated became wealthy.

Without the daily burden of defending his professional relationships with organized crime figures to the press and to the rank and file—as Hoffa had spent much of his career doing—Fitzsimmons used his free time backing up his union subordinates and making new friends in politics and big labor.

Things were going well for the IBT under Fitzsimmons. Its first- and second-level officials were happy, and so was the National Crime Syndicate. Then, in November 1968, Richard Nixon was elected President of the United States. Because the Teamsters had gone with the rest of organized labor and supported Hubert Humphrey that year, Nixon's election was bad news.

Nixon had formed a quid pro quo alliance with Hoffa during his 1960 presidential campaign against John Kennedy, brother of Hoffa's archenemy. Until he resigned to manage his brother's campaign, Robert Kennedy was chief counsel to the Senate Rackets Committee, which investigated the Teamsters in general and Hoffa in particular. The extraordinary pressure Kennedy placed on Hoffa personally during the committee's hearings, combined with rumors that Bobby Kennedy would become attorney general if his brother was elected, led Hoffa to put his union at Nixon's disposal. According to Ed Partin, a former Hoffa aide turned government informant, in September 1960 the crime boss of Louisiana, Carlos Marcello, contributed $500,000 to the Nixon campaign through Hoffa and his associates. Within a few weeks after the alleged payoff, Nixon managed to stop a Florida land fraud indictment against Hoffa.

So when Nixon finally won the presidency in 1968, it was no surprise to Fitzsimmons and the Teamster leadership that he was considering an early release for Hoffa. Unlike Fitzsimmons, Hoffa had supported Nixon in 1968 through his influence with remaining friends in the union.

For Hoffa, however, problems remained and they would be his undoing.

In Lewisburg he had made a prison alliance with dope trafficker Carmine Galante, the underboss of the Joseph Bonanno crime family of New York, which was in internal conflict over the line of succession. Although other mob families had at first been neutral in the "Banana Wars," which lasted from 1963 to 1969, their attitude quickly changed when they uncovered a plot to murder two other New York crime bosses, Carlo Gambino and Thomas Lucchese. Because Bonanno's son was implicated in the plot, the National Crime Syndicate's ruling council ordered the elder Bonanno to respond to the charge. When Bonanno refused to cooperate and began to raid other underworld jurisdictions, he was expelled from the ruling council, which quietly began supporting the rebels in the Bonanno clan. Fearful of mob reprisals and government prosecution, Bonanno arranged for his own disappearance, which lasted from 1964 to 1966. While underground he made a coalition with two other powerful organized crime figures, Santos Trafficante of Florida and Carlos Marcello of Louisiana. Moving his New York operations to Arizona—where he already had considerable influence—Bonanno, with his new friends, formed a triumvirate that rivaled the New York underworld's forces.

By making his prison pact with Galante, Jimmy Hoffa became a key figure in this North-South power struggle. As president of the Teamsters he had had a close working relationship with the New York crime families as well as Marcello and Trafficante, but his ties to the latter two mobsters were exceptionally close and personal.

After the Cuban Revolution in 1959, when Fidel Castro began throwing the American mob off the island, Marcello and Trafficante were among those exiled. Both lost their best heroin and gambling connection. Trying to recapture their lost territory, Trafficante and other gangsters—including Sam Giancana of Chicago and Russell Bufalino of Pennsylvania—agreed to work with the U.S. Central Intelligence Agency in a direct action against Castro. Strong evidence points to the fact that the original middleman between the CIA and the American underworld was Jimmy Hoffa, who used the union's financial machinery for arms sales to both sides in the Cuban Revolution.

There is solid evidence as well that Hoffa, Marcello, and Trafficante—three of the most important targets for criminal prosecution by the Kennedy Administration—had discussions with their subordinates about murdering President Kennedy. Associates of Hoffa, Trafficante, and Marcello were in direct contact with Jack Ruby, the Dallas night-club owner who killed the ''lone assassin'' of the President. Although members of the Warren Commission, which investigated President Kennedy's assassination, had knowledge of much of this information at the time of their inquiry, they chose not to follow it up. Marcello and Trafficante continued to support Hoffa after his convictions, offering bribes to a key witness to recant his testimony against Hoffa.

But while the southern underworld remained loyal to Hoffa, the New York mobs were shifting their alliances to Frank Fitzsimmons.

While Hoffa made friends with Galante and Bonanno did the same with Marcello and Trafficante, New York mob leaders began to realize that Hoffa's return to power in the union could wreck their business interests in the IBT. If Hoffa began favoring the Bonanno-Marcello-Trafficante alliance in the South—and there was every reason why he should, since he knew he was being betrayed elsewhere—there was a very real danger of a breakup of the National Crime Syndicate, with its traditional allotted spheres of interest. One indication of trouble to come was that in prison both Hoffa and Galante had brief fistfights with Anthony Provenzano, a captain in the Vito Genovese crime family, which had aligned itself with the New York families opposing Bonanno. A New Jersey Teamster leader, IBT vice president, and former ally of Hoffa, Provenzano had been an active participant in the battle up to the time he was jailed. He had ordered the locals under his control not to pay the Bonanno men who were on Teamster payrolls.

Knowing that if Hoffa was released from jail he and his allies would retaliate financially, the northern underworld and pro-Fitzsimmons union leaders turned their attention to President Nixon. Fitzsimmons' influence with the new President was minimal, but the Teamster president did know Nixon's attorney general, John Mitchell, with whom he had numerous conversations in 1969. It is reasonable to assume that the two men reviewed the situation between organized crime and the Teamsters Union, along with the underworld's growing internal problems; and that both men believed armed warfare could explode if Hoffa was permitted to return to power in the union. The prospect must have been deeply alarming to an attorney general serving under a President who had promised the American public law and order. At any rate, during 1969 the Nixon Administration balked at releasing Hoffa and kept him in prison.

In February 1969, less than a month after Nixon took office, the Banana Wars ended, and the Teamsters and the mob began to neutralize Hoffa by winning over his allies in both groups. Respected among all parties and put in control of the union's pension and welfare funds by Hoffa, Chicago underworld associate Allen Dorfman became Fitzsimmons' peacemaker. His job was to be sure that every section of organized crime got its fair share of the union's billion-dollar pension and welfare funds.

Hoffa's support within the underworld and among Teamster leaders whom the mob controlled dwindled steadily. By mid-1971 the White House had forced Hoffa to resign all his union offices in return for an early release. This set the stage for Fitzsimmons' election as IBT general president the following month, and for Hoffa's restricted commutation of sentence in December, which barred him from union office until 1980.

The Hoffa issue had drawn the White House, the Teamsters, and organized crime closer together. Although the Justice Department successfully prosecuted Allen Dorfman and associates of Marcello and Trafficante—all for misuse of Teamster funds—John Mitchell was personally responsible for numerous aborted prosecutions of underworld figures during his four-year tenure. Several investigations of Teamster officials, including one against Fitzsimmons' son Richard, were dropped without explanation.

As a result, Fitzsimmons, the IBT's general executive board, and the mob gave Nixon their full support during his 1972 reelection campaign. The only IBT board member who refused to back Nixon was named a White House ''enemy'' and had his income tax returns audited the following year. Fitzsimmons became personally involved in a dirty tricks campaign against Senator Edward Kennedy, a potential challenger to Nixon. Allen Dorfman chipped in a $100,000 contribution which he gave illegally to John Mitchell. And after the Watergate burglars began blackmailing the White House, the mob came through in January 1973 with a million dollars in hush money—delivery arranged by Fitzsimmons, Provenzano (out of prison since 1970), and Dorfman.

The press, which was concentrating on Watergate, did not notice for a while that Hoffa was patiently putting together the machinery for a comeback, which included a suit against the restrictions on his commutation. Although the battle between him and Fitzsimmons was for control of the international union, the battleground would be their home-town local, Detroit's Local 299. And in Local 299, as in the union at large, loss of support from both the underworld and top Teamster leaders left Hoffa surrounded by powerless allies, most of them rank-and-file loyalists who clung to the myth of Hoffa as their defender.

Although grandfatherly Frank Fitzsimmons was more amiable and easier to talk to than Jimmy Hoffa ever was or could be, that image never seemed to filter down to the rank and file. To them Fitzsimmons was Hoffa's shoeshine boy, who was handed and did not earn the number one spot in the union. By 1974, caught up in the drama of Hoffa's possible return to power, the press had picked up the theme and forever labeled Fitzsimmons as he was perceived by the membership. It was a bad rap to lay on Fitzsimmons, and it simply wasn't true. Defensive about being compared so unfavorably to Hoffa, Fitzsimmons drew further and further away from the rank and file.

In the years before he took over, Fitzsimmons had merely exhibited the loyalty that any subordinate should give his boss. A tough street fighter in the old days, a man who had held his own in all the brawls with rival unions, Fitzsimmons was a streetwise former trucker whom Hoffa had trusted and depended upon since the thirties. Perhaps that was reason enough for Hoffa to make Fitzsimmons his successor, but according to a Teamster official who was close to both men, Fitzsimmons was the Detroit underworld's choice. Certainly he was no stranger to the mob. The succession was allegedly arranged after Hoffa appealed to Detroit's top don to get rid of a local gangster who was having an affair with his wife. Soon after Josephine Hoffa's lover was sent to jail for stock fraud, Hoffa named Fitzsimmons his heir apparent.

Hoffa never operated in the heroic vacuum that was glamorized throughout his career. His successes and failures were in large part determined by who his friends and enemies were at each point in his life. Besides Fitzsimmons, two other men were of special importance in his rise to power: Dave Johnson and Rolland McMaster. Dissident truckers who, along with Fitzsimmons, joined and cleaned up Local 299 in 1935, Johnson and McMaster were major reasons for Hoffa's early victories. As his two top organizers they were probably more responsible than anyone else, even Hoffa, for pulling the entire midwestern trucking industry into the Teamsters during the 1940s and 1950s. They were partners who battled strikebreakers and rival unions on the front lines while Hoffa was by then sitting behind a desk calling the shots. Rewarded with top positions in the local—Johnson as recording secretary and McMaster as secretary-treasurer—they kept Local 299 functioning after Hoffa and Fitzsimmons went to Washington to run the IBT from its new headquarters. And when Hoffa and Fitzsimmons began their power struggle, no two people were more vital to it than Johnson and McMaster.

McMaster was the reason for the split between Hoffa and Fitzsimmons. It was his appointment as chief executive officer of Local 299 after his release from an extortion sentence that Hoffa protested from jail. Hoffa, who had decided that McMaster was probably a government informant, wanted Johnson, now secretary-treasurer, to hold major power in the local as his most trusted lieutenant.

One of the most serious problems Hoffa faced during his tenure as general president was the isolated pockets of rank-and-file resistance that challenged his leadership. Handfuls of bold rebels kept organizing in cities on both coasts, throughout the Midwest, and even in Detroit, forcing Hoffa to buy them off or physically intimidate them. But when new groups of reformers kept coming over the hill—some trying to overthrow their local union officials and others campaigning for decertification from the union—Hoffa had the IBT constitution revised to grant himself absolute control. Later, it was the Hoffa constitution that Fitzsimmons used to keep Hoffa out of power.

No match for the Teamsters' money and muscle, rebel movements struck hard but faded fast in the Hoffa years. Without a national organization the reform groups were crashing their heads into brick walls. Then in 1964 Hoffa himself gave the rebels the organizing tool they needed by negotiating the union's first national contract—a master collective bargaining agreement for Teamster members all over the country. From here on all Teamsters would have the same conditions and the same timetable for protest.

The first rebels to realize that Hoffa had handed them the common ground they needed were the steel haulers in Gary, Indiana, most of whom drove their own trucks and as owner-operators had long been exploited by the union. Too late to affect negotiations for the 1964 agreement, the steel haulers prepared for a full-scale revolt in 1967, when the next contract would be negotiated. That year the dissidents staged the first national wildcat strike in Teamster history. Giving Fitzsimmons his first major headache as acting president of the union, the rebels paralyzed the steel industry in eight states and affected the manufacturing of steel products all over the country. The protest failed to win them any real concessions from either union or management, but they had proved their unity and shown Fitzsimmons that he was just as threatened by the rank and file as Hoffa had been.

Formed during the 1967 strike, the Fraternal Association of Steel Haulers, centered in Pennsylvania and Ohio, split from the union and became an independent bargaining agent—but only after a bloody shoot-out with the Teamsters in October 1969 and a second national strike the following year.

An old hand at suppressing dissident uprisings, Rolland McMaster was appointed to handle the IBT's problems with FASH, but the owner-operators of FASH made a degree of common cause with the Detroit rebels and McMaster became increasingly unpopular with the rank and file. Knowing that Hoffa was plotting against him from Lewisburg, McMaster sent him a threatening letter warning him to stay out of Local 299's internal affairs. Outraged, Hoffa retaliated through Dave Johnson, who was ordered to get McMaster out of Local 299. Johnson's opportunity came in December 1970, when he and one of McMaster's organizers had a fight in the union hall. Johnson used the incident to have McMaster purged, and, to avoid mutiny in Detroit, Fitzsimmons went along. Johnson became president of Local 299 and McMaster vowed to get even.

Fitzsimmons had no intention of losing his top enforcer; McMaster remained the overall head of the union's battle against FASH. He established a thirty-man organizing team which had a dual role: to organize truckers and to watch Jimmy Hoffa after he got out of jail. During the two-year history of the campaign, bombings, shootings, and sabotage were commonplace against both antiunion companies and Hoffa supporters.

In February 1974, McMaster's national task force was disbanded after spending more than a million dollars of union money while organizing only 750 new members. It had served primarily as a smokescreen to get employers to pay for labor peace.

That same month the owner-operators shut down nationwide for the third time in as many months, protesting fuel prices. The massive demonstration also became a protest against Fitzsimmons, especially in Detroit. Some of the leaders of the shutdown had aligned themselves with Hoffa, who was now promising them better conditions if he returned as IBT president.

By now Hoffa's open attacks on Fitzsimmons and his appeal against the district court that had sustained Nixon's commutation restrictions had alarmed both the Teamster high command and the mob. In mid-1974, according to a former McMaster task force organizer, Fitzsimmons gave McMaster a ''blank check'' to make sure Hoffa did not return to power in Local 299, the necessary stepping stone to the IBT presidency. Johnson had indicated that if Hoffa's court battles were successful he was willing to give Local 299 to Hoffa. Thus Fitzsimmons' major target was Dave Johnson, Hoffa's only hope of regaining control.

Soon after the blank check was issued, Johnson's cabin cruiser was bombed at its mooring behind his home on Grosse Ile, near Detroit. The leading suspect in the government's investigation was a former member of McMaster's organizing task force.

With pressure mounting on Johnson to resign and forsake Hoffa, Richard Fitzsimmons announced that he was planning to run against Johnson for Local 299 president; he had earlier replaced his father as the local's vice president, a position the elder Fitzsimmons had held since 1946. McMaster was running as Richard Fitzsimmons' vice presidential candidate. With violence spreading as the election approached, the Detroit joint council proposed and Local 299's executive board agreed to bring the Hoffa and Fitzsimmons forces together in a coalition slate: Johnson would remain president and young Fitzsimmons would settle for the vice presidency again. McMaster was left off the ticket at Johnson's insistence. But after one of his organizers had stalled the election for a month by filing suit against the local, McMaster came back and announced as a candidate for president against Johnson. Furious, Johnson threatened to torpedo the coalition if McMaster remained in the race, and Fitzsimmons ordered McMaster to withdraw.

McMaster's strongarm men shuttled in and out of Detroit—two of them living rent free in a hotel owned by McMaster's closest business associates—and violence against Hoffa supporters increased. Then, on July 10, 1975—twenty days before Hoffa disappeared—Richard Fitzsimmons' union car was bombed. The government's two major suspects in that bombing were the two men from the hotel.

Possibly they were trying to stir up enough violence to give Frank Fitzsimmons justification for putting Local 299 into trusteeship—where it had been long ago, before the reformers, now rulers, cleaned it up. Fitzsimmons could then bring in his own batch of new officers and close Hoffa out forever. Or possibly the bombing was a theatrical device to set the stage—and confuse the audience—for Hoffa's disappearance. A few weeks before the bombing an interesting meeting was noticed at an airport near Detroit. According to an eyewitness, three men climbed out of a private plane and were greeted by McMaster, who drove them away and brought them back several hours later. One of the three men was identified as New Jersey Teamster leader Anthony Provenzano. The significance of this meeting could be somewhat better understood a few weeks later.

In mid-June, before the McMaster-Provenzano meeting, and a few days prior to his scheduled appearance before a Senate Select Committee investigating CIA-underworld plots to assassinate Fidel Castro, the Chicago mobster Sam Giancana was murdered at his home. A trusted underworld informant who was close to him told a House committee investigating the CIA that Sam Giancana was executed by underworld associates who had also been involved in the assassination plots.

According to a former Hoffa aide—later a government informant—who believes his boss was the CIA's initial go-between with the mob in the Castro murder plan, McMaster was Hoffa's liaison to Santos Trafficante during the planning of the assassination in the early 1960s. Russell Bufalino had also been among the mob chieftains whom the CIA solicited for direct action against Castro, and Genovese crime captain Provenzano had in 1974 come under the jurisdiction of gangland leaders, including Russell Bufalino, who were now trustees of the Genovese family.

On the final day of Hoffa's life, Bufalino was driven into Detroit early in the morning by Frank Sheeran, a Delaware Teamster boss who was a long-time friend of Hoffa. Along with several union rebels, Sheeran was a co-plaintiff in Hoffa's suit against the commutation restrictions. According to government investigators, later that day Sheeran picked up three of Provenzano's men—Salvatore Briguglio, Gabriel Briguglio, and Thomas Andretta—at a nearby airport and took them to the temporary residence of Hoffa's ''foster son,'' IBT general organizer Charles O'Brien.

O'Brien had been working across the street from Local 299, where he shared an office and a secretary with attorney William Bufalino, Russell Bufalino's cousin, who was president of the Teamsters' ''jukebox local.'' By eleven-thirty that morning both O'Brien and William Bufalino had left Teamster headquarters. O'Brien was doing errands; Bufalino was making arrangements for his daughter's wedding.

At one o'clock, Hoffa left his cottage at Lake Orion, Michigan. He stopped to see a business associate, who had already gone to lunch. Talking to an employee in the office, Hoffa mentioned that he was going to a meeting where Provenzano and Detroit mobster Anthony Giacalone would be present. Arriving a half-hour early for his two-thirty meeting—which he apparently thought was to be at two—Hoffa had to wait and began to think he had been stood up.

While the ex-Teamster boss fretted, O'Brien was with Giacalone at a nearby health spa, where O'Brien was picking up gifts for his children's birthdays. Leaving the club at 2:25 P.M., O'Brien, federal agents say, then drove a car borrowed from Giacalone's son to pick up Hoffa. He took Hoffa to the place he was staying, where Sheeran and the three Provenzano subordinates were waiting.

Within a few minutes Hoffa was dead.

A government informant has said that Hoffa's body was then stuffed in a fifty-five-gallon oil drum and transported to an unknown destination on a Gateway Transportation Company truck. Another underworld figure who cooperated with the government indicated that Hoffa had been killed by the same mobsters who had worked with the CIA during their plots to kill Castro. He said very specifically that Hoffa's body had been crushed in a steel compactor for junk cars.

On the day Hoffa vanished, Rolland McMaster was in Gary, Indiana, meeting with Gateway Transportation executives. His brother-in-law, the head of Gateway's Detroit steel division, confirmed the alibi.

On December 4, 1975, McMaster; his brother-in-law; Sheeran; and the three New Jersey men appeared before the federal grand jury investigating the Hoffa murder. All five pleaded the Fifth Amendment, as Giacalone and Provenzano had done earlier; all five were represented by William Bufalino.

The Hoffa Wars is a history of power in the Teamsters Union; how Jimmy Hoffa got it, kept it, lost it, and was prevented from regaining it. It examines the influences on his rise and fall by three of his earliest and closest union associates: Frank Fitzsimmons, Dave Johnson, and Rolland McMaster. And it shows how rank-and-file rebels, corrupt and honest politicians, and organized crime complicated the world of these four Teamster leaders.

This is the story of the wars fought by and among the Teamster leadership; and how these wars led to the murder of Jimmy Hoffa—which perhaps resulted from his role in two political assassination plots, including one against an American President, as well as from his inability to give up the struggle for personal power. Much of the story is told in the words of the participants themselves, through hundreds of hours of conversations and interviews in truck stops and union halls, in government offices and the storefront headquarters of rebel teamsters.

The narrative begins in 1932, in the depths of the Great Depression. It has national and international scenes and implications, but for the Teamster leaders themselves it starts, as it ends, in Detroit.

2 Rebel Hoffa

"No Work" signs dangled from crusty string along the strands of barbed wire above the gates of silent factories. Men and women facing another day of unemployment walked dejectedly toward the humiliating but merciful bread lines and soup kitchens supplied by the Red Cross and the Salvation Army. It was 1932, and American ex-doughboys who had fought to "make the world safe for democracy" bunked down in dingy subways or shacks made of flattened tin cans and cardboard, or hopped freight trains from town to town.

That same year President Herbert Hoover vetoed an emergency plan for veterans' bonuses, and veterans from all over the country marched on Washington. Hoover used the army, former comrades, to throw them out of the capital. All over the country people listened in stunned silence to radio news reports, and the marchers' puzzled bitterness reflected a national despair. The bitterness would last a lifetime. "Two of our men were killed by those bastards," one old-timer remembers. "Fourteen years later, after months of fighting in the Great War, no one seemed to care about us boys who came home."

With a hundred thousand businesses shut down, ten million people were unemployed. Most of them had already used up their life savings by the time the Great Depression reached its nadir. The federal government remained preoccupied with futile attempts to enforce Prohibition and collect war debts, apparently assuming that American business would discover a cure for America's economic illness. But the business community seemed just as helpless as the rest of the country. The beloved comedian Will Rogers summed up the situation: "We are the first nation in the history of the world to go to the poorhouse in an automobile.''

There was little for the average guy to cheer about in gloomy 1932, except maybe the local baseball team and the vivid reporting of Damon Runyon and Grantland Rice with such stories as Babe Ruth's ''called'' home run into the right-field bleachers when he led the Yankees to victory over the Chicago Cubs in the '32 World Series.

For most people poverty was a way of life. They spent their evenings near the radio, listening to the Amos and Andy program, Maxwell House Coffee's ''Showboat'' or the early big-band sound of Eddie Condon, or to young Bing Crosby croonin' into the night. The radio was addictive; its commercials for Palmolive Beauty Soap and ''Calll forrr Philip Morrr-ris!'' were part of the language. And there was Coca-Cola, the beer, wine, and liquor substitute when nothing ran through the basement still or filled the family bathtub.

Music lovers were listening to Tin Pan Alley's George Gershwin, who played his beautiful ''Rhapsody in Blue'' at Carnegie Hall that year. Some people shuddered over Aldous Huxley's latest novel, *Brave New World*. Others, at a nickel each, swamped their neighborhood movie houses to catch the weekly newsreels and the latest product from Tinseltown. They flocked to see newcomer Jean Harlow, the blond bombshell, and to watch James Cagney push half a grapefruit into Mae Clarke's doll face in *Public Enemy*, a glorification of a real-life Prohibition antihero, the Chicago gangster Hymie Weiss. Shoulders bouncing, fists up, Cagney popularized the cocky ''You dirty rats'' mobster, slugging dames and mugs indiscriminately. And in *Public Enemy* he achieved the ultimate fate of many of his counterparts—cut down by rivals in a gangland murder. As the film ended, his bullet-riddled body was leaning limply in his sweet mother's doorway, where the killers had maliciously left him.

Although the movies improved in 1933, the government's war against organized crime did not. Just two years earlier, in mid-September, the last of the ''Mustache Petes''—first-generation leaders of the American-Sicilian underworld—had been slaughtered on orders from an ambitious young mob leader named Charles Luciano, who retained the services of free-lance enforcer Meyer Lansky for the series of New York raids called ''the Night of the Sicilian Vespers.'' Among the forty dead was Salvatore Maranzano, who in April had declared himself the mythical *capo di tutti capi*, or boss of bosses, of the hoodlum empire that had thrived on gambling, illegal booze, and prostitution. Maranzano's claim had in turn followed the sudden death of his rival, Giuseppe Masseria, whom Luciano lured to a Coney Island restaurant to be murdered by his lieutenant, Vito Genovese, while the boss was in the bathroom.

Four days after the September purge, Luciano proposed to the other mob bosses that a nationwide criminal syndicate be set up. This was Lansky's idea, and the plan was to divide the United States and its cities into twenty-four subdivisions, each controlled by a regional coordinator, nine of whom would sit on a commission primarily to settle disputes. The organization was under discussion for three years before it was formally established.[1]

With the repeal of Prohibition in 1933, under President Franklin Roosevelt, the criminal underworld continued to flourish. Its illicit distilleries were legal now, and its fleets of liquor trucks could operate around the clock. The mob had money to invest in new areas, and with labor organizing encouraged by Roosevelt's New Deal policies, unions as well as businesses offered convenient money-making opportunities.

In Chicago, for example, looking for post-Prohibition investments, the underworld's heirs to the notorious Al Capone—finally jailed in 1931 for income tax evasion—tried to obtain a labor-and-industry monopoly in the milk distribution business. When they failed to buy off the established union's leadership and get favorable contracts for mob-controlled distribution firms, the syndicate established a rival union. Companies that refused to negotiate sweetheart contracts with the new truckers' union—which was stacked with mob henchmen—had to contend with strikes and continuing violence. Even if they gave in and bargained collectively with the crime-ridden union, many legitimate companies, paying decent wages and competing with those that were mob-controlled, were priced or strongarmed out of business.

At the same time the underworld supplied strikebreaking thugs hired by companies that honest unions were trying to organize. These goon squads were violent and expensive, but many company managements continued to be strongly antiunion throughout the country, especially in Detroit, center of the new automobile industry and a mecca for job hunters from all over the country.

One of the key strikebreakers in Detroit was Santo Perrone, a coremaker for a steel company, the Detroit Stove Works, who began his long career in "labor relations" when the Mechanics Educational Society of America tried to unionize the firm. Perrone quickly solicited the aid of his associates in the Detroit underworld, who battled and defeated the trade unionists.

"In return for his work," Vincent Piersante, head of the organized crime unit of the Michigan attorney general's office, told me in the 1970s, ''Perrone received some lucrative steel hauling contracts from the Stove Works. He didn't pay anything for the scrap he hauled away but was making over $4000 a month for keeping the company union-free.''

In spite of such tactics, the steel haulers went on trying to organize, and by 1933 there were two small, powerless Teamster locals on the scene. In April 1933 a third small local union, composed primarily of truck drivers who hauled general commodities around town, affiliated with the International Brotherhood of Teamsters, Chauffeurs, Warehousemen, Stablemen, and Helpers of America, AFL, and was chartered as Teamsters Local 299.

The International Brotherhood of Teamsters was itself a small organization, but it was growing quickly with the rise of the trucking industry. In 1898, twelve years after the American Federation of Labor was formed, the Team Drivers International Union was founded and received an AFL charter; its scant membership of 1200 drivers was serviced by eighteen local unions, with national headquarters in Detroit. In 1902 some Chicago members rebelled and established the rival Teamsters National Union, with a membership of 18,000 horse handlers. Appealing to both sides to settle their differences, AFL president Samuel Gompers arranged for a national team drivers convention, which was held in Niagara Falls, New York, in October 1903.

The two groups formed the IBT by merging their combined membership of 50,000 and treasury of $25,000 (members earned about $11.00 per 70-hour work week). International headquarters were in Indianapolis. The first president was Cornelius P. Shea.

In the midst of Shea's first and last term he was indicted for extorting money from team owners. Although he was acquitted, he was voted out in 1907 and replaced by a bull-voiced, stiff-necked Irish immigrant, Daniel Tobin of Boston, who exercised relatively little power over the widely decentralized union. Within this pattern of considerable autonomy, Teamster locals began springing up throughout the country.

Teamster history was turbulent from the outset. In 1905, after a Teamster walkout against the Montgomery Ward Company, the Chicago employers' association tried to use the incident to wipe out the infant union. The employers failed to destroy the organization, but they won the strike, and this caused another rebellion in Chicago. The Chicago dissidents and others allied against Shea and the Indianapolis leadership split from the IBT and started the United Teamsters of America. They tried to reunite with the international union in 1907, when Tobin took over, but he refused to readmit them; he wanted to punish the rebels and discourage future uprisings. After that, support for the United Teamsters disintegrated except in Chicago, where the dissidents kept their own separatist union intact in spite of IBT influence.

By 1933 there were some 125,000 Teamster members, heavily concentrated in industrial centers such as Chicago and Detroit. Dan Tobin was still president, and the locals still had enough autonomy to get into trouble. Detroit's Local 299 had serious problems almost at once. Joseph Campau and Al Milligan, the local's first president and secretary-treasurer, were under siege by rank and file members trying to prevent an election which they believed was rigged. Tobin sent out an accountant who examined the records and found misuse of the small local's finances. The IBT executive board removed Campau, Milligan, and other officers, put Local 299 into receivership, and lifted its charter. R. J. Bennett, secretary-treasurer of Local 247, which represented Detroit's coal haulers, was appointed receiver in 1936.

Among the three hundred members of Local 299 who had paid their ten-dollar initiation fee and two dollars a month dues was Rolland McMaster, a city cartage driver. Epitomizing the stereotype of a ''Teamster,'' McMaster was six-foot-four and weighed 245 pounds. His hands were as big and as firm as shovels, and his thick, protruding upper lip looked as if it had been struck repeatedly with a steel chain. His right eye was penetrating; it seemed to dissect and then analyze its targets while his left eye—which was made of glass—simply stared straight ahead into the distance.

This awesome-looking man was born in Onaway, Michigan, on March 23, 1914, and soon afterward moved to Detroit with his parents. His father found work at the Ford Motor Company and was able to support his wife and only child through lean years, but the boy had to go to work before he finished high school. After hitching a ride with a truck driver, he decided that hauling freight was what he wanted to do for a living. At sixteen he got his first job, making deliveries for the Michigan Cartage Company to and from the trains and boats around the waterfront of the Detroit River. Later he did the same kind of work for Keeshin Transport.

The huge, quiet but affable teamster was invited to an early meeting of Local 299. As soon as he had paid his dues McMaster was elected shop steward at Keeshin. ''I guess because I was so big,'' he told me with a smile. ''They explained to me what a union was, and that I should try to get everybody signed up at the company where I worked.

''There was practically no one in Local 299 at the time,'' McMaster went on. ''There was a sheet of paper on the wall that said it was a local union. Three Teamster locals rented the second floor of a big old building. And there was an old guy there, a custodian of the building and also the custodian of the money if you brought any in, if anbody had any.''

He succeeded in unionizing the drivers at Keeshin Transport, but ''the boss, Jack Keeshin, came in from Chicago and fired the whole bunch of us.

''So we went on strike, and I was elected chairman of the strike, and we came down and tied up the waterfront. We had a nice old free-for-all here, and everybody joined the union . . . And then we started to have union meetings, but we didn't know how to run 'em; nobody knew parliamentary procedure. So we just ran 'em, that's all. The loudest was generally the one that was boss.''

Other drivers loading and unloading their merchandise on the waterfront soon joined the union. Two of the early members were over-the-road, long-distance drivers, Frank Fitzsimmons for the National Transit Corporation and David Johnson for the United Truck Service.

''Yeah, and after that we were asked to come to the union hall for a meeting,'' Johnson says. ''Fitz and I joined the union the same day.''

Fitzsimmons, quiet and spectacled, was no one to be taken lightly. Despite his five-foot-six, 165-pound frame, the fiery-tempered Fitzsimmons, like McMaster, could take care of himself if he had to. And if he needed help there were always plenty of friends to pitch in.

Born in Jeannette, Pennsylvania, near Pittsburgh, on April 7, 1908, Fitzsimmons had come to Detroit with his family when he was a boy. At sixteen he had to quit school to help pay the medical expenses of his father, who was paralyzed after a stroke. He landed a job as a dock checker on the loading platform at Ternstedt Manufacturing Company, which made automobile hardware, where he worked thirteen hours a night. Young Fitzsimmons soon quit the docks to drive a double-decker bus for the Detroit Motor Bus Company, and at seventeen he got the job with National Transit.

''In those days you did everything,'' Fitzsimmons has said. ''Sometimes you worked on the dock, sometimes you'd work as a city driver, and sometimes you'd drive over the road at night.''

After joining Local 299 Fitzsimmons switched jobs again and became a long-distance driver for the Three C Highway Company, which operated between Detroit and Cleveland, Columbus, and Cincinnati. He was popular among the other drivers and became their shop steward in the new local.

"It was tough days for the union. You couldn't even wear your union button where it could be seen."

On those endless rainy nights of the long hauls, Fitzsimmons was reassured when he glanced in his rear-view mirror and saw his good friend Dave Johnson trailing close behind. At coffee stops, after joking with the other drivers, Fitzsimmons and Johnson usually stretched out in a booth to sip their coffee and eat their sandwiches, talking about their plans for larger homes, more kids, and a stronger union. Detroit was a growing community, and as the country began to slip out of the Depression and into war, the city offered big opportunities to those smart enough to take advantage of them.

Johnson, like Fitzsimmons, was from a small town near Pittsburgh. Born in Charleroy on New Year's Day 1908, Johnson was only five when his parents, who were natives of Finland, moved to southern Illinois, where he went to school and later worked in the coal mines for three years. As a member of the AFL United Mine Workers, Johnson admired men like its president, John L. Lewis, union leaders who could get the workers good contracts and a good wage. In the year of the crash on Wall Street, Johnson left the mines and came to Detroit, where he got a job as a produce hauler for the C. F. Smith Grocery Company.

In 1932 Johnson was laid off and returned to Illinois, but he came back to Detroit the following winter. For a few months he hauled produce for Scarpace Cartage Company, which contracted with the Kroger Food Company in Detroit. He would drive his rig over to Kroger's Green Street warehouse and watch the Kroger dock checkers working at top speed on the icy loading platform, making less money than he did as a driver.

"Man, those guys can have that kind of life."

The next summer Johnson got a job at Ford, working on the assembly line. "But I was really hired to play on their semipro [baseball] team." After lasting two seasons with Ford as a hard-hitting centerfielder—but unable to make the major leagues—Johnson returned to driving a truck in 1935. This time, working for United Truck Service, Johnson became an over-the-road, long-haul driver. Soon after beginning his new job Johnson joined Local 299, paid his ten bucks, and, like his good friend Fitzsimmons, was elected shop steward by his fellow drivers.

"It was the stewards who forced Local 299 into trusteeship," Johnson says. "We were raising all kinds of hell about the way Campau and Milligan were running things. So we forced a rebellion by the membership, and that's when R. J. Bennett came in."

"There were a lot of wild things going on all around here," Bennett explains. "The international sent in the auditor, who found that everything wasn't quite right with 299. Then he looked at my local's books and was impressed with what I'd done. So he gave me a good report and sent it to the international. The executive board then named me as Local 299's receiver."

Cleaning house was the first order of business when Bennett took over the local on January 6, 1936. The old union leaders were tossed out like the morning garbage. Knowing that coal haulers were earning only 47 cents per ton shipped, and that most other Detroit drivers were making the equivalent or even less, Bennett began to plan a well-oiled city-wide strike that would raise his union members' wages and attract more workers to the Teamsters. "So I started looking around town and began choosing my team to make it all happen," he says.

One of Bennett's first selections was Joseph M. O'Laughlin, a furniture van driver with close-cropped hair and cauliflower ears who had once been a sparring partner of Jack Dempsey. Too many shots to the head had taken its toll on ex-pug Red O'Laughlin, and his nose would bleed if he barely touched it. "Even though Red was a bleeder," Bennett says, "you just had to put a few slugs of booze into him, and he'd fight anybody over anything."

O'Laughlin and another Bennett appointee, Victor Tyler, a part-time driver for White Star Freight Lines, ran the day-to-day operations of Local 299 while Bennett—frugal, honest, and ambitious—counted the local's pennies and stored them in the union treasury, waiting for the big confrontation.

To round out his team, Bennett hired Al Squires, a Teamster he had fired from the coal haulers staff, and a rough little street fighter, James R. Hoffa, who was a warehouseman at Kroger.

"Squires jumped at the chance to work for the union again," says Bennett. "But Hoffa didn't want to work for me at first. With Kroger he was making $40–$45 a week, and I could pay him $30. But Jimmy was a guy who had a lot of guts, so I told him to come with me, because the union could work. Finally, he said he'd try it for a while."

Like the young rebel shop stewards, McMaster, Fitzsimmons, and Johnson, Hoffa had grown up the hard way. He and his brother had been the men of his family since his father, a coal miner, died when

Jimmy was seven. Born in Brazil, Indiana, on February 14, 1913, Hoffa moved to Detroit with his mother, brother, and two sisters in 1924. His mother worked in Detroit, as in Brazil, in a laundry.

Quitting school at fourteen, Hoffa got a job as a stock boy with Frank & Cedar Dry Goods and General Merchandise, where he made $12 a week. Later he started work on the loading platform at the Kroger Food Company for 32 cents an hour.

Dave Johnson, whose company used to haul for Kroger, recalls, ''Jimmy sometimes loaded my truck. I didn't actually meet him until a few years later, but he was the kind of guy you don't forget . . . He was a tough guy who kept himself fit. You knew he hated the damn job, because he always had this mean look on his face. But he did work hard, and all the other workers respected him.''

Hoffa had begun to earn that respect in 1932. His thick legs, heavy shoulders, and calloused hands were helpful in the grueling chores on the loading docks. Working conditions were rotten, so Hoffa and some of his fellow workers organized a work stoppage. Bargaining power for the 175 angry warehousemen was several hundred crates of fresh Florida strawberries which were only half loaded in refrigerator cars. If not put on ice quickly, the strawberries would spoil in the hot spring weather. When the Kroger night manager stepped onto the loading platform Hoffa gave him a list of the workers' grievances and he promised to set up a meeting with management the next day. Hoffa and the other men went back to work and finished their loading job.

Hoffa and his cohorts—the ''Strawberry Boys''—met with Kroger executives and, after several days of basic negotiations, received a one-page contract which included a raise of 13 cents an hour. It was the start of a one-company union and affiliated directly with the AFL, federal charter No. 19341. Heading the tiny local were president Sam Calhoun, a thirty-nine-year-old union radical who had received his baptism in such affairs while an employee of the Railway Express Agency; vice president Hoffa; and secretary-treasurer Robert Holmes, an English coal miner who came to Detroit via Canada.

''We used to meet at Connie's Beer Garden here in Detroit, and she let us hold meetings in the basement,'' Holmes remembers. ''We'd get ourselves a couple of pitchers of beer and start talking about the organization. But then Kroger refused to renew the contract, so we lost both our standing with the company and our union charter and were right back where we started.''

In 1935 the Kroger warehousemen were absorbed by the fish-peddlers' local, 674, which with Locals 299 (general freight), 247 (coal haulers), 51 (bakery drivers), 243 (furniture van drivers), and 285 (laundry drivers) made up Detroit Teamsters Joint Council 43. Their headquarters were all huddled together on the second floor of a big brick commercial building on the corner of Trumbull Avenue and Fort Street. When Bennett took over Local 299 in January of 1936, he lobbied with Joint Council president Sam Hurst to cut waste in the Joint Council by eliminating Local 674, feeding its membership into 299.

It was at this point that Bennett began to notice Hoffa, who was getting into more trouble with his bosses because of his rabble-rousing on the loading platform. When Hoffa was finally fired from Kroger in 1936, Bennett talked Hurst into hiring him as a joint council organizer, to work with haulaway drivers for Local 299.

Ever since his Strawberry Boy experience, Hoffa had shown leadership abilities and a union idealism that was rare in Depression-wracked Detroit. When he came on the joint council payroll he soon proved to be a potentially skilled negotiator, and he captured the respect of the city's most ardent trade unionists.

Respected leaders were essential in 1937, when several unions in the Midwest took hard stands against stubborn managements. It was the year of the Republic Steel Massacre in Chicago, when steel workers and their families demonstrating for union recognition were attacked by employer-hired legbreakers and the police. More than a hundred people were shot—many of them in the back—and ten were killed. In Detroit the charismatic Walter Reuther, who was fighting to get Henry Ford to recognize the United Auto Workers, was beaten almost to death during the "battle of the overpass" near the River Rouge plant. As in Chicago, hired guns brought in by the company led the charge against peaceful demonstrators.

In many ways the Detroit Teamsters were worse off than the steel and auto workers. They had less organization, fewer warm bodies, and very little money. Nevertheless, Bennett saw 1937 as the ideal year for his first union assault on management. Prices were rising steadily, wages were low and staying there. A union-sanctioned strike was the only answer.

With Bennett handling the logistics and O'Laughlin, Tyler, Hoffa, and Squires in subordinate roles, Detroit's first city-wide Teamsters strike was called in April.

"The strike lasted only about three days," says Bennett, "and the city drivers received a raise to sixty cents an hour and the over-the-road drivers started making five dollars for each trip to Chicago. Before that, management had kept the workers happy by giving them a handshake on most holidays and maybe a turkey on Christmas.'' Giving young Jim Hoffa credit for the success of the strike, Bennett says, ''It never would have come off without him.''

Hoffa's ability to make the protest click was not based on his organizing; the friendships he had made before becoming an organizer were more important.

During the early 1930s Hoffa had met and had a love affair with a darkly attractive woman named Sylvia Pigano, who had a clerical job with a labor union.

''In about 1934, Sylvia Pigano, after her affair with Hoffa, moved to Kansas City where she married the driver for a gangster-politician type,'' explains a Washington, D.C., law enforcement official who is an expert on organized crime. ''Her husband's name was Sam Scaradino, but he changed it to Frank O'Brien. Her child took the name of her husband and was called Charles O'Brien.

''To add to the strange situation, Frank Coppola, one of the most notorious gangsters in Detroit, became the boy's godfather. After old man O'Brien died, Coppola picked up where Hoffa left off and began having an affair with Sylvia. It was through her that Hoffa was introduced to Coppola and other members of Detroit's underworld.''

Through Sylvia Pagano and Coppola, Hoffa met Santo Perrone, who was by now the chief union buster in Detroit and had also spent two years in prison for liquor law violations. Perrone put Hoffa in touch with Angelo Meli, who was close to Perrone. In the 1930s Meli was head of a firm that was actually a ''drop'' for machine guns and rifles sent to the Detroit mob from New York. The large Meli family was related to both the New York syndicate and the top organized crime figures in Detroit. Arrested three times for murder and once for kidnaping, Meli had been convicted only once, for carrying a concealed weapon.

In 1936 Hoffa married Josephine Poszywak and bought a modest house on Robson Drive. Apparently, however, he did not abandon Sylvia Pigano's underworld connections. When the 1937 strike got underway, Hoffa used his influence with Perrone and Meli to persuade the mob to stay neutral in the union-management battle. ''It wasn't really that Jimmy had made any alliance with these guys during the 1937 strike,'' says Dave Johnson, ''because he didn't. It was simply a matter of knowing who was going to hurt you and then asking them to back off.''

Although the Teamsters' defense forces were only Hoffa's old drinking buddies, the Strawberry Boys, they were enough to repel all the muscle that management could recruit. With the mob out of the action it was hardly a fight.

What did the underworld receive for its cooperation? "Primarily, the mob got its foot in the door in the Detroit trucking industry," says crime authority Piersante. "Perrone's steel hauling interests were handled by his wife while he was in prison. She probably got some kind of break with the union—like it left the business alone. We also know that other crime families started getting into the trucking business during this period of time. It's hard to tell what kind of a deal was made. Most of the union records from that time were later destroyed."

Whatever bargains were struck, they must have been temporary. The union remained independent of mob control. Bennett was still in charge of Local 299 and doing a good job for the Detroit work force; Hoffa was still only an organizer for the joint council.

Because Local 299 had still not won the Kroger workers their long-awaited renewal contract, the warehousemen applied for their own charter from the IBT and in the spring of 1937 became Local 337.

The first thing the officers of the new local did was to call a strike against Kroger. It was a long and unsuccessful one, but the legendary reputations of the Strawberry Boys were built during those eighteen months of combat. Martin Haggerty was shot in the arm while he and Sam Calhoun were beating up a Kroger watchman. Bobby Holmes was jailed several times. And a Detroit attorney, George Fitzgerald, volunteered his legal expertise to get the strikers out of jail.

"I guess it was just after I had been bailed out," says Holmes. "Hoffa and I were having something to eat someplace and talking about our legal problems. Then, just like in the movies, George popped up and offered to help us."

Considering the times, it was no wonder that the Teamsters' heroes were guys who mauled the enemy and got shot up or thrown in the slammer. The cops and the courts were firmly behind management. As Hoffa said in later years, "Nobody can describe the sitdown strikes, the riots, the fights that took place in the state of Michigan, particularly here in Detroit, unless they were part of it."[2]

Hoffa himself was often jailed for his union work, and he was constantly harassed by management goons. He was viewed as a dedicated labor man, a major threat to Detroit employers. "My scalp was laid open sufficiently wide to require stitches no less than six times during the first year I was a business agent of Local 299," he said. "I was beaten up by cops or strikebreakers at least two dozen times that year.''[3]

After the 1937 strike Hoffa was shifted from the joint council to Local 299, to concentrate on over-the-road car haulers. Although many truckers were ready for anarchy, few were prepared for unionization. To some workers unions meant ''godless communism.'' Others believed that organized labor was part of a massive conspiracy by unknown forces, as Henry Ford implied when he said: ''Labor unions are the worst thing that ever struck the earth, because they take away a man's independence. Financiers are behind the unions and their object is to kill competition so as to reduce the income of the workers and eventually bring on war . . . I have always made a better bargain for our men than any outsider could. We never had to bargain against our men, and we don't expect to begin now.''[4]

Hoffa and the Strawberry Boys prided themselves on their ability to be at least as tough as any of the goons who tried to muscle them. But trying to sign up over-the-road drivers and the car haulers who drove loads of three to six automobiles from Detroit to dealers' lots all over the country was hazardous duty. Truckers in the Depression knew that they were easy targets for thieves and hijackers who roamed the highways, so when they parked their rigs along the side of the road to catch a little sleep, it was not uncommon for them to clutch mean-looking tire irons or even guns for self-protection. On the road, soliciting new members, Hoffa approached with the caution of a dog catcher trying to snare a rabid hound.

''I learned to identify myself with a rapid-fire introduction.

'' 'Hi,I'mJimmyHoffaorganizerfortheTeamsters,andIwonderifI couldtalktoyou.'

''Then I'd duck back.''[5]

When Hoffa could rouse the trucker's curiosity without being badly damaged, he would promote his union with candor and forthrightness; no set speeches, but an unparalleled enthusiasm for the rewards of ''teamsterism''—union democracy, rank-and-file control of officials and union policies.

Unlike some fast-talking salesmen, Hoffa was sincere. Discussing the drivers' incredibly poor working conditions, low wages, and lack of job security, Hoffa sounded like a great reformer, a rebel against a tired, cynical business-political establishment afraid to try to change the status quo. Even the skeptical road men had to nod in agreement when he spoke.

"Hoffa became popular among those of us who were tired of the 'Let's wait and things will get better' crap," says Bennett, his first boss at 299. "He seemed inspired to find better ways to make things work."

Hoffa saw himself as the rank and file's champion of justice, a working-class hero. Like other union leaders of the time, he was willing to make tremendous personal sacrifices to educate employees who recognized neither their own rights nor their bosses' responsibilities.

Within a year after the '37 strike, Bennett had signed up nearly four thousand new members and had put Local 299's treasury in the black for the first time since 1933. With the extra cash Bennett continued to enlarge the local's paid staff, and one of the new appointees was Frank Fitzsimmons.

"Fitzsimmons was one of those guys who wouldn't go to work for me at first because the money wasn't there," Bennett says. "He said that he was making more driving a truck. But one day, he came up to me and said, 'Ray, give me a job.' He knew there was a future in it."

Because of Hoffa's success in organizing long-haul drivers, Bennett and Red O'Laughlin asked him in late 1937 to go with them to a meeting in Minneapolis with Farrell Dobbs, a highly respected Minnesota Teamster leader who had led a violent but successful eleven-day strike in Minneapolis three years before.

Dobbs had already done miracles with his city drivers but was having difficulty organizing over-the-road truckers. He needed organizing help and also backing for his idea of setting up area conferences within the IBT which would provide additional bargaining and political strength for the union.

"Farrell kept preaching the fact that nobody could, in the future, nobody would be able to win in their own town or their own state, but had to have expanded coverage for the entire transportation, warehousing, and food industry," Hoffa said later in a television interview. "I realized how right he was and it had an impact on my mind as to the fact that you could no longer live, no matter how well organized, in a particular city or state."[6]

With Bennett's consent, O'Laughlin and Hoffa remained on Local 299's payroll while they led the midwestern organizing campaign for long-distance drivers. To help in his new crusade, Hoffa brought along several of his Strawberry Boys for moral support and physical persuasion.

By spring 1938, with the qualified approval of Dan Tobin—who respected Dobbs but was dubious about an avowed Trotskyist or any "red"—Dobbs had established what was to become the Central States Drivers Council, made up of forty-six locals in twelve midwestern states. Dobbs became the council's first secretary-treasurer, and its main goal was to work toward regional uniformity in the IBT's demands for shorter hours, higher wages, and better working conditions. The Teamsters' efforts were greatly helped by the passage in June 1938 of the Fair Labor Standards Act, which provided for a national minimum wage of 40 cents an hour and a maximum work week of forty hours with time and a half for overtime. Although the law exempted many workers, including over-the-road truckers, it provided a basis for negotiations.

Charged with negotiating for the CSDC's area, Dobbs and his bargaining committee faced their first problem: there was no central bargaining agent for the hundreds of trucking companies within their jurisdiction. Not even the American Trucking Association was authorized to speak for management in labor matters. Dobbs realized that Chicago could be the key, since all midwestern truck routes went in and out of it. A Chicago contract would help establish a region-wide standard.

Dobbs was right. At the union's demand, based on the requirements of the new law, three hundred Chicago companies, large and small, selected an employers' committee headed by John Bridge, vice president of the Interstate Motor Freight System, to conduct a series of talks with union representatives headed by Dobbs and Local 299's O'Laughlin.

In early October 1939 both sides announced the signing of a two-year contract, affecting thousands of truck drivers in the Midwest. There was a 9 percent wage increase for the first year and a further 9 percent raise during the second year. But the ceiling for drivers' time on the job was lowered only from sixty hours a week to fifty-four. The Chicago Independent Truck Drivers Union, a direct descendant of the old separatist United Teamsters, participated in the negotiations.

The most complicated provision of the contract dealt with the status of owner-operators, those who drove their own trucks. Dobbs had negotiated the 9 percent raises for them too, and the result was that the company drivers' pay increase amounted to a raise of ¼ cent per mile, while the owner-operators' increase was double that. The difference was due to the independent status of owner-operators, who were responsible for maintaining their own rigs, paying for their own gas and oil, and paying taxes on their moving property.

The Chicago negotiations brought to the surface a dilemma over owner-operators' standing in the union—whether they were really employees or independent contractors—that would be central to the Teamsters and the industry for years to come. It would lead to strikes, sellouts and bloodshed for the next forty years.

As Dobbs wrote about the CSDC negotiations:

> Firms holding carrier rights issued by the government employed many of these independents (owner-operators), paying them flat rates by the mile, ton, or trip for the rig and driver. It was truly a cut-throat setup. Diverse methods were used to heap inordinate trucking costs upon the owner-operators, thereby shaving down their earnings as drivers. At the same time, devious patterns were woven to confuse the true nature of the employer-worker relationship and turn the individuals in an anti-union direction.[7]

The legal status of owner-operators was somewhat clarified in the Motor Carrier Act of 1935, which ''helped the Teamsters by placing all trucks engaged in interstate commerce under the jurisdiction of the Interstate Commerce Commission,'' says Dave Johnson, who chaired Local 299's over-the-road drivers' grievance committee from 1937 to 1942. ''We were afraid of the unfair competition that owner-operators could give us if they continued to undercut established rates which company drivers' companies had to stick to.''

The act also gave the ICC authority to regulate minimum and maximum rates charged by owner-operators as well as common carriers—that is, fleet owners that hired truckers to use company-owned equipment. In addition, the ICC forced interstate owner-operators to obtain permits before they could lease their rigs to certified carriers, which, under law, had to hire them for at least thirty days. The law required that no driver be permitted to haul longer than ten hours during a twenty-four-hour period. This also helped to neutralize the threat to company drivers from the highly productive owner-operators, who were paid by the load instead of the hour.

Hoffa was with Dobbs in the Chicago contract talks, and his mentor explained to him the importance of regional negotiations and also of the owner-operators. Eager to learn, Hoffa and the other IBT leaders on the scene listened carefully to Dobbs's teachings.

But within the next two years many employers who had signed the CSDC agreement began to cheat their owner-operator drivers. David Lipman, chairman of the Chicago Truck Owners and Operators Association, wrote:

The International Brotherhood of Teamsters has sought . . . to correct [the problems of owner-operators] by placing employment responsibility where it rightfully belongs—on the shoulders of the operating company, which is now held responsible for the driver's wages, social security tax, compensation insurance, etc., regardless of whether he is employed by the operating company or through a small fleet owner.

Not least in importance in the general problem is the driver who is given a paper title to the truck by the operating company, usually on a deferred payment plan, and is then paid as an individual owner-operator, not as a legitimate business relationship, but as subterfuge to escape the payment of the union wage scale.[8]

Tobin and the IBT were fully aware of the situation but allowed it to continue into 1941, when the next contract was scheduled to be negotiated. Although Dobbs pledged to continue helping the owner-operators, other Teamster leaders changed to a policy of refusing ''to negotiate a profit for equipment,'' claiming that ''owner-operators complicate the bargaining process.'' In other words, the IBT abandoned the owner-operators' interests.

Since Dobbs was determined to keep owner-operators in the Teamsters, and to help them to boot, the IBT leadership decided he had to be crushed. And international events provided the means to do it the American way. Independence among the rank and file was not appreciated. The IBT would organize the owner-operators to control them, and would put them out of business whenever possible.

With war spreading in Europe and a high probability that America would be going to war as well, President Roosevelt feared internal subversion within the United States. Because the Soviet Union had made an alliance with Hitler's Germany (in force until the brutal assault on Russia in June 1941), the President wished to remove all ''reds'' as well as Nazis from positions of leadership in the country. Tobin, a close friend of Roosevelt, had supported a resolution passed at the 1935 IBT Convention to oust Communists from the union. So, for God and country, Tobin decided to garner public approval while grinding his own personal ax by eliminating Dobbs. The fact that Dobbs did not support Hitler—merely the German labor unions which had been double-crossed by Der Fuehrer when he took control—had no bearing. Having vocally pledged his support to Trotskyism and, perhaps even worse, to owner-operator truckdrivers—Dobbs had to pay the price.

Seeing the handwriting on the wall, Dobbs and his rebels voted to bolt from the union and join forces with the more militant Congress of Industrial Organizations, founded in 1935 by John L. Lewis after he bitterly "disaffiliated" from the AFL. The Dobbs group began organizing with Lewis's brother, Denny Lewis, who was head of the United Construction Workers Organizing Committee and in charge of the CIO's organizing drive in Minneapolis.

Needing some muscle to take on the combined Dobbs-CIO forces, Tobin and the IBT turned to the Detroit Teamsters for assistance. It seemed to Tobin that the ideal person to head the vigilante brigade was Dobbs's prize pupil, Jimmy Hoffa.

While Hoffa thought hard about what to do, Tobin started making promises about the young Teamster's future career. Some of them sounded pretty good to a fellow who was still making less than $75 a week.

"Right about that time I was chairing a grievance meeting for the over-the-road drivers in Detroit," Johnson remembers, "and a couple of guys from Minneapolis came in to observe us. We knew they were trouble, so everyone tried to ignore them. Hoffa was there, and when one of Dobbs's boys complimented us on the way we ran our meetings, Jimmy told them, 'Yeah, and we didn't need any of you damn Communists helping us.' "

Hoffa had made his decision.

Bennett's Local 299 agreed to handle the battle with the Minneapolis radicals, and Hoffa was chosen as the operation's field marshal. The Strawberry Boys and selected musclemen were his army.

In a television interview years later, Hoffa said, "I think that [Tobin] used our relationship because I had refused to go on a request, or on an order. When he ordered me to go to Minneapolis, I said I wouldn't go and it was none of my business. And then he put it on a personal basis, as a request, and brought up what he'd done for me and so forth, and what he was gonna do for me. And once the old man made a personal request at his age, you couldn't very well turn him down. Recognizing he was the General President, I went there . . . went into Minneapolis, went over, took over the office, brought in a hundred crack guys, had the war. We won every battle. And we finally took the union over and then Farrell left and went with the Socialist Party."

On the same show Dobbs replied, "Now it is true that Hoffa was among the IBT goon squads that Tobin sent into Minneapolis . . . That's actually true. But he says, he says in effect there *he* whipped us. For instance, he was helped by the Minneapolis Police Department, the courts of the city, the county, and the state . . . the mayor, the governor and an antilabor law that had been rigged and put through by the Republican governor of the state, and by the Federal Bureau of Investigation, the United States Department of Justice and Franklin Delano Roosevelt, who then happened to be President of the United States . . . Under those circumstances you got to admit Hoffa had just a little help, didn't he? The man exaggerates on this point. He exaggerates."[9]

After many violent clashes between the unionists, Dobbs and twenty-seven other Socialist Workers Party and union leaders were indicted by the Justice Department on charges of sedition under the Smith Act, passed in 1940. Eighteen were found guilty and Dobbs was sentenced to twelve to eighteen months in prison. Tobin quickly named Hoffa the negotiating chairman of the regional Central States Drivers Council, replacing Dobbs. R. J. Bennett became an IBT general organizer and received more locals to command.

Although Dobbs was defeated, Denny Lewis was not. He got a "catchall" charter from the CIO for his United Construction Workers Organizing Committee and in the summer of 1941 he set Locals 299 and 337 in Detroit as his next targets.

With the Minneapolis struggle behind him and Lewis dead ahead, Hoffa had graduated into the big leagues of organized labor. The two-fisted, beer-drinking Strawberry Boys were no longer enough for the larger-scale brawls of the future. "We needed some husky guys around," Bennett says. "What the hell, I didn't need no college graduates. I wanted someone who wasn't afraid to use his dukes. So I gave Jimmy the authority to hire Rolland McMaster. McMaster was tough like no one I've ever seen." McMaster had been in his share of battles since he joined Local 299 in 1933, but this was his first time on the Teamster payroll.

"We went together then," McMaster recalls, "because we had an attack from Denny Lewis's outfit. They wanted to take the Teamsters over. We had a real out-and-out battle with those fellows . . . and it was one of those old-fashioned fights with sticks. And it even got to the pistol business."

Hoffa decided that Local 299's day-to-day manager, Red O'Laughlin, and his assistant, Vic Tyler, had been too close to Dobbs to run the local during this critical time. McMaster, who was chairman of the city drivers' grievance committee, says, "We started having stormy, rebellious meetings. They weren't thinking the way we wanted them to think."

"That's right," Johnson agrees. "So we had a Policy Board

meeting, and all the stewards—me and McMaster included—decided to give Jimmy the authority to pressure O'Laughlin and Tyler out.''

Bennett, still the receiver of Local 299, consented to the coup, and O'Laughlin and Tyler were thrown out of the local. Because O'Laughlin still had some friends at IBT headquarters in Indianapolis, he was able to swing a job as an IBT organizer in North and South Dakota. Tyler, with no friends, bought a small farm; he never returned to union politics and never wanted to.

Hoffa had risen fast and far in less than a decade. He would be hard to stop from here on. And it had cost him only three betrayals— O'Laughlin and Dobbs, and several thousand owner-operators.

3 The Oppressed Become the Oppressors

Local 299's first headquarters, shared with six other locals, had been the second floor of an old three-story red-brick building in downtown Detroit. In 1941, with a growing membership and a sound treasury, the Detroit Teamsters moved into their own offices a couple of blocks north, on Trumbull Avenue. The new two-story building, of drab light-and dark-brown brick, was built like a fortress, with right angles and heavy, three-paned windows which symbolized the strength the Teamsters hoped to achieve.

Dan Tobin showed up on December 15 to dedicate the Teamster hall and surprised Local 299's officials by reissuing their charter. Bennett's receivership was a success; Local 299 had become one of the most respected locals in the Midwest. But as Tobin cut the ribbon and gave back the charter, Local 299's assets were in serious jeopardy.

Denny Lewis and his CIO catchall union had formally declared war on the Teamsters on September 4, 1941, at the Hotel Statler in Detroit. Announcing that the United Construction Workers Organizing Committee's first goal was the area's auto haulaway drivers, Russell Turner, an assistant to Lewis, claimed, ''We have a fair percentage of the employees of these firms organized right now,'' and added that the CIO had already put twenty-five union organizers to work in Detroit.[1]

Scoffing at Turner's cool confidence, Frank X. Martel, president of Detroit's AFL, replied that the Teamsters Union could take care of itself. ''Instead of being worried, we're inclined to laugh.''[2]

Martel's statement of confidence was premature. Undermanned

after the Minneapolis battles against Dobbs and the CIO, Locals 299 and 337 had to fight in Detroit without government forces on their side. Local 337 was, however, in better shape internally than it had been earlier. Its president, former Joint Council organizer Owen Bert Brennan, one of Hoffa's close friends, had been arrested three times before, for bombing trucks and businesses. He was arrested again in 1941, after a company that had signed with the CIO was bombed.

Brennan, whose trademarks were his wide-lapel trench coat and brimmed hat, jauntily cocked and pulled down to shadow his eyes, had been elected president when his predecessor was blamed for the local's failure to organize the Kroger Food Company after the long, vicious strike of 1937. Vice president Martin Haggerty and Robert Holmes, the British secretary-treasurer, survived the Local 337 shakeup, and Brennan was close to victory at Kroger—with the help of $250,000 in loans, most of it from Local 299.

On September 18, 1941, after Walter Reuther and most of the members of his UAW, which was also a member of the CIO, refused to support Lewis and the CIO's raids in Detroit, the *Detroit Free Press* published a prophetic editorial:

> Reports out of Chicago are that the International Executive Board of the UAW-CIO is divided over the support to be given to the Detroit CIO's Truck Drivers' Union in its membership drive. A delegation from the new union attended the Chicago meeting to urge all aid and assistance. Cooler heads, however, argued the obvious: That an all-out drive would necessarily include a raid against the AFL Teamsters Union; that such a raid would be violently resisted by the AFL; finally, that an almost certain result would be a bloody war locally between the two labor groups.
>
> Union business is union business, but such a prospect is definitely of concern to the whole Detroit public. It is one thing to "organize the unorganized"—the basic principle in the CIO's formation. It is quite another to begin guerrilla campaigns against established unions. They can only lead to serious trouble.

Clashes between Teamsters and CIO forces became "so common that pedestrians couldn't walk down the street without seeing a couple of union guys rolling around, thrashing each other," Holmes remembers. "There was no doubt about the fact that they wanted to tear us up and destroy us. When you consider the sweetheart contracts they were passing out to employers to make themselves attractive and acceptable, we, the Teamsters, were fighting for our survival." The Teamsters began to take the threat of the CIO more seriously when reports flooded the union hall that drivers who refused to stop and talk to CIO organizers were being fired upon.

As Bennett and Hoffa sent their army into the streets to combat the CIO thugs, the Teamsters, badly outnumbered, suffered heavy losses. At least one man was killed; scores were hurt. Dave Johnson was clubbed several times and nearly killed in one fight. ''That same day,'' he recalls, ''my friend Frank Fitzsimmons, who was a 299 business agent, got his head beat in, too. Because some of his hair was missing, we thought someone threw acid on him.''

One story that was told and retold in many versions began on a drizzly afternoon when city cartage grievance chairman Rolland McMaster and joint council organizer Tom Burke were walking away from a picket line with five other Teamster toughs armed with baseball bats and knives. As they got near their cars they spotted two CIO men sitting in a car nearby. When the two men saw McMaster and the others, they locked the car doors and tried to drive away. Unfortunately their car wouldn't start.

Frantically rocking back and forth in their seats, trying to move the two-ton automobile with sheer body momentum—and seeing McMaster looming larger and larger in the corners of their eyes—the CIO men must have seen their lives pass in review as McMaster, towering above the car, crashed his steely fists onto the hood. Then, with one mighty jab, he smashed his hand through the window, grabbed the driver by the hair, and pulled him through the shattered glass, tossing him into the street to Burke and the others. McMaster then opened the car door and dived at the other man, who couldn't open his door to escape; while Burke and the rest beat the driver with their baseball bats and sliced him up with their knives, McMaster tore out the gearshift handle and began beating the other union man.

Three off-duty motorcycle cops, roaring by, spotted the massacre, stopped and drew their guns to save a couple of lives while arresting the Teamsters for assault and battery. Later the case against McMaster and his friends was dismissed when the CIO men refused to testify for fear of further reprisals.

While McMaster was under indictment for the episode, Hoffa made him a business agent for Local 299. A month later, in December 1941, Dave Johnson became one as well. ''But we weren't enough,'' Johnson says, shrugging. ''The CIO had tougher guys than any of us expected. So Jimmy went to see Santo Perrone.''

Perrone, Angelo Meli, Frank Coppola, and other crime figures gave Hoffa the support he needed to drive the CIO raiders out of Detroit.

When their defeat was imminent Denny Lewis and the CIO told the press that "professional hoodlums and gangsters" were intimidating truck drivers into "joining the AFL Teamsters Union."[3] The CIO raiders were defeated by the end of the year. And considering the new players on Hoffa's team, it was a miracle that the CIO survived at all in Detroit.

There was jubilation in the Teamsters Union; its turf had been protected. But the victory was a tragedy for the American labor movement. The CIO's defeat, brought about by Hoffa's ringers, became the major factor in his rapid plunge from union reformer to labor racketeer. His pact with the underworld, no matter how tenuous at the time, took him out of the running as a potentially great leader of the Teamsters' rank and file.

"Jimmy dealt with the mob on a regular basis, beginning with his problems with Denny Lewis and the CIO in Detroit," says a close Hoffa associate. "There's no use debating it or dodging it. But even after Lewis was run out of Detroit, Hoffa still handled the mob in an independent way, at arm's length. They got something for their money, but he still tried to represent the union membership."

When war came to the United States on December 7, 1941, the Teamsters, like other labor unions, faced serious problems. Forbidden to strike by the 1943 Smith-Connally Anti-Strike Act, the labor movement was further hampered by the National War Labor Board, which was the final arbiter in labor-management disputes during the war years. While managements got huge defense contracts for the war effort, labor's pressure for better wages was filtered through the new laws and regulations. Without the ultimate weapon of the strike, the unions' bargaining power was substantially weakened.

The Teamsters, however, were better off than most. Just three weeks before the Second World War began Hoffa had negotiated a 13 percent wage increase for drivers within the twelve-state Central States Drivers Council, barely averting a strike. He then began to concentrate on his statewide organization, the Michigan Conference of Teamsters, which he had created in emulation of Dobbs and of which he had become head the year before. Hoffa had noticed the talents of Frank Fitzsimmons and selected him as the Michigan Conference's secretary-treasurer. Bright and tough, Fitzsimmons was highly respected, and he and Hoffa—along with Bert Brennan, now vice president of the Michigan Conference—fought to maintain the uniformity of contracts and continuity of negotiations that had been set up before the war.

The draft threatened to absorb much of Local 299's membership and most of its officers. When Hoffa received his 1-A classification he asked R. J. Bennett to ask the draft board for a deferment. Claiming that Hoffa's work with the Teamsters was vital to the transportation industry and thus to the country's war effort, Bennett successfully kept him out of the armed services.

Rolland McMaster was also trying to get a deferment and went to Hoffa for help. Hoffa wrote to the draft board, describing the business agent's activities as the

> settling of all labor disputes between management and labor and particularly through his extensive knowledge [which] was very successful in the careful handling of all jurisdictional disputes between various A.F. of L. labor organizations; also with the CIO, in particular of keeping a continuous supply of essential war materials flowing into our war industries.[4]

Hoffa also insisted that McMaster should be exempted because of his glass eye. Nevertheless McMaster was drafted. He was to spend three and a half years in Europe as a private first class in the military police, specializing, interestingly enough, in criminal investigations.

Hoffa was more successful for others in the hierarchy. On the basis that Fitzsimmons was too valuable and that Johnson, at thirty-four, was too old and had four children to support, Hoffa persuaded the board to defer them both.

During the war years the Detroit Teamster locals continued to organize, collect dues, process grievances, and represent the area's truck drivers and warehousemen. In Local 299 "we organized truckers, the guys on the loading platform, and others who were nonunion and who worked in federal stores, the local barns [of trucking companies], and the mills—about a thousand new members in all,'' Johnson estimates.

"We also worked with the government,'' he says "For the most part, our main obligation was to keep the trucks rolling and not to strike or anything like that. We also had to conserve our resources, like rubber and gasoline. To save the tread on tires, we put trailers loaded with cargo on barges and ships and sent them to different places on the Great Lakes.''

Truckers were also encouraged to join another government program, the U.S. Truck Conservation Corps, which promoted preventive maintenance for their rigs. Participants received a red, white, and blue emblem which was pasted patriotically on their cab doors.

Hoffa was less concerned with conservation than with construction. He spent the war years solidifying his empire in Michigan. Sometimes his enthusiasm got him into trouble. He was not jailed but he stood trial in 1941 and again in 1942. In the first trial he pleaded no contest to antitrust charges in connection with labor racketeering in Detroit's wastepaper industry, admitting that he had helped union companies prevent nonunion companies from operating.

The second indictment charged that he had extorted thousands of dollars from a ma-and-pa grocery store association which was hauling its own goods with nonunion labor. A letter to the city director of markets from a food distributor saying that local suppliers were being "threatened and intimidated by a bunch of racketeers" brought the racket into the open, and a reply from the director agreed that the charges were "essentially correct" and went into detail about how the shakedown methods worked: Hoffa, with the help of his friends in the mob, was forcing the grocery association members to purchase "permits" from the Teamsters.

"The local figured they had spent that much in establishing their own [association] and that outsiders wanting its benefits should pay for them," Hoffa retorted in his own defense. But after the felony charge was reduced to a simple misdemeanor, Hoffa pled guilty and paid a small fine.

During one of the grand jury investigations the vice president of Teamsters Local 247, Herbert Crimp, appeared to testify against Hoffa about the shakedowns. Afterward, as Crimp hurriedly left the grand jury room, Hoffa spotted him and shouted, "You dirty bastard! I'll have you killed for this! You won't live through the night!" Understandably frightened by the threat—which was heard by several people standing in the courthouse hall—Crimp requested and promptly received twenty-four-hour protection for himself and his family. Headlines read, "Threats Get Police Guard for Official" and "Jury Probes Threat to Teamster Witness." Detroit was beginning to take this fellow Hoffa seriously, and in the process helping to enhance his tough-guy reputation.

The Teamster leadership was proud of Hoffa. Tobin made him one of the three trustees of the IBT and offered him a job as an organizer with the international office. The organizer's job would have paid much better, but Hoffa knew that in Indianapolis he would be a subordinate while in Detroit he was king. Soon afterward, with the help of his new mob friends, he overthrew an old friend, Sam Hurst, who had given him his first Teamster job, and became the president of Detroit Joint Council 43.

Hoffa's incipient allies were getting richer. The black market and war-profiteering rackets were a boon to organized crime. Dealing in stolen ration stamps for gasoline and paying off officials for protection brought New York mobster Carlo Gambino into the syndicate's upper levels. Carlos Marcello, switchman for dope deals in New Orleans, and Santos Trafficante, Sr., Florida's pivot man in the drug traffic between Marseilles, Cuba, Tampa, and Kansas City, became the mob's narcotics czars in the South.

Joseph Bonanno, Thomas Lucchese, Vincent Mangano, and Joseph Profaci laid the groundwork for postwar expansion in Brooklyn while Frank Costello strengthened his operations in Manhattan and, with Meyer Lansky, began expanding south to New Orleans and west to Las Vegas, where they financed the Flamingo Hotel, first of a string of syndicate-supported casinos. Through his close friendship with Cuban dictator Fulgencio Batista, Lansky, organized crime's financial wizard, directed most of the gambling operations in Cuba with the full support of its government.

Costello was caretaker of the New York syndicate for Charles Luciano, who was serving thirty to fifty years for running a prostitution ring. Luciano had done only five years of his sentence when the war began, but this did not prevent his becoming one of the more uniikely heroes of World War II.

Facing the strong possibility of sabotage on the New York waterfront, U.S. Navy Counterintelligence asked Luciano to order his waterfront racketeers to guard against enemy infiltration. Prodded by Lansky, who was also involved in the scheme, Luciano cooperated, and he cooperated later on with the Office of Strategic Services (which later became the Central Intelligence Agency) in the invasion of Sicily in 1943. This was the first time on record that American intelligence worked with organized crime.

Presumably Luciano sent orders to his Sicilian subordinates to give the American army all possible help:

> The Mafia within its loose, localized hierarchies, wanted to help get the Axis forces off the island, get on well enough with the Allies, and get back to peace and prosperity for its own purposes. For example, *mafiosi* bravely volunteered to serve in large numbers as "native guides" for Allied forces. As the OSS official report on the Sicily campaign later stated: "It was

quickly found that agent personnel recruited and trained in the United
States for Secret Intelligence work could not be used on short-range, tactical
or combat intelligence missions. In contrast, selected natives, recruited,
trained and briefed on the spot, had not only natural cover for line-crossing,
but also an intimate knowledge of the terrain.'''

One of Luciano's henchmen, Vito Genovese, was firmly on the Axis
side, at least at the time. He had fled to Italy in the 1930s to avoid a
murder charge and quickly became a good friend to Benito Mussolini.
Genovese contributed a quarter of a million dollars to help build the
Fascist Party's central offices in Rome, and in 1943 he ordered the
murder in New York of Carlo Tresca, an antifascist newspaper editor
who was Mussolini's bitter enemy. Carmine Galante, a rising star in
the mob, was thought to be the killer.

When the Americans invaded Italy and the citizens strung up their
despot, Genovese quickly volunteered his services as an interpreter for
the U.S. Army. He returned to New York in 1945 and was arrested on
the old murder charge, but it was dismissed when the key witness
against him was found dead of poison.

Within months after the Allied victory, Genovese's boss, Charles
Luciano, was rewarded with a parole and deportation to Italy. Exiled
but far from retired, he soon established the most important narcotics
route to America, in partnership with a French-Corsican mob leader
named Antoine d'Agostino, a former Nazi collaborator. Two of
Luciano's key lieutenants were deported Detroit syndicate figures
Frank Coppola and Salvatore Vitale, both well acquainted with Jimmy
Hoffa.

''To all intents and purposes,'' says Charles Siragusa, a Bureau of
Narcotics officer who was the head of an American group investigating
the Italian drug connection, ''Detroit was the primary point of drug
imports, and the Detroit mob fed the rest of the country, even New
York. . . .

''Coppola and Vitale had a number of ways of getting the heroin to
their contacts in Detroit. Boats, planes, anything that could get across
the Atlantic was used. I remember that they often smuggled the stuff in
legitimate-appearing shipments of sardines.''

John Priziola and Raffaele Quasarano were the key receivers in
Detroit. Priziola, a five-foot-three native of Partinico, in Sicily, had
succeeded Coppola as head of the American segment of the Partinico
clan. Heroin from Coppola and Vitale came in to an importing com-

pany and from there to a nearby fish store owned by Peter Tocco, an ex-bootlegger who was both Priziola's son-in-law and the nephew of Angelo Meli. Narcotics officers believe that Meli was responsible for Detroit–New York cooperation in the smuggling through his close ties with Frank Livorsi, a major East Coast drug dealer whose daughter was married to Meli's son. Another Livorsi in-law, John Ormento, who owned a trucking company and had been convicted three times for drug trafficking, picked up heroin in Detroit and trucked it back East.

Quasarano, the other receiver, was Ormento's chief contact, because Meli refused to become directly involved. With his extensive arrest record for violating drug laws and for armed robbery, Quasarano was becoming an important figure in the Detroit syndicate.

As the narcotics business boomed, the members of the Detroit dope ring expanded into another growth industry, jukeboxes, an area to which Jimmy Hoffa had close ties.

Near the end of the war, Local 299 and Brennan's Local 337 lent Eugene James $2000 to reorganize Local 985, a small car-wash and garage workers' union which had been dormant for several years. The first thing James did was to put Hoffa's and Brennan's wives on his payroll, using their maiden names.[6] The second thing was to begin organizing in the coin-machine industry: jukebox, cigarette, and game machine employees.

Simultaneously the Detroit mob began buying up distributorships. Angelo Meli's nephew, Vincent A. Meli, bought the Meltone Music Company with $30,000 worth of help from his uncle. Peter Tocco, owner of the fish market *cum* heroin drop, opened the Jay-Cee Music Company with Quasarano and Michael Polizzi, John Priziola's son-in-law.

In 1945, Angelo Meli added another valuable connection to his family when a niece married William Bufalino, a young Pennsylvania attorney. Fiery-tempered and high-strung, Bufalino was a cousin of Russell Bufalino, underboss of the Joseph Barbara crime family of Pittston, Pennsylvania, which controlled mob activities in the northeastern part of the state.

''[The government says that] in the underworld, you either have to be born in it or you have to get in by marriage,'' William Bufalino says proudly. '' . . . I married a Detroit girl . . . If you want to charge me with something regarding Russell Bufalino, charge me with the fact that I selected him as my number-one friend . . . Because my daughter . . . is the godchild of Russell Bufalino and his wife. In other words, we selected them to be the godparents of my daughter. This is a closer relationship than a brother.''

Encouraged to get into the jukebox business with the rest of the Meli family, Bill Bufalino borrowed $20,000 from a Pittston bank and, with $25,000 from Peter Tocco's father, established the Bilvin Distributing Company. Bilvin's other stockholders—Angelo Meli, John Priziola, and other racketeers—put up another $96,000 to get the business in gear.

In the spring of 1947, Local 985's president decided that he could not work with the mobsters who had taken over the jukebox industry. James went to Hoffa for help and Hoffa suggested that he hire Bill Bufalino as his assistant. As soon as Bufalino was named to the post his company was closed down, and after Bufalino had been on the payroll for two weeks Hoffa deposed James and made Bufalino president.

As for Local 299, with its charter restored and the IBT's approval to hold elections, the membership had filed into the polls at the union hall and elected Hoffa president in December 1946. Frank Fitzsimmons was vice president, Dave Johnson recording secretary, Strawberry Boys Frank Collins and Sam Calhoun secretary-treasurer and trustee; Hoffa's old organizing partner, Al Squires, was the second trustee, and George Roxburgh, a newcomer to the leadership, was the third. In accordance with the IBT constitution, the three trustees were responsible for monthly examinations of the local's books. The seven officers made up the local's executive board, responsible for general administration as well as all policy decisions not voted upon by the membership.

Because of Hoffa's strong emphasis on statewide organizing the Teamsters had remained strong and at the end of the war were again in a position to challenge management. As he negotiated new contracts in Michigan, Hoffa's reputation and influence grew in other midwestern states. The machinery to bargain for and implement uniform regional agreements—the Central States Drivers Council—was already in place, and uniformity was desperately needed in the Central States. Wages varied from 75 cents to two dollars an hour, and work weeks ranged from forty to sixty hours. Some drivers had benefits like overtime, holiday pay, and vacations; others had nothing at all.

''We really had our work cut out for us, but we didn't have that many old-timers around to get things moving again,'' says Johnson. ''So when everyone came back from the war, Hoffa called a big meeting and brought a bunch of guys back with the local. One of those guys was McMaster.

''But Mac came back to Detroit with a kind of chip on his shoulder—being in the service and all—so he and Jimmy were always fighting at first about something . . . One of their arguments was because McMaster wanted to wear his army uniform—ribbons and all—when he was working a picket line.''

McMaster recalls, ''When I came back from overseas, I remember Jimmy was running the ship pretty well then. For some reason he was unhappy with me. But he gave me one company that had 99 people in it. He said, 'If you can build that up, you can stay here—we can afford you.' ''

The company was Transamerican Freight Lines, one of the many hauling businesses that used nonunion owner-operator truckers.

''So Hoffa said, 'Do you think you can do anything with these steel haulers and commodity carriers throughout the country?' And I said I didn't know. I went at it and started calling some meetings, and I made very good progress. And he gave me an airplane which I could use whenever I wanted to use it.''

He needed it—there were a lot of truckers to corral. After the war trucks that had been stockpiled by the military could be bought cut rate, and some drivers were able to finance a small fleet, hiring unemployed friends and relatives to drive the extra trucks.

''That's the way I started my career in this business,'' one small fleet owner explains. ''I needed a job after the war, so my uncle—who had bought several trucks from the government—asked me to drive one. Things were going well but then we were told by Hoffa that he didn't want us to own our own equipment. He said that if we didn't own it before the war, we weren't going to own it after.

''Hell, I had a dream of parlaying my own earnings into the purchase of my own truck and then maybe a fleet of them. I finally got it, but it was a hell of a fight.''

For the Teamsters the old problem of how to deal with owner-operators had become worse. Hoffa, as chief negotiator for the CSDC, now accepted the IBT position completely: those who owned their own trucks were independent businessmen and not employees.

''After the war, Jimmy really turned against the owner-operators in that he didn't want anyone to be one,'' Johnson says. ''Everyone should work for a certified carrier and use his equipment. Of course this made the owner-operators mad at the union and turned them against us.''

Most midwestern Teamsters quickly fell into line with Hoffa's contract demands—even those owner-operators who didn't understand how they were being compromised. But a considerable proportion of steel haulers in Ohio, most of them owner-operators, rebelled against Hoffa's authority.

"When we started making separate peace settlements with the companies we worked for and getting a better deal in the process, the word got around," an Ohio steel hauler remembers. "Soon there was an exodus of owner-operators from other states who swarmed into Ohio to set up their operation. And this was all happening just sixty miles south of Detroit, where Hoffa was brooding about the whole thing."

At the same time, nonunion owner-operators in Ohio increased their business by working for less than the established ICC rates and by hauling intrastate only to avoid federal wage-and-hour regulations. The Teamsters' problems were compounded when the Ohio carriers—the employers—began institutionalizing these practices by encouraging drivers to buy their own rigs and split load revenues with the company. With this arrangement the employer avoided all maintenance expenses for the trucks he didn't own. Some carriers even sold off their trucks and leased independents to haul the goods they had contracted to carry.

In addition, Teamster-style organizing was somewhat hampered by two new laws: the 1946 Hobbs Anti-Racketeering Act, which prohibited obstruction of goods involved in commerce or threats of violence for such purposes; and the 1947 Taft-Hartley Act, designed to outlaw jurisdictional strikes and prevent the use of strongarm tactics against the self-employed. Violators of these laws could receive a ten-year stretch and a $10,000 fine, or both.

"You can tell me all you want to about 'fair play' on the picket line," one Teamster organizer said about the legislation, "but violence and union organizing go hand-in-hand. Hell, it can't be avoided. Either the union, the employer, or the employees themselves will start it if the economic pressure is there."

Hoffa sent two of his best men to Ohio. Johnson and McMaster had the difficult assignment of organizing the owner-operators and forcing them to work at legal scales. With blackjack diplomacy still used but less blatantly, the Teamsters began allowing uncertified employers who cooperated with the union to make illegal interstate shipments. As one company owner puts it, "We were allowed to use union city drivers to participate in the steel haul." The Local 299 strike force also favored steel mills that loaded or unloaded company-owned trucks first, forcing owner-operators to wait long hours when they did get work.

"Unfair!" Union and nonunion owner-operators threatened to shut down the steel hauling industry until the illegal use of city drivers was halted.

"Frank Fitzsimmons, Hoffa's right-hand man, came down to Toledo with McMaster and Johnson and tried to talk us out of pulling a wildcat strike, along with the union owner-operators who were also being affected by all this shit," says a steel hauler who was at the meeting with Fitzsimmons. "He was shouted down time after time until he finally agreed to pull the city men off our loads."

Trying to protect themselves and their investments, in 1948 the Ohio owner-operators formed a dissident reform group, the Motor Truck Steel Haulers Association, and they got some support from drivers in Indiana, Michigan, and Pennsylvania. Concentrating on problems with regulatory agencies like the ICC, which the independents claimed allowed the Teamsters to run roughshod over their rights, the rebels were also concerned about taxes, permits, tariffs, and other major problems for owner-operators.

Fighting the Teamsters, who were right next door, and simultaneously battling it out with an immovable government bureaucracy, proved too much for MTSHA and the group faded and died within a year. Nevertheless, the Ohio owner-operators remained strong enough, individually, to resist Hoffa and the CSDC until 1952, when many of the independents gave in to Johnson and McMaster and became Teamsters.

Working together Johnson and McMaster had become close friends. They and their wives went to parties and even on vacation together. Noticing how well the relationship was clicking, Hoffa began to use the two men as a team on other union business around the country.

"Mac and I were really close," says Johnson. "And we were both very loyal to Jimmy. We worked in Jersey City, New Jersey, for a while. Then we worked in St. Louis and Indianapolis to put some locals in order and straighten out some problems for the drivers.

"Once we were attending a meeting in Buffalo with Jimmy and a couple of guys came running down the center aisle, shouting, 'We'll get you! We'll get you!' They tried to run Jimmy off the stage, but me and Mac stood beside him, slugging anyone who tried to get near him."

Another time, after muscling some troublemakers, McMaster and Johnson were seen walking triumphantly out of a union hall with their arms around each other's shoulders, like two high-school football heroes walking off the gridiron after one had thrown a touchdown pass to the other. Their adventures during organizing campaigns always made for great storytelling sessions back at Local 299, where they talked and laughed into the early morning hours.

One story they didn't tell was about one of their trips to cool the tempers of union members on the East Coast. Hearing that the pair was in New Jersey on business, an East Coast employer who did business in Detroit and was having trouble with the union asked his friend, Albert Anastasia, to ''discuss'' the matter with them. A member of the notorious Murder, Inc., of the 1930s, which handled all syndicate-authorized killings, Anastasia was also the chief racketeer on the Brooklyn waterfront. He was not a man to bad-mouth.

With two armed torpedoes standing beside him, Anastasia introduced himself and murmured to the two organizers, ''Listen, I understand that you've been giving a friend of mine some labor problems.'' The name Anastasia meant nothing to Johnson and McMaster.

As Anastasia's thugs clutched the cannons in their pockets, passing cold stares, one of the Teamsters responded curtly, ''Well, you're just gonna have to tell your 'friend' to get himself straightened out, pal.''

''And you can tell those two gorillas behind you that if they want to start something, we're ready,'' the other organizer added in defense of his friend. ''We work for Jimmy Hoffa.''

Harsh words and looks continued but somehow the encounter ended in a bloodless draw.

''Hoffa nearly died when he heard what had happened,'' so the story goes. '' 'Do you have any idea who that was? Do you have any idea who Albert Anastasia is?' Jimmy shouted.

''Me and my buddy didn't know before Hoffa told us, and we were scared. So Jimmy ended up hustling us out of New Jersey and checked us into a hotel in New York until Jimmy's friends cooled Anastasia down so we could go back to Detroit.''

Through his relationships with the local underworld, Hoffa had by now become acquainted with gangsters on the East Coast, including Meli's in-law Frank Livorsi, the New York narcotics trafficker. According to a close associate, Hoffa was involved with Livorsi's own in-laws, who included Tom and John Dioguardi and their uncle, James Plumeri. The Dioguardis and Plumeri, convicted extortionists in the labor rackets, were in turn part of a tightly knit clan that included Thomas Lucchese, a garment industry mobster and a close associate of Anastasia; Luciano's caretakers, Frank Costello and Vito Genovese; and Russell Bufalino in Pennsylvania.

Joe Valachi, a Genovese aide, later recalled:

Now the next thing I got to worry about is the union, so I go downtown to
the garment district to see Jimmy Doyle, right name Plumeri, or one of the
Dio [Dioguardi] brothers, Johnny or Tommy, I forget who, I think it was
Jimmy, but it don't make no difference as the Dios are his nephews, and
when you talk to one, you are talking to all of them. They are in Tommy
Brown's [Lucchese's] Family, and they are supposed to straighten out any
trouble with the union . . .

I'd say I was in the dress business for about twelve years, and we only had
a couple of complaints. If any union organizer came around, all I had to do
was call up John Dio or Tommy Dio and all my troubles were over.[7]

With allies in the East, Hoffa already had firm midwestern support
through his former mistress. Sylvia Pagano O'Brien had married again
and was living in Detroit with her husband, John Paris, a laundry
executive. Through Mrs. Paris—who was a frequent houseguest of the
Hoffa family—he met Morris Dalitz, a key figure in the "Purple
Gang," a bunch of young punk bootleggers whose leader was named
Norman Purple. A Jewish gang that preyed on the Jewish community—though it occasionally hired Sicilian gunmen for additional
firepower—the Purple Gang had fled from Michigan after two bloody
battles with a rival Jewish group. Dalitz, who went to Ohio, helped
organize the Cleveland syndicate, which soon became part of the
National Crime Syndicate founded by Charles Luciano and Meyer
Lansky.

"They said I knew Moe Dalitz," Hoffa once remarked, "and that
he was a big deal in the Mafia. Hell, yes, I knew Dalitz. I've known
him since way back when he owned a string of laundries in Detroit and
we threatened him with a strike."[8]

It was Dalitz who in the 1940s established communication between
the Teamster boss and members of the Cleveland organization, including Ohio jukebox czar William Presser, and Louis Triscaro, an ex-
boxer who chummed around with West Coast gangster Mickey
Cohen—who was originally from Cleveland. In 1948 Dalitz left
Cleveland for Las Vegas, where he built the Desert Inn, but he made
sure that Hoffa was well tuned in with his successor, Frank Milano.

Using one of his earliest friends in organized crime, Santo Perrone,
Hoffa met Paul Dorfman, a former Capone henchman who was in the
good graces of Anthony Accardo, one of Capone's successors in
Chicago. Perrone, still in the steel and scrap hauling business, had

done business with Dorfman, who was the president of the crime-controlled Chicago Scrap Handlers Union. He had assumed control of the local when its founder, Leon Cooke, was murdered.

"The first and only time I ever met 'Red' Dorfman was when he came to Detroit, trying to get Jimmy's help for some trucking problems he was having in Chicago," says one of Hoffa's aides. "After that, he and Jimmy became good friends. But it was something people didn't talk too much about."

Through Dorfman, Hoffa drew alliances with Joseph Glimco, a corrupt trustee of the Chicago cabdrivers' Local 777, who had been arrested more than thirty times—twice for murder; Paul DeLucia, another former Capone lieutenant who had become a power in the midwestern syndicate; and former bootlegger Sam Giancana, arrested more than seventy times, and convicted twice.

Hoffa justified such relationships as "pure common sense. I don't hurt them; they don't hurt me."

But Dorfman's kindness did not go unreciprocated. In early 1949 Hoffa set up the Michigan Conference of Teamsters Welfare Fund. In 1951 he persuaded the fund's two trustees—employee representative Frank Fitzsimmons and an employer delegate—to move the fund to the newly formed Chicago branch of Union Casualty Agency. The branch was owned by Dorfman's wife, Rose, and his stepson, Allen, a dapper ex-Marine with no experience in the insurance business. Solicited by Paul Dorfman, the New York parent company gave Allen his start in the lucrative industry and helped him set up the Chicago branch. Through his stepfather, Allen Dorfman met Hoffa and Local 337's president, Owen Bert Brennan.

When Union Casualty received fiduciary responsibility for the Michigan Conference Fund, Hoffa had already created a larger welfare fund, the Central States Health and Welfare Fund, which had also thrown its business to Union Casualty.

The two fund accounts made up 90 percent of the branch company's contracts.

During the first eight years of fiduciary management by Union Casualty the Dorfmans made more than $3 million in commissions and service fees. In one instance Allen Dorfman took $51,462 in premiums and simply deposited it in a special account which he maintained with his mother. There were no complaints from the Teamsters.[9]

In the early 1950s the members of the Detroit underworld, many of whom had helped Hoffa in his battles with the CIO and were now in the narcotics and jukebox businesses, were beginning to infiltrate legitimate businesses with the Teamster boss's assistance.

"There is little doubt about the fact that Hoffa, consciously and willingly, protected the rackets in Detroit by protecting their legitimate fronts with the Teamsters Union," Vincent Piersante says. "And that included those gangsters who were deeply involved in the drug traffic."

One new vehicle for the mob was the Star Coverall Supply Company, headed by Vincent H. Meli, son of Angelo Meli and son-in-law of Santo Perrone, who gave Vincent $6000 to start the business. Young Meli also received an additional $1500 from Peter Tocco's son Anthony.

"The operation of the coverall industry is really quite simple," a Detroit law enforcement official explains. "Companies in this field solicit business from local auto dealers and gas stations, for example, who have mechanics who wear coveralls while working. After a contract has been obtained by the supplier from a customer, the supply company is simply responsible for supplying, repairing, and laundering their overalls."

The coverall business was already overcrowded in Detroit, and Irvin P. Miller, with whom Star Supply contracted for laundry services, asked Meli and his associates why they got into the business. "At that time they told me that they weren't worried about competition because they had enough backing that they could get all the overall business they needed," Miller said.[10] "Pressure" could be delivered by Meli's father and by two other gangsters, Joseph Bommarito and Peter Licavoli. Miller met all three of them while talking to Vincent Meli in the Star Supply office.

Additional pressure came from Joint Council 43 organizer Herman Kierdorf, dispatched at Hoffa's directive, who warned prospective customers to do business with Star or face reprisals from both the Teamsters and the mob.[11] In several instances companies that refused to do business with Star Supply were struck and picketed by the Teamsters. Several victims of Kierdorf's tactics complained directly to Hoffa, who did nothing to help them.

The early 1950s were also the first time in United States history that Congress undertook formal investigation of the underworld. It began in 1950, when Senator Estes Kefauver's Senate Select Committee to Investigate Organized Crime in Interstate Commerce held its first hearings, and many of the legendary figures of America's underworld were paraded across the screens of America's new toy, television. Curious shoppers, cluttering the sidewalks outside department stores, watched the TV sets in display windows as they broadcast the 1950–51 hearings. The five-member crime committee traveled to fifteen cities investigating allegations that a nationwide network of mobsters existed in the enlightened second half of the twentieth century. With the likes of Carlos Marcello, Santo Perrone, and Morris Dalitz marching to the witness chair, the general public was reminded of the Fifth Amendment as gangster after gangster repeated, ''I refuse to answer that question on the grounds that it may incriminate me.''

New York racketeer Frank Costello clenched and fumbled with his famous, overexposed hands, describing his love for America, while the committee detailed his purchases of crooked cops and politicians.

Confirming the existence of a National Crime Syndicate, the Kefauver Committee reported:

> There is a sinister criminal organization known as the Mafia operating with ties in other nations, in the opinion of the committee. The Mafia is the direct descendant of a criminal organization of the same name originating in the island of Sicily. In this country, the Mafia has also been known as the Black Hand and the Unione Siciliano. The membership of the Mafia today is not confined to persons of Sicilian origin. The Mafia is a loose-knit organization specializing in the sale and distribution of narcotics, the conduct of various gambling enterprises, prostitution, and other rackets based on extortion and violence.[12]

An especially frightening statement was that

> these criminal gangs possess such power and had access to such sources of protection that they constituted a government within a government in this country and that that second government was the government by the underworld . . .
>
> This phantom government nevertheless enforces its own law, carries out its own executions, and not only ignores but abhors the democratic processes of justice which are held to be the safeguards of the American citizen.
>
> This secret government of crimesters is a serious menace which could, if not curbed, become the basis for a subversive movement which could wreck the very foundations of this country.[13]

In its Detroit hearings the committee also scrutinized Hoffa's growing empire in Michigan. Although this first examination was rather cursory, it inspired subsequent, deeper investigations by two

House subcommittees after the Kefauver Committee was shoved out of the spotlight by Senator Joseph McCarthy's infamous witchhunt.

In June 1953 Clare E. Hoffman, a Michigan Republican, chaired a House subcommittee investigating racketeering in Detroit. A focal point of the investigation was Detroit's Local 985, the "jukebox local," which was investigated for violence and extortion rather than as a front for businesses controlled by Detroit's top drug traffickers. The Hoffman committee concentrated primarily on Hoffa and on Local 985's president, William Bufalino.

In spite of the fact that Hoffa—whom the congressmen described as the "brains" of Bufalino's operation—had periodically destroyed Local 985's financial records, the subcommittee found enough evidence to report that

> there existed a gigantic, wicked conspiracy to, through the use of force, threats of force and economic pressure, extort and collect millions of dollars not only from unorganized workers but from members of unions who are in good standing, from independent businessmen, and, on occasion, from the Federal Government itself. . . .
>
> The teamsters union, Local 985, through its president William E. Bufalino, is the principal offender and perpetrator of the racketeering, extortion, and gangsterism . . . The union attempted, and to some extent succeeded, in obtaining a monopoly in the "juke-box" business.[14]

The subcommittee found that if a company refused to join Bufalino's union monopoly, then it faced the threat of picketing and bombing:

> Subsequent to the refusal to continue paying dues to the union, the establishment of one of these owners was bombed during August 1952 . . . Again in January 1953, the place of business of another one of these owners was bombed, resulting in serious damage to his building and his machines . . . At about the same time, two car-washing companies were also bombed. This was during the time that the teamsters union, local No. 985, was attempting to organize and unionize the car-washing industry in Detroit, Michigan.[15]

Like nonmob jukebox operators, the car washers complained to the subcommittee. Employees claimed that they paid 70 cents per week in dues but never received a union card, were never notified of a union meeting, and never saw their union steward. Earnings for one employee for his sixty-hour week had dropped from $30 to $18 after he joined the union.

The subcommittee found that after four bombing raids the companies involved learned that protesting accomplished nothing and capitulated, paying their monthly dues to Bufalino.

Although the Detroit Police Department took ''no effective action'' against Local 985—it advised one victim to ''arm himself with a gun for his self-protection''—Bufalino and a half-dozen others were indicted for extortion in the fall of 1953. Bufalino was then acquitted by a judge who, the year before, had received $100 a week from the Teamsters' health and welfare fund for being a guest on a Teamster-sponsored radio program. While Bufalino was under indictment the judge received a $6200 contribution from the union for his 1953 reelection campaign.[16]

Furious at the congressional hearings and the Bufalino grand jury investigation, Hoffa speculated that an informant was working inside Local 299, feeding information to federal agents. Hoffa telephoned John Dioguardi in New York and explained his fears. Dioguardi put Hoffa in touch with Bernard Spindel, a professional wiretapper, who promptly flew to Detroit and wired the telephones of Local 299's business agents.

''Jimmy thought someone in our office—we had about eighteen business agents at the time—was getting phone calls from outside people,'' Dave Johnson says. ''We were in another office, 'way far from Hoffa, down the hallway. We had a desk and a phone, and when we would have any telephone conversations with anybody, Jimmy had it rigged up so that he could listen in. No one knew it was going on; but most of us had nothing to hide anyway.''

More trouble lay ahead for Hoffa when another House subcommittee chairman, Wint Smith, a Kansas Republican, initiated a series of hearings at the end of 1953. Concentrating primarily on Hoffa's placement of the Michigan Conference and Central States health and welfare funds with the Dorfman family's Union Casualty Agency, the subcommittee disclosed that the two Teamsters' welfare funds had also ''invested a quarter-million dollars in preferred stock of Union Casualty. The record shows that . . . though it has paid no dividends or interest for 2 years, [Hoffa] still considers [the investment] a good one; but he failed to report it to his fellow trustees on the Central States funds.''[17]

The Central States fund's trustees had agreed to an audit, conducted by Union Casualty, which contended that the union was $249,000 behind in its insurance premium payments, which Hoffa had promised to increase—while drastically cutting benefits.

"The sum was paid," according to the subcommittee's report, "even though it could not be determined from the fund's own reports that the claim of Union Casualty was an accurate one. When the Central States employer trustees sought an investigation of Union Casualty's financial soundness, they were successfully resisted by Mr. Hoffa."[18]

During the four days of hearings Allen and Paul Dorfman took the Fifth Amendment 135 times. As a result the subcommittee recommended that the Dorfmans be cited for contempt of Congress, a charge that was later dropped for unexplained reasons.

Hoffa, at first arrogant and defiant during the hearing, quickly became defensive when questioned about the Test Fleet corporation.

Incorporated in Tennessee in 1949, Test Fleet, Inc., was preceded by the J & H Sales Company, which supposedly leased a single tractor-trailer unit to William O. Bridge and Carney Matheson, owners of the Baker's Driveaway Company, which had a contact—and labor difficulties—with the Teamsters. Registered in the maiden names of Hoffa's and Bert Brennan's wives, J & H changed its name to the National Equipment Company but continued to haul for Baker's Driveaway. The articles of incorporation for the Hoffa-backed dummy companies were prepared by Carney Matheson's brother, Albert Matheson, a Detroit lawyer for the National Automobile Carriers Association. Matheson also negotiated the sale of National Equipment, which was worth $6000, to Bridge, who purchased the company for $10,000 and quickly resolved his problems with the union.

With $4000 profit, Hoffa and Brennan, again in their wives' maiden names, created the Test Fleet corporation, which did business exclusively with Commercial Carriers Corporation, a Cadillac haulaway outfit which operated in, among other states, Michigan and Tennessee. And since Test Fleet had no equipment, Commercial Carriers lent it $50,000 to buy some.

Commercial Carriers' willingness to cooperate with Test Fleet was easy to understand, since its terminal in Flint, Michigan, was having trouble with its drivers, most of them owner-operators who were Teamster members. The men who drove their own trucks had been conducting a wildcat strike and had ignored Hoffa's order to return to work. When Test Fleet started getting the company's business, the owner-operators' hauling leases were revoked—with Hoffa's blessing, of course.

In the first seven years of the relationship between Test Fleet and Commercial Carriers, Mrs. Hoffa and Mrs. Brennan made a profit of $125,000 on their $4000 investment.

One of the saddest figures to testify before the subcommittee was Harold Cross, a Teamster owner-operator who had hauled for Commercial Carriers. After he was fired and heard that the union wasn't going to support him and the other drivers, Cross appealed to Hoffa in person for help in getting his job back.

"This was refused, although he was a paid up member. Thus, Teamster Cross could not work at his own trade, using his own equipment, because his own Teamsters' Union blackballed him."[19] After Test Fleet began working for Commercial Carriers, Cross was driven out of business. He lost both his truck and his home.

The subcommittee's hearings ended abruptly. One day in the midst of testimony Congressman Smith received a long-distance telephone call. When he returned to the hearing room he announced that the investigation had been called to a halt. Pointing to the ceiling, Smith told the shocked press people at the hearings, "The pressure comes from away up there, and I just can't talk about it any more specifically than that."

4 Stacked Decks and Dirty Deals

Jimmy Hoffa was not unlike Johnny Friendly, the union leader in Budd Schulberg's Academy Award-winning *On the Waterfront*. Hoffa's alliances with the mob and with ruthless employers showed his increasing dependence on illicit money and muscle to achieve his dream of a national Teamster contract. He had begun to use the union for personal gain and personal survival.

Hoffa and Bert Brennan already had Test Fleet, Inc., whose name was changed to the Hobren Corporation in 1955. With Hobren's profits Hoffa and Brennan bought a chunk of land in Iron Mountain, Michigan, and leased it to the "Lake 13 Hunting and Fishing Club," a nonprofit corporation composed of Detroit Teamster business agents. Though the land was owned by the "private club," Charles "Chuckie" O'Brien, Hoffa's "foster son," by then in his early twenties and a business agent for a Retail Clerks Union local in Detroit, was sent to Iron Mountain to supervise the construction of living quarters for the vacationing Teamster officials. Naturally O'Brien maintained both his status and his salary in the union while working for Hoffa's company.

Hoffa's love for the great outdoors increased when he and the Dorfman family together bought Joll Properties, a resort near Eagle River, Wisconsin. Renamed the Jack O'Lantern Lodge, the heavily wooded area included a sparkling lake, a large barn, and a quaint L-shaped lodge. Fifty feet in front of the lovely garden stood a security booth where an armed guard kept a watchful eye on those who drove up the 500-foot driveway spotted with bright snaggle-tooth jack o'lanterns.

"There were some awfully scary stories about some of the people and things that went on at the Jack O'Lantern Inn," an Eagle River shopkeeper remembers. "When Hoffa came to town the whole town knew it, because all his kind were swarming all over the place. They never caused any trouble or anything; we just don't like that kind around here."

An operator of a local bar-restaurant remarks, "Eagle River is a good place to go if you're hiding from the law. When members of Al Capone's gang got into trouble in Chicago, he just packed them up and sent them to some cubbyhole here in Eagle River. Some folks say that even John Dillinger ducked out here for a while when the feds were chasing him."

Hoffa, Brennan, and Dorfman also invested in an Ohio racetrack; a Detroit prizefighter; a real estate company (with Michigan's state liquor commissioner); and a small oil company. Hoffa invested in the stock market too, and at least three of those deals involved companies with which the Teamsters had collective bargaining agreements. He had $25,000 in Fruehauf Trucking Company stock and owned four hundred shares in ACF Wrigley Co., a Michigan supermarket chain, and 600 in McLean Industries, another trucking company.

One especially bizarre arrangement was basically a pure land swindle. Sun Valley, Inc., a strip of land in Titusville, Florida, near Orlando, was publicized as a golden-years paradise for Teamsters who were wise enough to invest in it when young. It was promoted by a Detroit wheeler-dealer, Henry Lower, an escaped convict and narcotics dealer with suspected ties to Santos Trafficante. The scheme offered 8000 lots, which Lower had bought for $150,000, or about $18.75 per lot. Using Teamster business agents as salesmen—at union expense—the privately owned Sun Valley corporation sold nearly two thousand lots at $150 each to eager rank-and-file members. After that the remaining 75 percent of the land was placed on the public market, priced at $550 per lot. As more property was sold, the price of the other lots rose steadily.

Hoffa and Brennan failed to mention to Teamster members that they had a hidden option to purchase up to 45 percent of the property at the price Lower had paid for it.

In August 1954 Lower's initial investment of $6000 was provided by a $10,000 loan from William Bufalino's Local 985, which had borrowed that amount from Hoffa's Local 299; the rest of the

$150,000 was financed through bank loans. As Lower made promises to improve the development by paving its roads and adding a water line, Hoffa ordered that $400,000 be pulled out of Local 299's account in a Detroit bank and immediately deposited in an Orlando bank. Taking $90,000 for his services, Lower diverted another $250,000 from Local 299 and deposited it among his other business interests in Detroit, with Hoffa's full knowledge and approval.[1]

"Sun Valley was high and dry," says George Roxburgh, a Local 299 trustee who purchased four lots and gave Hoffa $1000 to get the project started. "There was no water or sewer there; and the only people who made money were those who sold it to the highway department for the construction of Interstate 95, which ran up the east coast of Florida.

"There were a lot of really mad people when they knew they'd been taken. But Jimmy justified his position and didn't apologize to anyone. I loved the guy, but I do hold that against him."

Like his colleagues, Frank Fitzsimmons was concerned with financial security. In 1953 he was indicted on charges of bribery and extortion—specifically, a shakedown conspiracy with local trucking and construction companies involved in such major projects as the Detroit expressway system. Indicted with Fitzsimmons were Daniel J. Keating and Louis Linteau, president and secretary-treasurer of Teamster Local 614 in Pontiac, Michigan, which represented area drivers, warehousemen, and gas station attendants; and Mike Nicoletti and Samuel Marroso, president and business agent of the Detroit building workers and coal haulers Local 247.

At the IBT's insistence Hoffa removed all the indicted officials except Fitzsimmons, who remained as Local 299's vice president. Hoffa defied the international union, however, by moving the fired officers into other union posts. While under indictment and on the Teamsters' payroll, Keating and Linteau remodeled Hoffa's waterfront cottage in Lake Orion, Michigan. The funds for the renovation were taken directly from Local 614's treasury.[2]

During the trial a trucking company owner testified that he had given Fitzsimmons a "gift" of over $500, by personal check, in return for a favorable union contract for his firm. But even then Hoffa would not fire Fitzsimmons, whom he called "a very fine gentleman." During a conversation with Detroit's assistant prosecutor, Hoffa told him to back off Fitzsimmons or else he'd be framed for social or professional misconduct.[3]

Soon afterward Keating, Linteau, and Marroso pled guilty, presumably protecting Fitzsimmons, whose indictment was dropped.[4] In return for their cooperation the three convicted men continued receiving their union salaries in prison—a combined total of $85,489—and their joint legal bill of $30,000 was paid by the Detroit Teamsters.

Saved from prison, Fitzsimmons quickly became involved in another project, the Exhibitors Service Company, which delivered motion picture films to Detroit's theaters. Howard C. Craven, the elderly, nearly deaf owner of the company, had been having labor problems with the union. Approached by Fitzsimmons, Craven was promised a virtual monopoly over the Detroit film-hauling industry in return for 90 percent of his current net profits, which averaged $2000 a month. Fitzsimmons and Craven signed a three-page contract that met all Fitzsimmons' demands. Craven agreed to turn over Fitzsimmons' share to one of his company's truck drivers, John Curran. The man who drew up the contract was Albert Matheson, who had prepared the papers for Hoffa's and Brennan's Test Fleet corporation.

After Craven had paid several thousand dollars to Fitzsimmons— through his friend Curran—without a major increase in business, Fitzsimmons began to squeeze Craven for more money. He even ordered a union accountant to take control of the company's books.

Craven protested to both Fitzsimmons and Hoffa, and Fitzsimmons called a strike against the company. Union drivers parked their company rigs in the street, blocking the firm's entrances and exits. Consequently a $50,000 insurance policy on Craven's trucks was canceled and the local fire department demanded that they be removed from the streets as a fire hazard. In the midst of the picketing Fitzsimmons asked Craven for $500 to be sent through Curran. Again Craven sent the check, but the strike went on.

Financially destroyed, Craven decided to sell the company for the best offer he could get—which was $7000, including his four trucks. Unknown to Craven, the new owner was Frank Fitzsimmons, who put the new company, Theater Trucking Services, in Mrs. Hoffa's maiden name along with the names of Fitzsimmons' brother-in-law, nephew, and son. A union accountant handled the company's books and noted that the firm owed Frank Fitzsimmons, who was also the firm's union business agent, the purchase price of $7000.[5]

During a grand jury probe that followed the sale of the original company, it was learned that the union auditor Fitzsimmons brought in to seize Craven's books had "lost" all the company's financial records, but investigators recovered from a local bank a check for $500 endorsed by both Curran and Fitzsimmons. At that time, and later, Fitzsimmons denied ever having received money from Curran.[6]

Somehow Fitzsimmons escaped being indicted.

Like Craven, another film delivery company owner, Gustave LeVeque, had serious problems with Fitzsimmons, the company's union business agent, but before being completely ruined, LeVeque sold his firm to Fitzsimmons' nephew. In addition, upon Fitzsimmons' personal recommendation a third film distribution business, also having labor problems with Fitzsimmons, received a $12,000 loan from Local 299—disposition unknown.

Fitzsimmons picked up a few dollars more from Better Brands of Illinois, a Chicago beer distributor, which paid him $75 a week as a sales consultant, and several members of his family were helped financially through his union position. His wife was on the payroll of Detroit's Local 234, representing cooks and waiters, and his son Donald took over Theater Trucking. Fitzsimmons' other son, Richard, started the Trans-City Trucking Company, with twelve trucks whose drivers were represented by Local 299 business agent Rolland McMaster.

The real businessman of the Teamster trio—Hoffa, Fitzsimmons, and McMaster—was McMaster, who was now Hoffa's powerhouse on the Central States iron and steel negotiating and grievance committees.

In late 1949 McMaster filed a certificate with the state of Michigan indicating that he was planning to do business under an assumed name. Claiming to own and control the M & G Cartage Company, he placed the corporation in the maiden names of his wife and sister-in-law. Not surprisingly, the firm's address was that of McMaster's farm in Wixom, Michigan. He owned no trucks and had no employees; yet he made money, lots of it.

One business venture involved William Rumminger, owner of a Detroit company, Aero Cartage. In 1953 and 1954 Rumminger worried increasingly about his declining business, particularly with his major account, Douglas Trucking Lines, a local steel hauling outfit. The following year he approached McMaster, who was the business agent for Douglas's employees. Touched by Rumminger's sad tale about his failing enterprise, McMaster promised to help the salesman by "putting in a good word" with the McLouth Steel Corporation, one of the largest steel producers in the Detroit area.

As quick as you can say "shakedown," Rumminger had landed the steel hauling business from McLouth for Douglas, picking up a small fortune for himself in the process. But McMaster's services didn't come cheap; he and Rumminger made a deal. "It was more or less on a partnership basis," as Rumminger put it. "I split my personal net with him, which was about three percent, on the McLouth business."[7]

Rumminger paid all McMaster's "commissions" into M & G Cartage. In the first two years of their partnership, McMaster, according to his income tax returns, pocketed $19,711 from Rumminger's business alone.

McLouth's executives contended that any business Douglas Trucking received from McLouth via Rumminger was based upon the merits of Rumminger's Aero Cartage and had nothing to do with McMaster's intervention. As to McMaster's payoffs, the McLouth version was that Rumminger was a "pretty stupid businessman" to pay McMaster when he was going to get their business anyway.

McMaster also owned Powers Trucking Company, established in 1950; Reed Transportation Company, 1953; Ram Transport Corporation, Inc. (with an anonymous man known only as "Allen"), which succeeded Reed Transportation, 1954; and Aggregates Transport Company, which succeeded Powers Trucking in 1956. In 1951, with Local 299 trustee George Roxburgh and Local 337 official James Clift, McMaster founded Canter's, Inc., which owned a riding stable; and, with his nephews, the Enterprise Equipment and Leasing Company, which bought, leased, and sold trucking terminals.[8]

Incredibly enough, all McMaster's business ventures—even those involved with trucking—functioned with nonunion employees, when there were employees.

By the mid-fifties Hoffa and his top men had either ruined or bought their major enemies in labor and business. They had clawed their way from poverty to great personal wealth and, even more important to them, to power. They had also become tasty bait for ambitious politicians and investigators by the score. Slapping official inquiries away, like the countless dolls Cagney slapped in *Public Enemy*, Hoffa himself was the Cagney figure of the fifties.

Hoffa traveled first class but wouldn't let bellhops carry his luggage. He insisted on driving himself around town, and he remembered people, faces and names. His general defiance of "bourgeois respectability" enhanced his popularity among the workingmen who watched their cigar-smoking union leaders and bosses alike flee to country manors in sleek black chauffeur-driven limousines. Hoffa went on living in the modest house he had bought for $6800 after his marriage. Few union members knew of Hoffa's private defiance of bourgeois respectability: that his household contained a "foster son," Charles O'Brien, and often the foster son's mother, Sylvia Pagano Paris. Friends and associates who knew the family well thought that, because of Hoffa's fondness for teenage Chuckie, the boy was probably his own son. Apparently the strange household ran smoothly. According to a family friend, Mrs. Hoffa and Mrs. Paris were good friends, and the Hoffas' children, Barbara and James, got on well with Chuckie.

Although things were going well for Sylvia Paris, one of her ex-lovers, Frank Coppola, was looking for work. Coppola, like Luciano and others in the international drug traffic, had been nearly forced out of business by the cooperative effort of U.S. and Italian narcotics officers.

"Luciano ran the whole show," says Charles Siragusa of the Bureau of Narcotics. "He had the contacts with the Italian manufacturers of heroin and operated without challenge. Until we put an end to the traffic in the early 1950s, he had been traveling illegally to several countries, including the United States and Cuba, setting up additional drug routes."

Siragusa and his men had been closing down Luciano's drug outlets since 1950. The big bust occurred in April 1952, when narcotics agents intercepted a green trunk containing six kilograms of heroin, valued at $80,000. The trunk, which had a fake bottom and sides covered with old clothes, was on its way from Coppola to the Detroit receivers, John Priziola and Raffaele Quasarano.

That same year the Italian government indicted both Priziola and Quasarano in absentia for involvement in the dope ring. Records confiscated from Coppola and his partner, Salvatore Vitale, were evidence of the Detroit men's complicity.

"Since the Detroit mob was the principal supplier of heroin for the rest of the country—through Coppola and Vitale—it was the worst hit from the raids we conducted," says Siragusa. "Later, Vitale returned to the United States—California, where he had family—and was arrested and put in prison for a few years. When he got out, he accused Priziola and Quasarano of cheating him out of about $80,000 worth of heroin which the Detroit boys said had been adulterated. Because Priziola and Quasarano refused to pay, a big meeting of hoods was set up in California. There Priziola decided to give the old man $20,000—probably only because they were both related to the Matranga mob family out in California.

''But Vitale still wasn't happy, so he went to Detroit to collect and never returned. His son-in-law told me that he was killed by Priziola and Quasarano.''

Under extreme pressure from the American and Italian governments, the Luciano network had crumbled, and by 1954 it was replaced by French Corsican drug traffickers Giuseppe and Vincent Cotroni. The Cotroni brothers ran what was later known as ''the French Connection.'' Dope manufactured in Marseilles was routed to North America, where it was distributed and sold for street consumption.

Sixty percent of the heroin was shipped across the Atlantic, then through the St. Lawrence Seaway to Montreal. Needing protection and the contacts to handle the merchandise, the Cotroni brothers solicited the services of their American mob friend, Carmine Galante, the former Vito Genovese gunman who had become the underboss in the Joseph Bonanno crime family. Galante maintained two major distribution routes. The busiest was simply southeast through Buffalo, where it was handled by Steffano Maggadino, a former Bonanno bodyguard, and to New York City, where Galante did business with syndicate leaders Genovese and Thomas Lucchese.

The second major path was west from Montreal to Toronto, Ontario, then to Windsor, and across the river to Detroit.

Still maintaining strong relations with Lucchese crime captain John Ormento, the Melis' Long Island relative, Priziola and Quasarano remained in charge of Detroit's drug importing business. They were also co-owners of the Motor City Arena and the chief promoters of the boxer Hoffa and Brennan owned.

''Hoffa was not at all averse to using the Teamsters Union as a means of protection for those who were associated with the narcotics traffic,'' Vincent Piersante says. ''By protection, I mean he went as far as giving some of those involved jobs with the union. And others, like Priziola and Quasarano, were protected by Local 985.

Using Sam Gompers' ''reward your friends, punish your enemies'' philosophy, Hoffa went into the 1952 IBT convention in Los Angeles knowing that he was powerful enough to choose and then destroy the next Teamster president.

The headliner of the Los Angeles convention was Dave Beck, from Seattle. Pudgy and red-cheeked, Beck was the image of an overheated, beardless Santa Claus with sweat marks under the arms of his expensive suits. Since he controlled the Western Conference of Teamsters, it was appropriate that his moment of glory be staged in his own backyard. Old Dan Tobin, who had served the union well—or at least without major scandal—for forty-five years, had decided to retire in favor of Beck, his close associate. Although a grass-roots ''stop-Beck'' movement briefly upset the pro-Beck delegates, the little Michigan Teamster boss came to the rescue, quashed the phantom challenge, and sewed up the election for Beck. In return Beck promptly entrusted Hoffa with an IBT vice presidency and a seat on the Teamsters' general executive board.

Arrogant and brassy—nicknamed ''His Majesty the Wheel''—Beck had little direct contact with the operations of the union. For the first five years of his administration he remained aloof from it all, calling on his friend, President Dwight Eisenhower, at the White House and making speeches on U.S. foreign policy. Detached from the rank and file, Beck allowed Hoffa to represent him on union business.

''Jimmy was always out front, trying to develop as a national figure,'' McMaster says. ''Now we were happy with that, because we supported him. He was Beck's assistant . . . a troubleshooter for him. In other words, if there was trouble, he told Jimmy. Of course Jimmy would call his boys in.''

Hoffa's philosophy of organizing was indicative of his complex and pragmatic personality. Strikes for recognition on a regional basis, he often said, worked as much against the worker and his union as it did against management. ''So when Jimmy had difficulty getting some of the bigger companies to sign our contracts,'' Dave Johnson explains, ''he'd only strike five or six of them, letting the little companies operate. This would cause the employers to be fighting not only us but among themselves too.

''Hoffa told us a hundred times: If a company in New York is having problems with the contract and won't sign and it hauls into Michigan, then we've got to stop them in Michigan and other states that are key to their business. With all that pressure, the company usually came around. But several states, especially in the South, were causing headaches for Jimmy, and he had to do something about them.''

Antiunion sentiment was especially strong in Tennessee, one of the last holdouts from the Central States Drivers Council's regional contract. Hoffa sent McMaster to Nashville to change some minds. Taking with him Flint Local 332 business agent Frank Kierdorf—ex-convict, a Teamster torch and nephew of joint council organizer Herman Kierdorf—McMaster worked with local Teamster leaders against independent owner-operators and other nonunion factions.

Don Vestal, formerly of Dallas, Texas, led the Tennessee pro-Hoffa forces. Once arrested for attempted murder—he later pled guilty to a reduced charge of assault and battery—Vestal was the president of Nashville's Local 327. In 1952, because of his loyalty to Hoffa, he became the head of Tennessee's Joint Council 87, representing seven locals. As a close Hoffa confidant and one of five top Hoffa representatives, Vestal was given the money and manpower to neutralize his union's enemies in the state. With Hoffa's help he recruited heavies from trucking companies and formed a brutal goon squad which was involved in 173 known separate acts of violence against the nonunion opposition. Operating in several states, including Florida, Georgia, Kentucky, Mississippi, and even New Jersey, the special units of leg-breakers were led by William A. Smith, a Local 327 "assistant business agent" Vestal appointed in 1953. Smith, an explosives expert, had twelve convictions for a variety of strongarm crimes.

"McMaster and his enforcer, Frank Kierdorf, came down to Tennessee to supervise the action," Vestal says. "Plus Hoffa wanted to make sure that we weren't messing around with any of the companies owned by his friends in Chicago. And you just didn't mess with Mac. I once saw him hit a man so hard you'd have thought a mule kicked him."

After a long, violent campaign which included bombings, shootings, and sabotage, Tennessee, like other states around it, fell into the fold of the Central States Drivers Council, which within four years included twenty-two states. The victory in Tennessee was a milestone in Hoffa's career, and McMaster was now Hoffa's number-one strong-arm specialist.

During the Tennessee campaign the national IBT, at Beck's instigation and with Hoffa's enthusiastic approval, moved its headquarters to Washington, D.C., to be closer to national policy decisions that affected labor—and the politicians who made them. In 1955 the IBT moved into its brand-new marble palace, just a hop, skip, and a jump from the Capitol Rotunda.

Hoffa began to spend much of his time in Washington, running the union for Dave Beck. Frank Fitzsimmons, Local 299's vice president, assumed many of his boss's day-to-day duties in Detroit. With Hoffa's consent Fitzsimmons made his friend McMaster his "administrative assistant," a nonelected position. Thus McMaster was really third in command after Hoffa and Fitzsimmons.

"Because Jimmy was always in Washington, and he usually took Fitz with him, we had an executive board meeting," says McMaster.

"I was chosen to run Local 299. But because neither Jimmy nor Fitz wanted to give up any titles, they just called me 'the administrative assistant,' which meant that they came to the meetings to add dignity to everything while I did the work."

With aides like Johnson, McMaster, and Vestal working in the field, Hoffa began to assemble a Washington staff of union professionals. His top adviser was Hoffa antithesis Harold Gibbons, a scholarly, dignified liberal crusader. The youngest of twenty-three children, Gibbons had worked his way through a maze of government jobs and several labor organizations. He was with the Teamsters because in St. Louis his CIO union had been in competition with Teamsters Local 688; both unions were organizing the area's warehousemen. When Gibbons and the head of Local 688 went to Dave Beck for advice, he suggested a merger of the two locals. In 1948, providing some $78,000 in severance pay to Local 688's officers from his CIO local's treasury, Gibbons moved in and became president. He had literally purchased the union.[9]

As soon as he took over, Gibbons began to have problems with the St. Louis union dissidents—whom he calls "hoodlums"—and he went to Hoffa for help.

"Jimmy listened to my problem and told me just to place some of these fellows on my local payroll. Then, in a few months, I'd be taking orders from them," says Gibbons. "He also told me that I could grab the first one that walked in, take out my gun, and shoot him in the head."

Gibbons walked away shaking his head while Hoffa laughed; he continued to have problems until Hoffa finally came to St. Louis with Johnson, McMaster, and other musclemen and cleared up the situation. Then, through Beck, Hoffa put the entire St. Louis joint council into trusteeship to prevent a rebel takeover, selecting Gibbons as trustee. Soon after that Hoffa named Gibbons secretary-treasurer of the newly formed Central Conference of Teamsters, founded in 1953 to complement the already-established Southern and Western Conferences.

"Hoffa was an intense worker who knew the union from top to bottom," Gibbons says. "His working hours and demands on his staff's time were difficult to keep pace with. But he had a way of handling people which made them want to make the sacrifices. We didn't have as many problems as one would think we would, taking into consideration how different we were. But I always contended that labor unions were a movement; Jimmy viewed them as a business."

With the help of Gibbons and other union leaders in the jurisdiction of the Central States Drivers Council, Hoffa, now a seasoned bargainer, negotiated the 1955 over-the-road contract.

In a side deal during those negotiations, Hoffa, Fitzsimmons, and McMaster managed to sell out some owner-operators. McMaster, who had represented employees at Transamerican Freight Lines since the war, had a warm working relationship with its executives and was often accused of either owning a large chunk of the company or receiving payoffs to protect the firm against the Teamsters. He firmly denies both versions: ''I would much prefer a friendly than an adversary situation between me and an employer.''

McMaster's growing importance to Hoffa was perhaps best exhibited when Hoffa, as chairman of the CSDC negotiating team, allowed Transamerican to make a separate agreement with the Teamsters, a blatant violation of the master contract.

As secretly negotiated by Hoffa and McMaster, Transamerican's contract included none of the normally expected fringe benefits and instead forced employees to accept a mere 1½ cents per mile raise. Second, while the established grievance procedure called for processing complaints at the local level and, if necessary, sending them on to state Teamster committees and then to the area committee in Chicago, the arrangement with Transamerican provided for all grievances, no matter where they originated, to go directly to either McMaster or Fitzsimmons in Detroit. Because Transamerican operated principally with owner-operators, it was clear that Hoffa, McMaster, and Fitzsimmons remained consistent in their intention to get those who owned and operated their own trucks out of the industry.

Although the Transamerican grievance procedure didn't need ratification, the 1½ cents raise in lieu of fringe benefits did. The owner-operators knew that they were being taken and voted down the agreement. McMaster then made a ''goodwill tour'' of Transamerican's terminals in several cities, bringing with him a small group of his associates to provide varying degrees of persuasion. Sympathetic employees were persuaded to sit down with company and union officials, and it was decided to give the new agreement a twelve-week trial. Then a second meeting would be called at which a final judgment on the future of the contract would be considered. But when the twelve-week cooling-off period ended the second meeting was not held, and the owner-operators were stuck with the contract.

Although it did not have the immediate impact of the Transamerican deal, one provision of the 1955 Central States master contract had all the earmarks of being even more illicit. Introducing an innovation in workmen's benefits, Hoffa pushed through a provision that employers would contribute two dollars a week for each of their employees to a pension fund. Formally set up on March 16, 1955, the IBT's Central States, Southeast and Southwest Areas Pension Fund was a strong addition to Hoffa's massive war chest, which already contained the large sums accumulated in the Michigan Conference and Central States health and welfare funds. Intended to provide a $90 per month pension to supplement Social Security benefits for 110,000 elegible union members who were at least fifty-seven years old and had twenty years of unbroken service, the Central States Pension Fund was governed by a twelve-member board of trustees, composed of six Hoffa-loyalist union officials and six friendly executives from the trucking industry. The trustees of the fund were empowered ''in their sole discretion, to invest and reinvest the principal and income of the Trust Fund'' according to the CSPF's Trust Agreement, '' . . . and may sell or otherwise dispose of such property at any time and from time to time as they see fit . . . ''

Since the fund was authorized to do business in the state of Illinois, where its headquarters were, its trustees didn't have to look far for a fiduciary manager. Like the two welfare funds, the Central States Pension Fund was handed over to Allen Dorfman.

Through his friendship with Allen Dorfman's stepfather, Hoffa asked Paul Dorfman's associate, John Dioguardi, for help in gaining control over the eastern states. With Beck's blind approval and cooperation, Hoffa created seven ''paper locals'' in New York City, most of them with no membership and under Dioguardi's jurisdiction. Passing these dummy unions to his gangster buddies, the racketeer engineered the takeover of the city's Joint Council 16 in 1956. The margin of victory for the pro-Hoffa supporters came from the votes of the fraudulent locals.

The election in New York convinced Teamster watchers that if the growing power of the union remained unchecked, it could rival that of the U.S. government. Among those especially concerned was labor reporter Clark Mollenhoff, head of the Washington bureau of the *Des Moines Register and Tribune*. He persuaded Robert F. Kennedy, then the chief counsel of the Senate Permanent Investigations Sub-committee, to conduct a preliminary investigation.

''Bobby Kennedy was already investigating Johnny Dioguardi for his activities in the northeastern garment industry,'' Mollenhoff recalls. ''So the paper locals episode, plus the operations of Hoffa,

Beck, and the Teamsters around the country, made it fairly easy to talk Bobby into promoting a major study of the matter.''

Kennedy flew to Seattle, Dave Beck's home territory, and found documentation that proved that the Teamster president had used over $320,000 of union funds to construct his private home and swimming pool and pay off personal debts. Returning to Washington, Kennedy in turn persuaded his subcommittee chairman, John L. McClellan of Arkansas, to support the establishment of a bipartisan Senate select committee which would look closely at corrupt union and management practices.

On January 30, 1957, the U.S. Senate Select Committee on Improper Activities in the Labor or Management Field was created, with an initial budget of $350,000. Chaired by McClellan, the committee consisted of four Democrats—McClellan, John Kennedy of Massachusetts, Sam Ervin of North Carolina, and Pat McNamara of Michigan—and four Republicans—vice chairman Irving Ives of New York, Joseph McCarthy of Wisconsin, Karl E. Mundt of South Dakota, and Barry Goldwater of Arizona. It eventually had a staff of ninety-one employees.

Robert Kennedy was a competitor, the kind of guy who loosened his tie, rolled up his sleeves, and got down to work. Formerly assistant counsel to Roy Cohn during the Permanent Investigations Subcommittee's McCarthy hearings, Kennedy had resigned, accusing Cohn of running the hearings ''like a circus.'' After Senator McCarthy was disgraced by his colleagues, McClellan took control of the subcommittee and asked Kennedy to return as its chief counsel.

Excited about his new responsibilities, Kennedy led the new select committee into its first day of testimony on February 26, 1957.

What would become known as the ''Great Investigation'' inevitably focused on the AFL-CIO, which had merged only fifteen months earlier after a history of bitter conflict, with George Meany as its president. The AFL-CIO's Ethical Practices Committee insisted that union officials called to testify before the McClellan Committee not take the Fifth Amendment. Scandal was the last thing the newly merged group needed, and the AFL-CIO was willing to expel any member organizations that caused one. In 1954—perhaps helped by *On the Waterfront*—the East Coast longshoremen's union had been tossed out of the AFL for refusing to get rid of the hoodlums who ran it.

The committee's first witness was a Portland, Oregon, mobster who testified that the local underworld, the Teamsters, and the district attorney were working in collusion to promote racketeering. He was followed by long-time Beck associate Frank Brewster, who at once took the Fifth. Brewster was convicted on thirty-one counts of contempt of Congress, but the conviction was reversed on appeal.

Dave Beck followed Brewster to the McClellan Committee's hot seat and, like his associate, refused to answer any questions about his union or personal finances, taking the Fifth 140 times during the session. By the end of his March 1957 appearance before the committee—during which he went out of his way to praise Hoffa—the ex-newspaper boy turned truckdriver turned top Teamster was ruined. The President and the politicians with whom he had fraternized now claimed they had never liked or trusted him. Several months later, in federal district court in Seattle, he was convicted of embezzlement.

Beck's heir apparent had in fact been leaking information to Senate investigators about the Teamster president. Although Beck had never been a real threat to Hoffa, he was becoming bothersome. In Minneapolis, for instance, Beck relieved a Hoffa man of his duties as a local Teamster leader. Ignoring Beck's authority, Hoffa defiantly reinstated his friend and told Beck to mind his own business. Beck backed down, but Hoffa foresaw more problems if Beck decided to flex his political muscle in union affairs. According to an associate, Hoffa thought Beck might start taking his job seriously and decided to use the McClellan Committee to get rid of him. ''Jimmy knew he was next in line to succeed Beck,'' the associate says. ''It was just a matter of getting him out of the way. That's where the New York lawyer came in.''

While the staff of the committee was being selected, Hoffa got in touch with attorney John Cye Cheasty and offered him $18,000 to monitor the committee's work. Being a decent fellow, Cheasty ran to room 101 of the Senate Office Building and told Kennedy about the bribe offer.

Soon afterward Kennedy was invited to dinner by Edward Cheyfitz, a Washington public relations man who had fallen out with Beck. He was to meet Hoffa at Cheyfitz's suburban home. Sizing each other up, Kennedy and Hoffa circled each other like two bareknuckled prizefighters ready for a brawl.

''Both Cheyfitz and Hoffa met me at the door—Hoffa with a strong, firm handshake,'' wrote Kennedy.

Immediately, I was struck by how short he is—only five feet five and a half. We walked into the living room of Cheyfitz's elaborately decorated house, but chatted only a few minutes before going in to dinner. The three of us were alone. Hoffa, I was to discover, can be personable, polite and friendly.

But that evening, though friendly enough, he maintained one steady theme in his conversation throughout dinner and for the rest of the evening.

"I do to others what they do to me, only worse," he said.

"Maybe I should have worn my bulletproof vest," I suggested.

From that first meeting, it seemed to me he wanted to impress upon me that Jimmy Hoffa is a tough, rugged man.[10]

Hoffa's analysis of Kennedy wasn't much different:

Robert F. Kennedy was a man who always made a big thing out of how strong and how tough he was, how he had been a football player or something at Harvard, and how he always exercised and kept himself in top shape . . .

I was sure, by this time, that Kennedy was a hard-nosed guy who was so spoiled all his life that he had to have his way in everything no matter who got hurt. The kind of guy you had to be as nasty with as he was with you or he'd run right over you. But it's always been my theory that you keep the door open to your enemies. You know all about your friends.[11]

On March 13, 1957, several days after the quiet dinner, Hoffa met Cheasty near DuPont Circle in Washington. Hidden cameras manned by FBI agents recorded Cheasty handing Hoffa a large envelope as the Teamster boss slapped $2000 cash into Cheasty's hand.

Arrested on the spot and charged with bribery, Hoffa was taken to the federal courthouse, where Kennedy was waiting, smiling. Tense moments between the two men quickly ended when they began a somewhat friendly debate on who could do the most pushups. Hoffa, now forty-three, boasted that he could do thirty; Kennedy, at thirty-one, claimed fifty.

Few light moments occurred after that, as the war between them became hotter and deadlier.

With what appeared to be an airtight case, Kennedy jokingly promised to "jump off the Capitol" if Hoffa wasn't convicted of attempted bribery. "Cye Cheasty was a good and honest man. He had served his country with distinction," Kennedy wrote, "The evidence supporting his testimony—there were fast moving pictures of Hoffa receiving the documents and paying off Cheasty—was solid. I felt that Jimmy Hoffa was finished."[12] But Kennedy underestimated Hoffa's brilliant legal counsel, Edward Bennett Williams, who had previously represented Frank Costello, Joe McCarthy, and Dave Beck.

On July 19, 1957, after a one-month trial in federal district court in Washington, Hoffa was miraculously acquitted. The turnabout was

due principally to Williams's genius as well as some highly questionable courtroom theatrics for the jury.[13] Williams sent Kennedy a para-
chute in case he made good on his promise.

Kennedy had gone on to other investigations after Hoffa's arrest,
thinking he was no longer a threat. When Hoffa was found not guilty
the young chief counsel hustled one of his investigators, Pierre
Salinger, out to Detroit in early August to subpoena the records of
Local 299 from 1950 to 1957. After arriving at Detroit's Willow Run
airport, checking into a small hotel, and talking to the local FBI,
Salinger raced to Local 299, where he found Frank Collins, the
secretary-treasurer. Ordering him to come across with the information
he wanted, Salinger tossed a subpoena on Collins' desk.

"I was scared as hell, I'll admit it," Collins says. "So I called
Jimmy and told him what had happened."

After serving similar court orders on Brennan's Local 337 and
Bufalino's Local 985, Salinger returned to his makeshift office in
Detroit's federal building. Fitzsimmons called him at four that af-
ternoon.

"Jimmy wants to see you."

The meeting was arranged for ten o'clock the next morning and
Salinger telephoned Kennedy. Salinger was told that the committee's
chief accountant, Carmine Bellino, would go with him to the meeting.

"It was pretty tense in the room when the committee guys showed
up," Dave Johnson recalls. "A bunch of us business agents were in
the room, along with our attorney, George Fitzgerald, and a couple of
other people."

Seated in front of Hoffa's desk, with the crowd surrounding them,
Salinger and Bellino fanned themselves with more subpoenas while
Hoffa exploded. He felt they were part of a conspiracy to destroy organized labor and Bobby Kennedy was using it to further his own political ambitions.

"Over my dead body!" Hoffa screamed. "Bobby isn't going
anywhere."

"You . . . " Salinger tried to say.

"Shuddup!" yelled Hoffa, snatching the subpoenas out of their
hands.

But when Hoffa cooled down he agreed to produce Local 299's
records for the investigators to review. In Washington, Kennedy
ordered his staff to conduct a full-tilt investigation of Hoffa in
preparation for Hoffa's scheduled appearance before the committee on
August 20.

While the Senate investigators gathered data on the Teamster vice president, the senators were busy hearing testimony about Dioguardi's paper locals in New York. Dioguardi had recently been convicted of extortion but escaped conviction on a more dramatic charge. He was on trial for ordering an associate to throw acid in the eyes of labor columnist Victor Riesel as the reporter stepped out of Lindy's Restaurant. Earlier that day Riesel had featured rebel Teamsters from New York's Local 138 on his radio show.

Hearing of the attack, Hoffa, who was in Chicago, blurted out to his friends, ''That son of a bitch Victor Riesel. He just had some acid thrown on him. It's too bad he didn't have it thrown on the goddamn hands he types with.''[14] After Riesel's assailant was found dead and other witnesses to the assault refused to testify, that charge against Dioguardi was dismissed.

The McClellan Committee found that Dioguardi's phony locals

showed that Dio and those with whom he formed alliances brought 40 men into the labor movement in positions of trust and responsibility—men who, among them, had been arrested a total of 178 times and convicted on 77 of these occasions for crimes ranging from theft, violation of the Harrison Narcotics Act, extortion, conspiracy, bookmaking, use of stench bombs, felonious assault, robbery, possession of unregistered stills, burglary, violation of the gun laws, being an accessory to murder, forgery, possession of stolen mail, and disorderly conduct.[15]

When Hoffa began the first of his three days of testimony, Kennedy grilled him on his relationship with Dioguardi and their conspiracy against Joint Council 16 in New York. In the afternoon Kennedy stepped into another area of the Hoffa-Dioguardi friendship, the one involving the gangster's sending Bernard Spindel to Detroit to Local 299's headquarters back in 1953. Hoffa could not afford to take the Fifth Amendment, but he came as close as possible. To the best of his recollection, Johnny Dioguardi had never helped him, never sent anyone to help him in anything. Finally Kennedy pulled out a tape recorder and played a tape supplied by New York State law enforcement officials. It was a discussion between Hoffa and Dioguardi about Spindel and his wiretapping chores.

When the tape ended, Kennedy, now smiling, turned again to Hoffa and asked him about a reference to the four tiny recording devices Spindel had used:

Mr. Hoffa, what were these things that he was talking about?

Mr. Kennedy, I have read this [transcript] and listened to the recording, and I recognize my voice, and I believe it is Dio's voice. But after reading this, I cannot refresh my memory from the notes, to the best of my recollection, I cannot understand what he would be talking about, ''four of them,'' and I don't know whether or not he ever came to Detroit at that particular time.[16]

Because of Hoffa's evasive answers and his testimony, or lack of it, about his relationship with Dioguardi and Spindel, Senator McClellan asked the Department of Justice to investigate possible perjury charges, and a month later the Justice Department indicted Hoffa on five counts of perjury.

By then Hoffa was already under indictment in federal court in New York, charged with wiretapping his business agents' phones and with perjury before the grand jury that brought the indictment. Spindel and Bert Brennan were named as co-conspirators in the wiretaps. Like Hoffa and Brennan, Spindel had his legal bills paid by ''friends'' of the Teamsters Union. He received a total of $34,000 for his defense, including $10,000 in cash which Brennan handed to him in a men's room in Detroit.[17]

Frank Collins, who had altered a set of the local's 1953 minutes with a typewriter which the local did not own in 1953, was also indicted with Hoffa—but on a separate twelve-count indictment.

''Frankie and I were up before the grand jury in New York for about two weeks,'' says Dave Johnson, the local's recording secretary, who was not present at the meetings when the disputed minutes were taken. ''The government was trying to find some way to put one of us in jail, because they weren't having much luck with Hoffa.

''They asked me about some minutes that were taken in 1953. So when I came out of the grand jury room, Frankie said, 'Did they ask you about the '53 minutes?' I told him, 'Hell yes, I told them.' But I told them that Frankie had recopied the minutes—which I knew was legal. Except he had already told the grand jury that he didn't. So they indicted him.''

Collins, who was convicted and spent fifteen months in prison, says, ''Those damn minutes, I honestly couldn't remember which set had been retyped. But they had to get somebody in Local 299, and they had caught me making an honest mistake. I've never done anything wrong, intentionally, in my entire life.'' Collins went to prison in 1959 and McMaster replaced him as secretary-treasurer of Local 299.

Hoffa's trial for wiretapping ended in an eleven-to-one hung jury. During a second trial a juror reported that an unnamed person had tried to influence his vote. An alternate was seated and the case proceeded. While the verdict was being read Kennedy was hearing testimony in the Senate Caucus Room. Someone handed him a folded sheet of paper. When he opened it his face turned pale. The note, which he dropped on the table, read, ''Hoffa was acquitted.''

Resting his hopes on a conviction against Hoffa in his perjury trial, Kennedy was defeated for a third time when the Supreme Court ruled in a similar case that wiretap evidence obtained by state officials could not be used in federal court. That decision barred the use of the strongest evidence of Hoffa's perjury. The indictment had to be dropped.

Robert Kennedy was now more determined than ever to pry open the sealed casing that guarded the secret sources of Hoffa's power.

Hoffa saw himself as the rank and file's champion of justice, a working-class hero. May 5, 1937. (Johnson Collection)

Local 299 staff, 1940. (Seated left to right) Walter Carpenter, James R. Hoffa, David Johnson, Ed McHahn. (Standing left to right) Rolland McMaster, Frank E. Fitzsimmons, Steve Stasko, Floyd Hayes. (Johnson Collection)

"The CIO had tougher guys than any of us expected. So Jimmy went to see Santo Perrone." (*Detroit News*)

Raffaele Quasarano was John Ormento's chief contact, because Angelo Meli refused to become directly involved in the drug traffic. (*Detroit News*)

Johnson and McMaster had become close friends . . . Noticing how well the relationship was clicking, Hoffa began to use the two men as a team on other union business around the country. (McMaster, Clark Abbott of Fruehauf, Johnson) (Johnson Collection)

The Chicago Union Casualty Agency was owned by Paul Dorfman's stepson, Allen, a dapper ex-Marine with no experience in the insurance business. His company handled the Michigan Conference of Teamsters Welfare Fund and the Central States, Southeast, and Southwest Areas Health and Welfare and Pension funds. (Wide World)

The McClellan Committee was "convinced that if Hoffa remains unchecked he will successfully destroy the decent labor movement in the United States." At the committee table left to right are: Senators Barry Goldwater; Irving M. Ives; John L. McClellan, chairman; Counsel Robert Kennedy; and Senator John Kennedy. (UPI)

The delegates to the 1957 convention had been captured by the mysterious spell of the Teamster Pied Piper. (Stan Wayman, *Life* Magazine, © 1957 Time Inc.)

While the delegates wildly applauded their approval of Dave Beck's five years as IBT president, Beck, awaiting his prison term, savored one of his last moments of glory . . . Defeating the token opposition three to one, Hoffa went to the podium as the president-elect of the 1.5-million-member union. (Wide World)

Theorizing that an informant might be present in Nashville, feeding information to federal agents, Hoffa came to the conclusion that the infiltrator was Don Vestal. He turned to Partin and said, "Get a few guys together from Baton Rouge. I want Vestal killed . . . I want him cut down like a cottonwood tree!" (Vestal Collection)

As a *caporegime*, or captain, in the Genovese crime family, Anthony Provenzano (right) had the distinction of being both a high Teamster official and a high mob figure. In July 1961 he was voted a vice president of the IBT. (Wide World)

Former contract killer turned government witness Charles Crimaldi strongly implies that it was Hoffa who persuaded Russell Bufalino (*above*) to cooperate with the CIA. (Wide World)

Santos Trafficante, one of the most feared members of the underworld, succeeded his father, who died in 1954. Trafficante quickly became king of the Florida and Cuban rackets after Meyer Lansky laid the foundation. (Wide World)

Louisiana underworld chief Carlos Marcello (left,) who controlled one-third of the Cuban dope traffic, was introduced to Jimmy Hoffa by Detroit mobster Frank Coppola. (Wide World)

"Strongarm" Teamster Barney Baker (left), a former street brawler and prizefighter, was one of Hoffa's top aides, and served as a personal liaison to a significant number of underworld figures around the country. (UPI)

"We didn't plant Partin in there," Jim Neal says. "Hoffa brought him in without our participation. We didn't send him in there to be a spy . . . Partin was in there, telling us about efforts to bribe jurors. What else could we do?" Ed Partin (left) walks with William Bufalino, Hoffa, and Ewing King (right) as they leave the Nashville courthouse in 1962. (Wide World)

Local 299 officers, 1965. (Seated left to right) Rolland McMaster, Frank Fitzsimmons, James R. Hoffa, Dave Johnson. (Standing left to right) Joe Thomas, Bernard Friedman, Francis Russell, Don Taber, Martin Haggerty, Steve Riddle, Ralph Proctor, George Roxburgh, Otto Wendell, Richard Fitzsimmons, Larry Campbell. (Johnson Collection)

A month before the election, McMaster sent a squad into TBL headquarters . . . ''to smash this hall and inflict mayhem on any TBL member who tried to stop us,'' according to a statement from one of his men. After the fight on September 29, 1965, the dissidents signed up new members. (Charles Collins [left], Larry McHenry [center, background].) (*Detroit News*)

Twice arrested and once convicted for attempting to bribe police officers, Anthony Giacalone, a former numbers runner for Detroit mobster Peter Licavoli, was prominent in the Detroit organization, serving as an enforcer for Zerilli and William Tocco. His wife was a cousin of Anthony Provenzano. (*Detroit News*)

As the fifty-two-year-old Hoffa posed for photographers, holding Fitzsimmons' hand high in the air to symbolize the union's strength and solidarity, few expected this to be Jimmy Hoffa's last IBT convention, or that fifty-eight-year-old, grandfatherly Fitzsimmons would become his own man. (Wide World)

On March 7, 1967, at 9:00 A.M., Hoffa surrendered to U.S. marshals in Washington. A few hours later he had been transported to Lewisburg Penitentiary, in Pennsylvania. Chuck O'Brien (center, left) (UPI)

5 The Enemy Within

On September 17, 1957, the AFL-CIO's Ethical Practices Committee charged that the IBT "has been and continues to be dominated or substantially influenced by corrupt influences." It also accused Beck and Hoffa of using "their official union positions for personal profit and advantage, frequently to the direct detriment of the Teamsters Union membership." Criticizing Hoffa for using John Dioguardi and the New York paper locals to take over the city's Teamsters Joint Council, the committee charged that Hoffa "associated with, sponsored and promoted the interests of notorious labor racketeers."

On September 24 the Senate Rackets Committee began its second series of hearings, concentrating on the Detroit Teamsters. This time Hoffa was not required to appear because of his current indictments in New York. The committee studied the questionable activities of Hoffa's men in Detroit. With most of its leadership in Washington, Local 299 was functioning normally; Dave Johnson, its recording secretary, was one of the few leaders unscathed by the committee's work.

First to be called for committee testimony was Rolland McMaster, the hulking nonelected administrative assistant of Local 299. His attorney, George Fitzgerald, told the committee that McMaster was in Detroit's Providence Hospital and produced a letter from a Dr. Edward F. Draves that read: "Mr. McMasters [sic] has been complaining of pains in the chest and a chronic productive cough, sometimes blood tingled [sic]. He also had a fainting spell Saturday morning, with severe chest pains, so I admitted him to the hospital."[1]

While the senators registered disbelief, Joint Council 43 organizer Herman Kierdorf stepped to the witness chair. Well-built, graying, and gruff-voiced, Kierdorf was questioned extensively about the circumstances that led to his job with the Teamsters after his alleged involvement in a kidnaping plot and a bombing. Citing Kierdorf's hiring as proof of Jimmy Hoffa's strange practice of employing convicted felons, Robert Kennedy detailed Kierdorf's background.

Kennedy's investigators had found that after the Detroit bombing indictment was dropped, Kierdorf and his nephew, Frank Kierdorf, went to Akron, Ohio, where they were arrested for armed robbery of a department store. Although the charges against the nephew were eventually dropped, Herman Kierdorf was sent to prison. Frank's arrest for another armed robbery ended in another aborted prosecution in Youngstown, Ohio, after which he was arrested in Michigan for a third armed robbery, convicted, and sent to jail.

Within a month after Herman Kierdorf's release from the penitentiary he had gone to work for the Detroit joint council, which was then headed by Hoffa. When Frank Kierdorf was released from prison soon afterward, his uncle introduced him to Hoffa, who gave him a job as a business agent with Teamsters Local 332 in Flint.

Some years later, scowling at his critics, Hoffa told a television audience: "Now, when you talk about the question of hoodlums and gangsters, the first people that hire hoodlums and gangsters are employers. If there is any illegal forces in the community, he'll use 'em—strongarm and otherwise. And so if you're going to stay in business of organizing the unorganized, maintaining the union you have, then you better have a resistance."

Local 337 and Local 299 business agents James Clift and William Bell followed Herman Kierdorf to the witness chair and told the committee how they had been illegally selected as delegates to the IBT convention in Miami. They had been selected during closed sessions of their local executive board. Although the IBT Constitution provided for rank-and-file ratification of all delegates, Dave Beck had allowed delegates to be seated without evidence of ratification.

It seemed a small point at the time, in comparison to racketeering, but Clift's and Bell's admissions were to haunt both the union and Hoffa himself.

Frank Fitzsimmons, Local 299's vice president, was called next to testify about alleged shakedown schemes in Detroit's film-distributing industry. He seemed nervous and hesitant, but his hat-in-hand style soon turned to defiance as he became increasingly afflicted with memory lapses. Asked whether he had been extorting money from Howard C. Craven, the film distributor, and whether the money was funneled through John Curran, the company truckdriver, Fitzsimmons balked.

Senator Mundt: It would be much easier for me to accept your statement if you said, "No, I didn't get any money, directly or indirectly, or in any way, shape, or form."

Mr. Fitzsimmons: I think I made that statement to Mr. Kennedy in Detroit.

Senator Mundt: I would like to have it made under oath now, while we are here.

Mr. Fitzsimmons: Yes, sir; as far as I am concerned . . .

Senator Mundt: Here you are under oath. There you were not. That is why I ask you the question now.

Mr. Fitzsimmons: I say again, to the best of my knowledge, I never received no money, directly or indirectly, from John Curran.

Senator Mundt: Could you eliminate that qualifying phrase which vitiates your whole statement? Could you simply eliminate that "to the best of my recollection," and say categorically, "I never received any money directly or indirectly from John Curran"? Could you say that?

Mr. Fitzsimmons: To the best of my recollection . . .

Senator Mundt: It is no good. You might as well say nothing. I want you to say whatever you have to say to be fair to yourself and honest . . .[2]

After further sparring Fitzsimmons finally testified that he had never received any money "directly or indirectly" from John Curran, and Senator McClellan then handed Fitzsimmons Craven's check for $500 made out to Curran, who had endorsed the back of the check. Fitzsimmons' signature was just beneath Curran's.

Senator McClellan: Tell us whether that was "directly or indirectly." You handled the transaction. You describe it.

Mr. Fitzsimmons: As far as the check is concerned, to the best of my knowledge this is a check of wages. Wages is written on the top of it. I presume that John Curran got this check, asked me to cash the check, and I did cash the check and, in turn, endorsed it and either deposited the check . . .

Senator McClellan: Do you recall the transaction?

Mr. Fitzsimmons: Sir?

Senator McClellan: Do you recall the transaction?

Mr. Fitzsimmons: I recall it as vivid? No, I couldn't recall this . . .

Senator McClellan: How many other checks did you cash for him in this fashion?

Mr. Fitzsimmons: I wouldn't know. I don't think there was many if there was any more.[3]

Fitzsimmons' amnesia continued through the rest of his testimony.

Local 337 president Owen Bert Brennan, Hoffa's partner in such questionable business arrangements as Test Fleet and Sun Valley, said that he wanted to testify and could remember everything, but because of his indictment for perjury in New York, he was afraid his statements might be self-incriminating. Upon the advice of his attorney, George Fitzgerald, Brennan took the Fifth Amendment.

The school integration crisis in Little Rock, Arkansas, that fall drove the second Hoffa hearings off the front pages. Besides, the committee was asking about such things as several unexplained loans to Hoffa from Teamster business agents and Detroit trucking companies, as well as his exploitation of owner-operator truck drivers. This was less exciting for the media than last year's gangsters, with their descriptive nicknames and aliases, who either took the Fifth or spilled their guts about bombings and gangland murders.

Nevertheless, the subsequent testimony was not without interest. Former Hoffa associate Robert Scott, a short, roly-poly former official of Pontiac's Local 614, was ready to talk. He told the committee that when he was elected to union office the election had been rigged, and he went on to say that he had also been used for a good deal of Hoffa's dirty work.[4] As an amateur in state Democratic Party politics, Scott had been ordered to ask the governor to pardon Peter Camperionero, the father-in-law of Peter Licavoli. Another time Bert Brennan asked Scott ''to put the fix in with the Oakland County prosecutor'' so Sam Finanzo would have protection when he opened up a gambling joint in Pontiac.

This second set of hearings ended on September 28, 1957, and the McClellan Committee charged Hoffa with thirty-four additional improper activities. Committee charges now totaled eighty-two, ranging from labor racketeering to collaborating with organized crime figures. The most serious charges were still Hoffa's ownership of the Test Fleet corporation, which the committee regarded as a violation of the Taft-Hartley Act, and the bogus Sun Valley land deal.

Considering the fact that Hoffa always kept a pocketful of change to make phone calls and rarely charged them, wrote few letters, and systematically destroyed his own and his union's financial records, the committee had accomplished an amazing feat by documenting as much as it had against Hoffa.

In its first interim report the committee wrote that Hoffa was a "dangerous influence" in the American labor movement. "The power of the teamsters union president is so extraordinary that the committee finds the fact this power is now lodged in the hands of a man such as Hoffa tragic for the teamsters union and dangerous for the country at large."[5]

Two days after the summary accusations were made, seventeen hundred noisy delegates wearing "Win With Jimmy Hoffa" buttons crowded into Miami's luxurious oceanside Eden Roc Hotel for the seventeenth IBT convention.

Dave Beck thrilled the audience with attacks on the government for what he called its policy of denying individual freedoms and rights. While the delegates wildly applauded their approval of Beck's five years as IBT president, Beck, awaiting his prison term, savored one of his last moments of glory, reminding the assembly that under his leadership the IBT's treasury had grown by $12.5 million.

Then, changing key and speaking like the broken man he was, Beck pleaded:

> I am going to ask you to judge me as I would judge you . . . I only ask you to try, if you possibly can, just here and there, somewhere along the line, to see if you can't find something that I have done that is perhaps just a little bit over on the credit side—just a little.

As Beck walked from the podium all attention shifted to Hoffa, who was to defend himself against the accusations of the AFL-CIO's ethics committee. His prepared response was loaded with the classic non-denial-denials of his testimony before the Senate Rackets Committee. In regard to the charge that he had sanctioned the hiring of known criminals to administer Teamster business, Hoffa merely replied, "Matters with respect to alleged 'toughs' and 'hoodlums' in the Central Conference area which the [ethics] Committee charges Hoffa associated with, supported, or hired, will be discussed 'off the record' with the Committee."

With the responsibility of dealing with the AFL-CIO's critical report thrust upon them, the defiant IBT delegates loudly voted to strike the ethics committee's report from the convention record.

On Friday, October 4, the inevitable occurred. Old John English, the respected secretary-treasurer of the IBT, stepped to center stage and gave the AFL-CIO the Teamsters' final word.

> We are here today at the most crucial time in the history of the Teamsters Union. We are being watched by everybody all over the country. Yes, they have people here to our left and right from the FBI, the Senate Rackets Committee and probably the American Federation of Labor-Congress of Industrial Organization watching what we do. I am standing here today, telling you that we are going to place in nomination the name of James R. Hoffa, the champion of the Teamsters' movement . . . We don't care what other people think, we are nominating Hoffa for what he has done for the organization . . . There may be a little trouble going on here and there, but he will take care of that.

Defeating the token opposition three to one, Hoffa went to the podium as the president-elect of the 1.5-million-member union. After kissing his wife amid the roars of the delegates, he stood erect before the convention—his gray-green eyes gleaming, his lower jaw cocked and pointed over everyone's head.

> Brothers, brother Teamsters, one and all! I want to express from the bottom of my heart my thanks . . .
> If you are dissatisfied with anything that is being done, or in the way this union is being run, I want to hear about it from you. I believe in good honest trade unionism. I believe in the welfare of our members. This union will practice democracy in its fullest form, notwithstanding our enemies.

Hoffa went on to attack the McClellan Committee and other critics:

> I have no fight with the McClellan Committee. But when a Congressional committee concentrates on a personal attack or misuses its power, it can be dangerous for all of us.
> Something is wrong when a man may be judged guilty in the court of public opinion because some enemy or some ambitious person accuses him of wrongdoing by hearsay or influence . . .

And he ended with a call for unity that apparently did not ring ironically in the ears of the cheering delegates:

> Let us bury our differences; let us work together as a team; let us stand united; let us serve the interests and protect the welfare of our membership every hour of every day.

By closing ranks, by settling our differences peacefully and democratically within our own house, we can move forward to build a greater and stronger Teamsters International Union.

On October 14, the day before Hoffa was to take office, Federal Judge F. Dickinson Letts stunned organized labor by barring Hoffa from taking the presidency. Hearing a lawsuit filed by thirteen East Coast rank-and-file Teamster dissidents whose claims were based, in part, upon the admissions of two of Hoffa's Detroit business agents that delegates to the IBT convention were improperly selected, the court decided not to allow Hoffa to become president until the charges were fully investigated.

Ten days after Judge Letts's bombshell, the AFL-CIO Executive Council voted, twenty-five to four, to suspend the Teamsters, announcing that it would seek the final expulsion of the IBT at the December convention.

Subpoenas were falling on Hoffa like a heavy rain. His attorneys quickly filed an appeal against the court's injunction, but on November 4 the U.S. Circuit Court of Appeals upheld it and called for a speedy trial of the rebel Teamsters' charges.

As the December 5, 1957, AFL-CIO convention opened near the snow-covered boardwalk of Atlantic City, New Jersey, the Teamsters were the main topic of conversation among the delegates, whose central organization received over $750,000 annually from the IBT. From the first day, when George Meany shook his fist at a picture of Hoffa, the Teamsters' fate was never in doubt. Saying he would save the IBT from expulsion only if it dismissed its new president, Meany demanded a response from Hoffa. Hoffa's only reply, through the press, was ''We'll see.''

Waking up in the cold New Jersey morning on the second day of the convention, the delegates knew what they had to do when they walked to Convention Hall. And they would have to do it in Hoffa's absence; he was still on trial in New York. John English, an AFL-CIO vice president since Beck's ouster, clutched a floor microphone and demanded recognition from the chair.

Regardless of what you or anybody says, deep down in your hearts you know there is not a union connected here that is better than the Teamsters Union. For fifty years, when you were on strike and when you could not get it [support] from anybody else, when you knocked at the Teamsters' door, they helped you . . .

> Oh, it makes my blood run cold. I am coming near the end of my days. I never thought I would live to see this . . . I say to you, my friends, the Teamsters Union will get along. We won't forget our friends. Teamsters never forget their friends. As far as our enemies are concerned, they can all go straight to hell . . .

It was one of English's finest moments, but the impact was less than he must have hoped. Meany shouted that he was not at war with the Teamsters Union; in fact, "I'm for the Teamsters," he said, presumably the rank and file. He repeated that the AFL-CIO's door would always remain open to the union once it cleansed itself of "this corrupt control."

After that speech the roll-call vote was taken and the IBT was expelled by nearly five to one. English and the other Teamsters quickly left their seats and walked out of their last AFL-CIO convention, still defiant.

"It really made me red-assed. Because I found out that Kennedy had whispered in a lot of ears at the top," Hoffa wrote. "They sure as hell were scared they would be investigated if they crossed Kennedy . . . It was back-alley politics by the Kennedys."[6]

After the expulsion Hoffa and the IBT turned their attention back to the problem of the dissidents' suit. Edward Bennett Williams, representing Hoffa, proposed a compromise solution in late January 1958. He appealed to Judge Letts to allow his client to serve as provisional president of the union while a three-member board—a rank-and-file representative, a union official, and a third person, selected by Letts, to act as its neutral chairman—monitored the activities of the union until a new IBT convention could be convened and a new election held. The court agreed to try the idea.

At first the Board of Monitors seemed to work well. Handling hundreds of complaints from rank-and-file members throughout the country, it made several recommendations to Hoffa, who, surprisingly, cooperated. Although his reforms were mostly localized, without dramatic changes in the IBT's power structure, they ranged from election procedures to the way union meetings should be run. But later, when the board began to move against Hoffa's criminal associates in union leadership positions, Hoffa tried to subvert the board and its reform efforts.

"Within a few months of the appointment of the Board of Monitors," Hoffa said, "Robert Kennedy issued a gratuitous statement predicting that the monitors would gather enough evidence to have me removed from office.''[7]

The McClellan Committee was continuing its investigations, but some of its Republican members were now demanding that the investigation ease up on the Teamsters Union, which had supported Republican President Eisenhower in his 1956 reelection campaign. The Republicans insisted that the committee should also study alleged racketeering problems in Walter Reuther's UAW and other AFL-CIO unions that traditionally supported Democrats.

In 1958, as a result of the committee's AFL-CIO hearings, which concentrated on Reuther and the UAW, Senator Pat McNamara charged his Republican colleagues with harassment and resigned from the Senate Rackets Committee. With no mad rush to fill the vacancy— few senators wished to be accused of being antiunion—Senator Frank Church of Idaho was drafted to replace McNamara. Discredited redbaiter Joseph McCarthy had died, on May 2, 1957, and had been succeeded by Carl T. Curtis of Nebraska; Republican Irving Ives was replaced by Senator Homer E. Capehart of Indiana, and Karl Mundt became vice chairman. Chairman John McClellan and his fellow Democrats, John Kennedy and Sam Ervin, remained on the committee throughout its existence, along with Republicans Mundt and Goldwater.

While committee members battled each other along party lines—and Hoffa brawled with the government and the monitors—members of the underworld were adjusting to personal changes in their organizations since the early 1950s.

After the Kefauver hearings of 1950–51, the operations of organized crime in America had greatly expanded but its emphasis was much the same. It continued to function primarily in illicit gambling, narcotics, and prostitution, using its dirty money to infiltrate legitimate businesses.

The Kefauver Committee had recommended that a National Crime Commission be established to consolidate the federal effort against organized crime. But as Senator Kefauver noted in his book, *Crime in America*, J. Edgar Hoover objected vehemently, saying such a commission might lead to establishment of a national police force. In fact, the FBI director argued that the National Crime Syndicate did not exist. The National Crime Syndicate continued to flourish right under Hoover's bulldog nose, but he was not to admit its existence until the 1960s.

Although the mob's basic money-making enterprises hadn't changed since Kefauver days, some of its leadership had. Financial wizard Meyer Lansky left New York to set up a "syndicate in the sun" around Miami and to open the Casino Nacional in Havana, Cuba, with the help of his friend Batista. Albert Anastasia, formerly of Murder, Inc., took control of the Mangano crime family, reputedly by ordering both Philip and Vincent Mangano killed. Anastasia shared the New York hoodlum empire's spotlight with Joseph Bonanno and Thomas Lucchese.

Frank Costello was still running the family business for deported drug trafficker Charles Luciano, but Costello considered narcotics a secondary function of the mob, next to gambling. His lieutenant, Vito Genovese, on the other hand, put narcotics first; that was where the most money was. Because of this difference, Genovese shed few tears when Costello was indicted and convicted for income tax fraud in 1956 and he could take command.

By mid-1954 most of the other mob bosses were as pleased as Genovese at the steady flow of illegal drugs. It was a good time to celebrate, and the opportunity came on August 18, when Joseph Bonanno's son married Rosalie Profaci, the niece of Joseph Profaci, a Brooklyn don who had been arrested several times—once for rape—in his native Palermo, Sicily, and had been convicted in the United States for drug law violations.

The Bonanno-Profaci families held an enormous wedding reception at the Astor Hotel in New York, in certain circles *the* social event of the year. Northeastern Pennsylvania mob leader Joseph Barbara was there; Anastasia came, of course, and so did Anthony Accardo and Sam Giancana.

Profaci's two daughters were already married to the sons of Detroit mobsters William Tocco and Joseph Zerilli. The Bonanno-Profaci marriage tied the Detroit mob even closer to the New York families.

In 1957 the party was over, at least temporarily. Frank Costello had retained Edward Bennett Williams to appeal his tax case and was released on bail through Williams's smooth legal maneuvering. Within a month after Costello was released on May 2, he met with a Genovese aide in a New York restaurant. After discussing business, Costello finished dinner and went smiling to his apartment building. He rushed for an elevator when a gunman, hired by Genovese, shouted, "This is for you, Frank!" and fired a .32 caliber revolver at point-blank range.

Costello slumped to the floor while his assailant hustled out of the building. Although the blood was draining down the left side of his head, Costello was quite alive. His scalp wound was quickly patched up at a hospital. Genovese reportedly hired forty bodyguards to protect him from reprisals, but Costello refused to retaliate or even to identify his would-be killer in court.

Rejoicing, Genovese laid claim to the number-one slot in the old Luciano family, naming Gerardo Catena, in New Jersey, as his right-hand man, and began to push himself as the underworld's boss of bosses. The dope was flowing faster because by mid-1957 the Cotroni brothers in Corsica had further expanded their drug kingdom.

"The Cotronis placed three of their men, who were also Corsicans, in Havana to receive the heroin from their new southern drug route," Charles Siragusa explains. "Because they also needed protection and muscle, Meyer Lansky and Santos Trafficante—who were on excellent terms with the Batista regime—were asked to provide these things by the Cotroni brothers. So Lansky and Trafficante began doing the same thing in Havana that Carmine Galante was doing in Montreal—keeping the junk safe and distributing it among their connections in the United States."

Willing to share the action, Lansky made sincere efforts to bring America's racketeers into the Cuban trade in return for their money and muscle. Responding enthusiastically, crime families began investing heavily in the lucrative drug traffic as well as Cuban gambling. New Orleans don Carlos Marcello was able, with Lansky's help, to monopolize at least a third of the Cuban dope business.

But according to federal agents, Anastasia, wanting more than he was offered, tried to muscle in on Lansky's territory.

"At first Anastasia had refused Lansky's repeated offers to control some of his Cuban empire," says Ralph Salerno. "But then when Anastasia saw how lucrative the business was, he wanted in—immediately. Lansky told him that now there was a waiting list. So when Anastasia started making waves, Lansky sent his number one boy, Santos Trafficante, to see him."

Anastasia and Trafficante discussed the problem in a room at the Warwick Hotel, in New York, but could not agree. Trafficante packed his bags and returned to Florida.

An hour after Trafficante went home, Anastasia left the Warwick and walked to the nearby Park-Sheraton Hotel for a haircut and shave. He had been sitting in the barber's chair for ten minutes, relaxing with a hot towel over his face to soften his rough beard, when two masked men—allegedly Larry and Joseph Gallo—walked into the barber shop and opened fire with automatic handguns.

Salerno believes that ''the decision to hit Anastasia was made by Genovese and Carlo Gambino—who was to replace Anastasia—at the same time the decision was made to have Costello hit. Genovese, in particular, was afraid of trouble with Anastasia since he and Costello were close friends.

''But those decisions to have these men killed weren't made unilaterally. Think of the mob like you would three Venezuelan colonels who were planning a coup in Venezuela. Before making a move, they would have to make sure that they had the support of the U.S. State Department, so that their new government would be recognized. It's the same thing with the organized crime families. Before you make a move to have someone purged or killed, you get permission from everyone else—even if it's just a display of respect.''

Consistent with Salerno's theory, police wiretap information disclosed that Genovese had met with Thomas Lucchese and Carlo Gambino just before Anastasia was murdered. And two weeks earlier Joseph Bonanno, Frank Coppola, Carmine Galante, Charles Luciano, and Vito Vitale, among others, attended a meeting in Palermo, Sicily, at the elegant Grand Hotel des Palmes, to discuss the problems Anastasia had been causing. It is also known that Trafficante and Lansky were informed of the killing beforehand.

''After Anastasia had been hit and Costello neutralized, a former bodyguard for Bonanno who had become boss of his own crime family in Buffalo said he wanted a meeting of mob bosses,'' Salerno says. ''He was concerned about the void Anastasia's death had left as well as Genovese's new ambition to become 'boss of bosses' of the entire criminal syndicate. Also there was a need to discuss the acceleration of narcotics and gambling enterprises in the Caribbean, particularly in Cuba, and problems the mob was having in the Northeast garment industry.''

For these reasons the mob called what became known as the Apalachin Conference, as far as we know the most impressive assemblage of underworld power ever held. By a quirk of fate, routine police work in upstate New York led to unique revelations of the interrelationships among new and old figures in organized crime.

Investigating a bad check written to a motel near Apalachin, Sergeant Edgar Crosswell of the New York State Police saw Joseph Barbara, Jr., son of the mob leader, making reservations for three rooms for November 13 and 14, 1957. Barbara charged the rooms to his family-owned franchise of the Canada Dry Bottling Company, said he didn't know the names of the future occupants, and asked for the room keys in advance.

Routinely checking out a register of the motel's guests, Crosswell learned that a car owned by Cleveland mobster John Scalish was parked in a nearby lot. The police had earlier identified other automobiles owned by organized crime figures parked near the Barbara estate. Suspecting some sort of meeting of the underworld, Crosswell and several officers went to Barbara's home to investigate.

"We drove in and everybody started running in all directions . . . " Crosswell later told the McClellan Committee. "A lot of men ran from around the barbecue pit and around this corner and some ran for the house, and some came out of the house and ran the other way, and everybody got all excited and all worked up."[8]

The sight of all those gangsters—in silk pinstripe suits, wide-brimmed hats, tailor-made shirts, expensive hand-painted ties, and pointy shoes—running like hell for the pine woods around Barbara's home was a memorable spectacle for those who watched it. As the mobsters sprinted through the trees they were caught by members of the police dragnet who were waiting with open arms and loaded guns. Some of the fleeing hoodlums ran down a road which led to a washed-out bridge and were caught there. One had to be gingerly picked out of a barbed-wire fence.

Some escaped, but fifty-eight hoodlum conventioneers were captured. Of that number

50 had arrest records; 35 had records of convictions, and 23 had spent time in prisons or jails as a result of these convictions; 18 of these men had been either arrested or questioned at one time in connection with murder cases. Other illegal activity noted in the survey included narcotics (for which 15 had been arrested or convicted); gambling (for which 30 had been arrested or convicted), and the illegal use of firearms (for which 23 had been arrested or convicted).

As to legitimate business activities, a study of the men who attended the Apalachin meeting showed: 9 were or had been in the coin-operated machine business; 16 were involved in garment manufacturing or trucking; 10 owned grocery stores or markets; 17 owned taverns or restaurants; 11 were in the olive oil-cheese importing or exporting business; 9 were in the construction business. Others were involved in automotive agencies, coal companies, entertainment, funeral homes, ownership of houses and racetracks, linen and laundry enterprises, trucking, waterfront activities and bakeries, and one was a conductor of a dance band.[9]

The Apalachin Conference was the largest known gathering of American racketeers. The McClellan Committee considered it "symptomatic of the growing power of the American underworld. This growth is reflected in expanding economic enterprises, the continuing operation of vast illicit enterprises, and the infiltration of top hoodlums into labor, management, and management associations."[10]

Those arrested at Barbara's home included Joseph Bonanno, Vito Genovese, Joseph Profaci, and Carlo Gambino, all from New York; Barbara and his underboss, Russell Bufalino of Pennsylvania; Gerardo Catena from New Jersey, and Santos Trafficante from Florida. Law enforcement officials also believed that Chicago crime boss Sam Giancana and Carmine Galante were among those who escaped.

All these criminals except Giancana and Galante were among the twenty-seven men indicted on a charge of obstruction of justice. Later, however, the twenty who were convicted celebrated when the appeals court overturned the convictions.

Members of the Detroit mob were conspicuously absent from the conference, but Salerno says that Joseph Zerilli and Anthony Giacalone were on the way to the affair in a rented car. They stopped near Binghamton, New York, presumably after hearing about the raid on the radio. "Even if they'd decided not to show up at all they still would've been pretty well represented [through their family connections in the East]. Zerilli, the recognized leader of the Detroit syndicate, was Tocco's brother-in-law and both were related to Joe Profaci. Giacalone was sort of Zerilli's 'man in the street.' If Giacalone said something, everyone knew that old man Zerilli was saying it too.

"A couple of other interesting things were that telephone records showed that calls were made to Raffaele Quasarano in Detroit from Joe Barbara and from Johnny Ormento, the big drug dealer for the Lucchese family in New York."

Aware of the importance of the Detroit drug traffic, Robert Kennedy tried with some success to establish that Hoffa was at least indirectly involved in the dope trade through protection and other favors for those directly involved. One connection had to do with the boxer whom Hoffa and Bert Brennan had owned. He was promoted by Quasarano and during one of his bouts in New York, Brennan and Quasarano were registered in the same room at the Hotel Lexington.

Under tough questioning Hoffa admitted only that he had known Quasarano for about ten years. He couldn't recollect any business associations with him. When Quasarano was called to testify, Kennedy tried to pin him down on his relationship with the Teamsters.

Mr. Kennedy: Do you know Mr. James Hoffa?

Mr. Quasarano: I refuse to be a witness against myself.

Mr. Kennedy: . . . Could you explain why it was that the Teamsters began [an] organizational drive of the LaSalle Distributors, and that they then got in touch with you and that the organizational drive was then called off?

Mr. Quasarano: I refuse to be a witness against myself.

Mr. Kennedy: Could you tell us why the LaSalle Distributors have sold over 1,000 watches that have been distributed to union officials?

Mr. Quasarano: I refuse to be a witness against myself.[11]

During other testimony Kennedy focused on William Bufalino's operations in Local 985, maintaining that Quasarano and his partner, John Priziola, "were the ones behind Mr. Bufalino's being established in the jukebox business in Detroit. . . . It shows once again the close relationship of not only gangsters but the lowest type of gangsters, those dealing in narcotics, being interested in certain elements in the Teamsters Union, namely in this case, Mr. Bufalino."[12]

When Bufalino appeared to testify before the McClellan Committee he was defiant and argumentive, defending his criminal associations and alliances. He also wrote a letter to a national magazine in which he defended his "number-one friend" and his daughter's godfather, Russell Bufalino:

> For your information, I have known Mr. Russell Bufalino since childhood, and it is impossible to conceive the injustice heaped upon [this] one individual by the press. This can probably only be attributed to careless statements printed without regard to their accuracy or degree of veracity, since I know him to be of high moral character and a person of honesty and integrity.[13]

Hoffa himself was haunted from the beginning of the hearings by the undisputed allegation that Detroit Locals 299 and 337 had purchased the Long Beach, Indiana, home of Paul DeLucia, a former henchman for Al Capone who had taken over part of the Capone interests with Anthony Accardo and Sam Giancana. DeLucia, an ex-con with a long string of arrests, was a key man in Chicago's dope ring. Although the estate was valued at only $85,000, the Teamsters had agreed to pay $150,000 for it. Claiming that he purchased the place to use as a "school for business agents," Hoffa failed to mention that in Long Beach it was illegal for a labor union to own real estate.[14]

The committee pointed out that DeLucia needed the money because he was having financial problems with the Internal Revenue Service and that he was permitted to live on the grounds for over a year after the deed had been turned over to the Teamsters.

In its second interim report the committee stated that it was

> convinced that if Hoffa remains unchecked he will successfully destroy the decent labor movement in the United States. Further than that, because of the tremendous economic power of the Teamsters, it will place the underworld in a position to dominate American economic life in a period when the vitality of the American economy is necessary to this country's preservation in an era of world crisis. This Hoffa cannot be allowed to do.[15]

In the meantime J. Edgar Hoover was still refusing to recognize the existence of the National Crime Syndicate. "In the fall of 1958 twenty-five numbered copies of an FBI report on the Mafia—the first and only time the FBI has acknowledged the Mafia's existence—were distributed to the top twenty-five officials in government concerned with law enforcement," Victor S. Navasky, then a *New York Times Magazine* editor, disclosed in his book, *Kennedy Justice*. "The day after they were circulated, J. Edgar Hoover had each copy recalled and destroyed. He denounced the report as 'baloney,' and it was never heard of again."[16]

With Hoffa's close connection to organized crime under scrutiny by the committee, he could do nothing more than try to defend his operations. Claiming that he had access to the mob but no direct control over its actions, Hoffa later remarked during a television interview, "I think, more or less, not tellin' 'em—you can't tell those kind of people nothing—I think, more or less, you develop a relationship with 'em to where you don't interfere with their business and they don't interfere with your business . . . I can pick up the phone in Detroit and call anybody, and I can talk to and have a meeting with them; and I'll prevail upon 'em not to become involved in breaking anything, any of our strikes here.

"But at the same time, that don't mean they control or run the union . . . So when people talk about who do you know. We make it our business—and a man who's head of a union's a fool if he don't—to know who are your potential enemies and how can you neutralize 'em. If you don't, then ultimately they will bankrupt the richest union by . . . constantly harassing you, by using strike breakers in your strikes."

On August 3, 1958, Teamsters Local 332 business agent Frank Kierdorf stumbled into St. Joseph's Mercy Hospital in Pontiac, Michigan, with 85 percent of his body burned. The professional torch was now running a protection racket with area laundries, and he had been caught in a flash fire he had set at the Latreille Dry Cleaning Company.

Photographs of Kierdorf in the hospital appeared on front pages, and the public waited to see if he was going to make any deathbed statements incriminating Hoffa. Committee investigators rushed to Michigan for a final interview with Kierdorf, who had appeared before the panel several months earlier but had taken the Fifth Amendment.

''You only have a few hours to live,'' a Michigan law enforcement official whispered to the bandaged mass. ''You are about to face your Maker, your God. Make a clean breast of things; tell me what happened.''

Breathing thinly, Kierdorf began to murmur something. The agents bent lower, their ears close to the bandages around his charred lips.

''Speak a little louder if you can, Frank.''

''I said''—it was barely audible—''go fuck yourself.'' Kierdorf died soon afterward.

Information about Kierdorf was flooding police headquarters, and a pick-up order was issued for Frank Fitzsimmons, Local 299's vice president, who the day before the fire had approved the sale of a $4800 union-owned Cadillac to Herman Kierdorf for $1500. The elder Kierdorf had vanished immediately after the fire, with the Cadillac, and was thought to be one of the two men who had been seen with Frank Kierdorf at the scene of the blaze.

Herman Kierdorf did finally reappear a few days later, but neither he nor Fitzsimmons could shed any new light on the investigation. The circumstances of Frank Kierdorf's death remained a mystery.

Hoffa knew, perhaps better than anyone, that Kierdorf's death was—and would be portrayed as—indicative of the way he ran Teamster business. As pressure to eliminate racketeers and hoodlums from the Teamsters Union increased, however, Hoffa chose more cosmetics. In August 1958 he set up an ''anti-racketeering commission'' with former U.S. Senator George Bender, a Republican from Ohio, as its head. Bender had been accused of accepting a $40,000 bribe from the Ohio Teamsters in 1954 to drop contempt charges against that state's Teamster leaders, William Presser and Louis Triscaro.[17] Soon after the case was dismissed, the Ohio Teamsters decided to support Bender in his winning campaign for the Senate seat vacated by the late Robert Taft.

Bender met Hoffa at an ''Italian banquet'' in Akron and was quickly selected to chair the anti-racketeering commission, for which he received $5000 a month. Senate investigators were at a loss a year later to find a single hoodlum expelled from the union as a result of Bender's work.

Mr. Kennedy: Has anybody been ousted from the Teamsters Union, Mr. Bender?

Mr. Bender: Well, I recall . . .

Mr. Kennedy: That is, on your recommendation has anybody been ousted? . . .

Mr. Bender: I am not going to get into that. My report is to Mr. Hoffa . . .

Mr. Kennedy: Did you recommend that William Presser be ousted?

Mr. Bender: No; I did not . . .

Mr. Kennedy: You have not recommended him. Have you recommended anything on Mr. Triscaro, that he be ousted from the union?

Mr. Bender: I have not.[18]

In the summer of 1958 the committee was focusing on the Detroit Teamsters even before Kierdorf's much publicized death. This time McMaster seemed fit enough when a Senate investigator approached him with a second subpoena on July 23, 1958.

Joseph Maher, a slim former FBI agent and Navy war hero, tells the story. ''I was doing my job and walked up to McMaster who was standing near a bunch of his friends in the Teamsters' building. We exchanged some words—he called me a Communist or something—then the others started moving toward us. With the crowd around us, McMaster grabbed me by the throat and threw me against the wall. Damn, that guy was strong, really strong. Anyway, all these Teamsters were shouting, telling McMaster to whip me. With all those guys there and McMaster's hands around my throat—his hands were really big, too—you know, I was really scared.

''So we fought near the edge of the stairway, then I just swung and broke his grip and ran like hell down the stairs.''

As McMaster tells it, Maher had illegally seized his personal records without his permission. Then ''he said something to me, I said something back, and we got into a rassling match. I don't know if all that happened, but I did take him on.''

Maher tried again and managed to serve the subpoena. On January 27, 1959, McMaster appeared before the committee.

Senator McClellan: What is your business or occupation?

Mr. McMaster: Mr. Chairman, I respectfully decline to answer because I honestly believe my answer might tend to incriminate me.

Senator McClellan: You honestly believe that if you stated what your business or occupation is, that a truthful answer to that question might tend to incriminate you? Is that what I understand you to say?[19]

Again McMaster took the Fifth.

After seven questions from Kennedy, to which McMaster pleaded the Fifth seven times, Kennedy began calling witnesses to provide background.

One of the witnesses was Joe Maher, who testified about McMaster's 200-acre farm in Wixom. The investigator had learned from McMaster's income tax returns that as the income from his illegal dummy corporations increased from 1955 to 1957, the farm's losses increased at the same rate. McMaster's wholly owned ''trucking companies'' maintained no equipment and no employees and were merely used as a means to extort money from employers in return for labor peace.

''Maybe Mr. McMaster had become what is called an agriculturalist,'' remarked Senator Ervin, ''who is a person who makes his money in the city and loses it on the farm.''

McMaster was soon recalled to testify and proceeded to take the Fifth to the next thirty-four questions. In one encounter McMaster was asked whether Yvonne McMaster was his wife—to which McMaster again took the Fifth.

''Did I understand you correctly when I understood you to testify that you honestly believed that it might tend to incriminate you in the commission of some criminal offense if you admitted that you were married to your wife?'' asked Ervin.

McMaster conferred with his attorney and again took the Fifth.

Ervin replied, ''I will leave it up to you to answer her when you get home.''

By the end of the day McMaster had taken the Fifth Amendment more than fifty times.

On Tuesday, July 14, 1959, McMaster was recalled as a witness. Hoffa had just been grilled about the Transamerican Freight Lines sweetheart contract with the Teamsters. As McMaster and Hoffa passed each other to and from the witness stand, Hoffa told McMaster how to testify by flashing five fingers at him and whispering, "Take five."

"That wasn't very fair of him doing that, was it?" McMaster inquired years later. "This really made me look a little bad."

McMaster's lawyer tried to make a deal with McClellan and the committee that was consistent with McMaster's wishes to answer some questions and take the Fifth on others.

> Senator McClellan: We can probably do without testimony in some respects, but if it is going to be clouded up otherwise by the fifth amendment on other matters within the witness' knowledge, I don't know how much credit should be given to his answers anyway. Let's proceed, Mr. Kennedy, with your questions.
>
> Mr. Kennedy: Mr. McMaster, have you received any moneys, directly or indirectly, from any of the companies for whom you are processing grievances?
>
> Mr. McMaster: Sir, I respectfully decline to answer because I honestly believe my answer might tend to incriminate me . . .
>
> "Well, if you were in my union and I was president of the international," McClellan exploded, "you would be fired before you left the witness stand! I don't know what would happen to you!"[20]

Kennedy then called another Senate investigator, Harold Ranstad, who testified that McMaster's father owned a half-interest in the farm in Wixom; the other half was owned by McMaster and his wife, Yvonne. The 200-acre property—valued in 1959 at $200,000—had been purchased by the McMasters in 1952 for $23,000. In 1955 Mrs. McMaster had purchased another 160-acre farm near Hartland, Michigan, for $20,000.

McMaster had received six head of Black Angus cattle from the president of the Hofer Trucking Company in Toledo, Ohio, which had a contract with the Teamsters. In all, McMaster owned fifty-five head of registered Black Angus cattle for which he had paid less than $12,000. Mrs. McMaster had bought a half-interest in a slaughterhouse and in a suburban Detroit restaurant. Her business ventures, presumably on her husband's behalf, included the purchase of another home in Bloomfield Hills, a well-to-do Detroit suburb.

Finally Ranstad disclosed that McMaster had been receiving payoffs from William F. Wolff, the president of Youngstown Cartage Company, through McMaster's Ram Transport of Royal Oak, Michigan, another dummy corporation.[21]

The committee estimated that overall, between 1953 and 1957, McMaster had made over $56,000 in sideline trucking deals.

McMaster took the Fifth to three more committee questions and was excused.

The committee also showed great interest in the business empire of the Dorfman family. Through its control of the Teamsters' health and welfare and pension funds, Allen Dorfman's Union Casualty had expanded into twelve insurance companies and ten noninsurance enterprises, including banks, a resort hotel in the Virgin Islands, oil wells, slum real estate, and the buying and selling of tax liens. Subpoenaed to testify were Allen Dorfman, the head of most of the family's interests, and Dorfman's stepfather, Paul Dorfman, who had been expelled from the AFL-CIO at the same time as the Teamsters for misusing funds from the Chicago Wastehandlers Union, of which he had been president.

During Paul Dorfman's tenure as boss of the wastehandlers he had a close relationship with the union's major employer, Theodore Shulman, president of Sanatex Corporation and executive director of the Waste Trade Industry of Chicago, which consisted of employers under contract with the wastehandlers' union. Shulman had successfully negotiated a sweetheart contract with Teamsters Local 705.

Although both Dorfman and Shulman invoked the Fifth Amendment about their relationship during their appearances before the McClellan Committee, Robert Kennedy produced a letter from Shulman to the members of his employer association about a new union contract:

> In the fall of 1951, a number of our members faced the problem of being forced to increase rates paid to employees not hired as truckdrivers, but who occasionally operate trucks in the course of their daily work. Through [the] cooperation of Mr. Paul Dorfman, our own union representative, a compromise agreement was reached with the Teamsters Union whereby certain drivers may continue to be paid a rate lower than the $1.75 per hour union scale established by the Chicago Teamsters Union, Local 705.[22]

In return for Dorfman's services Shulman helped out Allen Dorfman's insurance company: Shulman had two people on his payroll whose only job was to sell insurance for Dorfman.

Paul Dorfman's troubles with the AFL-CIO began when he was caught taking funds out of the union's health and welfare reservoir and, among other things, started paying personal bills with the membership money. Of course Dorfman and Shulman were the only two trustees of the fund. In addition, Dorfman had deposited $150,000 of health and welfare money in a bank owned by a friend, George Sax, who did not pay the union a cent of interest. The committee learned that Sax was the owner of the Saxony Hotel in Miami, which was a meeting place for Hoffa, Dorfman, Shulman, and others when they visited southern Florida.

Described by the committee as a "major figure in the Chicago underworld," Dorfman had introduced Hoffa to such associates as Paul DeLucia and Joseph Glimco, another heir to Al Capone. Glimco and DeLucia maintained close working relationships with their colleagues Anthony Accardo and Sam Giancana.

Kennedy subpoenaed Glimco, who was also a trustee of Chicago's cabdrivers Teamsters Local 777 and had been arrested thirty-six times, twice for murder.

> Mr. Kennedy: Did you ever do anything to help the union membership, one thing?
> Mr. Glimco: I respectfully decline to answer . . .
> Mr. Kennedy: You were one of the major supporters of Mr. Hoffa, and he is one of your major supporters. Is it because of this background that you have?
> Mr. Glimco: I respectfully decline to answer . . .
> Mr. Kennedy: You can have a lot of tough people call up witnesses, poor businessmen, poor members of the union, who can't afford to protect themselves, and have them intimidate these people, but you can't come before this committee and answer any questions, can you, Mr. Glimco?[23]

As to the Dorfmans, the committee reported that Allen Dorfman—who also took the Fifth—and Rose Dorfman, Paul's wife, received more than $3 million in commissions and service fees on Teamster insurance in eight years.

> This is indeed a handsome return for a set of insurance brokers who had absolutely no experience in the field and no office space until a few months before Hoffa successfully maneuvered the insurance business to them in early 1950 and 1951. . . . While Teamster members were literally digging into their jeans to assure comfortable living for the Dorfmans and their

cronies, the benefits available to them under the health and welfare plans were drastically reduced.[24]

While the Rackets Committee hearings were going on, Senator John F. Kennedy chaired a joint House-Senate conference committee which wrote the Labor-Management Reporting and Disclosure Act, commonly called the Landrum-Griffin Act. Meant to insure union democracy and curb the illicit use of union funds, the law was passed by the Congress on September 9, 1959.

Speaking of both the new law and the court-ordered Board of Monitors, Jimmy Hoffa said scornfully, "If the Landrum-Griffin law had adequate provisions for protecting the rank and file of union membership from undemocratic practices, why should the Teamsters be denied the right to hold a convention and an election under the provisions of that law?"[25]

On March 31, 1960, the Senate Select Committee completed its three years of work. During its 270 days of hearings, the testimony of 1526 witnesses filled 46,150 pages; 343 of those appearing took the Fifth Amendment. The ninety-one committee investigators traveled over 2.5 million miles, served more than 8000 subpoenas, photostated 128,204 documents for use in its 253 active investigations. At a total cost of $2 million, it was the biggest congressional investigation since the Teapot Dome scandal of the 1920s.

In its final report the committee was still strong, but more philosophical, in its criticism of Hoffa.

Hoffa's whole record is, indeed, a model of inconsistency. He argues vociferously on the one hand that using his constitutional powers to rid the union of thieves, extortionists, dynamiters, thugs, and dope peddlers would seriously undermine traditional lower level autonomy under which members supposedly have inalienable rights to choose their own leaders.

On the other hand, Hoffa's rise to the higher echelons of union command has been accomplished through a remarkable ability to concentrate negotiating power and control over contracts into the hands of himself and a selected clique subservient to his will. Thus, under his aegis, areawide master agreements have become instruments that have operated to strip local unions of virtually all autonomy in contract matters.[26]

While he was managing his brother's presidential campaign, the former chief counsel to the McClellan Committee published a best-selling book, *The Enemy Within*. In it he wrote:

The Teamsters Union is the most powerful institution in this country—aside from the United States Government itself. In many major metropolitan areas the Teamsters control all transportation. It is a Teamster who drives the mother to the hospital at birth. It is the Teamster who drives the hearse at death. And between birth and burial, the Teamsters drive the trucks that clothe and feed us and provide the vital necessities of life. They control the pickup and deliveries of milk, frozen meat, fresh fruit, department store merchandise, newspapers, railroad express, air freight, and of cargo to and from the sea docks.

Quite literally your life—the life of every person in the United States—is in the hands of Hoffa and his Teamsters.

But, though the great majority of Teamster officers and Teamster members are honest, the Teamsters union under Hoffa is often not run as a bona fide union. As Mr. Hoffa operates it, this is a conspiracy of evil.[27]

Thanks to Robert Kennedy, Jimmy Hoffa had become America's latest anti-hero.

ⓑ The Making of Two Presidents and One Angel

The Teamsters' world was still shaking long after the McClellan Committee hearings adjourned. During the three-year ordeal 141 Teamster officials had been implicated in "improper activities," and many of them were being indicted. Others were being pursued by the Board of Monitors, which continued to try to oversee the union, including its $40 million treasury. From the time when the board tried to purge Bert Brennan for the boxing interest he and Hoffa shared with Raffaele Quasarano, Hoffa worked hard to immobilize the monitors and subvert the dissidents whose suit had caused the board to be set up.

In 1959 the leader of the rebel group, truck driver John Cunningham, had such a change of heart after being placed on Hoffa's payroll that he filed suit against the rank-and-file representative on the board. Financed by the union and backed by Hoffa supporters, the suit charged that Godfrey Schmidt had once been the attorney for a trucking company, which allegedly constituted a conflict of interest.

Pressure on Schmidt increased when Hoffa refused to pay the monitors' legal fees of $210,000, which by court order were to be paid by the IBT. Since $105,000 of that money was earmarked for Schmidt, Hoffa tried to use the money issue as leverage to force him to resign. Schmidt, who had litigated the dissidents' original claim against Hoffa, was a relentless crusader and the prime mover of the charges against Brennan. He had also been critical of Hoffa's brainchild, the Conference of Transportation Unity, through which the Teamster boss hoped to bring the IBT and the East and West Coast longshoremen's unions—both outside the AFL-CIO—under the same banner.

But Schmidt remained on the board long enough to help the rank and file win a major victory in federal court.

Martin O'Donoghue, a former attorney for the IBT, was made chairman of the Board of Monitors by Judge Letts. At first strongly criticized by the Senate Rackets Committee and the press, O'Donoghue worked hard and proved himself a genuine reformer. After several run-ins with Hoffa—who at first had been pleased with the appointment—O'Donoghue reminded him that the board was not only an advisory body but could actually insist that certain reform measures be taken. And when Hoffa and the Teamster board member blocked repeated attempts to remove certain officials—including Brennan—Schmidt and O'Donoghue took the problem back to Letts's court in Washington.

In the midst of the debate over the status of the monitors, a federal judge in Cleveland, who had formerly represented the Ohio Teamsters, ruled that three rebel leaders in Youngstown who were running for union office were ineligible because their dues—checked off their paychecks by their employers—had arrived at the union hall too late. The dissidents were trying to overthrow Local 377 boss Joseph Blumetti, a convicted white-slaver who was a top ally of both Hoffa and William Presser.

Soon after that Judge Letts handed down his decision on the role of the monitors:

> The Court does not subscribe to the view that the duties and privileges of the monitors were merely advisory . . . [They] are empowered to exert every known method of achieving the basic purpose set forth in the consent order, to wit: that a new convention would be free of corruption and in recognition of the rights of the membership.

He added pointedly that the union had no right to stop rank-and-file Teamsters from running for union office because their employers, who were susceptible to sweetheart contracts, were late in having employee dues checked off.

Hoffa appealed the decision and lost, and the monitors filed charges against him for his role in the Sun Valley land scheme, in which $400,000 of Local 299's treasury was being held in a Detroit bank, at no interest, as collateral for a loan to the privately owned Sun Valley project, which had borrowed $395,000 from a Florida bank.

In March 1960, Hoffa named William Bufalino to replace the IBT's representative on the Board of Monitors. Bufalino's assignment was to disrupt the board. For instance, he insisted that no mail addressed to the board be opened if he wasn't present. During one episode Bufalino grabbed a letter out of the hands of a staff member and then quickly left the office. A few hours later he called a press conference at which he appeared with a bandaged hand and claims that he been assaulted by the staff worker.

At a news conference O'Donoghue said that such incidents "reveal clearly the plan to utilize Monitor Bufalino, not in the proper performance of his duties as an officer of this court, but as a tool for creating dissension and controversy in order to hamstring the board."

Further harassed by late-night telephone calls from Bufalino and Hoffa, as well as badgering written complaints that demanded prepared responses, O'Donoghue resigned, and his resignation led to the collapse of the board by February 1961. But before leaving O'Donoghue detailed the Sun Valley charges against Hoffa for the Justice Department, which was planning to prosecute.

In the fall of 1961, trying to bail out of the fraudulent land deal, Hoffa began manipulating the Central States Pension Fund, which now had more than $200 million. He made desperate loans to shady operators in real estate and the construction business. In return for the money the recipients agreed to kick back 10 percent of the loan to Hoffa. Finally, after giving out millions in loans, he raised the necessary $400,000 to replace the collateral money that Local 299 had put up for Sun Valley.

Hoffa seemed to be off the hook. The Board of Monitors was gone and the most embarrassing debt paid. But the Justice Department, now under the new Kennedy Administration, proceeded with the Sun Valley case.

The fall before, while former McClellan Committee member John Kennedy was running a colorful and hard-hitting campaign, lame-duck President Eisenhower's vice president, Richard M. Nixon, was a lackluster presidential candidate. Choosing to remain close to a small circle of proven allies whose opinions and judgments he had learned to trust and respect, Nixon was a marked contrast to the young, boyish Irish Catholic who sought out bright young men and women, many of them friends and acquaintances from the days of the Senate Rackets Committee.

While Robert Kennedy ran his brother's campaign, Murray Chotiner had a similar, though far less public, role in Nixon's. Chotiner was one of the earliest and most interesting members of the Vice President's inner group.

During the early years of Nixon's rise to power it was Chotiner who introduced the ambitious California Republican to the underworld. Known as master attorneys in syndicate bookmaking and gambling cases, Chotiner and his brother Jack handled some 221 cases of known mobsters arrested or indicted between 1949 and 1952. During this three-year period Nixon rose from congressman to senator to vice-presidential hopeful under the watchful eye and guidance of Murray Chotiner, who had also managed campaigns for Earl Warren, then governor of California. Nixon had been sent to seek advice from Chotiner after he was selected by southern California businessmen to challenge Jerry Voorhis, a popular liberal Democrat, for his seat in Congress.

As far back as 1946, while Nixon—at Chotiner's direction—was basing his first congressional campaign on redbaiting Voorhis, Chotiner solicited and received a $5000 campaign contribution from West Coast mobster Mickey Cohen, who also provided office space for "Nixon for Congress" headquarters in one of his buildings. In 1950, during Nixon's senatorial campaign against Helen Gahagan Douglas— a campaign that also relied heavily on the red menace—Chotiner asked Cohen to give a fund-raising dinner for Nixon at the Knickerbocker Hotel in Los Angeles.

"Everybody from around here that was on the pad naturally had to go to the dinner. It was all gamblers from Vegas, all gambling money, there wasn't a legitimate person in the room," according to Cohen.

Trying to raise $75,000 for Nixon, Cohen learned during the dinner that the fund was still $20,000 short. "There were three entrances to this banquet room. I says, 'Close them.' Then I got up and I said, 'Lookit, everybody enjoyed their dinner, everybody happy? Well, we're short for this quota and nobody's going home till this quota's met.'

"All the guests seen the doors were being closed, so the quota was met over and above and that was it. Then Nixon made a speech. He made a hop, skip, and a jump speech because the guy that really done all the speaking was Murray Chotiner."[1]

Nixon grew in strength, building his reputation by accusing government officials and respected citizens of being Communists—who were more feared during the cold war years than the romantically portrayed criminal underworld. He parlayed himself into being the candidate for vice president on General Dwight Eisenhower's ticket, and when a secret-fund scandal threatened to remove Nixon from the campaign in 1952, Chotiner conceived of the "Checkers Speech," which captured the hearts of millions of Americans who listened to Nixon's well-timed theatrics on national radio and television.

By 1956, Chotiner was functioning as a special assistant to the vice president. But he was not too busy to do a favor for South Jersey and Philadelphia mob leader Marco Reginelli, an ally of Vito Genovese and Gerardo Catena. Chotiner was Reginelli's personal emissary in his deportation case. While Reginelli's lieutenants were in a violent struggle over who his successor would be, Chotiner quietly met with several Justice Department officials, including William Rogers, then an assistant attorney general, who helped reverse the deportation ruling and allowed Reginelli to remain in the country.

Nixon made other influential friends during the late 1940s and early 1950s. As early as 1948, he and his congressional chum from Florida, Representative George Smathers, maintained close contact with Charles "Bébé" Rebozo and Tatum Wofford—with whom Nixon often went yachting. Wofford, a Florida underworld figure with close ties to the New York syndicate, opened the Wofford Hotel in Miami, which became the Florida headquarters of Frank Costello and Meyer Lansky.

Rebozo and Nixon became fast friends, and Rebozo's circle of syndicate cronies got to know the young politico from California who was becoming famous as the nation's leading crusader against communism. By 1959, when the Cuban Revolution brought Castro to power and the mob back to the mainland (and to the Bahamas), Rebozo was thickly involved with the Miami community of right-wing Cuban exiles who served as recruits for the Lansky-Trafficante mob army in Florida. An American citizen of Cuban descent, Rebozo participated in many of the antirevolutionary activities that followed Castro's victory. He was a close business associate of Al Polizzi, a drug trafficker related to Detroit's John Priziola and formerly a member of the Cleveland syndicate. Polizzi, Morris Dalitz, and their associates had relocated in Florida, Nevada, and Cuba with Lansky's cooperation. Later they also migrated to California. In 1943, when Polizzi was convicted of black-market liquor violations in connection with a Cuban rumrunning ring, the Rebozo family had helped him get a federal pardon. Polizzi was also a business partner of Tatum Wofford in the mob-run Sands and Grand hotels in Miami.

In 1958, Jimmy Hoffa and the Teamsters began taking over the Miami National Bank, setting up a banker named Lou Poller as its principal owner.

A former syndicate figure turned government informant later wrote that Hoffa had recommended that he go to see Poller for some fast, clean money:

> [Hoffa] asked me if I'd ever heard of a guy named Lou Poller. Poller worked for the Miami National Bank, and his specialty was taking money that had been gotten illegally and "washing" it—cleaning it up and legitimizing it. Whatever money you'd put with Poller, he'd take 10 percent. It might take him a year or two, but if you gave him ten million or one million, that money would be invested for you in something legitimate. You'd be able to pay taxes on it. No one knew how he did it—he had his own ways—but he was a master at it. Hoffa offered to write me a letter of introduction to Poller.
>
> Poller, I found out later, was one of Meyer Lansky's men, and he washed the mob's money through the bank. It came out in the form of real estate, apartment buildings, and business ownership, like motels or hotels or mobile-home companies. The government could trace all day and never find anything illegal.[2]

The key man in negotiations for the Teamsters' purchase of the Miami National Bank was Hoffa's good friend Arthur Desser, who had connections of his own with the Lansky and Trafficante groups. In 1958, when Desser wanted to buy 547 acres of rich land in Key Biscayne, Florida, for $13 million, he was given a $5 million loan from the IBT's Central States Pension Fund. Richard Nixon later (in 1967) purchased two lots of Desser's Key Biscayne property for $50,000; each was then worth more than $75,000.

Before the revolution Nixon was a frequent visitor to Cuba. He met Fulgencio Batista several times and occasionally stopped in a Havana casino with friends. In April 1952, with Dana Smith—the administrator of the secret "Checkers" slush fund—Nixon made a late night visit to a casino in Havana where Smith quickly lost $4200 gambling. Playing on credit, he wrote a check to cover his losses, but when he returned to the United States he stopped payment on the check. The casino initiated legal action and had a good case, but Senator Nixon intervened with the State Department and the charges were eventually dropped.

While the Teamsters were taking over their Miami bank, Hoffa was in the midst of his trouble with the Sun Valley deal. His Florida attorney, Frank Ragano, also represented Santos Trafficante, who had a large investment in Cuban gambling and narcotics.

When Castro was hiding in the Sierra Maestra, planning his final assault on Havana, organized crime felt that the Cuban revolutionaries might be accommodating if they won. For a while the mob shipped arms to both sides. Jimmy Hoffa also helped both Batista and Castro, while presumably picking up some dollars for himself.

Edward Partin, a Teamster leader in Louisiana—a close Hoffa aide during the late 1950s and early 1960s, and later a government informant—explains the operation: "Hoffa, Bill Presser, and another person had bought a bunch of arms and were selling them to anyone who wanted them in Cuba. They bought some planes from the army surplus, and they were ferrying these weapons and planes from Florida to Cuba."

The other person in the triumvirate, according to Partin, was I. Irving Davidson, a dapper Washington public relations specialist who did business with government officials in Israel and Latin America. Although Davidson is just as insistent that he didn't do business with Hoffa as Partin is that he did, Davidson concedes, "I sold a tremendous amount of tanks and whatnot to Batista in 1959. About a month or two before Batista fell, I delivered a big package to him."

Presser refused to respond to Partin's statement.

Hoffa and Davidson had met in Washington during the McClellan Committee hearings, introduced by an official in the Pittsburgh Teamsters. Their friendship proved mutually beneficial.

In mid-December 1959, Davidson helped to set up a meeting between Hoffa and former California Congressman Allan Oakley Hunter, who was a friend of Nixon. Hunter wrote to the Vice President explaining who Davidson was and how a covert alliance with Hoffa could help in Nixon's bid for the presidency.

With an okay from Nixon, Hunter met Hoffa in Hunter's suite at the Americana Hotel in Miami Beach. During the discussion Hunter conveyed Nixon's admiration for Hoffa's courage and endurance against Robert Kennedy. Hoffa was willing to support almost anyone if he was running against John Kennedy, but he knew that an open endorsement could only hurt Nixon's chances. Hoffa agreed to lend support by attacking Kennedy "because of his support of anti-union legislation," as Hoffa later wrote in the IBT's *International Teamster*. Hoffa considered both Kennedys simply "young millionaires who had never done a day's work."

Satisfied with the conversation, Hunter wrote Nixon:

Hoffa is definitely of the opinion that the Department of Justice under Attorney General Rogers is harassing him and that the large number of investigators and attorneys who have been assigned for special duty in connection with the Teamsters Union activities are working up nothing more than nuisance suits. This, he charges, is discriminatory and unfair. Again, he said, he expects no privileges or special treatment; he just wants to be treated like anyone else. These nuisance suits, he says, have cost the Teamsters Union a great deal of money. He said that the Florida land case [Sun Valley], for example, he would win, but that it would cost money and might involve considerable time in court. He said that it's an easy thing to get a Grand Jury indictment but convictions are a different matter. He says as far as he is personally concerned he has absolutely no worries because he leads a clean life, pays his taxes, and obeys the law.[3]

Davidson was as active among Democrats as among Republicans. At the 1960 Democratic Convention in Los Angeles, Davidson arranged a private meeting between Hoffa and Senate Majority Leader Lyndon Johnson's old Texas friend John Connally. During the meeting Hoffa promised to support Johnson in the general election if his last-minute try for the nomination was successful. But the late challenges by Johnson and Adlai Stevenson failed, and Kennedy received the nomination.

Hoffa quickly met again with Hunter to restate his firm support for Nixon, and on September 7, 1960, the IBT's general executive board gave the Republican candidate the union's official support. Announcing the board's decision, Hoffa wrote that John Kennedy ''presents a very real danger to our nation if he is successful in buying our country's highest office.''[4]

That same month, before the first of the Kennedy-Nixon debates which began on September 26, Hoffa quietly made a trip to New Orleans to meet Carlos Marcello, another close associate of Davidson.

''I was right there, listening to the conversation,'' says Partin. ''Marcello had a suitcase filled with $500,000 cash which was going to Nixon. It was a half-million-dollar contribution. The other half [of the million promised] was coming from the mob boys in New Jersey and Florida.''

With a grand jury investigating Hoffa's role in the Florida Sun Valley Scheme and authorizing the Justice Department to indict him, the anti-Hoffa forces were pretty sure that there would soon be a direct hit on their evasive target. Sun Valley was an open-and-shut case.

But during the presidential campaign, in which Hoffa was covertly supporting Nixon, the Justice Department suddenly withdrew the indictment. Hoffa was still leading a charmed life.

That fall, when John Kennedy was elected thirty-fifth President of the United States, Hoffa reflected bitterly:

The Kennedys poured a ton of money into that election campaign, along with their usual hoopla and that ''beautiful people'' bullshit, and still they barely beat Richard Nixon. It's part of political history how maybe Nixon got a short count in some critical precincts . . .

There was bad news for me, of course, when JFK won the presidency. Because that's when little brother Bobby demanded, and was handed on his usual silver platter, the appointment of attorney general of the United States. With this added power in the hands of the greedy little rich kid, it meant that Hoffa was in the soup worse than ever. Nobody had to tell me that he was really going to go after my scalp now.

I knew that my worst days were still in front of me.[5]

Hoffa wasn't wrong. Soon after the election lame-duck Attorney General William Rogers reconsidered the grand jury data against Hoffa and indicted him for the Sun Valley matter.

Union insiders say that Hoffa felt Nixon had double-crossed him. It would not be the last time. On January 4, 1961, however, columnist Drew Pearson wrote in the *Washington Post* that Nixon had intervened with Rogers on Hoffa's behalf and that after Hoffa's indictment Allen Oakley Hunter wrote to him:

Dear Jim,

I was sorry to hear of the indictment against you in the Orlando matter. I know for a fact that your side of the case was put before the Vice President and that he discussed the case with the Attorney General, Bill Rogers.

I do not know what was said by the Vice President to Rogers. I do know, however, that the Vice President has been sympathetic toward you and has felt that you were being subjected to undue harassment by certain parties.

It would be my surmise that Bill Rogers acted as he did for reasons of his own. Mr. Nixon lost the election, I doubt that he has since been in a position to exercise any decisive degree of influence. As Vice President he had no authority to order the Attorney General to do anything.

Soon after Kennedy was inaugurated the new administration was in full swing. The Justice Department, under Robert Kennedy, Hoffa's relentless adversary, was especially active.

''Under the Kennedys . . . the U.S. government considered itself at war with Jimmy Hoffa and the Teamsters,'' wrote Victor Navasky in *Kennedy Justice*. ''They regarded him as a political saboteur who had the power, at any moment, to bring the nation to a halt.''[6] Kennedy also knew more than most people about the power of organized crime.

As a direct result of the Senate hearings and the raid on the 1957

Apalachin Conference, many of the illicit activities of the underworld had been exposed, forcing organized crime members and even some of its leaders out of business and, in many cases, into jail.

"From 1958 to 1961, some of the most devastating blows to the criminal syndicate were leveled by the Bureau of Narcotics," says Charles Siragusa. "During those three years we were able to arrest and convict top-ranking members of four of the five mob families in New York. And that included gangsters like Vito Genovese, John Ormento of the Lucchese family, Carmine Galante of the Bonanno clan, and [a captain] in Carlo Gambino's organization. We had slowly chipped away at most of the narcotics traffic which the French Corsicans had been dealing in since 1953."

Indictments, convictions, prison sentences, and deportation hearings were the fate of numerous racketeers whose exploits in the underworld had become infamous or legendary, depending on the point of view. In narcotics alone, 40 percent of Lucchese's crime family, 20 percent of the Gambino mob, and 19 percent of the Genovese group were under indictment.

Genovese was among the casualties of the Narcotics Bureau's raids, sentenced to a fifteen-year stretch. Both Galante and Ormento, who had fled to escape prosecution, were apprehended, convicted, and sent to prison for twenty and forty years respectively.

Gambino and Lucchese were fighting deportation orders; so were Hoffa's other friends: Russell Bufalino, Carlos Marcello, and Paul DeLucia.

Proud of his record as chief counsel of the Senate Rackets Committee, Robert Kennedy made no secret of the fact that the war against Hoffa and organized crime was the Justice Department's top priority. In view of Hoover's continuing resistance to the idea of a National Crime Commission, Kennedy started a program of coordinating the intelligence-gathering capacities of twenty-seven government agencies which could contribute to the blitz on the underworld. Centralizing this flood of information in the Organized Crime and Racketeering Section of the Justice Department's Criminal Division, Kennedy increased the unit's legal team fourfold, from fifteen attorneys to sixty.

Within the Organized Crime Section the attorney general placed some of his most talented assistants in its Labor and Racketeering subdivision. Heading this unit was a man whom the attorney general had learned to admire and respect while supervising his work as investigator during the Senate hearings. Walter Sheridan, once an FBI agent, had earned a reputation as a Hoffa tracker perhaps second only to Kennedy's. The quiet, unpretentious investigator, whose piercing stare seemed to bore holes through the mobsters and racketeers before the select committee, had one primary job: Get Hoffa.

"I know Sheridan," Hoffa said in a television interview. "A rat; a slimy, sleazy rat."

While the "get Hoffa squad" of Sheridan and several other brilliant attorneys traced Hoffa's continuing role in the Sun Valley scam and searched for evidence of influence peddling and jury tampering in Hoffa's two wiretap trials, Hoffa rid himself entirely of the Board of Monitors. Judge Letts allowed the Teamsters to proceed with their convention, scheduled for July 3–7, 1961.

As the convention approached, Hoffa continued his normal routine of waking up at 6:30 A.M.in his Woodner Hotel suite in Washington and doing thirty pushups before planning the business day over breakfast. He still dressed modestly, though he now had diamond cufflinks which he wore occasionally. Once at the office, sitting in his white leather chair in the IBT's "marble palace" in Washington, he usually held a succession of meetings that went late into the evening. Sometimes his only break was to eat dinner on the run. It was rare that he had time to pull up a seat in a restaurant and eat his favorite meal, a well-done porterhouse steak.

Hoffa's daily pace was grueling, but as his associates said, it inspired others. Sometimes unlikely others. Somebody on Robert Kennedy's staff reported that once, while he was with the McClellan Committee, Kennedy was driving past Teamster headquarters in Washington late at night and saw the light in Hoffa's office still on. Kennedy turned around and drove back to work.

About five weeks before the Teamster convention, Bert Brennan died suddenly. In filling the IBT vice presidential slot for Michigan, Hoffa narrowed his selection of Brennan's successor to two choices: Frank Fitzsimmons, Local 299's vice president, and Robert Holmes, secretary-treasurer of Local 337. The decision was difficult for Hoffa because both men had been loyal supporters since the 1930s. Union old-timers say that he resolved the problem by calling a meeting with the two candidates.

"Both of you have been my friends for a long time," said Hoffa. "And I can't choose between the two of you who will become the next vice president.

"So I'm going to flip a coin, and whoever wins will be the next international vice president."

Fitzsimmons won the toss and was immediately appointed to take

Brennan's place. He was later elected in his own right at the convention.

Another new vice president was a rising New Jersey Teamster boss, Anthony Provenzano. As a *caporegime*, or captain, in the Genovese crime family, Provenzano had the distinction of being both a high Teamster official and a high mob figure. Moving up fast in the Teamsters since 1958, he had gone from president of Union City's Local 560 to president of New Jersey's Joint Council 73 to IBT vice president in three years. When elected an international vice president, Provenzano was under indictment resulting from Robert Kennedy's charges during the McClellan hearings that he had extorted money from New Jersey trucking companies in return for labor peace. He had been among the union officials whom the Board of Monitors tried to depose.

At the convention Hoffa named his gunrunning buddy, William Presser, as one of the international's three trustees. The other two were Raymond Cohen, from Philadelphia, under indictment for embezzlement at the time, and Los Angeles Teamster leader Frank Matula, previously convicted of perjury.

Hoffa's choices were ramrodded through the convention. Union democracy was nonexistent as the handful of rebel voices were flicked off by the microphone control panel at Hoffa's fingertips.

"Hoffa adopted a public-be-damned attitude," wrote Clark Mollenhoff, who had won a Pulitzer Prize in 1958 for his investigations of the labor rackets. "He told the 2,000 delegates to the convention he didn't care what the press, the public or the Kennedy Administration thought about his actions. This attitude was against the advice of close associates who felt it was only courting more trouble."[7]

Like a feudal lord ruling over the serfs on his manor, Hoffa made a mockery of rank-and-file demands; he centralized absolute authority over the members and the convention in his own hands; he raised his own salary by 50 percent to $75,000, with an unlimited expense account; and he decreed that all legal expenses of IBT officials resulting from either criminal prosecutions or civil suits be paid by the membership—whose dues were, of course, increased.

Hoffa empowered himself unilaterally to put rebel locals into trusteeship, to remove all renegade officials and replace them with handpicked trustees. In addition, to make it more difficult for dissenters to infiltrate future conventions, Hoffa shoved through a resolution which provided that local union officials were automatic delegates to conventions, which by union law selected the general president and other members of the general executive board.

Cheers rose from the floor of the convention to the little president perched high on the podium. The delegates had been captured by the mysterious spell of the Teamster Pied Piper, who—just in case of wakefulness—had an army of goons stationed at every door, standing in every aisle.

After rewriting the IBT constitution to his own taste, Hoffa was easily reelected as the union's general president—by acclamation—after the only person to run against him, Milton Liss of Newark, withdrew during the roll-call vote.

The undisputed king of the Teamsters rejoiced again when, a week after the convention, he received word that a federal judge had ruled that the Sun Valley grand jury had not been properly empaneled; the indictment was dismissed. Bolder and more defiant than ever before, Hoffa was free to keep enlarging his domains.

Not all rank-and-file members were awed at Hoffa's overall power. One dissident was James Luken, a brilliant union leader in Ohio who had been speaking out against Hoffa since the early 1950s. Tough and courageous, the respected president of Cincinnati's Local 98 and his followers decided that they were finished with Hoffa and the Teamsters. They would get out of the IBT and affiliate with the AFL-CIO.

Luken's departure from the union was one indication of a trend that was beginning to develop in the union: rebellious rank-and-file members were organizing, forming countless groups with assorted acronyms, to combat the autocratic rule of Hoffa and the Teamsters.

In Chicago a tough reform leader, Dominic Abata, a former cab driver who was the founder and first president of Local 777, had already formed the Democratic Union Organizing Committee. Driven from the union by the mob and forced to open a small grocery store to make a living, Abata bounced back with DUOC, organizing militant cab drivers in their effort to purge Hoffa's friend Joseph Glimco from Local 777.

In Philadelphia's Local 107—the fourth largest Teamster local in the country—the leadership was almost entirely corrupt. During the McClellan Committee hearings a few dissidents formed a Betterment Committee, but with the local's money against them they could not accomplish very much. Although the Betterment Committee lost an election and failed to dethrone long-time Hoffa supporter Ray Cohen, the rebels regrouped after the government hearings and changed their name to "The Voice of the Teamsters Democratic Organizing Committee." Reformers in nearby Teamster locals were among the "Voices." After a second defeat by Cohen—who, like New Jersey's Provenzano, was under indictment for extortion while holding union office—The Voice began to campaign for a split with the Teamsters, the step Luken and the Cincinnati dissidents had taken.

There was dissent in Local 560 in Union City, too, but Provenzano had a knack for handling his opposition. In 1960 a rebel leader opposing the New Jersey Teamster leader for president was beaten and had to be hospitalized; the next year he was slugged with a claw hammer and nearly killed.

On June 3, 1961, Anthony Castellito, another dissident, was lured to his own country home in Ulster County, New York.[8] A Provenzano assistant hammered Castellito's head in, and to finish the job, Salvatore Briguglio, a Local 560 business agent, garroted him with a nylon cord. A third man then buried the body in an unmarked grave. Provenzano had arranged the killing but was in Florida at the time it occurred.

Briguglio's view was that the government was just interested in "headlines." His explanation was that "what they want is a Provenzano or a Briguglio, or any name they can build up. What they actually do is build you up to knock you down. So they can make a name for themselves. They're not interested in crime in the streets."

On a visit to the West Coast after the convention to explain a local contract, Hoffa was greeted with boos and angry yells from discontented members in two San Francisco locals. He managed to subdue those protests but was less fortunate in Los Angeles, where hundreds of Local 208 militants actually got up from their seats and walked out on him while he was explaining a contract to them.

To add to Hoffa's troubles, he was reindicted on October 11, 1961, in Orlando, again for misuse of union funds in the Sun Valley scheme.

In Detroit, things weren't much better.

The last election of officers in Detroit's Local 299 had been in 1958. Although there were virtually no dissident movements in Detroit at that time, both Hoffa and his administrative assistant, Rolland McMaster, feared that there would be as the Rackets Committee's hearings went on. Hoffa and McMaster devised a plan.

"We bought all of our membership a jacket," McMaster recalls. "Jackets cost about $15.00 each—$50,000, yeah—we voted on it in the [299] executive board meeting.

" 'Give everyone a jacket,' they said. Some of 'em got two. The election went smooth as hell.''

As the 1961 local elections approached, there was trouble, but it was caused by only one man.

Melvin Angel was a quiet family man, not a barroom brawler like many of the car haulers he worked with. He could easily have passed as a desk jockey who worked with an adding machine all day. Nevertheless, Angel was the first person in Local 299 to challenge Hoffa's local authority actively and persistently—right on Hoffa's own stamping grounds. Angel had been a rebel since the late 1950s, when Hoffa began allowing the railroads to haul more automobiles from the Detroit assembly lines, which caused unemployment among haulaway drivers, both company truckers and owner-operators. Angel questioned the new policy so often and so strongly that the local had Angel fired, and soon afterward he was expelled from the union.

In return Angel established Transportation Information Services, appointing himself its president, and began to write, print, and distribute a crude newsletter that informed local car haulers of contract matters and the situation with the railroads. Although rank-and-file members were reluctant to support Angel's anti-Hoffa rag, the publication infuriated most of the area's Teamster leadership. A Local 337 business agent filed a $100,000 libel suit against Angel after the newsletter accused him and Hoffa of accepting $10,000 worth of bribes, paid in fifty-dollar bills, from local employers. The case was later dismissed.

Problems between Angel and Hoffa came to a head in Hoffa's Local 299 office when Angel came in to discuss the car haulers' contract. As the two men argued, Rolland McMaster, who was passing by, heard the commotion and opened the door to see what the problem was. According to Angel, just as McMaster stepped in Hoffa shouted to the rebel, "Stay out of Teamster affairs!" Then he darted across the room and grabbed Angel by the throat. Startled, McMaster picked Hoffa up by the shoulders and tossed him across the room like a sack of potatoes.

Still steaming, Hoffa again attacked Angel, whose hands were on his knees while he gasped for air, trying to recover from the first assault. Before Hoffa could strangle Angel, McMaster pried the two men apart again and ordered Angel to get the hell out of the union hall before he got killed.

As several business agents crowded around Hoffa's door, McMaster led the little rebel through the doorway and to the street. Angel thinks that probably saved his life. Hoffa's henchmen might all have been willing to take their shots at Angel, but no one—not even Hoffa—had the balls to tangle with McMaster.

When he left the union office Angel drove straight to the Michigan Labor Mediation Board to file charges against Hoffa. He was told that he should report the incident to the police instead, and he did so. He also took and passed a lie detector test. With Angel's accusations written out and signed, the local police began a quiet investigation of the matter.

The trouble was that Angel didn't know the name of his big benefactor. Two days after the fight he went back to Local 299 to look for the witness. This time two detectives from the Detroit Police Department were along, but as luck would have it, Angel found McMaster standing around with a dozen business agents.

McMaster denied witnessing the fight, and Hoffa's "foster son," Chuck O'Brien, who was standing next to McMaster, charged out of the crowd and attacked Angel. As the two police officers tried to break up the one-sided fight, McMaster shoved his way through the crowd, grabbed both cops simultaneously, picked them up and threw them against the wall. He kept the detectives at bay while O'Brien pounded Angel, and the other business agents clasped hands and made a circle around the two men rolling over and over on the tile floor.

Again it was McMaster who saved Angel's life. He shoved the two struggling cops aside and pulled O'Brien off Angel, and the rebel and his two escorts fled at a dead run from the union hall.

Citing a "lack of witnesses," the Detroit prosecutor—who had received an $11,000 campaign contribution from the Teamsters—stalled as long as he could but finally indicted McMaster and O'Brien for criminal obstruction of justice and assault and battery. He still refused, however, to authorize Hoffa's arrest. Hoffa claimed to have been at Detroit's convention center, Cobo Hall, at the time of the second fight, and he had two friendly witnesses—Teamster lawyer George Gregory Mantho and Chuck O'Brien—who insisted that he was in a second and third place at that same time. The authorities dismissed the complaint against Hoffa.

Wanting his boys to be well represented, Hoffa provided McMaster and O'Brien with three Local 299 attorneys, Larry Burns, George Fitzgerald, and William Bufalino. As it turned out, they were not needed for long. Because the policemen who were with Angel on the day of the second beating had gone into the Local 299 offices without a search warrant, the court dismissed the charges against McMaster and O'Brien.

"The union had nothing against this guy," is McMaster's comment about Angel. "We tried to help him."

Angel was at once legendary as the man who stood up to tough Jimmy Hoffa. He decided to attend the 1961 IBT convention and raise some hell.

After landing a job on the work crew at Cobo Hall, making $3.65 an hour, Angel paid his union dues by registered mail and again became a bona fide member of Local 299. He wrote to Hoffa demanding time to speak to the convention delegates and propose several resolutions on behalf of the rank and file.

On June 28, a week before the IBT convention, Angel was hard at work, driving a forklift in Cobo Hall. A man reputed to be a member of McMaster's growing stable of goons asked Angel to get a ladder for a woman who was putting up decorations for the National Square Dance Convention, to be held that evening. As he drove his forklift into the dark corridor where ladders were stored, two other McMaster men pulled him off his vehicle, beat his face in, and kicked him in the legs, back, and stomach until he was unconscious.

While Angel lay in a hospital bed, the Detroit City Council swung into action, proposing a committee investigation into the lack of security at Cobo Hall. All that was really needed was more security for Mel Angel.

Angel managed to get out of the hospital in time for the IBT convention on July 3. He flew to Miami and rented a car which he covered with posters reading, "Rank and File Teamsters Want End to Hoffaism." Pro-Hoffa delegates and goons tore them off twice.

With black eyes, bruised ribs, and a stiff right leg, Angel limped into the Deauville Hotel and passed out his literature in the lobby: "Give rank-and-file members a greater voice in Teamster activities and prevent hoodlums and criminals from holding union office." "Hoffa is becoming a dictator through the constitutional amendments being passed here."

His trip to Miami was financed by a few friends in Detroit, but Angel made his stand against Hoffa alone. And he wouldn't quit. His next move, in the hope of severing Detroit's five hundred haulaway drivers from Local 299 and creating an independent union of transportation workers, was to align himself with Dominic Abata's Democratic Union Organizing Committee, which had led one of the first major revolts against Hoffa by overthrowing Joseph Glimco. Abata's Chicago group had instigated rebellions in St. Louis, Milwaukee, and Youngstown, and prompted Chicago Teamster leader John T. O'Brien to announce that plans were being laid ''to drive all these rebels out of our union and prevent them from getting jobs anywhere.''

Taking his lead from Abata, Angel proclaimed that ''the union belongs to the rank and file, not to any one man. If we can't get our just due in the Teamsters Union, we will get it outside that outfit,'' and he filed suit against Hoffa for ''breach of trust under the Landrum-Griffin Act,'' specifically in regard to the handling of Local 299's car haulers.

Soon after the suit was docketed, McMaster charged Angel with simple assault, saying that the little rebel had walked up to him in June and threatened, ''I'm going to get you and put you away.'' He was so afraid of Angel, said McMaster, that he had asked his attorney to obtain a gun permit for him, and he added that he had learned that Angel was willing to call off the feud for $20,000.

McMaster's recital was heard in stunned silence followed by roars of laughter in the Detroit prosecutor's office as police officers pictured Mel Angel calling out the big, rough, tough McMaster. In the end even McMaster had to laugh, and the charges against Angel were dropped.

In September 1961 Angel finally received some support when he and a fellow dissident filed another suit against Hoffa and Local 299 after both men were thrown out of a union meeting.

The significance of the litigation was certainly not in the charges—which, of course, were later dismissed by the courts. Rather, it was the first major rebel activity of Lawrence McHenry, Angel's co-plaintiff and a man who was to figure prominently in the future of Local 299.

While dissidents like Angel and McHenry fought their lonely battle against the Teamsters' high command, Hoffa's men were in trouble all over the country.

In Ohio William Presser had been charged with obstruction of justice; New Jersey's Anthony Provenzano was still under indictment for extortion; Central Conference organizer Barney Baker faced a prison stretch for shaking down a Pittsburgh newspaper; even Puerto Rico Teamster kingpin Frank Chavez, formerly of Los Angeles, had been picked up for attempted murder. It was symbolic that former general president Dave Beck began serving his five-year term, disgraced and appeals exhausted.

In Hoffa's home local, trustee George Roxburgh was indicted and convicted of extortion for taking payoffs from executives of the Interstate Motor Freight System. Because he had cancer of the throat the court ordered a two-year probation, suspending his prison sentence and levying only $2500 in fines. Roxburgh resigned as a trustee and business agent for his probation period.

Local 299's long-time secretary-treasurer, Frank Collins, had been imprisoned for two years for perjury. When he got out after fifteen months he returned to Detroit to get his old job back, but his replacement, Rolland McMaster, refused to yield. Collins had to get a job with a trucking company until Hoffa finally stepped in and made him administrator of the Michigan Conference Pension Fund.

Like Hoffa, McMaster was under relentless pressure from Robert Kennedy. McMaster also hated the President's younger brother. At one private meeting in particular McMaster thought he was playing games. ''I had a lovely session with him,'' McMaster remembers. ''Like they say in the psychiatrists' books or someplace, Kennedy got on a high chair—I remember it well—he sat up there and was looking down at me. And he sat there with his legs whipped across him while he leaned back on the chair. He looked at me for five minutes. He just stared. So I really got upset. I looked at my attorney and said, 'What the hell is going on here?' Kennedy didn't speak to me. Later, we got into a big argument and my attorney talked me into settling down.''

In 1961 a federal grand jury accused McMaster, Local 299, and the Southern Michigan Leasing Company of conspiring in a labor extortion scheme. Locked in the company's gray steel file cabinets was the evidence that would prove it, but when company owner Elaine Mastaw was subpoenaed to produce her financial records in court, McMaster surprised everyone by marrying her. The indictment was quashed when the new Mrs. McMaster refused to testify against her husband. Yvonne McMaster had died just forty-five days earlier, in May 1961.

McMaster was indicted again on October 30, 1962, on thirty-two counts of labor extortion. His co-defendant was William F. Wolff, Sr., president of Youngstown Cartage Company, an Ohio steel hauling outfit with offices in Detroit.

The case was simple and its details had been uncovered by investigators for Robert Kennedy during the Senate Rackets Committee hearings. McMaster was accused of parking a broken-down flatbed truck on the property of Youngstown Cartage's Detroit terminal. While the rig gathered dust, Wolff paid McMaster ''rent'' and, in return, the company remained nonunion. Money was sent to the Ram Transport Company—incorporated in McMaster's first wife's name— between December 1956 and July 1959; payments totaling $9000 in all ranged from $25.62 to $230 per month.

"Bobby Kennedy sent me to Detroit to help conduct the investigation and try the case," says William French, then a special assistant to the attorney general. "During the trial we called nearly forty employees of Youngstown Cartage, who, more or less, testified that McMaster's 'phantom' truck was wholly owned by him and his wife, and that Ram's only employees were his wife and sister-in-law. The thing that was really incredible was that McMaster was an official of Local 299 during the entire time that he owned this 'trucking company.' "

Although some of the truckers called were "frightened to death to testify," according to French, it was their testimony—particularly that of Mike Boano, a Youngstown Cartage steward—which was the most damaging to McMaster.

"Everyone knew that it was some kind of shakedown," Boano says, "because that truck just sat there and never did anything or went anyplace."

Al Harrison, a Cleveland driver who also testified against McMaster, recalls, "It took a special kind of courage for all of us to get up on that stand and say what we did about McMaster, and what we knew about the thing. McMaster had a reputation for getting real ugly when he got mad, and I'll always remember that glare in his eye when he looked at us while we were testifying. You could wind up real dead crossing a guy like that."

But as the trial wound down, it was McMaster who sealed his fate by taking the stand in his own defense. "McMaster is really kind of a pleasant-appearing guy just to sit down and talk to," French says. "You'd never guess that he had the reputation he has. But when the government attorneys got him on the witness chair, his cool and calm façade just crumbled away. And all that remained in the eyes of the jury was one very guilty man."

After two and a half hours behind closed doors on November 19, 1962, the jury returned to the courtroom with its verdict: guilty as charged.

Facing $500,000 in fines, plus a year in prison for each of the thirty-two counts, McMaster was given an eighteen-month sentence and a

$10,000 fine. But as it is a crime to receive a payoff, it is also a crime to pay one, so Wolff was given the same sentence and fine.

McMaster quickly appealed, hoping he wouldn't lose his precious freedom; Hoffa was hoping that he wouldn't lose his top muscleman.

Things were never the same again.

7 Teaming Up Against Castro

Jimmy Hoffa enjoyed his rough-and-tumble existence, including his relationships with the tough people who contributed to his survival both inside and outside the union. A shrewd gambler who knew when and how to play his best and worst cards, he was defiant in defeat, arrogant in victory.

"You had to love the guy," says one of his closest advisers in Detroit, smiling and shaking his head in respect. "If he had decided to go into something other than the union thing, maybe he would've made a great prizefighter. Not that he was all that tough, but you kinda have to admire a guy who—win or lose in the ring—would always want to go outside after the bout and fight the other boxer in the alley."

A brawler with extensive street-fighting experience, Hoffa could and did fight behind the scenes as well.

At the time Hoffa's friends in the underworld viewed Fidel Castro as a potential ally, the syndicate had shipped arms and ammunition to the revolutionary forces as well as to Batista, hoping that if Castro took over his cooperation could be bought in advance. Edward Partin says that Hoffa, with several Teamster officials and union associates, was in the business of ferrying arms from south Florida to various points in Cuba. "I was right there on several occasions when they were loading the guns and ammunition up on the barges," he recalls. "Hoffa was directing the whole thing."

After Castro overthrew the old regime, Hoffa tried unsuccessfully to obtain a $300,000 loan from the IBT's Central States, Southeast and

Southwest Areas Pension Fund on behalf of a group of gunrunning friends. They formed a corporation, Akros Dynamics, which was selling a fleet of C-74 airplanes to the new Cuban government.

"The whole [Akros Dynamics] thing was purely and simply Hoffa's way of helping some of his mob buddies who were afraid of losing their businesses in Cuba," says Partin. "So they were trying to score points with Castro right after he moved in."

Although Hoffa's friend from the Miami National Bank, Meyer Lansky, quickly fled from Cuba because of his commitment to Batista, Santos Trafficante, Lansky's alter ego, remained behind, hoping to salvage the mob's interests.

Balding and hook-nosed, Trafficante was one of the most feared members of the underworld. Succeeding his father, who died in 1954, Trafficante quickly became king of the Florida and Cuban rackets after Lansky laid the foundation. A brutal man who was implicated in but never convicted for his alleged roles in several gangland murders— including the 1957 slaughter of Albert Anastasia—Trafficante was deeply devoted to Lansky. This devotion was best dramatized by his declaration upon being formally inducted into the criminal syndicate:

> With an ancient Spanish dagger—none from Sicily was available— Trafficante cut his left wrist, allowed the blood to flow, and wet his right hand in the crimson stream. Then he held up the bloody hand:
> "So long as the blood flows in my body," he intoned solemnly, "do I, Santos Trafficante, swear allegiance to the will of Meyer Lansky and the organization he represents. If I violate this oath, may I burn in hell forever."[1]

Having control of Florida's "bolita lottery," a Cuban numbers game, Trafficante recruited young Cuban citizens to sell chances. In 1954, after two attempts on his life by rival gangsters, he was arrested and convicted of bribing a police officer, to whom he had given a new car, a television set, clothing, and cash in return for protection. The honest cop who received the goods played along, with the knowledge of his superiors, and later collared Trafficante. But after he was sentenced to five years in prison an appeals court overturned the decision.

The earliest known contact between Trafficante and an important Hoffa assistant was in 1957, a year before the Teamsters began taking over the Miami National Bank and the same year Trafficante was arrested at the Apalachin Conference. Hoffa had sent his number-one organizer, Rolland McMaster, to Miami to establish Local 320, which served as a front for many of the mob's gambling and narcotics activities. Trafficante—who, according to union officials, was also instrumental in setting up the local—occupied a small office in the union hall.

The key man who helped McMaster start Local 320 was an assassin for Sam Giancana named David Yaras, once a pinball and slot machine concessionaire under Al Capone. Roberty Kennedy called Yaras "a notorious Chicago racketeer who had been involved with many of the leading racketeers in the Midwest."[2]

According to Siragusa, "Davie Yaras was probably one of the first members of the Chicago underworld to 'discover' Florida after Capone was sent to jail. During his stay down there, he was second only to the Lansky-Trafficante people in the number of Cuban contacts he had. He ran a number of gambling operations on the island and was also the Chicago mob's liaison to the Cuban exile community after the fall of Batista." Arrested fourteen times and a suspect in several mob executions, Yaras was indicted with his partner, Leonard Patrick, in 1947 for the murder of James M. Ragen, a Chicago racketeer.

Through electronic surveillance the FBI some years later overheard Yaras and two other syndicate executioners describe a forty-eight-hour torture session before they killed their victim, a 350-pound suspected government informant. Yaras spoke of having shot the accused in the knees, stripped him naked, and, with his colleagues, cut his limbs open with an icepick. Then they hung him on a meat hook and beat him with baseball bats. Yaras then tormented the informant with a cattle prod, buzzing his testicles—but never enough to kill him. After that they seared his body with a blowtorch, and burned his penis off. Finally they removed him from the hook and disemboweled him.

A year after McMaster and Yaras set up Miami Local 320, McMaster, with Hoffa's approval, made a convicted New York extortionist, Harold Gross, the head of it. Gross was a close friend of McMaster and a former associate of the syndicate hit team, Murder, Inc. His duties included passing out sweetheart contracts and shaking down taxicab companies, service stations, and parking lot owners.

McMaster set up several other locals in the Miami area and packed each one with talent almost equal to that of Local 320.

Hoffa's use of middlemen like McMaster and Yaras to deal with the underworld was understandable. His fear of being caught in compromising situations was perhaps best explained in a sympathetic Hoffa biography, which stated that during the later 1950s and early 1960s

Hoffa's life was dominated by his fear of "that little monster," Robert Kennedy. Under Kennedy's direction, Hoffa believes, FBI agents followed him wherever he went, tapped his phone, opened his mail, and beamed electronic listening devices on him from half a mile away, aided by invisible powder they had rubbed into his clothes. During the Miami Convention in 1961 Hoffa warned the delegates that Kennedy had sent female spies to pry secrets out of them and ordered them to avoid strangers . . . He is convinced that officials of his own organization, including at least two Vice Presidents, reported to the FBI . . .[3]

McMaster was a wise choice for a front man. Few government investigators and reporters who knew the big, angry secretary-treasurer of Local 299 suspected that he was as important or as powerful as he really was. They knew him only as Hoffa's bodyguard at IBT conventions and just another fall guy during the McClellan Committee hearings.

"McMaster was Hoffa's bodyguard as a front," Partin explains. "Any time anyone tried to link the two of them together in something, someone would always say, 'Hell, McMaster is just Hoffa's bodyguard.' " In reality, according to Partin, McMaster was a personal Hoffa liaison to Meyer Lansky, Santos Trafficante, the Dorfman family and the syndicate in Chicago, and the Genovese mob of New Jersey and New York. With his collection of muscle now available from the Midwest to Puerto Rico, the towering, massive McMaster handled most of Hoffa's rough stuff.

"McMaster and Hoffa were in several businesses together," Partin continues. "Hoffa would get things done through him, since he himself was under surveillance by the government. McMaster had the contacts with the strong people directly. So if Hoffa wanted something done, he would get McMaster to do the contacting. Next to the mob, he was the strongest arm behind Hoffa."

A former Local 390 president in Miami says, "Rolland McMaster was as powerful as he wanted to be. He had a stable of goons that were top-notch. Plus, when you considered his ties with organized crime, he was terribly strong . . . definitely one of the strongest in the union."

Although he refers to himself as only "distant friends" with various mob figures, McMaster says, "Jimmy really never dealt with organized crime people as such. Jimmy had a very cunning mind. He knew that organized crime people could hurt him and his organization. So he got along with them. He knew that in our country you have different boss groups. Take those on the East Coast, Florida, New

Orleans, Chicago, and out West—you have five groups to go to. I'll tell you, if you don't have some of those friends, you could get ate up, and you wouldn't know what happened to you.

"Hoffa used 'em. He was a short guy and wanted his organization to be tough and strong. He seemed to cater to them."

While Hoffa catered to the underworld, Fidel Castro was one man who didn't. Although he allowed selected casino operations to remain in business after he came to power, he was quoted early on as saying, "I'm going to run all these fascist mobsters, all these American gangsters, out of Cuba. I'm going to nationalize everything. Cuba for Cubans!"

The aide who quoted him says that after Castro's statement he himself warned Trafficante that Castro was planning to double-cross the mob. "Not in this world," Trafficante responded. "You think he's going to close up a hundred million dollars' worth of business that we got? We generate over ten thousand people working. He's going to put all these Cubans out of work? He'll never do it." [4]

Nevertheless, Castro began systematically shutting down most of the underworld's casinos and putting dope peddlers in prison. Among those jailed were Trafficante and former Detroit racketeer Frank Cammarata, who was related to both John Priziola and Angelo Polizzi. Cammarata had been deported in 1959, and before that Hoffa had tried to get the governor of Michigan to pardon him while he was serving time in a state penitentiary. [5]

And just as the mob was growing impatient, so was the American government. On December 11, 1959, the Western Hemisphere Division head of the Central Intelligence Agency wrote a memorandum to Allen Dulles, the CIA chief, advocating the "elimination" of Castro. A portion of the division leader's letter read:

> Thorough consideration [should] be given to the elimination of Fidel Castro. None of those close [to] Fidel, such as his brother Raul or his companion Che Guevara, have the same mesmeric appeal to the masses. Many informed people believe that the disappearance of Fidel would greatly accelerate the fall of the present Government. [6]

Dulles approved of the plan in a handwritten note, but on January 13, 1960, during the first serious meeting about Castro's overthrow, he emphasized that a "quick elimination of Castro" was not under consideration. Others, disagreeing, pushed for a strategy of having Castro, his brother, and Guevara "eliminated in one package . . . " [7]

Both President Eisenhower and Vice President Nixon were informed of these discussions during meetings of the National Security Council, of which Dulles was a member. Perhaps because he "knew" Cuba, Nixon was delegated to be the White House's liaison to the CIA on the matter.[8]

Although those who attended these top-level meetings have refused to admit that the actual physical liquidation of Cuba's leadership was discussed, they have confirmed the sessions' minutes, which indicate "that the discussions involved a general consideration of a proposal to train a Cuban exile force to invade Cuba and . . . the problem of creating an anti-Castro exile force strong enough to ensure a non-Communist successor to the Castro regime."[9]

It is possible that outright murder was not the first option discussed, since there is evidence that from March to August 1960 the CIA tried to send an LSD-like chemical to be used against the Cuban leader—via an invisible spray—"to undermine Castro's charismatic appeal by sabotaging his speeches."[10] Further tests, however, showed that the drug was too unpredictable to be practical. Another brainstorm followed, when the CIA's technical staff conceived of somehow dousing an unwitting Castro with another chemical, which would make his famous beard fall out and thus destroy his public appeal. That plan was scotched when Castro canceled a trip during which the chemical was to be used.[11]

The failure of these attempts led to more drastic plans than forced day-tripping.

In the summer of 1960, Charles Siragusa, deputy director of the Bureau of Narcotics, was sitting in his Washington office making small talk with a friend who was a CIA agent. Siragusa, the bureau's liaison with the CIA, recalls the conversation.[12]

"We were just shooting the breeze, and then out of nowhere he says, 'We are forming an assassination squad.'

"I thought he was joking around, so I just said, 'You're kidding!' and smiled.

" 'Since you have a lot of contacts with the underworld, we'd like you to put together a team to conduct a series of hits . . . There's some foreign leaders we'd like dead.' "

Startled, Siragusa said nothing.

" 'We're prepared to pay a million dollars per hit.' "

Somewhat embarrassed, rustling about uncomfortably in his brown vinyl chair, glancing around the room but not at his friend, Siragusa replied softly, ''This is peacetime. If we were in war, maybe I could do it. But not like this; I just couldn't do it.''

The CIA agent left soon afterward and never brought the subject up again.

''As soon as he said 'foreign leaders,' '' Siragusa added years later, ''I knew exactly who he was talking about—Fidel Castro.''

Killing the Cuban leader was discussed at some length before the approach to Siragusa, but apparently it was not until August 1960— during a conversation between Richard Bissell, the CIA's deputy director of plans, and Colonel Sheffield Edwards, its Office of Security director—that the use of the crime syndicate was decided upon.[13]

In late August or early September, James O'Connell, a support chief under Edwards, got in touch with Robert Maheu, Howard Hughes's right-hand man and a former FBI agent who worked in counterintelligence during World War II.

''Jim O'Connell came over to my house and asked if I would be willing to help the CIA on a project related to the planning of an invasion of Cuba,'' Maheu explains. ''I said, 'Sure.' Then he told me that he wanted me to contact someone who could arrange the assassination of Fidel Castro.

''I couldn't believe it, and I was hesitant at first. But when I finally said I'd do it, I kept wondering to myself 'What the hell am I getting involved in?' '' O'Connell had been Maheu's case officer during the Hughes aide's previous work for the CIA. In the mid-1950s Maheu had broken into the room of an entrepreneur doing business with a Middle Eastern government and had photographed some sensitive documents. Later he is said to have made a skin flick ''purporting to depict a foreign leader with a woman in the Soviet Union.''[14] The film was to be shown as though the Russians had produced it. Maheu agreed to help the CIA and informed Hughes that his job was ''to dispose of Mr. Castro in connection with a pending invasion.''[15] A staunch anti-Communist, Maheu explains his decision: ''I was willing to kill ten Castros if I knew that it would save a single American life.''

A few days after O'Connell and Maheu met, Maheu got in touch with Chicago gangster John Rosselli, a member of the Midwest syndicate who maintained close ties with the Las Vegas mob community. When they met at the Brown Derby restaurant in Beverly Hills in early September, Maheu asked Rosselli to participate in a plan to ''dispose'' of Castro.

Maheu had known Rosselli for a couple of years. About 1958, while

Maheu was working as a consultant in Washington and living in Virginia, Hughes had sent him to Los Angeles. There Maheu saw a lawyer friend who offered him a free, all-expense-paid trip to Las Vegas for a weekend. In return the attorney asked Maheu to serve a subpoena on the owner of El Rancho Vegas, a local hotel-casino. After failing to get reservations at the hotel, Maheu called another lawyer friend, Edward Bennett Williams, who had been a teammate with Maheu on the college debating team at Holy Cross. Using his connections in Las Vegas, Williams got in touch with Rosselli, who then called Maheu. Rosselli proceeded to arrange accommodations for Maheu and his wife at El Rancho Vegas through its owner—the man Maheu had been sent to subpoena.

"I had a quick decision to make," Maheu remembers. "Was I going to be a son of a bitch and serve the subpoena? Or was I going to go back home and explain what happened? To me it wasn't a big decision. There was no way in the world that I was going to compromise my friendship with Ed Williams and the man I had just met, Johnny Rosselli, under those circumstances."

Maheu stayed mum about the subpoena, enjoyed his first weekend in Las Vegas, and when he returned to Los Angeles he reimbursed his client for the expenses of the trip.

"[The Los Angeles lawyer] laughed like hell, and subsequently he told the story to Rosselli. Then Rosselli said he wanted to find out more about this guy Maheu. After that we became friends . . . When he and I began discussing the Castro plots, I was straight up with him. I wasn't about to cross this guy or any of his friends."

Maheu adds that he explained to Rosselli that cooperation with the CIA in the matter "was a natural for them. There were legitimate business reasons for them to participate, considering what they'd lost in Cuba."

That idea wasn't completely new. Several months before Maheu got involved in the Castro murder plot—while the CIA was planning the Cuban invasion authorized by President Eisenhower in March 1960—the CIA had learned of losses taken by other underworld figures and tried to capitalize on them.

Russell Bufalino had had an interest in a race track and a large gambling casino near Havana during the Batista regime. His partners were New York underworld figures Salvatore Granello and James Plumeri, two crime captains in the Lucchese army. The latter two had been helping McMaster, Yaras, and Gross get Miami Local 320 started. Plumeri and Granello were also in business with Hoffa at the time, splitting kickbacks on loans from the Central States Pension Fund to enterprises in Florida, New Jersey, and New York.

According to a report in *Time*, when Castro purged Batista and closed down the business interests of Bufalino and his associates, the organized crime leaders left $450,000 with friends for safekeeping. Another $300,000—which had been skimmed by Granello and Plumeri—''was buried in a field outside Havana.''[16]

When the CIA learned of this while it was planning the Cuban invasion, the mobsters were approached by a middleman—his identity is still unconfirmed—who suggested that in return for their coopera- tion they might be able to recover their money. The three men gave permission for some of the $450,000 to be dispensed among ''their old contacts on the island to set up a small network of spies,'' and the CIA then asked them ''to pinpoint the roads that Castro might use to deploy troops and tanks in meeting the attacking forces.''[17]

During the preliminary stages of the CIA's invasion plans, other underworld figures also tried to cash in on the CIA arrangements. Among them were two western Pennsylvania mob leaders, John La- Rocca and Gabriel Mannarino, who had interests in Bufalino's Havana casino and the $450,000.[18] Like the others, they were both well con- nected. Mannarino had earlier sold his interest in Cuba's Sans Souci casino to Trafficante; and in the 1950s, after being convicted of receiv- ing stolen goods, LaRocca was pardoned by the governor of Pennsyl- vania during his deportation hearings.

Associates of the Zerilli and Tocco crime families in the Detroit laundry and overall business, LaRocca and Mannarino, according to Ed Partin, had been involved in the same Cuban gunrunning operations in which Hoffa participated. And during this same period of time, Hoffa had begun negotiations for a Central States Pension Fund loan with a Detroit development corporation financed in part by the local under- world. Subsequently Granello, LaRocca, Mannarino, and Plumeri par- ticipated in the split of the 10 percent kickback. But regardless of the success of their business coups with the Teamsters, Bufalino, who had also received union favors, and his four associates apparently contrib- uted nothing but worthless information to the CIA's planning of the Cuban invasion.

Although Maheu openly admits that he was responsible for bringing Rosselli into the intelligence agency's strategy to subvert the Cuban government, he denies having any role in or any knowledge of the covert activities by the five New York-Pennsylvania mobsters.

According to Charles Crimaldi, a Chicago syndicate contract killer turned government informant, whom Charles Siragusa and other investigators consider "absolutely reliable," Jimmy Hoffa was the "original liaison" between the CIA and the mob.[19] This strongly implies that it was Hoffa who persuaded Bufalino, Granello, LaRocca, Mannarino, and Plumeri to cooperate with the agency.

Maheu says that he first met Hoffa soon after he had become IBT general president in 1957. Edward Cheyfitz put them in touch. "I was hired by Hoffa to 'sweep' his new office, looking for 'bugs.' After that he asked me if I'd come to work for the Teamsters in a public relations capacity. I told him I couldn't do it."

Although he has no knowledge of Hoffa's participation in the CIA's plots to subvert the Cuban government, Maheu concedes that "things were happening before I became involved, and therefore I might not know about them."

"From the outset," says Ralph Salerno, the organized crime expert, "the CIA knew that guys like Rosselli didn't have the muscle or the pull to influence the Cuban exiles, who were expected to man the invasion force and pull off Castro's assassination. If Hoffa was involved—and I don't have any information that he was—then his role was the same as Maheu's: get to Santos Trafficante, the man who did have those contacts."

Although Hoffa did have Trafficante's ear, allegedly through McMaster and Yaras, it is quite possible that the CIA feared that further involving Hoffa, who was under growing government surveillance, could endanger the entire project.

After Maheu was selected—possibly as Hoffa's replacement—and proposed the idea to Rosselli in Beverly Hills, Rosselli refused to make a commitment but agreed to discuss the matter again. He was promptly asked to attend a meeting with CIA support chief O'Connell in New York, while Castro was appearing before the United Nations in late September 1960. At that meeting Rosselli consented to cooperate with the agency and was told to recruit right-wing Cuban refugees in Florida for the operation.

A few days after the second meeting, Bissell and Edwards informed Dulles that the initial "contact had been made with the Mafia."[20] But soon afterward, in early October, Rosselli complained to O'Connell that the job was too big for him to handle alone; O'Connell suggested that he approach Trafficante.

A short time later Rosselli introduced the support chief to two men whom he called "Sam Gold" and "Joe." "Joe" was said to have the

Cuban contacts and be able to make the necessary arrangements while "Sam Gold" would serve as "Joe's" back-up man.

"Sam Gold" was Sam Giancana; "Joe" was Trafficante.[21]

Simultaneously in Washington rumors were beginning to spread. On October 18, 1960, J. Edgar Hoover sent a memorandum to Richard Bissell:

> . . . during recent conversations with several friends, Giancana stated that Fidel Castro was to be done away with very shortly. When doubt was expressed regarding this statement, Giancana reportedly assured those present that Castro's assassination would occur in November. Moreover, he allegedly indicated that he had already met with the assassin-to-be on three occasions . . . Giancana claimed that everything has been perfected for the killing of Castro, and that the "assassin" had arranged . . . to drop a "pill" in some drink or food of Castro's.[22]

Although Hoover was not told how deeply involved Giancana was in the murder plot—or that he was working with the CIA—Hoover's cooperation later became vital.

Giancana was having an affair with a singer-actress living in Las Vegas. Suspecting her of having a simultaneous affair with a well-known comedian, Giancana asked Maheu to have the comedian's room in the Desert Inn bugged. Maheu hired a friend to do the job and waited for reports to feed to Giancana.

As in a late-night movie, the melodrama was complicated by a hotel maid who discovered the electronic surveillance equipment and called the cops. The wiretapper was quickly collared and thrown in jail. At police headquarters, he called Maheu. "What the hell were you doing with a wiretap instead of a bug?" Maheu snapped at the surveillance expert. "I don't know of anyone who makes love while talking on the telephone." Still angry, Maheu called Rosselli, who posted the man's bond.

Learning that Maheu and Giancana were somehow involved, the FBI began an investigation of the matter.

While the FBI inquiry plodded along, John Kennedy became President-elect and soon afterward attended a meeting with top CIA officials, including Bissell and Colonel Edwards, during which he was briefed on the "Bay of Pigs" Cuban invasion which was planned for mid-April. Kennedy was not told of the CIA's murder plots against Castro.[23]

Seventeen days before the new President took office, the United States broke off all diplomatic relations with the Cuban government.

Within a month after Kennedy was inaugurated, and without the President's knowledge, Rosselli made contact, through Trafficante, with an aide to Castro designated to administer the poison pills. ''The aide went back to Cuba and sent his family to the United States,'' Maheu explains. ''Then he lost his stomach and left the island, too. The pills were then given to a leader of the Cuban exile forces.''

The Cuban was Antonio de Varona, a former president of the Cuban Senate, who had been training the exile forces in Guatemala. Rosselli gave de Varona a set of pills which, if consumed, would cause death without detectable cause. Rosselli had hoped to kill Castro before the Bay of Pigs invasion.

In spite of all the careful plans and unsavory alliances, the April 17–20 Bay of Pigs invasion was a dismal failure. In the CIA heads began to roll almost at once. Both Allen Dulles and Richard Bissell were fired by President Kennedy by the end of the year.

The President, accepting full responsibility for the fiasco, had in fact considered scrapping the project from the outset. But ''If we decided now to call the thing off,'' he had told an assistant several days before the invasion, ''I don't know if we could go down there and take the guns away from them [the Cuban exile forces].''[24]

Kennedy had a point. According to *Washington Post* reporter Haynes Johnson, the exiles had been told by their CIA trainers to conduct a ''spontaneous'' mutiny if the President tried to stop the invasion.[25]

In the wake of their defeat the bitter Cubans turned their wrath against the President, who, they claimed, had not given the troops enough air support. However, according to an official government inquiry into the matter, the real reason for the overwhelming defeat was the failure of the CIA to provide the Cuban rebels with enough ammunition. The report added that the CIA had, unilaterally, stopped a convoy of supplies and ammunitions to the troops—without the permission of the President.[26]

Meanwhile, on the second day of the invasion the FBI was told that the CIA had been behind the wiretapping of the Las Vegas comedian's hotel room. Maheu was telephoned by an FBI agent that day, but Maheu would only tell him to ''see Colonel Edwards'' of the CIA. There was no mention of Giancana or the plots to kill Castro.

A month later J. Edgar Hoover sent Robert Kennedy an internal memorandum about the Las Vegas wiretap case. He wrote that in a discussion with Colonel Edwards it had been learned that the CIA, through Maheu, had solicited Giancana's assistance ''in attempting to accomplish several clandestine efforts in Cuba.''[27] There was no mention that Giancana and other members of the underworld had been hired to kill Castro, presumably because Hoover, like the President and the attorney general, had been unaware of the plots.

Robert Kennedy wrote an angry marginal note on the Hoover report: ''I hope this will be followed up vigorously.''[28] He knew that such associations would be very bad for the crime-busting Kennedy Administration.

In November, John McCone, a California industrialist who had been head of the Atomic Energy Commission, replaced Allen Dulles as head of the CIA. McCone was never briefed on the assassination plots by either Dulles, Bissell, or William Harvey, who had succeeded James O'Connell as the coordinator of operations against the Cuban leader.

In November also, the President, in a speech at the University of Washington, said, ''We cannot, as a free nation, compete with our adversaries in tactics of terror, assassination, false promises, counterfeit mobs and crises.''[29]

Soon after that speech, Kennedy issued a memo notifying selected government officials of his decision to ''use our available assets . . . to help Cuba overthrow the Communist regime,''[30] but there is no evidence that he sanctioned either assassination or any sort of government alliance with the underworld. The program—code named ''Operation MONGOOSE''—was designed to infiltrate and organize the Cuban population to incite a counterrevolution.[31]

In February 1962, Bissell was succeeded by his deputy director, Richard Helms. Soon after the change in command—and without McCone's knowledge—William Harvey discussed the murder plots against Castro with Helms.[32]

On February 27, Hoover sent a memorandum to Robert Kennedy and Special Assistant to the President Kenneth O'Donnell stating that Colonel Edwards had objected to prosecutions in the Las Vegas case. The memo went on to say that during the FBI investigation of Rosselli's role in the matter, the Bureau had found that he had maintained a relationship with Judith Campbell, who had also been having affairs with Sam Giancana and President Kennedy—simultaneously. Hoover had cross-checked the allegation by reviewing the woman's phone records, which showed that calls had been made to the general White House number.[33]

On March 22, Hoover and President Kennedy had a private lunch during which the Campbell matter was presumably discussed.[34] And, since the FBI had just uncovered some kind of working relationship between the CIA and the underworld, it is probable that they discussed this as well. Later that afternoon the President made his last call to the woman. The next day Hoover wrote to the CIA's general counsel recapping the status of the Las Vegas wiretapping investigation. He explained that Colonel Edwards had asked the FBI not to pursue the case and added that "We were also informed that introduction of evidence concerning the CIA operation would be embarrassing to the Government."[35]

The FBI inquiry into the wiretapping activity of Maheu, Giancana, Rosselli, and their cohorts was dropped a month later.

Within two weeks after Hoover wrote to the CIA, Helms ordered anti-Castro coordinator Harvey to sever the CIA's ties with Giancana and Maheu but to continue the relationship with Rosselli and Trafficante, whose names had not surfaced in the FBI's investigation. "Helms probably didn't know everything that was going on because O'Connell and I had severed our relationship with the people involved in the plots after the Bay of Pigs invasion," Maheu says. "We had been very critical about the fiasco, and it was a mutual decision among all of us that we leave. Rosselli and Harvey handled everything after that." Following the Hoover memorandum Harvey met with Rosselli and passed another set of four poison pills for delivery to de Varona, the Cuban exile leader. The targets this time were Fidel Castro, his brother Raul, and Ché Guevara.

On the afternoon of May 7, 1962, Robert Kennedy met first with Helms, then three hours later with Edwards and Lawrence Houston, the CIA's legal counsel. During these meetings the attorney general was informed of the assassination plots with Rosselli and Giancana through Robert Maheu.[36] Apparently there was still no official indication that Trafficante was involved. Kennedy was told that the plots were meant to complement the Bay of Pigs invasion and had been called off when the operation failed, but while the meetings were going on Rosselli was reporting to Harvey that the lethal pills had been gotten safely to de Varona.

Kennedy was horrified at the fact of a government-mob tie-up. As Lawrence Houston put it, "If you have seen Mr. Kennedy's eyes get steely and his jaw set and his voice get low and precise, you get a definite feeling of unhappiness.''[37]

''I trust,'' Houston quoted Kennedy as saying slowly and deliberately, ''that if you ever try to do business with organized crime—with gangsters—you will let the Attorney General know.''[38]

Kennedy met with Hoover two days later. Commenting on the meeting for his personal file, Hoover wrote,

> The Attorney General told me he wanted to advise me of a situation in the Giancana case which had considerably disturbed him. He stated a few days ago he had been advised by CIA that in connection with Giancana, CIA had hired Robert A. Maheu, a private detective in Washington, D.C., to approach Giancana with a proposition of paying $150,000 to hire some gunmen to go into Cuba and to kill Castro.[39]

Still neither Hoover nor Kennedy had learned the true story; gunmen were never involved.

Hoover's memo gave two reasons for the attorney general's rage: First, the CIA had put itself in a position where

> it could not afford to have any action taken against Giancana or Maheu. [Second,] Stated as he [Kennedy] well knew the ''gutter gossip'' was that the reason nothing had been done against Giancana was because of Giancana's close relationship with Frank Sinatra who, in turn, claimed to be a close friend of the Kennedy family. The Attorney General stated he realized this and it was for that reason that he was quite concerned when he received this information from the CIA about Giancana and Maheu.[40]

Frank Sinatra, a close friend of Giancana, was the person who introduced Judith Campbell to President Kennedy. Years later Judith Campbell Exner—an attractive brunette with a pretty smile—wrote a self-serving, undocumented autobiography in which she claimed to have met John Kennedy in early February 1960 at the Sands Hotel. She insisted that at that point she did not know either Giancana or Rosselli. Between March 7 and April 12, 1960, she wrote, she had slept with Kennedy on three occasions and he had telephoned her almost daily.[41]

In 1962 the FBI's discovery that any part of this story might be true carried the potential of grave scandal for the presidency. And the mob aspect was equally staggering. Campbell had surely exaggerated the relationship, but even if the President had met with her only once, there was a strong possibility that Giancana or his associates would blackmail the White House and the Justice Department. It is possible that Hoover, an old master of wiretapping and fully aware of the Maheu-Giancana wiretapping episode, was afraid the President might have been trapped the same way. And in any case, Judith Campbell was not noted for keeping secrets.

Years later, questioned by a reporter about what he knew about the Kennedys' sex lives, Jimmy Hoffa responded, " . . . I already had a tape on Bobby Kennedy and Jack Kennedy which was so filthy and so nasty—given to me by a girl—that even though my people encouraged me to [release] it, I wouldn't do it. I put it away and said the hell with it. Forget about it."

"Question: What was on the tape?

"Hoffa: Oh, their association with this young lady and what they had did, and so forth. I got rid of the tape. I wouldn't put up with it. [Pause.] Pure nonsense."[42]

Hoffa's closest union associates as well as a family spokesman have denied the existence of such a tape. One associate, Harold Gibbons, says flatly, "If Jimmy had something on the Kennedys, he would have used it. The pressure was on him, and he would've done just about anything to turn it off."

The fact that Hoffa didn't use the tape—not even for a careful leak to the press—indicates that he never had such a tape. It is inconceivable, in view of Hoffa's pragmatic nature and his hatred of the Kennedys, that he "got rid of the tape" and "wouldn't put up with it." A more likely explanation for Hoffa's familiarity with John Kennedy's alleged affairs is that he heard about them directly from someone close to those involved, or from the actual participants in the CIA plots.

Whatever leverage Hoffa and his underworld friends supposedly had against the Kennedys was not enough to keep him out of trouble. On May 19, 1962—twelve days after Robert Kennedy learned about the CIA-underworld connection—Hoffa was indicted for his part in the Test Fleet labor extortion scheme and an October trial date was set. In the meantime one of Hoffa's attorneys, Frank Ragano—also counsel to Santos Trafficante—got an indefinite postponement of a Sun Valley swindle indictment against him.

Another indication that the Kennedys did not feel unduly threatened came in September 1962, when a soldier in the Vito Genovese family, convinced that he was being targeted for a mob execution, began speaking candidly about the underworld with a representative of the attorney general. Joseph Valachi had twice been convicted of narcotics violations and he was serving a life sentence for murder in the federal prison in Atlanta. There he was in the same cell block as Genovese, in jail for dope dealing. After Valachi's second narcotics trial he was constantly interviewed by federal narcotics agents, which gave Genovese a bad attack of paranoia. He began to believe his subordinate had violated the underworld's oath of secrecy. One day Genovese told Valachi, ''You know, sometimes if I had a barrel of apples, and one of these apples is touched . . . not all rotten but just a little touched . . . it has to be removed or it will touch all the rest of the apples.''[43] Genovese then gave Valachi the fabled ''kiss of death,'' indicating that he was marked to be killed.

Trying to dodge the Genovese loyalists in the prison—including John Dioguardi, who tried to lure Valachi into an empty shower stall— Valachi, out of his own fear, struck and accidentally killed a man he thought was an assassin. Convicted of murder and sent back to Atlanta to certain death, Valachi offered himself to U.S. Attorney Robert Morgenthau, in New York, and Morgenthau put him in contact with the Bureau of Narcotics.

''Bobby Kennedy called me in Washington,'' says Charles Siragusa, ''and asked me if the Justice Department could question Valachi. So we gave him access to Valachi, who was turning out to be one of our best sources of information. Then, before you knew it, Bobby Kennedy, because of his hatred of the mob, had completely taken possession of Valachi. Frankly, we were pretty upset about it, because Valachi was helping to make a number of our cases.'' By September 1962, Valachi was singing tunes that were music to Robert Kennedy's ears.

That month, as word of Valachi's cooperation leaked out, Carlos Marcello met with his top henchmen in a cottage near New Orleans. During the meeting Marcello, according to a report, was in a frenzy about Robert Kennedy, and especially Marcello's own recent ''kidnaping,'' which had been engineered by the attorney general near the time of the Bay of Pigs invasion. Both Marcello and Russell Bufalino had gotten deportation orders and were battling the government with the same attorney. In the Marcello ''kidnaping,'' federal agents sent by the attorney general arrested and handcuffed Marcello as he was walking down a New Orleans street. They drove him to a nearby airport, loaded him onto a private plane, and flew him out of the country. Since he carried a Guatemalan birth certificate it was assumed that he was a native. After two months in Latin America, Marcello illegally flew back into the United States on his private plane, piloted by

David Ferrie, an anti-Castro activist. Back in America, Marcello began his successful appeal to fight permanent deportation, claiming that he had been sent away with no opportunity to call either his family or his lawyer.

Marcello reportedly worked himself up over the incident and finally shouted an ancient Sicilian death threat against the Kennedy brothers, *"Livarsi na petra di la scarpa!"*("Take the stone out of my shoe!")[44] He then announced that John Kennedy was going to be assassinated, and that a "nut" was going to be hired to handle the job.[45]

That same month Marcello's friend Trafficante, still involved in the CIA murder plots, was talking to José Aleman, a Cuban exile financier who was a respected FBI informant, about his hatred of the President.

"Have you seen how his brother is hitting Hoffa, a man who is a worker, who is not a millionaire, a friend of the blue collars? He doesn't know that this kind of encounter is very delicate. Mark my words, this man Kennedy is in trouble, and he will get what is coming to him."

Aleman, who was talking to the underworld leader about a $1.5 million Central States Pension Fund loan which Hoffa had personally cleared for Trafficante, responded that President Kennedy would probably be elected to a second term.

"No, José," Trafficante said firmly. "He is going to be hit."[46]

8 Coincidence or Conspiracy?

In 1962 the Soviet Union was pouring economic and military aid into Cuba, as it had been doing ever since the Bay of Pigs invasion. On September 13, President Kennedy announced that the Russian deliveries on the Caribbean island included short-range defense weapons. He warned that the use of Cuba as an offensive military installation would constitute a serious threat to American security, and that the United States was prepared to do ''whatever must be done'' to protect itself.

By October 16 the Kennedy Administration had ''hard'' evidence that a nuclear buildup in Cuba included offensive weapons with a first-strike potential against the United States.

On Monday, October 22, the eve of Hoffa's trial in Nashville, Tennessee, President Kennedy went on national television to announce his decision to order American ships to quarantine the Caribbean island. The Cuban missile crisis lasted until October 28, while the world held its breath, paying little attention to Hoffa and the Teamsters.

Nevertheless, the Hoffa delegation in Nashville had to do their best to keep their minds on the boss's immediate problems when the trial opened as scheduled on Tuesday morning. The indictment charged Hoffa and the late Bert Brennan with receiving illegal payments from the nationwide auto haulaway firm, Commercial Carriers Corporation, through Test Fleet, Inc., whose ownership was in their wives' maiden names. Commercial Carriers pled no contest and paid a fine. Hoffa was pleading innocent; the misdemeanor carried only a one-year sentence but could cost him the IBT presidency.

Hoffa had brought his entourage of lawyers and union officials to Nashville and they set up headquarters in the Andrew Jackson Hotel. Represented by William Bufalino and James Haggerty—with Frank Ragano assisting the defense—Hoffa claimed that his wife's interest in Test Fleet was legal because he reaped none of the company's profits.

While the Test Fleet jury was being selected, Hoffa summoned Allen Dorfman. Dorfman came, with West Virginian moving and storage executive Nicholas Tweel in tow. In the group from Detroit, Local 299 business agent Charles O'Brien was the most visible Teamster besides Bufalino. Local 299's only black business agent, Larry Campbell, who was born in Nashville, was also present—but in the guise of organizing drivers at the Louisville General Electric Company, which was not by any stretch in Local 299's jurisdiction. Rolland McMaster was also quietly in and out of Tennessee. Under indictment in Detroit on a similar charge, McMaster coached defense witnesses and carried messages in and out of the state.

Other Hoffa supporters included Local 327's president, Ewing King; Toledo's Larry Steinberg, who ran the makeshift headquarters; Edward Partin, up from Louisiana; Frank Chavez, head of the Teamsters in Puerto Rico; Irving Davidson, Hoffa's public relations friend; David Wenger, accountant for the Central States Pension Fund; and numerous other Hoffa partisans who dropped by to give Jimmy their best wishes.

One Teamster, Don Vestal, had already run out of best wishes. In 1955, after the IBT set up the Central States Pension Fund, Vestal was appointed by Hoffa as one of two ''advisory trustees'' who were responsible for assessing real estate which might qualify for loans from the Central States Fund. ''For instance,'' Vestal says, ''I went back to Dallas and checked out the Dallas Cabana Motel for a possible loan. It looked like a pretty good investment, so I recommended to the fund's trustees that they come across with the money; and they did.''

But after a quarrel with another Southern Conference official over pension fund allocations, a bitter Vestal quit the fund in 1958 and had a falling out with Hoffa two years later. This was after Robert Kennedy, during the McClellan Committee hearings, had accused Vestal of being a dynamiter for Hoffa. In late 1960 Hoffa supported an insurgent slate, led by Ewing King, against Vestal's leadership in Local 327. When King won the election Vestal's supporters filed a petition with the IBT asking for a separate charter.

As the Test Fleet trial opened, Donald Vestal's rebels were tearing Local 327 apart, neutralizing much of Hoffa's badly needed union support, which could influence press coverage of the trial.

Another enemy, as yet unacknowledged, was Ed Partin, an informant inside the Hoffa camp. While the jury was being selected, Walter Sheridan, as Robert Kennedy's chief assistant in matters related to Hoffa, received a telephone call from Partin, who said bluntly, ''They're fixin' to get at the jury.''[1]

''It was almost too good to be true, having an informant right in Hoffa's camp,'' Sheridan says. ''Most of the sources I had dealt with in the past had asked for anonymity and for promises that they'd never be called to testify. Partin made no such request.''

Partin told Sheridan that he had heard Hoffa telling Dorfman and Tweel that a local friend, Dallas Hall, could help them influence the jury. Although Hall had a list of the jurors and their backgrounds, there was no evidence then that the plot went any further than that.

But soon afterward one of the jurors, a local insurance broker named James Tippins, was offered $10,000 to vote for acquittal. The next day Tippins walked into Judge William E. Miller's chambers and explained that a neighbor, Lawrence Medlin, had offered the bribe. Outraged, Judge Miller took Tippins off the jury and ordered Hoffa, his attorneys, and the government prosecutors to his office. Without directly accusing any of them of jury tampering, Judge Miller warned against any attempts to subvert the proceedings.

''Judge Miller was a fair and honest judge from the outset,'' says the government prosecutor, James Neal. ''He knew that, considering the devices Hoffa's attorneys had used in the past to clear him, every ounce of patience and tolerance he could muster up would be necessary for those few months. The last thing we wanted was a mistrial for any reason.''

Soon after Tippins was dismissed from the jury, Partin reported to Sheridan that Hoffa, after returning from the meeting with Judge Miller, was ''motherfucking'' everyone because Tippins couldn't be bought.

''That's when I really started to take him seriously,'' Sheridan says. ''He had known the whole story about the attempt to bribe the jury before Tippins was even approached.''

Partin then told Sheridan that Ewing King had hinted in conversation that he was planning to approach a woman juror whose husband was a highway patrolman. Sheridan went through the biographical material on each juror and found a Mrs. James Paschal—whose husband was a highway patrolman.

"So, one night," Sheridan goes on, "four FBI agents in two cars followed King and a man named George Broda. The two men stopped at this little restaurant outside of Nashville. When they came out, they switched cars, apparently to throw off anyone who might be following them.

"The agents were thrown off the track for a few moments. But when they recovered, Broda, in King's car, was acting as the decoy while King, in Broda's car, drove to a Nashville truckdriver's home. The truckdriver, a guy named Oscar Pitts, had already gone out to meet James Paschal. Pitts set up a meeting between the patrolman and King, then King left Pitts's home in Broda's car and met Paschal on a deserted road."

Paschal denied that he was asked to influence his wife's vote but admitted that King had offered him a promotion in the local police department in return for a favor which he did not explain. Judge Miller removed Mrs. Paschal from the jury.

"There was no fix," says William Bufalino. "And if there was, it came directly out of Bobby Kennedy's office."

Such charges by the Hoffa forces were groundless, and the wheels that would convey Hoffa to jail turned at a quickened pace with Ed Partin's information at their hub.

While Hoffa's men ran around Nashville with pockets full of change, plotting strategies in pay telephones to avoid traceability, Sheridan and Partin met covertly on dark street corners and in hidden alleyways to plot theirs. The stakes for both sides had grown enormously. The Test Fleet scheme was a misdemeanor; jury tampering was a felony.

After Mrs. Paschal was taken off the jury Partin reported to Sheridan that Local 299 business agent Larry Campbell, who was living in a cottage owned by his uncle, Tom Parks, was influencing Parks, who in turn was influencing a seventy-year-old black juror, Gratin Fields. Partin, the "doorkeeper" of Hoffa's room, said that Hoffa walked in one day and said, "I've got the colored male juror in my hip pocket. One of my business agents, Larry Campbell, came into Nashville prior to the trial and took care of it."

"There were a few of us in Detroit who knew why Larry went to the Nashville trial," says a Local 299 Hoffa man. "But what the hell were we going to say? Jimmy, don't do it?"

Sheridan checked Partin's story by tracing the long-distance calls

Campbell had made to Hoffa before and during the trial; Campbell hadn't been using pay phones as he had been instructed to do. By retracing Campbell's steps, Sheridan and his staff learned that, through his children, Fields had been given a $100 down payment on a $10,000 bribe. Tom Parks had passed the money.

When Fields was removed from the jury—the third juror replaced— the basis for Judge Miller's action was a sworn affidavit, signed by Partin, who detailed his intimate knowledge of all Hoffa's attempts to fix the Test Fleet jury. Hoffa's defense attorneys claimed that the sealed envelope, given to and viewed by Judge Miller exclusively, was really filled with information from government-authorized wiretaps. They had a right to be paranoid. Everything they were saying in confidence was being repeated to the government.

Theorizing that an informant might be present in Nashville, feeding information to federal agents, Hoffa came to the conclusion that the infiltrator was Don Vestal. He turned to Partin and said, "Get a few guys together from Baton Rouge. I want Vestal killed . . . I want him cut down like a cottonwood tree!"

When Sheridan learned from Partin that he was supposed to have his old friend hit, Sheridan advised him to stall. The government could use Vestal as a decoy.

"I guess I was a patsy," Vestal recalls. "It all started one night while I was driving through Nashville, and I noticed a couple of guys in a car, tailing me. I knew the area and tried to lose them. After I shook 'em, I went home and got my gun. I knew something was up. Then Walter Sheridan showed up at my front door, and he told me that there was a contract out on me. He said that the government was trying to give me some protection, and that the tail I had shaken earlier in the night was really FBI agents."

On December 5, 1962, Hoffa's own life was jeopardized when a man in a raincoat walked calmly up to Hoffa while the jury was out of the courtroom, pulled out an air pistol, and fired several point-blank shots. Hoffa instinctively blocked the flying lead with his muscular forearms and, while people threw themselves to the floor for protection, lunged at his assailant and punched him hard on the side of the head. As Hoffa stumbled after the blow, Chuck O'Brien grabbed the attacker, threw him down, and began pounding him while a U.S. marshal hit the gunman with his pistol.

"When I saw that damn gun go off," says O'Brien, "all I could think of was that the 'old man' had been killed."

Very much alive, Hoffa nursed the spray of welts on his neck, forearm, and shoulders where he had been struck by the pellets. His attacker—after Hoffa, O'Brien, the U.S. marshal, and everyone else got through with him—was a lump of bloodied flesh on the courtroom floor.

"It turned out that the guy's name was Warren Swanson," Hoffa said, "a drifter who had worked on and off as a dishwasher. He was nutty as a fruitcake, saying he had 'a message from a higher power' to kill Jimmy Hoffa."[2]

The incident, concealed from the jury but headlined in the press, did not hurt Hoffa when he returned to Detroit the following week to run for reelection as Local 299's president. The shooting only heightened the bizarre Hoffa mystique. With token opposition from haulaway driver Ira D. Cooke, Jr., and Chuck O'Brien, who ran "only to split any anti-Hoffa votes, which might have all gone to Cooke," Hoffa won easily by ten to one. Rolland McMaster, whose extortion trial had ended in conviction, was reelected secretary-treasurer. Frank Fitzsimmons and Dave Johnson were also reelected.

When Hoffa returned to Nashville for the final part of the Test Fleet trial, his defense was confident of acquittal. But at that point the trial had become incidental to what was happening behind the scenes.

Although the government attorneys were thorough, their efforts failed to convince the jury, which after a forty-two-day trial announced on December 23, 1962, that it was unable to reach a unanimous verdict. Doubts lingered as to whether all the bribed jurors had been removed. It was the government's fifth defeat at Hoffa's hands since 1957.

Hoffa's jubilation over the hung jury was short-lived. The government had methodically built a solid case for a jury-tampering charge, and Walter Sheridan had Ed Partin to testify that Hoffa was directly involved in the conspiracy.

"Regarding the justice in all of this," says Jim Neal, "my only concern was that there was an informant in Hoffa's camp who was reporting directly to Walter Sheridan. That, on its face, could potentially be an area of great abuse . . . Obviously this concerned us: whether we were getting close to violating Hoffa's rights.

"The answer was that we didn't plant Partin in there. Hoffa brought him in without our participation. We didn't send him in there to be a spy. Moreover, we did everything we could to be fair. Partin was in there, telling us about efforts to bribe jurors. What else could we do?"

Within three weeks after the trial, Judge Miller, with information about jury tampering, ordered another grand jury investigation of Hoffa. Partin, like Hoffa's other men, took the Fifth Amendment and promptly left the grand jury room.

On May 9, 1963, Hoffa, Ewing King, Larry Campbell, Allen Dorfman, Nicholas Tweel, Lawrence Medlin, and Tom Parks were indicted on five counts of jury tampering. Hoffa was charged with being the overall mastermind of the conspiracy in count one. Hoffa and Medlin were charged with trying to influence insurance executive James Tippins in count two. Hoffa, Campbell, and Parks were accused of attempting to sway the vote of juror Gratin Fields in count three. Count four charged that Dorfman and Tweel had conspired with Dallas Hall in an effort to fix the jury. And in count five Hoffa and King were charged with trying to influence Mrs. James Paschal through her husband.

Cocky after the no-verdict decision in the Test Fleet trial, not seeming to take the new indictments seriously, Hoffa went to Philadelphia to squash the rebellion in Local 107. The Voice was due for a second NLRB election in which the local members would decide whether to bolt the IBT and petition the AFL-CIO for affiliation. In the first election, with nearly 7000 votes cast, the rebels had lost by only 600 votes. But Hoffa had a new momentum and a promise to raise pension benefits, and the rebels were badly defeated in their second try.

During both elections Robert Kennedy provided support and encouragement to the dissidents. In response Teamster-hired pickets demonstrated in Washington, walking back and forth on the sidewalk outside the Justice Department in Washington with large signs that read, "U.S. ATTY. GEN. KENNEDY USING HIS OFFICIAL POSITION TO PRESSURE LOCAL OFFICIALS OF PHILADELPHIA TO FAVOR ONE SIDE AGAINST THE OTHER IN AN NLRB ELECTION. IS HE TRYING TO TAKE OVER ALL AGENCIES OF THE STATE AND FEDERAL GOVERNMENT?—TEAMSTERS JOINT COUNCIL 53."

The *New York Times* viewed the rebellion as "striking evidence of rank-and-file discontent with the brand of union leadership provided by James R. Hoffa and his lieutenants."[3]

Nevertheless, Hoffa had licked Kennedy again, and it was quite beside the point that soon after the second election Ray Cohen, president of Local 107, was convicted of embezzlement of union funds and sent to jail.

On June 4, 1963, Kennedy authorized an indictment of Hoffa and seven other Teamsters for defrauding the Central States Pension Fund of over $20 million, $1 million of which had been diverted for the personal use of Hoffa and his associates in the Sun Valley scheme.

In addition, further pressure had been placed on Hoffa and the Teamsters by Kennedy's attempts to influence companies that bonded union officials against doing business with the IBT. The requirement that union officials with access to union funds be bonded against loss or theft of them was part of the 1959 Landrum-Griffin Act. All bonding companies had to be government-approved, and violators of these requirements could be sent to jail for a year and fined $10,000.

Again accusing Kennedy of impinging on Teamsters' personal freedoms, Hoffa said,

> This is another step of the Attorney General in an endeavor to remove the officers of the international union and local union officers by means other than court procedures—in which he has failed so far. And it is a continuation of the vendetta of Bob Kennedy using his office in violation of the oath he took to do by use of his powers rather than the court's ruling to accomplish what he has not been able to accomplish up to date, namely remove Hoffa from office . . .[4]

In reality, according to Victor Navasky in *Kennedy Justice*,

> The fundamental reason for the Teamsters' bonding problems was their insistence on seeking bondage only through a specific brokerage which had changed its name five times since September 1959 when the bonding requirement was enacted and which had ties to the underworld and an unfavorable reputation in the insurance business.[5]

The Teamster-supported brokerage firms were controlled by Allen Dorfman, who had been indicted with Hoffa for jury tampering, and Irwin Weiner, a bail bondsman who was under indictment for extortion in Miami with one of Sam Giancana's associates, Felix Alderisio.

Seething at Robert Kennedy's "vendetta" against him and the President's verbal and economic support for the attorney general, Hoffa began a national campaign for a new Teamster political action program, DRIVE (Democratic, Republican, Independent Voter Education), which was aimed primarily against "President Kennedy and other anti-union politicians."

To launch the campaign Hoffa spent three days in Dallas, at the Cabana Motel—built with money from the Central States Pension Fund—meeting with the IBT Southern Conference leader, Murray W.

Miller, and other key Teamster officials. On July 16 he held a press conference at which he again denounced the Kennedys: "Bobby Kennedy, being what he is, has constantly brought about indictments knowing full well there was no basis for them."[6] He also criticized Kennedy's policies on desegregation and accused him of stirring up racial tensions in the South.

Hoffa was now saying publicly some of the things he had been saying privately about the Kennedys. But there were other things that only Ed Partin repeated outside the Teamster-mob circle. Partin had turned against his boss just before the Test Fleet trial because of a discussion with Hoffa about the Kennedys.

In September 1962—the same month mob figures Santos Trafficante and Carlos Marcello hinted that President Kennedy was going to be assassinated—Partin got in touch with two Louisiana law enforcement officials to tell them about a conversation in Hoffa's Washington office in August. Hoffa had been thinking out loud, weighing the merits of two separate murder plans aimed at Robert Kennedy.[7]

The first plan, the one Hoffa was then leaning toward, involved firebombing Hickory Hill, Robert Kennedy's Virginia estate, with extraordinarily lethal plastic explosives. Hoffa was careful to note that even if Kennedy somehow survived the explosion, he "and all his damn kids" would be incinerated, since "the place will burn after it blows up."

The second plan was apparently a backup scheme, and in retrospect it is "the kind of thing that makes you wonder just a little bit," as Sheridan puts it. Kennedy would be shot to death from a distance away; a single gunman would be enlisted to carry it out—someone without any traceable connection to Hoffa and the Teamsters; a high-powered rifle with a telescopic sight would be the assassination weapon.

According to Partin, "Hoffa had a .270 rifle leaning in the corner of his office and Hoffa said, 'I've got something right here which will shoot flat and long . . .' "

The "ideal setup," Hoffa went on, would be "to catch [Robert] Kennedy somewhere in the South," where extremist "segregation people" might throw investigators off the track by being blamed for the crime. The "ideal time" to hit Kennedy would be while he was driving his "convertible." Partin thinks that the Kennedy brothers' crusade against Hoffa had driven him to desperation. "Somebody needs to bump that son of a bitch off," he recalls Hoffa saying. "Bobby Kennedy [has] got to go."

Kennedy's aides were skeptical at first, but Partin's veracity was soon borne out by a meticulous FBI polygraph examination. In addition, while Partin was at a Holiday Inn in Baton Rouge, federal officials taped a telephone call between him and Hoffa, who was in Pittsburgh, in which Partin told Hoffa he had gotten the plastic explosives and Hoffa asked him to bring them to Nashville.

A kid from a poor Mississippi family with a bad conduct discharge from the Marine Corps, Sheridan's informant, an ex-boxer, looked typical of the pugs Hoffa had surrounding him. Big and tough, he had been a Hoffa confidant since the 1957 IBT convention. "Hoffa trusted and liked me because he respected me," Partin says. "I wasn't like a lot of the guys around him who nodded their heads, agreeing with everything he said whether they believed it or not." But "Hoffa always just assumed that since I was from Louisiana I was in Marcello's hip pocket."

Most of the people in Robert Kennedy's "get Hoffa" group were working on Partin's information about jury tampering, but there was concern about Hoffa's threat to kill Robert Kennedy, and it increased as Partin's accuracy became more obvious.

By early February 1963, Partin's account of his midsummer conversation with Hoffa had apparently filtered through to the President. The President's close friend, Benjamin Bradlee, who was then with *Newsweek*, noted in an entry in his journal for February 11 that the night before, at a private dinner party, the President had confided that Hoffa's Teamsters had planned to send an assassin to Washington to kill his brother.

The murder plan that the President talked about did not involve firebombing but it was intended to be carried out by an assassin equipped with "a gun fitted with a silencer." Bradlee wrote that he found the President's story somewhat "hard to believe, but the President was obviously serious."[8]

Bradlee has said he can't remember exactly what Kennedy said about where he got the information, but former aides of the attorney general think it was almost certainly based upon Partin's disclosures four months earlier; the RFK men couldn't recall reports of any other Teamster assassination plan during that period. Bradlee tends to agree that the President was in fact speaking of the grisly Partin account of Hoffa's assassination discussion.

What other thoughts the President had about the possibility of Jimmy Hoffa's having a member of the Kennedy family shot to death are not known. As some veteran chroniclers of Hoffa's violent career have noted, a reasonable observer might wonder to what lengths the Teamster boss could go if he was already at the point of discussing the murder of the second most powerful official in Washington, the President's brother and closest adviser.

In any event, Hoffa apparently discarded his 1962 plans to murder the attorney general. Ed Partin is sure his boss never again brought it up in his presence, but he believes this subsequent silence may well have been a result of his own obvious discomfort when Hoffa brought it up. "I think he could see I was sort of turning a little green over it."

Another possible factor in Hoffa's presumed abandonment of the 1962 assassination plans relates to the simple question of potential accountability. There was at least one obvious flaw in the Teamster president's thinking as he discussed his views with his assistant. In a detailed account of Hoffa's darker activities (the *Life* article that first publicly disclosed the Robert Kennedy assassination scheme), Partin wrote that Hoffa had initially seemed confident of not being connected to the proposed killing. Hoffa had said that RFK "has so many enemies now they wouldn't know who had done it . . . " But as Partin said, "As smart as Hoffa was—and he was very, very smart—he must of sat himself down . . . and thought no matter how many enemies Bobby had, he [Hoffa] and his boys were the best known . . . and the most likely."[9]

"If Bob Kennedy's house had blown up back then, [or] if he had been shot," says Walter Sheridan, "there's one name we'd have put at the top of the list, in about five minutes . . . Jimmy Hoffa."

Ed Partin, more familiar than most with Hoffa's murderous impulses, strongly agrees that one Kennedy assassination plan might have indeed developed into another. And he became the Kennedy Justice Department's single most reliable source within the shadowy Teamster empire, developing a close and trusting relationship with Robert Kennedy's aides.

"In my honest opinion, I think that Hoffa would have [gone] to any extreme . . . " to get the Kennedys off his back. "He hated Jack as much as Bobby . . . After all, he was the man who'd always been in charge of Bobby. . . . I knew the man close enough to know how bad he hated [President] Kennedy . . . he'd fly off [when] the name was even mentioned . . . I think he would have died himself if he knew he could have gotten them [both] killed."

Partin remembers that in the discussion about firebombing the attorney general, Hoffa had thought the plots through enough to consider the possibility of having the assassin "hide out" in Puerto Rico after the killing. Then, Partin recalls, Hoffa reconsidered, because it might be too obvious a hiding place. "The thing for the person that did it would be to lay low for a while, and not . . . run off to . . . Puerto Rico, but just lay low." Hoffa would have found a hideout easy to arrange through one of his close Teamster associates, Frank Chavez, the hawk-faced leader of Puerto Rico Teamsters Local 901. That fall Chavez was under indictment for obstruction of justice—having passed out defamatory literature about Robert Kennedy to members of a grand jury investigating his local. He switched lawyers and hired Frank Ragano, counsel to both Hoffa and Santos Trafficante. In October, Chavez was released from custody when the trial jury was unable to reach a verdict.

A violent man with a long criminal record, Chavez, according to Partin, was the man Hoffa had in mind when he considered firebombing Robert Kennedy's home in Virginia. Among the crimes Chavez had been charged with over the years was murder—by firebomb. Justice Department records indicate that Chavez had also been identified as the leading suspect in another firebombing while Hoffa was trying to organize Puerto Rican workers. In early 1962, Hoffa and Chavez had been involved in an intense feud with the island's Hotel and Restaurant Workers Union, AFL-CIO, which Hoffa was trying to take over. In February 1962, the San Juan headquarters of the union was blown up and completely destroyed by a carefully coordinated firebombing. Though Frank Chavez was never charged, investigators were confident that he had been responsible for it. Shortly thereafter the Teamsters were finally successful in taking over the remnants of the Puerto Rican union.

In September 1962, Joseph Valachi, who had been brought to Washington to detail the history of the "Cosa Nostra," began testifying in public before the Senate's Permanent Investigations Subcommittee, chaired by Senator John McClellan.

Valachi's appearance before the committee was arranged by Robert Kennedy, who called Valachi's information the "biggest single intelligence breakthrough yet in combating organized crime and racketeering in the United States."

As the first witness called by McClellan, Kennedy said,

> Because of intelligence gathered from Joseph Valachi and from informants, we know that Cosa Nostra is run by a commission and that the leaders of Cosa Nostra in most major cities are responsible to the commission. We

know that membership in the commission varies between nine and twelve active members and we know who the active members of the commission are today.

. . . We know that the commission makes major policy decisions for the organization, settles disputes among the families, and allocates territories of criminal operations within the organization.[10]

In 1961, Attorney General Kennedy had ordered bugs placed in organized crime hangouts throughout the country. Crimes that had baffled police departments and government agencies were being solved by gangsters themselves who discussed their complicity in such crimes and were unknowingly being recorded.

For example, on the afternoon of February 11, 1962, David Yaras had the misfortune of being overheard in a discussion with fellow mob executioner John Cerone. The two men were formulating plans to kidnap and murder a Chicago boss of a city and county workers' union, Frank Esposito. One of the underworld's most feared killers, Cerone had, according to law enforcement officials, carried out several other mob murders with Yaras.

> Yaras: I wish . . . we were hitting him now, right now. We could have hit him the other night. We went to prowl the house . . .
> Cerone: Yeah, that would have been a perfect spot to rub him out . . .
> Yaras: Leave it to us. As soon as he walks in the fucking door, boom! We'll hit him with an ax or something. He won't get away from us.
> Cerone: Yeah . . . We can have everything with us, the ax and everything.[11]

A key "non-Italian associate" of the Chicago mob under Giancana, according to the Justice Department, Yaras was also a close friend of a Dallas night club owner, Jack Ruby.

Ruby first became acquainted with Yaras during the late 1930s or early 1940s. Yaras described Ruby, then named Jack Rubenstein, as a " 'Romeo' who was most successful in picking up girls."[12]

At about this same time Ruby also became acquainted with Paul Dorfman, head of the Chicago Waste Handlers Union, in which Ruby worked as an organizer. Dorfman took over the union just after its previous head, Leon Cooke, was shot to death by Ruby's union colleague, John Martin. Although the Chicago police were suspicious about Ruby's possible complicity in the murder—and he was held for questioning—Martin was subsequently acquitted for the killing on grounds of self-defense.

Paul Dorfman stated that Ruby left the union "about two months" after Dorfman took over the local. He "never considered Ruby as a friend or associate," said Dorfman. Ruby was "an emotional type person who was either easily excitable or not capable of dealing with people."[13]

After a three-year hitch in the Army Air Force, Ruby moved to Dallas in 1947. He was one of many who did so. According to the Senate Rackets Committee:

> The invasion of Chicagoans . . . came after a change of administration in Dallas resulted in local racketeers being run out of town. First to arrive in Dallas was Paul Roland Jones, who had served time in Kansas for murder. Jones had also been involved in narcotics traffic and had been associated with the Chicago syndicate in black-market and counterfeit ration stamp operations during the war years.[14]

Another hoodlum who moved to Dallas was Sam Yaras, "a former Chicagoan and brother of Dave Yaras, about whom the committee already had received testimony indicating he had taken over unions in the Miami area and had also moved into Cuban gambling."[15]

Paul Roland Jones told government investigators that the Dallas Police Department was cooperating with the underworld during the 1940s, and that when a new police chief came in Jones had been indicted and convicted for trying to bribe a law enforcement officer. Jones met Ruby and "assisted" him in the establishment of his first night club, the Silver Spur, which Jones occasionally patronized when doing business in Dallas. Jones also knew Ruby's sister, Eva Grant. He explained that he was willing to help Ruby because he had been "some kind of organizer for the [Chicago] Scrap Iron Workers Union," and Jones was aware that "the syndicate" had an interest in this union.[16]

In 1947, Ruby was questioned by federal narcotics agents investigating his possible role in the drug traffic to Chicago. Although Ruby denied that he was trafficking drugs and was never prosecuted, Jones was indicted and convicted.

Another key "non-Italian" Chicago mob associate was Leonard Patrick, a close friend of Ruby, Yaras, and Jones. In 1947, Patrick and Yaras were indicted together for the murder of James M. Ragen, the underworld boss of the racing wire service in Chicago. Two witnesses against them were murdered, two others refused to testify, and the case was dropped. Later, the police captain who instigated their indictment was found dead in his garage, his jaw torn off by a .45 caliber bullet.

According to Eva Grant, Ruby talked with Patrick in the summer of 1963, though Patrick claimed that he hadn't seen Ruby in "ten to twelve years."[17] Mrs. Grant said her brother had phoned Patrick for help with labor difficulties at his night club. "He called him for the purpose to see if he could fix him up with the [Variety Artists] union . . . I got his number," said Mrs. Grant. "This guy [Patrick] is not a holy man by far . . . He's a gambler."[18]

Gambler or not, Patrick in 1963 was lying low in Chicago after being credited by law enforcement officials with the murder of Benjamin F. Lewis, a political protégé of Mayor Richard Daley and the first black alderman elected from the city's Twenty-fourth Ward. Ben Lewis, at the age of fifty-three, was viewed as one of the most promising black politicians in Illinois.

Lewis's promising political career came to an end in the early morning hours of February 28, 1963, when he was found lying face down in a four-foot-wide pool of blood on the floor of his campaign headquarters. The back of his head had been shot off by three bullets fired at close range. Lewis's wrists had been handcuffed over his head before the killing, and he had also been beaten.

Federal investigators learned that Lewis had become financially entangled with Patrick but the investigation got no further, and Lewis's death became merely a statistic: the 977th unsolved underworld hit in Chicago since the early 1900s.

"Jack himself never had any connections with gangsters for money, for business, for sociability," said Ruby's sister. He never had any real "Mafia" connection.[19]

But it is known that in 1959 Ruby visited a Dallas gambler, Lewis McWillie, in Cuba on at least two occasions. On both trips McWillie picked up the tab for Ruby's expenses. Ruby made the first trip just after Castro turned on the mob and tossed Trafficante, McWillie's boss, in jail in April 1959. Ruby, according to confirmed reports by the FBI, went to Cuba again. This time he offered $25,000 to Robert McKeown, a gunrunner who had been a chief supplier to Castro during the revolution, in return for the release of three (unidentified) prisoners in a Cuban jail. According to the FBI report, Ruby claimed that the source of the money was gambling interests in Las Vegas who knew that McKeown was close to Castro.[20]

Within a month after that trip Ruby met McKeown in Houston and offered him several hundred jeeps—from an unnamed Louisiana source—in return for help in influencing Castro to release the three prisoners.

Another possible piece of the Jack Ruby puzzle comes from a CIA memorandum of November 26, 1963, which reports that a British journalist, John Wilson, informed the American Embassy in London that while in a Cuban prison in 1959 he met ''an American gangster-type named Ruby.'' Wilson, jailed by the Castro government and then deported to England, said that he had also become acquainted with ''an American gangster-gambler named Santos who could not return to the U.S.A. because there were several indictments outstanding against him. Instead he preferred to live in relative luxury in a Cuban prison.'' It was Santos whom Ruby ''visited frequently.''[21]

Wilson's ''Santos'' was a perfect description of Santos Trafficante, who was indeed in a Cuban prison during mid-1959 and had criminal charges against him in the United States.

Although Jack Ruby and Jimmy Hoffa shared some of the same friends—including Paul Dorfman and David Yaras, as well as associates of Sam Giancana, Carlos Marcello, and Santos Trafficante—that alone does not represent a direct relationship between them.

Interestingly enough, however, on October 26, 1963, Ruby placed a long-distance call to Chicago, to SH 3-6865. FBI records establish that this twelve-minute call went to Irwin S. Weiner, a veteran member of Hoffa's closest circle of underworld advisers and the major bondsman for the Teamsters Union. By the late 1950s, according to Walter Sheridan, ''Weiner was representing himself as the exclusive agent for the Teamsters Union bonding.''[22]

Speaking from his still thriving bonding business in Chicago, Weiner says that he and Ruby were personal friends. ''Ruby was a friend of mine. He called me. I talked to him. What I talked to him about was my own business. And I just don't want to, don't feel that I should discuss it with anyone. It has no relation, it has no bearing on anything.''

Weiner adds that he had known the Ruby family since the early days on Chicago's West Side when Ruby's brother, Earl, was one of his best friends. ''I was in fairly regular touch with Earl. He was one of my closest friends from back in school. Later he moved to Detroit where he opened up a laundry business [Cobo Cleaners] in about 1961.''

Four days after the call to Weiner, at 9:13 P.M. on October 30, Ruby called CH 2-5431 in New Orleans and spoke to Nofio Pecora, a key member of Carlos Marcello's tightly knit apparatus. Pecora's brother-in-law, D'Alton Smith, was Marcello's closest underworld adviser and front man. Smith was, incidentally, associated with two other Dallas friends of Jack Ruby. Second, Pecora's sister-in-law was the wife of Joseph Poretti, who managed some of Marcello's real estate holdings, coordinating them with the mob boss's half-billion-dollar-a-year gambling network. And Pecora's wife, formerly in business for herself, was now Marcello's secretary. In an analysis of the Marcello empire, Aaron Kohn, a respected authority on organized crime, noted that "Nofio Pecora is an ex-convict, with extensive past history in the heroin trade . . . he and his wife directed a call-girl ring between [Louisiana] and . . . Mississippi."

On November 7, at 2:12 P.M., Barney Baker, a former street brawler and prizefighter who was one of Hoffa's top aides before Robert Kennedy put him in jail, called Ruby from Chicago. There is no record of an initial call to Baker from Ruby, although Baker claims that he was simply returning a call from a Dallas night club owner whom he did not know.

Baker said, in an interview in 1978, "I called back, and I says, 'Is this Ruby?' and he says, 'Yeah.' I says, 'My name's Baker and I don't recollect knowing of you. What's it about?' He says, 'Well, a mutual friend . . . told me you have connections with the Actor's [American] Guild of Variety Artists. There's a guy here puts on local burlesque shows, and they won't let me do it.'

"And get this now. So I says to him, 'I'd like to help you, but I can't.' He says, 'Whaddaya mean?' 'First off,' I says, 'who's the mutual friend?' He says, 'Well, I don't wanna mention no names.' "

Baker says he then told Ruby that since he had been paroled from prison in June 1963 and had received parole restrictions on future labor activity, he couldn't be any help.

"He says, 'Why can't you do it?' And I said, 'Well, I just got out of the federal detention.' So he says, 'Well, I didn't know nothin' like that.'

"So I said, 'I'm sorry, I'd like to help you, but I can't.' And we hung up and that was it. That was the extent of the whole thing . . . That was the extent of the whole thing. Truly."

A big man whose weight ranged from 350 to 500 pounds during his long Teamster career, Baker was known as one of Hoffa's toughest guys. Like his friend Rolland McMaster, Baker served as personal liaison to a significant number of underworld figures around the country.

"Sometimes the mere threat of his presence in a room," Robert Kennedy wrote, "was enough to silence the men who would otherwise have opposed Hoffa's reign.''[23] Describing Baker as one of Hoffa's ''roving emissaries of violence,'' Kennedy wrote that Hoffa had merely chuckled as he listened to Baker tell the McClellan Committee about various mob executioners he knew.

There were others who chuckled over Barney Baker in those days—though very few who had ever tangled with the man. The committee staff had spent months just trying to track down the colorful Hoffa enforcer to arrange for him to appear. Each time they found him, Baker was checking into a hospital for ''medically urgent'' weight reduction, supposedly to keep from dying of obesity. Baker hadn't always been as successful in losing weight as he claimed; Kennedy's staff recorded the fact that Baker had once eaten ''38 pounds of meat at one time.''

Although the committee found plenty of documentation of Baker's lethal exploits, the most surprising testimony about his association with such powerful organized crime figures as Meyer Lansky came about through what Baker himself called ''the double whammy of a woman scorned.'' As the crowded spectators in the Senate Caucus Room listened in amazement, two witnesses who knew Baker well were called to testify about his activities: Baker's divorced wife, Mollie, who linked him to a kidnaping conspiracy; and Baker's former lover, Ruth Brougher, five times convicted for murder, who linked him to several leading underworld figures during his work for Hoffa.

On November 8, 1963, the day after Baker's call to Ruby, Ruby telephoned Murray W. Miller at 4:48 P.M. As head of the powerful Southern Conference of Teamsters, Miller was also one of Hoffa's deputies, entrusted with a number of delicate assignments. He was the key Teamster official in union operations in Dallas as well as New Orleans and Nashville.

Ruby's call went to JE 2-2561, in Miami, where Miller was conducting his business from the Eden Roc Hotel. According to FBI records, Ruby's call to Miller lasted four minutes.

Although Miller has refused to discuss the phone call, Barney Baker says he was fully aware of that call, too. Ruby called Miller for the same reason he called Baker—to ask for some assistance with his labor problems. Baker suggests that Ruby may have ''mentioned my name'' when he called Miller: ''Like Barney sent me [or] told me to see you. That's probably what he did. And Dusty [Miller] didn't do a damn thing for him. You know what I mean?''

The day before Ruby's call to him, and the same day Ruby called

Baker, Miller called and made an appointment to see Walter Sheridan at the Justice Department on November 7, 1963, while Sheridan and other Kennedy aides were finishing preparations for Hoffa's jury tampering trial. Sheridan noted that the visit came at a time when Hoffa suspected that one of his confidants was an informer for Attorney General Robert Kennedy's staff. By November, Sheridan thinks, Hoffa had begun to suspect that Ed Partin, rather than Don Vestal, was the inside source. If so, Hoffa's recollection that he had discussed the assassination conspiracy with Partin would have worried him.

In any event, Miller's sudden visit seemed to be a very subtle effort to find out the Kennedy staff's attitude toward—or relationship with—Partin. Sheridan wrote,

> When Miller left we were convinced that he had been trying to feel us out about Partin and that that was the real purpose for his visit. We also felt reasonably sure that we had passed the test . . . We felt it was likely that they were checking out different people . . . to assure themselves about there was no one they had to worry about.[24]

Thirty-one minutes after Ruby called Miller on November 8, Ruby called Barney Baker again, according to FBI records.[25] Baker says, "I don't remember. And if he did [call again], I, ah, I, I, ah, must have gone through the same routine again. But I don't remember . . . All I remember is me calling him back and that ended it." Having at first said "it's possible" that he spoke to Ruby a second time—"It might be; look, I'm not gonna say no"—Baker ended up flatly denying that such a second conversation ever took place. Told that FBI records showed a fourteen-minute call from Ruby to Baker's home phone number in Chicago at 5:22 P.M. on November 8, Baker denied any knowledge of RA 8-4031: "I don't know that number. Honest to God. It must be a mistake, pal . . . I remember vividly me calling him back [on November 7]; I don't remember him calling me again . . . He must have talked to somebody else. It couldn't, it couldn't possibly have been me. Because I ended that real abruptly . . . If I could remember that, I would sure tell you . . . Believe me, I would do that."

Asked about a November 21, 1963, call to David Yaras, Baker admits that this call might have taken place. "Yeah, Davie, I liked Davie. And it's possible I did call him." Yaras was "a nice guy socially, a very nice fellow socially, he was a hell of a nice fella." Baker further stated that this call to Yaras was probably in regard to Yaras's son's laundry business in Chicago.

Reminded that Yaras was a friend of Jack Ruby, Baker said, "Yeah, [but] only from here, from Chicago. He knew him from Chicago . . . years ago. He [Ruby] was a hanger-on, this guy. Believe me, he was."

Ed Partin has said that he "saw David Yaras having dinner with Allen Dorfman and Rolland McMaster at the Andrew Jackson Hotel in Nashville, in the fall of 1963." In that part of the world, Partin says, Yaras was known as a go-between for Trafficante and Marcello.

Also, on or about the evening of November 20, Yaras's close friend from Chicago, Paul Roland Jones, visited Jack Ruby at his Dallas night club. At 11:00 P.M. the following night, Ruby went over to the Cabana Motel to have drinks with some friends from Chicago and New York.

Just two months earlier, the girl friend of one of the Chicago friends had had a phone call from New Orleans. Telephone records from Southwestern Bell's New Orleans office established that David Ferrie, Carlos Marcello's pilot-investigator, had called her home on September 24, 1963.[26]

Ferrie was renting an office suite in New Orleans in the same building and on the same floor as another guest at the Cabana Motel on November 21—Jim Braden. On September 10, 1963, Braden had changed his name from Eugene Hale Brading. A month later he divorced his wife, the widow of a Chicago Teamster official. Braden had been arrested some thirty times and had served several prison sentences. He allegedly had numerous connections with organized crime figures. He admits that he was among the first members of the Carlsbad, California, La Costa Country Club, owned by Morris Dalitz and built through loans from the Central States Pension Fund. Although he owns a condominium there, he denies knowing either Hoffa or any other underworld figures. "I was asked to join La Costa by a golf pro I was friendly with," says Braden. "I don't even know what organized crime is."

Surprisingly enough, government investigators later alleged that both Braden and Ruby had been in the offices of the H. L. Hunt Oil Company at approximately the same time on the afternoon of November 21.[27] Although Braden says that he was in Dallas for his "oil business," he denies being where the investigators claim he was.

At 12:30 P.M., CST, on November 22, 1963, President Kennedy's motorcade, traveling through Dallas at eleven miles an hour, made a sharp left turn into Elm Street. As the procession drove past the Texas

School Book Depository, on the corner of Elm and Houston streets, Lee Harvey Oswald, perched in a window on the sixth floor of the building, allegedly fired three shots in rapid succession.

As the driver of the President's limousine sped from the scene with his passenger mortally wounded, the police converged on two buildings, the Depository and the Dal-Tex building, which is on the northeastern corner of the Elm-Houston intersection.

At the moment of the assassination Braden says that he was with his probation officer in an office two blocks away. ''I walked over to the federal courthouse to check out with him, because I was going to Houston, Texas.''

The U.S. Parole Officer, Roger Carroll, denies that this meeting ever took place.

Braden says that after leaving Carroll, he stopped at a sandwich shop and ate. ''I came out and proceeded on down the street, looking for a taxicab. I couldn't find a cab, and the next thing I knew, there were people running toward me, screaming and yelling, 'My God, the President's been shot!'

''So I figured, well, Jesus, I'll call my family . . . So I proceeded around and asked a girl, 'Is there a telephone around here anywhere?' She said, ''Upstairs, where I work [in the Dal-Tex building]. Come on in through here with me.' We went through a passageway and into an elevator, freight elevator . . . So we proceeded to the third floor. I got out. I go over there, and there's a telephone hanging on the wall. A woman was trying to use it. I said, 'Does that telephone work?' 'No.'

''I tried it, it didn't work.''

Braden then walked back into the elevator.

''So I get in there, and I'm going down. Now he [the elevator operator] begins to look at me . . . He had a little radio, and the voices are coming over that, screaming and yelling that the President has been shot and that whole business. Now he looks at me, and he's scared to death. He said, 'You're a stranger. I shouldn't have let you up in this building.' And with this, he takes off and runs for the cop.''

In a few moments Braden was stopped by C. L. Lewis, a local deputy sheriff, who asked Braden to come to headquarters because he was ''behaving suspiciously.'' Braden was released after his record was checked for prior arrests and there were none. The police did not know that he had changed his name three months earlier.

Carlos Marcello—who had allegedly claimed the year before that Kennedy was going to be assassinated, and that a ''nut'' would be hired to do it—was in a New Orleans courtroom at the moment of the shooting, being found innocent of possessing a fraudulent Guatemalan birth certificate. David Ferrie was in the courtroon with him.

An anti-Castro activist, Ferrie, up to 1963, was associated with the Cuban Revolutionary Council at 544 Camp Street in New Orleans, collecting food and money for the organization. Antonio de Varona, the Cuban exile leader who had been given the poison pills to kill Castro, was a co-founder of the Revolutionary Council, whose headquarters were in the same building as the Fair Play for Cuba Committee. Soon after Lee Harvey Oswald was captured he was linked to that pro-Castro group.

Four days later, after a report was filed with the FBI by a Ferrie associate, it was alleged that Oswald and Ferrie had planned the President's murder, and Ferrie was picked up by the FBI and questioned. According to the FBI report, Ferrie

> said that since the end of August, 1963 and up until November 22, 1963 he has been working on a case involving Carlos Marcello who was charged in Federal Court in connection with a fraudulent birth certificate . . . He stated that on November 9 and November 16, 1963, he was at Churchill Downs [in Louisiana], which is a farm owned by Carlos Marcello, mapping strategy in connection with Marcello's trial.

There was no solid evidence of any relationship between Ferrie and Oswald, and Ferrie was released.

On the afternoon of the assassination, Harold Gibbons, Hoffa's top assistant in Washington, was having lunch at Duke Zeibert's when he heard that the President had been shot. By the time he'd paid his check, rushed out the door, and gotten back to Teamster headquarters, the news was flashing over the radio that the President was dead.

"I immediately ordered all the employees home, brought the flags down to half-staff, and sent a message to Kennedy's widow. Then I called Hoffa in Miami where he was doing business, and I told him what I'd done.

"He started screaming at me, 'Why the hell did you do that for him?' and 'Who the hell was he?'

"I listened to him for a while, and then I explained that it was the best thing to be done and the right thing to do. Well, he started up again, so I said, 'Listen, Hoffa, when you get back here, you can get yourself a new boy. I don't have to take this shit from anybody.' "

Gibbons's resignation was on Hoffa's desk when he returned from Florida. IBT general organizer Dick Kavner resigned with Gibbons.

Later, during an interview, Hoffa was asked why he acted as he did after the assassination.

"I have no sympathy for Kennedy," Hoffa said coldly. "Either as a man or as a President. Just because he got shot that didn't mean we should close our building down or lower the flag. It was a matter of opinion and I told them not to do it."[28]

Jimmy Hoffa's name would probably never have been brought up in the endless speculation on the Kennedy assassination if Jack Ruby had not lunged between a reporter and a detective and fired a .38 Colt Cobra into Oswald's abdomen, silencing the alleged assassin forever on Sunday, November 24, at 11:20 A.M.

Like millions of his fellow citizens, Barney Baker, who had talked to Ruby so recently, saw it on television: "Now get this, pal, and you're getting this straight from the horse's mouth . . . Now I forgot about it [his contact with Ruby] and I don't know, a little bit later, we're watching TV. All of a sudden, we see this idiot throw shots at, uh, Oscar, uh, what's his name? Uh, Oswald. [That's] it."

Barney Baker had laughed when he said that "it would take both hands" to count the number of his former associates who went to the electric chair. But he grew heated and argumentative when he was asked directly if James Hoffa and his underworld associates could actually have been behind the murders of the President and Oswald.

"They can throw that up in the air, and forget it, and tear it up! Aaaah, believe me, that's so ridiculous it ain't even funny. You can bet your bottom dollar, and you can bet everything that you have, that this guy [Oswald], as far as Jimmy Hoffa and all of that, forget it! Tear it up! It never existed!

"And the Mafia, all that bullshit, they don't go for that crap. That ain't their cup of tea. They'll fight amongst themselves, but dammit if they'll step out on a thing like that.

"And one thing they [are], they're Americans. They're not communistic, you know? Over there, you make one mistake, you die! In America, you make a mistake, and they give you another chance."

Baker had "never heard [Hoffa] say anything" about killing either John or Robert Kennedy. "Jimmy was all, uh, he was all heart . . . He had principles that were astounding," and murdering people was simply alien to the basic character and nature of James Hoffa. "You know what? I knew Jimmy, and I knew him well . . . Jimmy was no killer. Jimmy'd punch you in the nose . . . But Jimmy never went in for that kind of trash! Never went in for that homicidal crap! Believe me. And wouldn't have anyone around him that would . . . think like that. Not in this business.''

Unfortunately, Hoffa did in fact have some men around him who ''went in for that homicidal crap,'' and some were men who worked quite closely with Barney Baker. Among the more interesting of the other enforcers were Frank Chavez, the Puerto Rican Teamster official, and Anthony Provenzano of New Jersey.

An FBI report of December 2, 1963, raised some intriguing speculation about Chavez. On November 26, Leopoldo Ramos Ducos, a former aide to Chavez, stated in an interview that his boss had been in contact with Jack Ruby. Ducos said that before the assassination he

heard Frank Chavez . . . mention the name of Jack Ruby as someone connected with [the] Teamsters Union . . . Sometime in about September, 1961, Frank Chavez told . . . Ducos that Chavez had an appointment to meet Richard Kavner, International Vice President of the Teamsters Union, and Jack Ruby as well as a third Teamsters official whose name . . . Ducos could not recall. [FBI agents believe the third man was Provenzano.][29]

Richard Kavner, the IBT general organizer who, according to Ducos, was to have met with Ruby and Chavez, was another key member of the Hoffa circle; another member who carried a gun. He was rather well known in connection with a series of dynamite bombings which had occurred in Wichita, Kansas, during a Teamster cab drivers' strike, a strike that Kavner and Barney Baker coordinated. During the McClellan Committee hearings Robert Kennedy had noted that Kavner was ''in Puerto Rico on Teamster business'' at the time his doctors were claiming that he was too ill to testify. Explaining Kavner's absence, his attorney, Morris Shenker, plaintively told the committee that ''whenever [Kavner] is under emotional strain, he is subject to attacks which consist of a sudden loss of consciousness followed by severe sweating and pain.''[30]

Another small piece of information about a possible link among Chavez, Provenzano, and Ruby appears in a Justice Department memorandum of November 26, 1963. The memo contains only basic biographical material about various associates of Jack Ruby, and it refers to ''a connection between Rubenstein [Ruby] and Frank Chavez and

Tony Provenzano.'' The specific information alluded to was not included in the memorandum.

Despite Ducos's interview and the FBI memo of November 26, the
Warren Commission, convened in early 1964 to find the truth about
the Kennedy assassination, never pursued possible connections between the Teamster officials and the events in Dallas.

The FBI did, however, pursue the Barney Baker aspect after obtaining Jack Ruby's telephone records from Southwestern Bell.

On January 3, 1964, Chicago FBI agents John Bassett and William
Hood were dispatched to interview Baker, who was ''advised that . . .
he had many friends [who] were . . . high ranking hoodlums.'' Baker
maintained that Jack Ruby was not one of them; he stated that Ruby
had been a complete stranger to him until he received a telephone call
from him ''on November 11, 1963.'' Baker then said that Ruby had
called him ''at his home phone of RA 8-4031'' and his wife had taken
the call. According to Baker, Ruby did not give his real name during
the call, but simply gave Mrs. Baker his Dallas phone number and
asked her to have her husband call back when he came home and to
''ask for Lou.''

Baker added that he had returned ''Lou's'' call later that same day,
from his office phone in Chicago, and that when he asked for ''Lou,''
Ruby answered with ''That's me. My name is . . . Ruby.''
Thereupon, according to the FBI report, Ruby asked Baker if he could
give him some help in a labor dispute he was having with competing
Dallas strip-joint operators. Baker said that Ruby told him that some
unnamed ''mutual friends'' had recommended him as a man who
could help Ruby settle the problem he was having with his night club
competitors—who Ruby said were ''giving me a headache.'' Baker
told the interviewers that he turned down the Dallas stranger's en-
treaties and ''concluded the conversation by firmly declining to offer
any assistance in the matter.'' After this brief FBI interview of January
3 was reported, the Ruby-Baker investigation was dormant for several
weeks.

By late February of 1964 the Warren Commission had compiled a
long confidential memorandum on ''Jack Ruby—Background,
Friends, and Other Pertinent Information.'' The memorandum
noted—amid lengthy sections dealing with numerous other Ruby
associates—that ''Ruby called Barney Baker, a Chicago hoodlum who
was reputedly a muscle man for Jimmy Hoffa . . . to ask Baker to give
him assistance'' in a labor dispute. The memo also listed the Team-

sters Union as the first entry on a list of six groups that might have been interested in the assassination of President Kennedy.[31]

A copy of the memorandum was sent to Richard Helms with a formal request for CIA assistance on the various areas outlined in the memo. The CIA never responded to the request for help in probing the background of Ruby and his associates. (Helms sent back a brief note of five sentences more than six months later.)[32] More important, the CIA never informed the commission of the agency's plots to assassinate Fidel Castro and subvert his government—in cooperation with Santos Trafficante, Sam Giancana, Russell Bufalino, John Rosselli, and, perhaps, Jimmy Hoffa. Nor did the CIA share John Wilson's information that Ruby had visited ''Santos'' in a Cuban jail.

In March a few more interesting connections came to light, and they brought Barney Baker and his close relationship with Hoffa back into investigative focus. In the second week of March the Dallas office of the FBI obtained a complete compilation of Jack Ruby's recent long-distance telephone records. This set of records provided a much more extensive list than the agency had gotten earlier. During the same week the Chicago FBI office was busy too, with Barney Baker's telephone records—a list of all long-distance telephone calls made on his home phone during the two months before the President's murder.

These two sets of records showed at least two useful things: First, Jack Ruby had actually spoken with Barney Baker twice, with Baker having received a second lengthy call from Ruby on November 11, 1963—a call which seriously contradicted the story Baker had given the FBI in January. Second, Barney Baker had been in touch with another old friend of both Jimmy Hoffa and Jack Ruby on the day before the assassination, an acquaintance who happened to be a leading mob executioner, David Yaras.

The first Baker-Ruby telephone contact had occurred on November 7, 1963, four days earlier than Baker said in his FBI interview. Additionally, while Baker said he had merely returned the call of a Dallas night club owner who was unknown to him, the phone records brought that story into question as well. They showed Baker talking to Ruby for seven minutes on the afternoon of November 7, but they failed to show any preceding call from Ruby to Baker. Thus the Hoffa's enforcer's claim that Ruby had initiated the contact with him—rather than the other way around—was seriously undermined.

The second Baker-Ruby phone call raised even more serious questions. The phone records showed that Ruby had called Baker at his home on November 8, 1963, the day after their first conversation. The records further showed that this second conversation had lasted some fourteen minutes. As to Baker's conversation with the deadly Yaras, the Chicago phone records showed that Baker had called Dave Yaras in Miami at 6:17 P.M. on the eve of the assassination.

Although the Warren Commission had access to this information, it never followed up on these investigations. Ruby was not asked about the two Baker calls during his testimony before the commission, and neither the commission nor the FBI ever went back to Baker for an explanation of the numerous discrepancies between his interview and the phone records.

"Yes, we did a shitty job on that," a former staff counsel for the Warren Commission recalls, "but do you want to hear the reasons? That period, March and April 1964, was really our busiest period," and also, "Maybe we didn't understand what Baker really was. I mean, the real punch of Hoffa and these Mafia associates.

"In our defense," he says, "Bobby Kennedy's guys lived and breathed Jimmy Hoffa . . . they should have been the ones to follow up on this stuff on Ruby."

Reminded that Attorney General Kennedy's aides were excluded from the Warren Commission's investigation—and that FBI and commission personnel maintained exclusive access to most of the documentation on both Ruby and Oswald—the former commission counsel replied, "Well, I think that was, well, that was generally the case. But they could have expressed an interest. They never did to me. I know that."

That, too, is puzzling, since Robert Kennedy did have knowledge of the CIA-underworld plots to murder Fidel Castro. Although Kennedy had been told in May 1962 that they had ceased the previous year, questions must have lingered as to whether one plot evolved into another. This probably explains the lengthy conversation in Washington between the attorney general and CIA director John McCone immediately after the assassination. McCone, like Kennedy, had been told that the Castro plots had been stopped. For unknown reasons, both decided not to reveal the information to the Warren Commission.

Ruby's longest testimony was given during a session in which attendence was substantially reduced. Of the seven commissioners only Chief Justice Earl Warren and Congressman Gerald R. Ford were present, in addition to staff attorneys J. Lee Rankin, Joseph Ball, and

Arlen Specter, plus Leon Jaworski, who was there representing the state of Texas.

During a long day of testimony before the commission on June 7, 1964, Ruby discussed his numerous telephone calls in general terms. He did not mention names nor provide any specific information about what was discussed, though he rather defensively conceded that he had been in touch with a number of rather questionable individuals. And he told the commission that the calls were made ''a long time prior to what has happened.''[33]

Ruby maintained that the only purpose of the various phone calls was to get assistance in the labor problems he was having with his night club competitors:

> . . . I had to make so many numerous calls that I am sure you know of. Am I right? Because of trying to survive in my business. . . .
>
> Every person I called, and sometimes you may not even know a person intimately, you sort of tell them, well, you are stranded down here and you want some help . . .
>
> All these calls were related, not in any way involved with the underworld, because I have been away from Chicago 17 years now in Dallas.
>
> . . . I want to set you gentlemen straight on all the telephone calls I had. This was a long time prior to what has happened. And the only association I had with those calls, the only questions that I inquired about, was if they could help me with . . . [Ruby's strip tease] shows in Dallas. That is the only reason I made those calls.[34]

Why did Ruby think that Jimmy Hoffa's men could help him with his small-time night club? How did he manage to have the unlisted numbers of people such as Barney Baker and Murray W. Miller, who was staying at a Miami hotel when Ruby called him? Why did the calls occur at the times they did? Why did Baker deny receiving a second call from Ruby? If he didn't field the call, who did and why?

During the commission's investigation, Luis Kutner, a Chicago attorney and a former staff lawyer for the Kefauver Committee, testified that Jack Ruby had appeared before the Kefauver staff in 1950 and they had learned that Ruby was ''a syndicate lieutenant who had been sent to Dallas to serve as a liaison for Chicago mobsters.'' Other commission witnesses stated that Ruby was known as ''the payoff man for the Dallas Police Department.''[35]

One organized crime expert explains that ''the practice of paying off a police officer is greatly misunderstood by the general public. Most simply think that, say, a gambler exchanges money to the cop in return for protection of his interests. And that's as far as the relationship goes. Really, it goes one step further. The criminal will also give the policeman information about his underworld competitors. The cop goes out and busts them, allowing his illicit source of income to develop nothing less than a 'privileged sanctuary.' With all these other arrests under his belt, the cop compiles a respected reputation while his other relationship grows.''

If Jack Ruby was a payoff contact for police officers in Dallas, fronting for the underworld, then, according to Kutner, that relationship had begun in the late 1940s, the same period when two of Ruby's friends were Chicago mob executioner Leonard Patrick and Paul Roland Jones—both of whom Ruby had seen not long before the assassination.

Disconcertingly enough, however, the Warren Commission Report referred to Patrick, Jones, and David Yaras as character witnesses for Ruby. The commission used Patrick's statement that his old friend was an honest man to corroborate its central conclusion about Ruby's ''underworld ties''—that they weren't ''significant'': ''Based on its evaluation of the record . . . the Commission believes that the evidence does not establish a significant link between Ruby and organized crime.''[36]

In support of this important commission finding, the Warren Commission Report made two further statements that turned out to be based in part on Patrick's personal views. First: ''Some of Ruby's childhood friends eventually became criminals; however . . . virtually all of Ruby's friends and acquaintances who were questioned reported that he was not involved with Chicago's criminal element.'' Second: ''Virtually all of Ruby's Chicago friends stated that he had no close connection with organized crime.'' Both statements were accompanied by footnotes citing the documentation that supported them.[37]

Turning to these citations one discovers that the record of Patrick's brief FBI interview (Exhibit 1202) was included as a corroborative documentary source for each of the two footnotes: ''He [Patrick] did state he was certain Rubenstein (Ruby) had never operated a book or had anything else to do with any racket. Patrick stated that 'no matter how much you investigate, you'll never learn nothing, as he had nothing to do with nothing.' ''

Barney Baker blames the media for allowing various theories of possible Teamster–organized crime involvement in the assassination to gain a measure of credence. ''No, no. There's no theory at all. It was the most ridiculous, stupid . . . thing. Only . . . the papers and the movies and the many articles that have been written'' have fed the speculation.

''With the Kennedy thing, they did nail that guy [Oswald]. And they did have, they did have the rifle and whatnot . . .

''I'll tell you the truth, just as an ordinary layman, reading and thinking: I think the screwball was on his own. And got away with it. And I think the guy would go to some communistic country and say, 'I'm the guy that done it. Put a badge on me!'

'' . . . They say there was another guy in the bushes. Nothing turned up! . . . I can't see nobody with this guy.''

Regardless of Ruby's bizarre telephone calls, and regardless of ''this guy knows that guy, therefore . . . '' theories, the subject of a possible connection of Jimmy Hoffa and the underworld to President Kennedy's assassination is of course highly speculative. But it has so far been as poor in streetwise methodical investigative work as it has been rich in tempting conspiracy-theory melodrama—and chilling irony.

One aspect, however, goes far beyond speculation: the cold bureaucratic numbers that represent the flaming heat which the Kennedy Administration brought to bear on Jimmy Hoffa's criminal empire and on organized crime in general.

Robert Kennedy early established what became known as a ''hit list'' of underworld figures and their associates for investigation and prosecution. The list—which included Hoffa, Marcello, Giancana, and Trafficante—grew from forty in early 1961 to more than 2300 by the time he left office in 1964. The number of racketeer indictments totaled twenty-four during the first six months of the last year of the Eisenhower Administration, 1960; during the first six months of 1963 the number climbed 700 percent, to 171. Similarly, the number of actual convictions had risen 400 percent, from a total of 35 in 1960 to 160 in 1963.

Hoffa's own indictments were a tiny fraction of the sweeping federal effort against IBT corruption: 201 Teamster officials and co-conspirators were indicted during the Kennedy period, and more than 125 were convicted by the end of 1964.

One victim of Kennedy's wrath, convicted of extortion and sent to prison, relaxes now in his office suite—provided by his employer, Allen Dorfman—and talks about the past investigations.

"It does something to you," Barney Baker says. "It gets you sort of nerved up and sick. And you say, 'For what?' Am I associated with somebody they don't like? Am I a fat man that looks like a tough man? You know what I mean? They made me a bad man. You know what I mean?

Frank Chavez wrote Robert Kennedy the following letter:

Sir:

This is for your information.

The undersigned is going to solicit from the membership of our union that each one donate whatever they can afford to maintain, clean, beautify and supply with flowers the grave of Lee Harvey Oswald.

You can rest assured contributions will be unanimous.[38]

Ralph Salerno sums it all up when he says, "There is no solid evidence yet that Carlos Marcello, Santos Trafficante, Jimmy Hoffa, or any other criminal or criminal associate had been involved in a conspiracy to kill President Kennedy. Regardless of whether they knew or not, they should have built the largest statue in the world to Lee Harvey Oswald. No one man has ever done as much damage to this country's war on the underworld as he did. Because the bullet that killed John Kennedy killed Bobby Kennedy's dream to destroy the organized crime society."

Hoffa seemed to agree when he told a Nashville reporter on the day Ruby murdered Oswald, "Bobby Kennedy is just another lawyer now."

9 Mob Wars and Paper-Napkin Contracts

Jimmy Hoffa's jury-tampering trial began on January 20, 1964, fifty-eight days after the President's assassination. Because of pretrial publicity the site was shifted from Nashville to Chattanooga. Judge Frank W. Wilson, a highly respected southern jurist, was presiding.

Harold Gibbons consented to return to Washington to administer the union's day-to-day operations in Hoffa's absence—though he insisted on remaining on the payroll of his home local in St. Louis and "tore up the final check Hoffa ever gave me." Retired as Hoffa's official trial attorney, William Bufalino headed the IBT's staff in Chattanooga, which leased the ninth floor of the Patton Hotel. Hoffa's trial team was a Detroit lawyer, silver-haired James Haggerty, and Harry Berke, from Chattanooga. Frank Ragano served as backup as he had during the Test Fleet trial, and St. Louis attorney Morris Shenker was helping with the defense along with several others.

On January 16, four days before the trial began, Hoffa met in Chicago with bargaining representatives from the trucking industry to negotiate the first National Master Freight Agreement, a milestone in the union's history. The contract established uniform wages, working conditions, and fringe benefits on a national basis, covering Teamster members employed in over-the-road and local cartage operations for three years. It guaranteed a 45-cent per hour raise plus increased fringe benefits. This was achieved nearly twenty-five years after Farrell Dobbs first proposed the creation of a nationwide bargaining system.

The signing of the National Master Freight Agreement was Hoffa's finest hour. Within a month he was to experience his worst.

Two weeks into the trial, the prosecutors thrashed away at Hoffa's associates, providing the court with solid evidence of their attempts to fix the Test Fleet jury. Hoffa, however, was confident of his own defense; the government attorneys had yet to implicate him in the scheme. The man who could do just that, Edward Partin, was hidden in a remote area on Lookout Mountain. As the government wound up its case, Partin would be the prosecution's final witness.

"Hoffa was his usual cocky self and his attorneys were highly optimistic," Clark Mollenhoff reported.

> Then, at 1:50 P.M. on February 4, Ed Partin, who had been hidden on the outskirts of Chattanooga for three days, stepped through the rear door of the courtroom as the principal prosecution witness.
>
> Hoffa glowered with shock and rage. Partin was one of the last Teamsters he had expected to talk. Within a few minutes after Partin was given the oath, his testimony had implicated Hoffa, Ewing King, and Larry Campbell as having knowledge of the jury tampering in Nashville. Thomas Parks was the only defendent whose name was not brought into the testimony by Partin. With Hoffa prodding them, the nine defense lawyers made a frantic effort to suppress Partin's testimony.[1]

Because prosecutor James Neal had evaded the underlying reason why Partin decided to give evidence against Hoffa, the defense pushed for a closed hearing to discuss the matter. With the jury out of the courtroom, Neal informed the judge and Hoffa's defense attorneys that in September 1962 Partin had reported that Hoffa was making plans to have the attorney general murdered.

"We have no objection [to that testimony]," said one of Hoffa's lawyers. "We think it is so fantastic and unbelievable we are not going to try to suppress it."

Nevertheless, Judge Wilson ruled that the information was not relevant to the jury-tampering case.

When the jury returned, Allen Dorfman's attorney evaded the judge's decision, pressing Partin and the two Baton Rouge law enforcement agents who had first heard his story. When the defense succeeded in getting the allegation that Hoffa had discussed "an assassination plot" into the trial record, the lawyers tried to use it to discredit all of Partin's testimony.

Neal then obtained testimony that Partin had willingly subjected himself to a lie detector test and passed. It was proof enough that at least Partin wasn't a screwball.

Efforts to refute Partin's testimony on Hoffa's complicity in jury tampering were equally unsuccessful, and on March 4, 1964, Hoffa, Parks, Campbell, and King were found guilty of jury tampering. Dorfman and Tweel were acquitted.

Eight days later, during the hearing for sentencing, Judge Wilson sternly told Hoffa: ''You stand here convicted of seeking to corrupt the administration of justice itself. You stand here convicted of having tampered, really, with the very soul of this nation. You stand here convicted of having struck at . . . the very basis of civilization itself, and that is the administration of justice . . . ''

Despite Hoffa's shouts of innocence, Judge Wilson sentenced him to eight years in prison and a fine of $10,000; the others received lesser sentences. Hoffa quickly appealed.

Robert Kennedy's Justice Department had finally licked the elusive Jimmy Hoffa. But Kennedy knew already that the Johnson Administration would not give him the backing his brother had offered. Nevertheless, Kennedy continued to push for a second Hoffa conviction. On April 27, 1964, Hoffa—his Chattanooga conviction on appeal—and seven others went on trial in Chicago for defrauding the Central States Pension Fund of over $20 million—diverting over $1 million for their personal use. The case stemmed from the aborted Sun Valley indictment of 1960, and involved Hoffa's efforts to bail out of the land scheme, which had used Local 299's money as collateral for Hoffa's private investment.

Although Hoffa was one of sixteen pension fund trustees who approved the loans, he was the only trustee indicted. The government's charge, like that against his co-defendants, was that Hoffa was a direct beneficiary of the kickback money, and that there had been a misuse of union funds and mail fraud.

Before the trial Hoffa told reporters, ''The plea of not guilty entered by my counsel [Morris Shenker] I'm sure will be substantiated by the evidence that we will be able to produce in this court and I hope and trust that all those who are involved in the pension fund will not have any anxiety until this trial is over. Because ultimately they will find that this is another propaganda scheme of Mr. Robert Kennedy.''

According to the indictment, the mastermind was Benjamin Dranow, a Florida wheeler-dealer. Dranow had been among those behind Hoffa's earlier attempts to obtain a $300,000 loan from the pension fund to purchase several C-74 airplanes which a mysterious corporation, Akros Dynamics, had promised to deliver to Castro soon after the Cuban revolution. Frank Ragano represented Dranow's business partner, Abe Weinblatt, another of the eight men on trial.

Also on trial were Miami Beach builder Calvin Kovens, who allegedly had ties to Trafficante and Lansky; Zachary A. Strate, Jr., an associate of Carlos Marcello, who had received $4,675,000 to build the Fontainebleau Hotel in New Orleans; S. George Burris, a New York accountant; his son, attorney Herbert Burris; and Florida real estate man Samuel Hyman. Hyman and the Burrises had been given millions from the pension fund in return for helping Hoffa out of the Sun Valley pinch.

On July 26, 1964, Hoffa and his co-defendants were all found guilty of misusing union funds. Three weeks later Judge Richard B. Austin sentenced Hoffa to five years in prison, to run consecutively—not concurrently—with his eight-year stretch for jury tampering. Dranow also received five years; the others got lighter sentences.

Government attorney William Bittman said, "I think the proof in that case clearly indicated that Mr. Hoffa, as one of the trustees of the pension fund, made material misrepresentations in connection with the pension fund loans that were made, that he concealed material facts which were relevant in connection with the pension fund trustees' determination of what loans to be made, and substantial amount of pension fund loan proceeds were directly traced from those loans to Mr. Hoffa's benefit in connection with a project called Sun Valley in Florida, in which he held a secret interest."[2]

Eternally defiant, after his second conviction Hoffa announced to reporters in Washington, "I'm going to prove eventually, number one, I was not guilty in Chattanooga; I cannot be held legally responsible for what other people did in Chicago, and eventually somewhere down the line there'll be decisions coming out of the Supreme Court, not for a Hoffa but for other people, we'll be able to use in our case and overturn it. I'm not going to give up."

With this second victory under his belt, Robert Kennedy resigned as attorney general on August 1, 1964, and later that month announced his decision to run for the Senate from the state of New York. He survived a huge onslaught of Teamster propaganda and manpower that fall, and was elected in the Johnson-Humphrey landslide of 1964.

Facing thirteen years in prison, Hoffa battled in the courts to keep his freedom. Nearly every tactic his defense could pull out of its dirty bag of tricks was used. Government witnesses and jurors from both trials were accused of having sex with prostitutes, who provided affidavits to Hoffa's attorneys. One streetwalker gave a Hoffa partisan a tape recording accompanied by the claim that the heavy male breather in the background was Judge Wilson.[3] Such maneuvers were repudiated by most of the politicians and newspaper editors whom the union tried to use to publicize the allegations.

More serious charges flooded out of the Teamsters' camp, too. There were allegations of illegal wiretapping in the Nashville, Chattanooga, and Chicago trials. These accusations were also without substance, but they led to legitimate questions by responsible people and institutions about how far the government could be allowed to go in order to convict someone.

''I had no concern with the allegations of wiretapping, bugging, or violations of attorney-client privilege,'' Jim Neal says. ''That sort of thing simply did not exist during the Hoffa trials. However, my own concern was that any time the government goes flat-out to convict a man, it's going to get him—sooner or later.''

Ironically, Hoffa and his hoodlum friends became symbols, to some, of the government's infringements of personal rights and freedoms. On the other hand, *Life* magazine subsequently accused Senator Edward Long of Missouri of illegally utilizing his power on Hoffa's behalf. While Long was chairman of a subcommittee investigating the abuses of government eavesdropping, Morris Shenker had paid the senator $160,000 in return for some legal work. Earlier, however, Long admitted to a reporter that he hadn't practiced law since the mid-1950s.

Robert Maheu was among those scheduled to testify at Long's hearings, but he ''applied pressure on the [CIA] in a variety of ways—suggesting that publicity might expose his sensitive work for the CIA.''[4] The CIA's general counsel then notified Long, in unspecific terms, that Maheu had worked with the agency. Consequently the subpoena for Howard Hughes's assistant was quashed.

The use of electronic surveillance was often criticized, but the Justice Department used it from 1961 to 1965, to monitor the activities of, among others, a notorious New Jersey gangster, Sam DeCavalcante, and the results were fruitful. With recording equipment hooked up to his headquarters, investigators obtained a wealth of information about the operations of the underworld, much of which confirmed Joseph Valachi's detailed disclosures of 1963. One of the DeCavalcante recordings included a conversation about Anthony Provenzano.

A Provenzano henchman, discussing a building contractor with DeCavalcante, bubbled:

> Right now the picture is ideal for you, Sam . . . I told the guy he's gotta be one hundred percent union . . . I got the pickets ready and everything.
> Tell him you'll close his job and stop all trucks.
> . . . I told him if [he] didn't go union he was gonna have a headache.
> Tell him you'll stop all the trucks . . . Tony [Provenzano] called me up the other day . . . anything I want I can have from him . . . in the Teamsters . . . call him direct. I got his private number.

As Clark Mollenhoff wrote:

> When Tony Pro's boys go out on strike, it is dangerous to cross the picket lines. Although it isn't always fatal, it is definitely unhealthy. There's very little reason to risk the wrath of the Teamsters anyway. A few days without supplies coming in, no deliveries or dumpings going out, means no work can be done on the strike site.
> Not only can the Teamsters precipitate a strike against a recalcitrant employer, but the union can break a strike by an unfriendly union against a favored contractor. Tony simply calls off Teamster services to other sites where the offending union has men employed.⁵

Through similar monitoring in Detroit law enforcement officials learned that the local mob had grown enormously with the help of Jimmy Hoffa.

Surveillance of the Home Juice Company—owned by mobsters Anthony and Vito Giacalone, who received a half-million-dollar loan from the Central States Fund—revealed that the underworld considered Hoffa ''our connection'' with the union's multimillion-dollar fund.

''Mike Polizzi said that he would have never gotten his loan of $630,000 without Jimmy,'' Vito Giacalone told his brother. ''Mike said, Tony [Giacalone] got this for me through Sylvia. Mike said he could have never gotten this loan from nobody, and he wanted to pay 10 percent. Mike said that Jimmy Hoffa had to put his stamp on it in order to [force] these guys [the fund's trustees] to give it to him. Hoffa took a shot with it.''[6]

"Sylvia" was Sylvia Pagano Paris, who was now having an affair with Anthony Giacalone. He instructed her to make regular reports on Jimmy Hoffa's activities: ''Sylvia is the only person that can handle Jimmy Hoffa,'' Giacalone said proudly.

An FBI memo states that ''Giacalone, who visited Sylvia almost daily, began bringing a friend, Tony Cimini . . . to provide companionship to Mrs. Hoffa.''[7]

''It was a little more than that,'' explains a Michigan law enforcement official. ''Cimini was having an affair with Josephine Hoffa during the early 1960s. It was a double-dating situation in which Cimini and Mrs. Hoffa would go out with Giacalone and Sylvia Paris. Hoffa found out about the affair and, not wanting to handle the matter himself, went to Joseph Zerilli for help.''

Although Hoffa was one to beat his breast about his devotion to his family, he maintained the double standard. Long before Mrs. Hoffa and Cimini began seeing each other, Hoffa was having an affair with a redheaded union secretary. Teamster aides and associates in Detroit, Las Vegas, and Washington agree that Hoffa was anything but completely devoted to his wife. ''There were times when it became nauseating to hear about Hoffa's 'close family life,' '' says a friend in Las Vegas, ''and he bragged about it as well, which made it even more sickening. A more appropriate posture for him would have been 'catch me if you can.' ''

Left at home a good deal of the time, with her husband's ex-lover for company, Mrs. Hoffa could easily be forgiven, though perhaps not by her husband.

''Just before Cimini was arrested in 1963 for peddling stolen securities, there was a sitdown,'' the Michigan investigator says, ''and he and Giacalone were told to break off their relationships with their mistresses. They refused and Cimini was arrested. The feeling was: 'If you don't do as you're told, you're going to get screwed one way or another; and that doesn't necessarily mean getting killed.' ''

It is doubtful that any such action was taken against the other lover. Twice arrested and once convicted for attempting to bribe police officers, Anthony Giacalone, a former numbers runner for Detroit mobster Peter Licavoli, was prominent in the organization, serving as an enforcer for Zerilli and William Tocco. Besides, his wife was a cousin of Anthony Provenzano.

Although Giacalone remained a friend of Hoffa's—and even derailed a 1963 plot to "grab that Jimmy Hoffa" being discussed by Zerilli's son—the Teamster leader was badly harmed by the way he dealt with his wife's affair.[8]

"Jimmy was completely ripped up over hearing about his wife's thing with that guy," a close Hoffa associate says. "When he ran to old man Zerilli for help, he lost face with the local mob. When you lose their respect, you're nothing."

If it is true that Hoffa lost prestige that early among the respected Detroit underworld, then he must have lost it nationally as well. During the 1960s the Detroit mob was increasingly viewed as an important neutralizing force in two wars among the crime families of New York.

Between 1960 and 1963, Joseph Profaci had gone into battle against two subordinates who were demanding more money. When a majority of the members of the National Crime Syndicate's nine-member commission voted that the Profaci war was an internal family matter, all eyes turned to Profaci's relatives in Detroit, the Zerillis and the Toccos, and, in New York, to the Bonanno family, to see whether the commission's decision would be defied.

"Wisely, the Detroit gangs chose to stay out of the shooting war and acted only as conciliators upon request," Salerno says. "In 1962, when Profaci died, Zerilli was rewarded by being appointed Profaci's successor on the commission."

Joseph Bonanno, on the other hand, quickly came to the aid of Profaci, whose niece had married Bonanno's son. Then the commission learned that members of the Bonanno family were involved in a conspiracy to kill two high-ranking commission members, Carlo Gambino and Thomas Lucchese. Consequently other crime families began actively arming and supporting the renegades from the Bonanno family. Again, although distantly related to Bonanno and sharing criminal activities with him in Arizona, the Detroit mob remained neutral.

If Hoffa had lost face among some elements of the organized crime community by the end of 1964, he was still highly regarded by others. Aside from his attorneys, who were appealing his convictions, the brains and money behind the "keep Hoffa out of jail" movement in 1964 were Carlos Marcello and Santos Trafficante.

Marcello and Trafficante, who had long been business associates in the drug traffic, had become closer than ever. They even shared the same New Orleans doctor, according to law enforcement agents. When they were not in direct communication with each other, David Yaras served as a respected go-between for them.

Marcello and Trafficante were arrested together on September 22, 1966, along with other mob figures, during a meeting at La Stella restaurant in New York. Also present was Frank Ragano, the Hoffa-Trafficante attorney.

Edward Partin, still in Marcello's territory at great risk, was offered several bribes—including one for a million dollars from a New Orleans municipal judge—in return for a signed affidavit admitting that he had perjured himself in Chattanooga.

One of Marcello's bagmen, according to Partin, was Hoffa's "foster son," Charles O'Brien, who allegedly was among those offering large sums for help.

Later, during an interview, Hoffa denied that Marcello was his chief money man: "They said my good friend Carlos Marcello called the mob together and put up $1,000,000 to get Hoffa outta jail. What kind of bullshit is this? Where'd they get those figures from? . . ."[9]

When Partin refused to yield, his enemies got tough.

In early 1967, New Orleans district attorney Jim Garrison opened his own investigation of the Kennedy assassination, which became an ideal means of intimidating Partin.

One of Garrison's first "revelations" was that David Ferrie had conspired with Lee Harvey Oswald to murder the President. Claiming that the CIA was directly involved in the conspiracy, Garrison was taken seriously after Ferrie was found dead in his apartment, on his first day of freedom after being in protective custody for four days. The coroner determined that Ferrie had died from a massive brain hemorrhage. Earlier that same day, a close friend of Ferrie, also active in the anti-Castro movement, had been murdered. However, there were at the same time other revelations that Garrison had actively protected Marcello's rackets. Aaron M. Kohn, director of the city's crime commission, said before a U.S. House subcommittee, "We have been in repeated public conflicts with Orleans District Attorney Jim Garrison who denies the existence in our city of provable organized crime. He and his staff have blocked our efforts to have grand juries probe the influence of the Cosa Nostra and other syndicate operations."[10]

The obvious question was: If Garrison is protecting Marcello, why would he implicate a Marcello man in the conspiracy?

''It is quite possible that Garrison didn't realize Ferrie's relationship with Marcello,'' says one assassination investigator. ''Garrison, who later claimed to know Marcello and a Marcello lieutenant from whom Garrison had purchased his home, said that he had received little cooperation from the FBI. And it was the FBI which had the information that Ferrie was a Marcello aide.

''Marcello probably had a fit when Garrison started throwing Ferrie's name around. It is conceivable, considering their relationship, that Marcello, through his middlemen, let Garrison know that he didn't like what was going on. This quite possibly happened, because it wasn't long until Garrison began flying off walls in his investigation.''

Later, on June 23, 1967, Garrison, according to WJBO in Baton Rouge, claimed, ''We know that Jack Ruby and Lee Harvey Oswald were in New Orleans several times . . . there was a third man driving them and we are checking the possibility it was [Edward] Partin.''

Sensibly, Partin was scared. Not only was he being pressured by Jimmy Hoffa and Carlos Marcello; now he was being implicated in the Kennedy assassination.

''Soon after that, Frank Ragano called me,'' Partin says, ''and he said he could get Garrison off my back. In return he wanted a signed affidavit saying that I lied in Hoffa's trial. Naturally, I didn't sign. But later it came out that Ragano was in touch with both Trafficante and Marcello during that period of time.''

Years later, when asked whether he thought Garrison was ''just a kook,'' Hoffa replied, ''No, siree! Jim Garrison's a smart man . . . Goddamn smart attorney . . . Anybody thinks he's a kook is a kook themselves.''[11]

Bold Ed Partin could not be bought or intimidated. Hoffa was still en route to jail.

Within the Teamster leadership, small conspiracies against Hoffa increased—without a recognized leader or a public plan. The first one had developed during the Chicago trial, when the IBT general executive board voted to stop payment on Hoffa's legal bill, now almost half a million dollars. But seeing Hoffa still walking around with the likes of Anthony Giacalone, and knowing that Marcello and Trafficante were helping him stay out of jail, the Teamster high command made only very subdued efforts to get rid of Jimmy Hoffa.

Among those who continued to be openly loyal was Frank Fitzsimmons, who had remained relatively clean (or at least unconvicted) through all the government investigations of the Detroit Teamsters. Nevertheless, he was a close friend of several Detroit underworld figures, including Raffaele Quasarano, and a frequent visitor to a Detroit mob hangout, Market Vending, which was operated by two local labor racketeers.

FBI transcripts indicate that Fitzsimmons was also well acquainted with Anthony Giacalone. On February 24, 1964, Giacalone called Fitzsimmons in Detroit because the union was going to audit the books of a friend's trucking company. Giacalone hoped that Fitzsimmons could ''fix it up.'' Because the surveillance device was a room bug and not a telephone tap, only Giacalone's side of the conversation was recorded:

''Tony calling. Let me talk to him, will you please, miss. Alright [sic]. What do you say, Fitz, how are you? Okay. Listen, I have a man here that I was born and raised with you know. No, no, no. In here . . . this man here, he's trying to make a living . . . [and a Teamsters representative] would like to go through my friend's books.

''What the [expletive] is he [the Teamsters representative] supposed to be, the government? Uh? I'll see you personally when you come back. Now in the meantime, I'll give you the name of the company. [Giacalone spells out the name of his friend's trucking firm.] Alright, give him [the union representative] a call and tell him to sit tight till you come back and then we'll sit down with him.

''Just tell him that I would like to sit down with him when you get back. Alright? Okay.''[12]

''The Detroit mob had a high regard for Fitz, because he was easy to get along with,'' says Vince Piersante. ''He'd do whatever they wanted him to do. 'He's our kind of guy' is what they said about him. Anything they wanted, they got. Whereas, with Hoffa, it was always a tough negotiation.''

It is speculated that Fitzsimmons was groomed as a possible successor because of his friendship with the Detroit underworld, and at least one Hoffa associate says it was true: ''Sure, Fitzsimmons and Hoffa got along good. But you have to remember that Hoffa also had his eye on Dusty Miller from the Southern Conference and on Harold Gibbons from St. Louis.

''When Jimmy went to the Detroit Mafia for help when his wife was messing around with Tony Cimini, in return the mob made a 'this for that' proposition to Hoffa. The mob took care of Cimini, and Jimmy left a friendly guy [Fitzsimmons] in his place.''

Rolland McMaster, a Hoffa and Fitzsimmons assistant, denies that the Detroit mob picked Fitzsimmons. ''Jimmy demanded absolute loyalty from his men. And if he didn't get it, he could get pretty ugly. But Fitz was really loyal to Hoffa and deserved to replace him . . . Gibbons and Miller were always his second choices. Gibbons was a smart man but he defied Hoffa after the Kennedy assassination on that lowering of the flags deal. 'Too independent,' Jimmy said. 'He can't be controlled.' ''

McMaster was another one who couldn't be controlled. In the absence of both Hoffa and Fitzsimmons, who spent a good deal of time in Washington, McMaster, as secretary-treasurer, ran the affairs of Local 299 in Detroit. Appointed to the post after Frank Collins was sent to prison, and elected in his own right a week after his conviction for labor extortion in 1962, McMaster, like Hoffa, battled to stay out of jail. ''The strongest arm behind Hoffa,'' as Ed Partin calls him, McMaster had begun to blame his boss for his legal problems, but he resisted heavy government pressure to turn state's evidence against Hoffa in return for a reduced sentence.

''I was down in the federal building,'' McMaster remembers, ''and some guy gave me a slip of paper. I didn't know who he was. The paper had a number on it, so I took it to Hoffa. He said, 'That's Bob Kennedy's office.' I said, 'What the hell would he want me for?'

''Hoffa told me to go see what they wanted.''

McMaster says he had two meetings with several representatives of the attorney general and was offered his freedom in return for cooperation.

William French, one of the prosecuting attorneys at McMaster's trial, was present at both meetings. ''That's not quite the way it happened,'' according to French. ''It was McMaster who asked for the meeting. He really didn't want to go to jail, and we understood that. But although he didn't specify why he wanted to see us, we were under the clear impression that he wanted to make a deal with us.''

After first meeting in a restaurant, McMaster went with French, Sheridan, and Carmine Bellino to a room at the Howard Johnson Inn, near the Detroit airport. McMaster says, ''Everyone took their shoes off, called me 'Rolland,' and expected me to talk.''

''Well, Rolland, you're a big boy and you understand things real well,'' McMaster quotes Sheridan. ''We need some help, and you can help us.''

''Well, what the hell do you mean I can help you?'' McMaster asked. ''Do you want me to phony up a charge to get out of the trouble I'm in?''

''You're a big boy,'' Sheridan responded.

McMaster says he was offered his freedom in return for incriminating information against either Hoffa or Fitzsimmons, and he shouted back, ''I'll tell you what, I gotta stay a hell of a long time before I'll do anything to hurt Hoffa or Fitz.''

McMaster later said, ''I did not accept. No, sir. I absolutely did not. I could've walked away from the whole thing. And I don't like to do time.''

French says, ''McMaster did refuse to cooperate. It was strange, though, that he wanted the meeting in the first place. McMaster always had a general reputation of being a really tough organizer with a deep devotion to Jimmy Hoffa.''

Whether or not McMaster tried to swing a deal with the government, Hoffa thought he had, and thus their relationship began to change dramatically. ''Hoffa and McMaster were so tight and had pulled so much shit together and had so much on each other that it was hard to imagine them splitting up,'' an IBT vice president recalls. ''But [Hoffa] thought it nonetheless. I remember sometime in the mid-1960s, I was at a banquet or something, talking to Hoffa. When McMaster walked by, Hoffa pointed to him after he'd passed and said, 'That son of a bitch is a goddamn informant on me.' I kinda laughed and said something like he had plenty of dirty laundry of his own. But Jimmy was dead serious. He said that McMaster wanted him to cool off in jail for a while.''

''See, you have to know Jimmy and his character and be with him for a while to understand him, his quest for power,'' McMaster says. ''I watched him [since] 1936–37 when he tramped over anyone who got in his way . . . He used everyone. Fitz, like most of us, went along with him, because not to go along with him was nothing but a goddamn problem.''

McMaster's court appeals were unsuccessful, and he began to face the fact that he was going to jail. Twisting the knife, Hoffa told him he didn't want any ''jailbirds'' in office at Local 299. When McMaster protested and pointed out that Hoffa was also on his way to prison, Hoffa replied, ''Yeah, but I'm still running this local, and you're out.''

Ordering McMaster to withdraw as a candidate for reelection, Hoffa turned to Dave Johnson and told him that he would run in Mc-Master's place, and that if Hoffa went to prison and Fitzsimmons had to be in Washington, Johnson would run Local 299.

McMaster was outraged and threatened not to cooperate. He demanded a promise of reinstatement as secretary-treasurer when he returned from prison.

Not wanting to push McMaster too far, Hoffa set up a meeting among Fitzsimmons, Johnson, and McMaster at Detroit's Pont-chartrain Hotel and authorized his two representatives to sign an agreement with McMaster that when he returned he'd get his old job back. Ominously, Hoffa neither attended the meeting nor signed the accord, which was written on a hotel napkin.

McMaster put the napkin in his pocket and withdrew from the race. Johnson was elected secretary-treasurer in December 1965. McMaster was given a job organizing steel haulers for the Central Conference of Teamsters until he went to prison late the following year.

In July 1966, at the IBT's nineteenth convention, Hoffa created a new union post: ''general vice president.'' Frank Fitzsimmons was promptly given the position. Hoffa merely said of Fitzsimmons, ''He believes in the same philosophy that I do.''

Like Dave Beck nine years before, Hoffa stood before the union's delegates with a prison term hanging over him. Nevertheless, with loud support from the same people he'd cheated and stolen from, Hoffa was reelected IBT general president for a third time. His term would expire in mid-1971, and by then or sooner he hoped to be out of jail and back in control of the Teamsters. In the meantime Fitzsimmons would be his caretaker.

To ease the pain of being imprisoned, the delegates voted Hoffa an increase in salary from $75,000 to $100,000. In addition, resolutions were passed that permitted the IBT to pay all legal bills of prosecuted Teamster officials—totaling $1.25 million by now—and raised membership dues by 20 percent!

As the fifty-two-year-old Hoffa posed for photographers, holding Fitzsimmons' hand high in the air to symbolize the union's strength and solidarity, few expected this to be Jimmy Hoffa's last IBT convention, or that fifty-eight-year-old, grandfatherly Fitzsimmons would become his own man.

On December 12, 1966, the Supreme Court turned down Hoffa's final appeal and in January 1967, negotiations for the second National Master Freight Agreement opened in Washington. Hoffa was tired but still defiant as he pounded the table, emphasizing his demands to the trucking management.

In the midst of bargaining, Hoffa's last-chance appeal to the Supreme Court to reconsider its decision was unsuccessful.

On the evening of March 6, Hoffa summoned his top aides from all over the country to his Baltimore hotel for instructions. Arriving in droves, leaders and union associates came to pay their respects to the leader and brother who would be in jail by nightfall the next day.

That night Fitzsimmons, Robert Holmes, and Dave Johnson met privately with Hoffa in his hotel room. Turning to Johnson, who recalls the scene, Hoffa said, "Dave, you know more about the trucking industry than any business agent I've ever had. You take over Local 299, and see that it runs smoothly."

Hoffa then put his hand on Holmes's shoulder and gave Bert Brennan's successor as president of Local 337, and vice president of the Michigan Conference of Teamsters, control over the Michigan Teamsters.

Finally, "Fitz, I'm going to jail, and I want you to take over my duties," said Hoffa.

"Well, Jimmy, when you get out, the keys will be right here," Fitzsimmons responded. "You come right back, don't worry about a thing."

Fitzsimmons, looking around the room for something to write on, found a paper napkin and scribbled on it a promise to do everything he could to get his boss out of jail and to step down when Hoffa returned.

For safekeeping the napkin was given to Holmes, whom both men trusted. "It was just a symbol of good faith," Holmes says. "Fitzsimmons loved Jimmy and knew what he was going through. He wanted him to feel comfortable as he went away."

Ironically, default on the 1965 napkin agreement with McMaster was to lead to default on the 1967 napkin agreement between Fitzsimmons and Hoffa.

On March 7, 1967, at 9:00 A.M., Hoffa surrendered to U.S. marshals in Washington. A few hours later he had been transported to

Lewisburg Penitentiary, in Pennsylvania, and was wearing his prison wardrobe, long, baggy pants, short, narrow work shoes. Inmate No. 33298, facing a thirteen-year stretch, was assigned to the mattress shop, where he stuffed and repaired bedding. Sometimes his job was to ticket the guards' uniforms for cleaning. To keep in shape he walked in the prison yard and lifted weights in the recreation center nearly every day after his seven hours of work. Returning to his cell—its walls covered with family photos and cards from well-wishers—he sat alone inside the eight-by-ten-foot cubicle which contained a washbasin, table, chair, toilet, and small radio.

Lewisburg was known as a country-club prison, and the social strata were as complex as those outside—just a little different. The top con in Lewisburg at the time Hoffa was there was Carmine Galante. Former mobster Vincent Teresa described the scene:

> Now the Capo di Tutti Capi [boss of bosses] of Mafia Row . . . Lillo, Carmine Galante. Lillo was the underboss to Joe Bananas [Joseph Bonanno] until he was jailed on a narcotics rap. He was doing twenty years. He's a stone killer. I think he took care of at least eighty hits himself. He is about five-foot-three, bald-headed, and he walked around with a mean look on his face. Lillo was fifty-seven years old, but he didn't have an ounce of fat on his body. He was always playing handball and he was as trim and lean as any athlete you could name. While we were at Lewisburg together, he never had much to say that was good about anybody, and he talked to even fewer people. I was one exception; so was Jimmy Hoffa, the labor leader. There were a few others, but damned few.
>
> In or out of prison, Lillo is Mr. Big, and anyone who thinks different don't know what makes the mob tick.[13]

Blaming Bonanno's enemies, including Genovese, for his loss of prestige during the Banana Wars, Galante bided his time, waiting for his release from prison. Jimmy Hoffa tried to do the same.

The Lewisburg scene was also ornamented by one of Hoffa's old associates, Anthony Provenzano, who had allegedly arranged the murder of rank-and-file dissident Walter Glockner during the extortion trial that had brought Provenzano to prison. Glockner had been recruited by the government to testify against the Local 560 union boss. Although federal investigators claimed that Thomas Reynolds, a relative of Provenzano, was a witness to the murder, no indictments were ever handed down. According to law enforcement authorities, Provenzano had actively participated in the Banana Wars by ordering the locals under his command to stop paying all the Bonanno men who were on the Teamster payroll. Provenzano was due to be released in 1970, but until then the Genovese crime captain had to co-exist with Galante.

With whom would Hoffa be aligned?

As the top dog in jail, Galante provided the best protection against prison violence and homosexuality. Hoffa needed protection from both. Further, Galante's boss had gone to Arizona and made alliances with Hoffa's friends, Carlos Marcello and Santos Trafficante. That was perhaps the most persuasive consideration. After all, Hoffa did not feel as close to Provenzano as he once had—there had been some disagreements over the allocation of pension fund money.

For all these reasons Hoffa made his important choice and allied himself with Galante.

It was a fateful decision.

PART TWO

PART TWO

1○ The 1967 Revolt

The rust-colored carbon vapors from towering smokestacks of steel mills billowed into the skies over Gary, Indiana, while their grimy residue covered the city below. Impoverished steel haulers could only look to the filthy heavens for relief from their low wages and poor working conditions; it seemed clear that the Teamster high command and the steel carrier bosses—via their respective bargaining agents —would be no help as they wrapped up the final round of talks and established the next three-year contract for the steel hauling indus- try. The crucial bargaining point for Gary was the steel addendum of the 1967 National Master Freight Agreement, and that was not the triumph that the IBT was calling the master contract proposals as a whole.

"All I know is that every three years we get a lot of promises; but none of them are ever kept," one frustrated driver said to me. "The talks are like a baseball game, except we have to ride the bench. When we finally get a chance to go to the plate, they won't put a bat in our hands. We just can't win."

If he had continued with his figure of speech, he might have outlined the opening of the crucial 1967 season this way: Heading the Teamsters' ball club during the negotiations of the steel addendum was Donald Sawochka, secretary-treasurer of Gary Local 142. Crowned czar of his local after the death of his father in 1964, Sawochka had been pitching in relief of Rolland McMaster, former chief hardballer of the Teamsters' iron and steel negotiating team, who was caught throwing spitters and imprisoned in late 1966 for taking payoffs from employers. On the mound for management was George Gregory Mantho, player-manager of the sixty-eight-member National Steel Carriers Association and owner of a Chicago steel hauling outfit. Mantho had once been a slugger for the other side, serving as Detroit Local 299's legal counsel until 1961, when he jumped leagues.

It was April 1967. Jimmy Hoffa, who had opened the negotiations in January, had gone to jail in March. Frank Fitzsimmons had taken over three weeks before the contract expired on April 1.

Testing the acting general president, management took a hard line and pushed negotiations past the expiration date, which caused speculation that the country was heading for its first nationwide Teamsters' strike. Trying to avoid this, Fitzsimmons agreed to a settlement on April 13 which the Chicago Independent Truck Drivers Union considered quite inadequate. Joined by IBT Locals 705 and 710, the Chicago independents demanded more money, and in response the Chicago employers locked them out. Within the first week of the lockout, groups of trucking companies came to terms with the Chicago locals—with wage increases higher than Fitzsimmons had obtained. When the remaining Chicago employers succumbed, an embarrassed Fitzsimmons was forced to renegotiate the contract for the rest of the country in accordance with the terms the Chicago locals had held out for. To many Teamster insiders the impressive display of Chicago strength was a classic case of the tail wagging the dog.

As the largest mail referendum in the union's history went out to the membership, Teamster leaders were confident of approval because the contract could be rejected only if two-thirds of the membership voted against it. The leadership was right, but among the 70 percent who returned ballots an astonishing 25 percent voted to reject the contract.

Although Teamsters throughout the country had their own separate contract sections—depending upon their work and geographic location—their union did not allow them separate ratification of the individual addenda. Each Teamster simply voted ''yes'' or ''no'' on the entire master contract. The same ''yes'' or ''no'' vote also approved or disapproved of the contract's thirty-two addenda. Thus a worker on the loading platform in San Francisco voted for or against not only the section that would govern his wages for three years but for or against the section that covered steel haulers in Gary and over-the-road drivers in New Jersey. Because drivers and warehousemen who hauled or handled freight for trucking companies and used company-owned equipment composed the overwhelming majority of those covered by the NMFA, their approval of the contract nullified any possibility of contract rejection—even if all the truckers affected by the other addenda were to vote 100 percent against the NMFA. If freight drivers and dock loaders were pleased with the contract and voted to ratify, the NMFA was strike-proof. Hoffa's top priority—and that of Fitzsimmons after him—was to take care of the Teamsters who would assure ratification of his contracts.

As in years past, again in 1967 the hardest hit Teamsters were the 30,000 steel haulers, particularly the owner-operators who drove their own trucks. When the negotiations opened in Washington in January, Hoffa's position of twenty-six years was clearly articulated when he told these drivers, numerically only one out of every eighty in the country, "We represent you as a worker and a worker only. Don't come to us asking us to negotiate a profit for your equipment."

Treated as an outcast, the Teamster member/owner-operator was upset. He hadn't been given a square deal since the first Central States Drivers Council agreement in 1939. Although few owner-operators had reputations for storming down the center aisle, chest out, shaking their fists at Hoffa, they were nevertheless the orphans of the trucking industry, living under a set of rules they had no voice in creating.

But many of these owner-operators were of a unique breed; they believed that they were their own bosses—small independent businessmen, not employees—with the power to determine their own destinies. They mortgaged their futures, and those of their families, to be free by investing $30,000 or more in a truck. Unlike homeowners with similar investments and years to pay, these truckers had to complete their payments to banks or loan companies in four or five years at a rate of at least $650 a month. Those who couldn't afford a new truck bought an underpowered used truck and dreamed of parlaying it into a brand-new diesel. Until then they tried to avoid state inspectors and spent most of what little free time they had keeping their rigs in running condition. Overcommitted and underfinanced, the owner-operators were naturally concerned about that next haul and its relation to their next truck payment.

Owner-operators had to keep moving to make ends meet. They broke speed limits, hauled longer than the ten hours a day the government permitted, and sometimes popped pills to stay awake.

Pushing themselves to the brink, some drivers broke under the strain, destroying their family lives or themselves. No statistics are available on the number of drivers who crash into bridges and are killed during the week a truck payment is due.

"Trade that damn white elephant in, and come to work in the factory," your friends say. One answer is, "I'd like to, but hell, I owe more on it than its market value. I'd have to find another dummy, like me, to buy it." Only that isn't usually the whole answer.

Bill Kusley didn't like the conditions of the industry but would give anybody who told him to leave it a "fuck you" scowl as he climbed into his rig to deliver another load of steel. A part-time farmer and son of a United Steel Workers organizer, Kusley was a barely literate "deez" and "doze" person who talked constantly, insufferably about the truckers' revolution.

"If deez sonobitches runnin' ya 'round, we'll strike da mothafuckas. Take his fuckin' tires; shut 'em down."

Truckers were sitting around a bar, swigging beer, listening to the little militant—half their size and not drinking—talking about the 1967 steel addendum. No big thing. Kusley had been talking like that since the 1964 contract was negotiated.

"Dat was a sellout, an' so's dis!"

Sometimes he scared the hell out of the bigger men with his talk of reform.

He had been fired from his company, Yellow Transit Freight System, Inc., in Gary, three times, ostensibly for breaking minor rules but really for being a troublemaker. Each time the union refused to support him and he was eventually reinstated by the courts or the National Labor Relations Board. His wife and four children had their share of obscene, threatening telephone calls in the middle of the night.

In 1964, with thoughts of provoking a national shutdown at all of Yellow Transit's terminals thanks to Hoffa's nationwide bargaining procedure, Kusley had started an "education program" among owner-operators in the company's steel division. His bitterness was aimed not only at Yellow Transit but at the Teamsters Union, which was not enforcing the few favorable provisions of the contract. For instance, according to ICC regulations, an owner-operator can lease his trucks only to carriers with proper permits; he can't go out and solicit business for himself. Sometimes carriers would do "rate cutting"—lowering the price of moving goods to attract more business—but the reduction usually got passed down to the owner-operator. Truckers often found their union reluctant to back them up against this illegal practice. Consequently the employers simply told their drivers, ''Either you take the cut or you lose the business.'' Forced to drive in illegally overloaded rigs, drivers also found little comfort in employers' promises to pay overload fines and bail if the trucker was jailed. ''Either you take the risks or you lose the business.''

''Big fuckin' choices!'' Kusley screamed. ''We call ourselves small businessmen, an' the only damn thing we decide is whether or not to take a damn load. An' if we refuse a bad load, the worst ones are yet to come.''

Although heads nodded when Kusley spoke, he could still muster only a handful of steel haulers to demonstrate for a better contract in 1967. Their demands were simple. They wanted to be paid for the required cumbersome chore of covering their loads with a large tarpaulin wrapped in heavy steel chains. They wanted separate ratification for their steel addendum and recognition of the steel hauling industry as a separate IBT division; they wanted 79 percent of the total hauling costs in lieu of a token rate increase—which would be cut anyway by their employers; and they wanted $15 an hour after the first two hours of waiting at the steel mills to be loaded or unloaded.

The Teamsters' contract proposals had asked for an increase from 72 to 75 percent of the gross revenue and $10 an hour after four hours of waiting time. When the steel haulers learned in late May that the national contract had been ratified by the membership, they were angry when it was discovered that they had received none of their demanded concessions.

Between December 1966 and July 1967, there were at least seven meetings between Kusley and company and/or union officials. Quiet support was brewing among the drivers, who were beginning to recognize that Kusley was fighting for them. Then Kusley stumbled across what was to become his tool to incite his dreamed-of truckers' revolt—an ordinary mimeograph machine. He juiced it up, started cranking the handle, and began to educate the downtrodden trucker. In a month Kusley spent $500 of his own money to flood the streets of Gary with propaganda. Later he got a list of Yellow Transit drivers' addresses and enlisted some friends and relatives who were amateur writers to help him put out a newsletter.

Encouraged by the favorable response, Kusley started going around to other companies to investigate the problems of other owner-operators. Not to his surprise, their complaints were similar to those of the drivers at Yellow Transit. When Kusley completed his tour he asked in his newsletter that Yellow Transit's drivers participate in a letter-writing campaign urging Frank Fitzsimmons to prevent their company from imposing the steel addendum upon them. Fitzsimmons of course refused, but the exercise was enough to spur Kusley to call a one-day wildcat strike in Gary on June 2.

The demonstration was held in front of Local 142 and it had the support of drivers from several companies in the area. It was one of the first overt steel hauler displays of dissidence against the united forces of the steel carriers and the Teamsters Union, and it also produced the first hard core of steel hauling militants. Behind Kusley were Tom Gwilt, Dick Grinell, and John Hack of Gary; and Jim Leavitt, a Yellow Transit steel hauler from Detroit. The most exciting moment of the brief protest was the appearance of two dozen Local 142 business agents with blackjacks dangling from their back pockets. Kusley simply gave the goons the finger and went on walking the picket line.

The June 2 wildcat strike ended with personal assurance from Donald Sawochka, secretary-treasurer of the local, that the steel haulers would have an audience with Fitzsimmons to air their grievances. Before they left, Kusley and the others tried to obtain copies of the steel addendum in its final form. All the rank and file had ever seen were the union's proposals. Kusley was told curtly that they had been fully briefed about the contract at a meeting of the local—before the contract was approved by the membership—and thus had no legitimate reason to see the actual steel addendum.

The meeting with Fitzsimmons never materialized—which further agitated Kusley—but the rebel force did meet in Chicago with Dave Johnson and other union officials who were members of the Central States Drivers Council's grievance committee. Although the drivers' grievances were discussed, none were resolved.

Meanwhile, Johnson and Local 299 were having their own problems in Detroit. McMaster had been paroled from prison in early April and, over the protests of Johnson and other Hoffa supporters, Fitzsimmons had appointed him his administrative assistant and chief executive officer of Local 299. Johnson had agreed that McMaster should have his old job back, but that was before Hoffa appointed Johnson to run the day-to-day affairs of the local. He had not agreed to become the number-three man, behind Fitzsimmons and McMaster. At the same time Fitzsimmons made McMaster the director of organizers, specializing in steel haulers, in the Central Conference of Teamsters. Since Fitzsimmons was well aware of Hoffa's new distrust of Mc-Master, these appointments indicated some conflict between Fitzsimmons and Hoffa already.

McMaster's responsibilities were short-lived; two weeks after he started work the Labor Department ordered him to resign his union posts. Knowing that he would be in violation of his one-year parole and be sent back to jail if he refused, McMaster complied and retreated to his Wixom farm.

With McMaster's official departure from union politics, Johnson was reinstated as the chief executive officer of Local 299. Nevertheless, Fitzsimmons' defiance of Hoffa had planted the seed for a vicious power struggle. McMaster was shoved to the sidelines for only a year; he would be back, and the prelude to his return to power would be felt quite soon by the dissident steel haulers.

When his meetings with Teamster officials proved fruitless, Kusley's mimeograph machine rolled off thousands of fliers during the first week in August. The drive was centered on Yellow Transit and other Gary companies, but the rebels found time to send literature to other steel hauling areas asking drivers to set up picket lines at their home locals on August 21 at 10:00 A.M.:

> The Teamsters have got our equipment nothing to speak of over the years! They won't even enforce their own contract! We have numerous grievances in, and can't get them processed. We have no alternative but to take drastic action, and picket the Teamsters.

Thus the Teamsters, not the carriers, were again the primary object of the protest.

After spending most of the weekend of August 18 parking their flatbeds and making picket signs, Kusley and Gwilt were disappointed when only twenty-six drivers showed up for the protest in front of Local 142. Leavitt, who had returned to Detroit to picket Local 299, had even fewer men supporting him. The rebels' problems were further complicated when John Hack and Dick Grinell, two leaders of the June 2 protest, decided to bolt the movement before the wildcat strike began. Grinell became a business agent for Local 142 soon afterward.

At the Gary union hall news people milled around the em-
barrassingly small number of protesters. Kusley's demands upon the
union were promptly challenged by Sawochka, who came to talk to the
press, not the rebels, and who pointed out that since the Teamsters'
contract had recently been ratified by the membership, the union could
do nothing until the next contract negotiations came up three years
hence. Off camera Sawochka stood near the steel haulers with a mob of
business agents around him and taunted them: "You men can walk
until you wear your legs off, but it won't do you any good."

Tom Gwilt, in desperation and rage, led eight of his pickets to
Gary's U.S. Steel Works plant and established a picket line there,
semiblocking its entrances and exits. Holding picket signs that read
"Teamsters Protest" and "Steel Haulers: Stop and Talk," they
explained the issues and their demands to their colleagues. The mood
of the protest began to change. The drivers returned to their terminals,
parked their rigs, and joined the revolt. The rebel leaders directed the
new onslaught of picketers to cover the other steel mills in the city.

"No drinking, no harassment, and no violence," were the orders
from Kusley, the spokesman for the strike. Within a matter of hours
Gary's steel hauling industry was virtually shut down. Nearly a
hundred striking steel haulers met in an old church hall, usually used
for accordion-and-polka wedding receptions, and chose grievance
committees to present their views to management, company by
company.

The employers—especially those who depended exclusively upon
owner-operators, and many of whom had sweetheart agreements with
the Teamsters—began pressuring the union to get the men back to
work. But union orders did not deter the protesters. The wildcat strike
grew.

On the second day the employers called the police, on grounds that
picketing at the steel mills constituted an illegal secondary boycott.
The sheriff's office began hauling strikers off the picket line and
putting them behind bars. (Later, claiming that their constitutional
rights had been violated, the steel haulers filed an unsuccessful $5
million suit against the Gary steel mills.) The demonstrators were in
jail only a few hours before bail was provided, but they were more
seriously hampered by scab truckers, who viewed the strike as an
opportunity to pick up a few extra bucks.

When the strike appeared to be lost, Jim Leavitt, back in Gary after
the Detroit protest fizzled, telephoned Mike Parkhurst, publisher of

Overdrive, a glossy-paged trucking magazine based in Los Angeles, California. Parkhurst was in Europe, so Leavitt asked to speak with Jim Drinkhall, a writer for the magazine. Drinkhall flew into Chicago and the dissidents met him at the airport.

"I told these guys that they had to make up their minds, but that they had no business being in the Teamsters Union. Instead they should join *Overdrive*-Roadmasters [a trucking organization] or form their own union," Drinkhall says. "When I was talking to them, I was doing it as a reporter. But Parkhurst was out of the country and there was really no way to reach him. And I could sense that this was a pretty important thing that was happening.

"You know, I did something I had no right to do—commit the magazine. But I was trying to put myself in Mike's mind—what would he do?"

Kusley and Leavitt, both members of Roadmasters, nevertheless wanted to reform the Teamsters Union, not leave it. But both knew they needed the support of Parkhurst and his Roadmasters.

A former owner-operator who had hauled furniture and produce for ten years and a million accident-free miles, Parkhurst was well qualified to help the rebels. A native of Philadelphia, the six-foot, brown-haired, blue-eyed former trucker had foreseen the necessity for an organization of owner-operators in 1961, when he founded *Overdrive*.

"I wanted the magazine to be the forum and tool for the association," he explains. "At that time there was only a little newsletter for the drivers which came out of Indiana, gossiping about which trucker was playing around with which truck-stop waitress."

After financing the publication of 2500 copies of *Overdrive*'s first issue, Parkhurst distributed them at selected truck stops around the country. The first edition was only twenty-four pages, sold for a dime, and told its readers what to do when stopped by the cops and where to chow down. But in pursuit of his dream of an association, Parkhurst told truck-stop managers to keep the 10-cent cost of the first issue and report whether there was an interest in the idea. The gamble worked, and Parkhurst printed 10,000 copies of the second issue, which dealt with more substantive matters, including truckers' problems with the ICC and other regulatory agencies.

By 1962, Parkhurst had moved his operations from Philadelphia to Los Angeles, where he was joined by his good friend Jim Drinkhall, who had ridden with Parkhurst as a teenager. An aspiring writer who had attended Villanova and Columbia universities, Drinkhall served as the magazine's bookkeeper while Parkhurst founded the Independent Truckers Association.

Even with no required dues or fees, few names trickled into the *Overdrive*-ITA West Coast offices; clearly there was little interest in an independent organization. To jar the drivers out of their apathy, the colorful publisher went on strike against, of all things, his readers—who, unlike ITA members, were rapidly increasing. To demonstrate the plight of the truckers, he climbed aboard a strong stallion and galloped from Los Angeles to Tucson over a two-month period, protesting archaic speed limits by carrying a sign that read "20th Century Roads—19th Century Law."

By November 1966, *Overdrive* was flourishing but the ITA had still not gotten off the ground. Parkhurst decided to scuttle the association and start a new one. "We had done some good things, but not as much as I'd hoped to accomplish," he says. "And since *Overdrive* had first coined the term, 'trucker'—to upgrade the demeaning connotations of 'truckdriver'—I wanted to call a new organization something that was a notch above trucker, so I started 'Roadmasters.' "

The new *Overdrive*-Roadmasters association was meant to be a liberation movement for truckers. For $36 a year members received an identification card; coupons for tires, truck equipment, and even food valued at much more than the yearly fees; legal aid against employers; and a bold Roadmasters decal for the drivers' cab doors. *Overdrive* and Roadmasters worked to dispel all the negative stereotypes of truckers. The only stereotype Parkhurst wanted to portray was the trucker as the new American cowboy, a tough hombre who was nevertheless a sensitive romantic.

Roadmasters who were also Teamster members were frequently accused of dual unionism by the IBT, but it was no secret that Parkhurst had no use for the Teamsters Union. On the cover of the January 1967 issue of *Overdrive*, Parkhurst proclaimed, "This Is the Year Truckers Stand Up for Their Rights!"

Although the steel haulers' situation in Gary was certainly an opportunity to increase Roadmasters' membership and *Overdrive*'s circulation, Parkhurst was more interested in helping the truckers make their first stand against the union. When Drinkhall was able to get in touch with him, he returned to the United States and immediately dispatched his legal staff to Gary. Bernard A. Berkman, of Cleveland, became the rebels' chief counsel.

On August 30, when the wildcat strike was in its tenth day, *Overdrive* sent a bulletin to truck stops around the country. Titled "Steel Haulers Shut Down in Determined, All-Out Effort to Have Their Rights Recognized," the bulletin stated:

After 30 years of being stepped on, disregarded, disrespected and slowly starved, the steel haulers have taken immediate, effective and all-out action.

The steel haulers in the midwest are shutting down their equipment until their just and long overdue demands are met. THIS HAS NEVER HAPPENED BEFORE IN THE HISTORY OF TRUCKING.

"Shut down the whole damn country!" was the battle cry of the wildcatters as the strike churned into its second week. By then Paul Dietsch and a group of Wisconsin truckers had come to Gary to join the protest, and it had finally caught on in Detroit. Dave Johnson called the strikers a radical minority, "a bunch of crooks out of Chicago" who were exaggerating their support and numbers.

When the strike reached Middletown, Ohio, where the gates of Armco Steel Company were picketed, the revolt was not led by burly steel haulers but by three women, Virginia Bradley, Bernadine Peterstein, and Betty Tillson, whose husbands were in Gary. In northeastern Ohio a Youngstown driver, Mike Boano, led the dissident forces as the wildcat strike spread into the eastern states, which in turn added to the momentum in the Midwest.

With Dietsch and Gwilt in charge of the pickets and Kusley manning the telephone, the protest moved headlong into its third week. Because CB radios were rare in 1967, the strikers had to depend on the telephone and on Kusley's newsletter to reach affected areas in eight states containing nearly 200 Teamster locals. As long as the communications network held up, the strike would continue to move.

In the mills, coils of steel were gathering dust; turnpike revenues were down; and railroad companies were forced to pick up the 50 percent of the nation's steel normally hauled by the striking truckers.

Because the strike was not sanctioned by the Teamsters Union some drivers continued to haul, but even Teamster loyalists began to park their rigs as violence spread around the country. Moving trucks were riddled with bullets, which also endangered other traffic, including that of private motorists. In several cities police were fired upon when escorting scabs, and trucking terminals were bombed. Millions of dollars worth of public and private property was destroyed. A firebomb was thrown into the cab of a Gateway Transportation Company truck in Detroit, badly burning the driver; a scab trucker shot and seriously wounded a protester who blocked the entrance of a toll area in Somerset, Pennsylvania; a rock shoved from a viaduct came through the windshield of a truck on Route 23, near Flint, Michigan, and killed the driver. The National Guard was called out in several states.

"All we've been gettin' is bad publicity 'bout violence that's not our doin'," Kusley said. "It's the damn union goons behind most of it."

In other times Rolland McMaster would probably have been the man assigned to get his "boys" together to break heads and the strike. Now, however, he was legally unable to engage in union business in the United States, although that did not mean he was out of the union business. One of the addresses he maintained while on probation was Teamsters Local 880, in Windsor, Ontario—just across the Detroit River. He also bought and sold real estate, invested $150,000 in a short-term diamond venture, and helped some friends in the trucking business. He accepted an offer from a Michigan specialist in acquisitions and mergers, Harry S. Berman, to locate a common carrier which one of Berman's clients could buy. In return Berman promised McMaster a finder's fee. Consequently McMaster swung a deal whereby Berman's client, U.S. Industries, Inc., would purchase 95 percent of the outstanding stock of Baltimore and Pittsburgh Motor Express, Inc., one of the largest general commodity haulers in the nation. His finder's fee was to be paid on completion of the B & P purchase in late 1968.

While McMaster was making his business deals, Ralph Proctor, a Local 299 business agent and a close friend of McMaster, was recruiting "organizers" from trucking companies in and around Detroit. Volunteers were promised $400 a week plus expenses in exchange for their services. After roughing up a few wildcatters in Pittsburgh, the legbreakers were arrested at the Beaver Valley Truck Stop by state and local police.

One of the now unemployed legbreakers submitted a written statement to a Detroit attorney which indicated that B & P Motor Express was also involved:

When enough members become aware of the corruption of union officials, the taking of "keep the labor peace" money from the companies, the sweetheart contracts and the on-the-side arrangements, the under-the-table arrangements, the behind-the-scenes secret deals, their numbers begin to grow, and this the union cannot tolerate. This is why the leaders and staunchest members of the dissident group, who have done nothing more than express dissent, are beaten, their lives threatened, their cars and homes dynamited.

This is the democratic process under which this union continues to function.

I know because until I finally became aware of this situation I was a part of it.

. . . In 1967, I was sent to Pittsburgh, Pennsylvania, with a squad to break up a strike by dissident teamster steelhaulers. This little venture was financed by the B & P, Baltimore and Pittsburgh Trucking Company, and, in fact, we were flown to Pittsburgh in a private plane owned by B & P Company.

Although B & P executives denied that they were involved in any goon squad activities, federal investigators in Pennsylvania confirm that the company had been brought into the physical end of the struggle by Rolland McMaster. It was no coincidence that when B & P was bombed during the 1967 strike, the IBT quickly stepped up and offered a $25,000 reward for the arrest and conviction of those responsible.

To insiders aware of the situation, it had become quite clear that, probation or not, the granddaddy of stompin', strike-breakin', head-bustin' goons was back in business.

''McMaster showed up at *Overdrive*'s offices in Los Angeles during the strike,'' Jim Drinkhall remembers. ''He sat down in a room with Parkhurst and me, and he was his usual soft-spoken self. And then, all of a sudden, he got himself all worked up, swinging his arms. He said, 'If this happens again, the Teamsters won't take it sitting down. We're going to come out swinging, and a lot of people are going to get hurt.' ''

The strike, however, was still effective, and rumors were circulating that there might be an independent steel haulers' union.

In mid-September a newsletter blown by the fall wind across the barren Pennsylvania Turnpike and found lying on the side of the road read:

This movement began in Gary, Indiana 3 weeks ago and has spread in all directions. Detroit, Chicago, Cleveland, Toledo, Youngstown, Erie, Buffalo,

Canton, Cincinnati, Steubenville, Weirton, Wheeling, Pittsburgh, Harrisburg, Philadelphia and most every city east of the Mississippi River and many of the smaller cities are feeling it's [sic] effects. The movement is enormous. We never had a movement like this before. We may never have another like it again.

The Teamster leadership was still telling the strikers, "Go back to work, and then we'll discuss your problems," but the union leadership was hurting badly. Criticism of Fitzsimmons' handling of the strike—his second major test as acting IBT general president—was common among Teamster loyalists: "This shit wouldn't be going on if Jimmy was still here."

Fitzsimmons repeated the "go back to work and we'll talk" rhetoric on September 20, after he agreed to meet with the steel haulers' protest committee while he was at the Edgewater Beach Hotel, in Chicago. The "back-door" meeting was predictably farcical. Mike Boano's best joke was to plead with Fitzsimmons for a job as a union organizer: "Make me one of your boys, Fitz; I'll show you how to handle steel haulers!" Outside the door was Boano's personal bodyguard, known only as "Big John"—a towering, twitching thug out of the thirties—packing an awesome-looking .357 magnum. Although nothing was accomplished at the meeting, many of the steel haulers saw Fitzsimmons' willingness to talk with the strikers as a sign of desperation.

It looked as if the wildcatters might bring the steel industry, its carriers, and the Teamsters Union to their knees. The home-town boys, Kusley and Gwilt, became folk heroes in Gary—two little guys battling the vicious, fire-breathing, three-headed dragon.

Then, as in a bad dream, the steel haulers' revolt began to crumble under the weight of each participants' self-gratification. Suddenly the noble revolution became the stepping-stone for personal crusades.

Overdrive attorney Bernard Berkman warned the members of the protest committee that they might be "over the crest" and stood to lose both Cleveland and Toledo if the strike lasted much longer. The lawyers, not unlike the Teamsters' leadership, were recommending going back to work while negotiations with the union and the carriers were in progress. Knowing that they had not yet reached the peak of their bargaining power, the protest committee quickly overruled the idea, but similar suggestions from the *Overdrive* lawyers kept coming up at meetings. One such proposal was a "ninety-day cooling-off period"; another was to allow a "trickle" of trucks to return to work as a sign of "good faith" with the Teamsters. In each case Kusley had strong objections. "The hell with you," he shouted. "If anything, we'll go back to our areas an' tighten up!"

When he demanded a vote among the members of the committee, Kusley's position was unanimously supported, but an Ohio delegate, Daryl Duncan, ordered the state's area leaders in Middletown to remove their pickets from Armco Steel. Although the area leaders ignored the order, the split among the leadership was becoming obvious.

Viewed by some as the major stumbling block to a settlement, Kusley's hard line on the issues was increasingly unpopular. Separatists who wanted to use the strike as their reason for leaving the union were afraid that if the Teamsters lost more face they would quietly negotiate a settlement, and with a few extra bucks in their pockets the drivers would become reluctant to leave the union. Thus the strategy of those who wanted to leave the Teamsters was: Put up a good fight and earn the respect of the steel hauling community; prove to the drivers that reform is impossible within the union; and persuade the rank and file, particularly the steel haulers, to split with the Teamsters and create their own labor organization.

"Frankly, I had two different directions that I considered," Mike Parkhurst says. "Number one, I knew that you weren't going to get rid of the Teamsters Union, but I thought there should be reform from within.

"But number two, it was such a big and powerful organization—and corrupt—that there never would be reform from within; and I don't think there ever really will be—unless you really have a union version of *Overdrive* working. It's too easy. People get too lazy; they get too fat, too rich, too content with the status quo. As a result, those Teamster presidents or officers who might have some fire in their veins lose it after a while, especially when they see some of the apathy among their own members. So, I guess, it feeds on itself. It's a terrible situation where one is responsible for the other."

Kusley had probably been unrealistic about the possibility of reforming the Teamsters. His plan of revolt against the union tyrants was based on the assumption that the rank and file was willing to fight the money and resources available to the union, but he was practical about Teamster membership: "What about all the money that's in the Teamsters' pension fund? If you leave the union, you won't see a nickel of it. And that's somethin' to consider if you have a few years of service under your belt and especially if you're gettin' ready to retire.''

Maintaining the hard line, Kusley led the face-to-face negotiations with the Teamsters.

On October 3, in a meeting in Pittsburgh with union negotiators selected by Fitzsimmons, Kusley's complete dedication and also his lack of diplomacy became evident. The steel hauler listed his demands and then passionately attacked union representative Norman Kagel, president of Pittsburgh's Joint Council 40. Outraged, Kagel jumped off his chair and crashed his fist onto the bargaining table. Pointing at Kusley, he screamed, ''Do you want a bloodbath, you motherfucker? Do you? The Teamsters Union will give you blood, by God! We got 10,000 organizers and business agents out there!''

As Kagel stormed out the door, Kusley stood up, turned to the steel haulers, and said, ''Well, you heard Kagel. What do you think? I say if they want war, let's give 'em a fucking war!''

Kusley walked out of the room, leaving the rest of the delegation still in a state of shock. Reporters outside stopped him to ask what had happened, and Kusley issued orders that everything on the road be stopped, ''except wheelbarrows and bicycles,'' until the strikers' demands were met.

It was the climax of the protest. The Teamsters Union hadn't been hit so hard from inside since the Philadelphia rebel group, The Voice, tried to break from the Teamsters and affiliate with the AFL-CIO. But The Voice, recognizing the union's manpower, had chosen to battle the Teamsters through an NLRB-sanctioned election; Kusley had apparently provoked a shooting war.

Acting as the spoiler—perhaps in a heroic sense, perhaps not—to Kusley's ambition of forcing a final clash between the Teamster leadership and the steel haulers, Bernard Berkman called an emergency meeting of selected members of the protest committee in early October—Kusley not among them. The lawyer insisted that Kusley's behavior in front of the television cameras and the press constituted a violation of the Hobbs Act, which prohibits any interference with interstate commerce, and that Kusley had acted recklessly and irresponsibly, using ''Hitlerlike tactics.''

''Listen, I've had it,'' Berkman told several members of the committee. ''Either Kusley goes or I go!''

The steel haulers looked at each other, considered the alternatives, and decided that Kusley had to be removed. Perhaps their decision was also affected by the fact that their two-room-and-cellar headquarters in Pittsburgh had been bombed just after Kusley's interview.

Even Kusley's old supporters—those like Tom Gwilt, who had agreed with the ''chin-on-chin'' philosophy of the wildcat strike—left his camp. Only Jim Leavitt of Detroit remained an advocate of a dramatic showdown with the Teamsters.

During a private meeting of the full protest committee later that week, Berkman told Kusley, ''We have appreciated your courage, Bill. But now it's time for common sense.''

''Who are you kiddin', Berkman?'' Kusley retorted. ''This is the men's strike; lawyers are here to advise. There's too much publicity that we're gonna break with the union. If you wanna draw battle lines, let's first draw 'em there!''

Then the story began to come out among the rebel insiders. Parkhurst and Berkman had fostered the split among the dissidents because they thought a separatist union would seem more feasible to the rank and file in the wake of a lost strike. Paul Dietsch, a Wisconsin steel hauler who helped lead the Gary revolt in the early days of the protest, and William J. Hill, a rugged and articulate owner-operator who was calling the shots in the East, had cooperated with the Roadmasters by quietly organizing a third faction in the protest committee.

''For us to announce at that point that we wanted to leave the union and form our own would have been heresy to many of our followers who still clung to some kind of belief in the Teamsters,'' Dietsch explains. ''We fully intended to let the system take its course—with us working inside it—and when it finally beat us, then we could turn to the owner-operators, particularly the steel haulers, and say, 'There, we tried it their way and it still didn't work. Now what?' ''

But Parkhurst, when he discovered the third force's intentions, had other ideas. ''Since we had the only association going—Roadmasters—and if they wanted to spin off a group which was basically going to accomplish the same thing, I thought that we could create 'Steelmasters' within the *Overdrive*-Roadmasters organization.''

But differences between the two separatist groups would have to be worked out later. Now that Kusley's support had deteriorated, there was a wildcat strike to settle.

While the dissidents' internal troubles were kept from the public, Governor Raymond P. Shafer of Pennsylvania called a governors' conference in Pittsburgh to discuss the economic chaos the strike was causing. The eight governors set up a committee of labor department heads from each state, with William Hart, Pennsylvania secretary of labor and a former official in the United Steel Workers, as its chairman. With a "nonparticipatory" representative of the Teamsters Union sitting on the committee, Hart announced that the rebels could stay out "until hell freezes over." A few days later Hart's summer home was bombed. No one was injured.

Negotiations among the protest committee, the Teamsters' negotiating committee, and a carriers' group representing eighty-two companies seemed likely to bring a quick settlement. Berkman's legal advice to the committee was that provisions of the National Master Freight Agreement, ratified by the rank and file in May, could not be renegotiated because the union could be accused of price-fixing.

As a result the steel haulers received none of their demands, nothing more than what had been negotiated in the spring by men such as Sawochka and Mantho. The only concession was a promise from the Teamsters and management that there would be no reprisals against the strike leaders.

Still the mouthpiece for the dissidents, but reading only what he was told to read, Kusley expressed his frustration privately, saying, "Next week this thing will be cold coffee. When we go back to work, they're gonna start fuckin' us all over again." And because in the name of solidarity he announced the results of the negotiations—which he opposed from start to finish, still wanting to battle it out with the union—he received the blame for them.

Within two months after the strike ended Kusley was fired from his job at Yellow Transit for alleged tardiness. When he went to his union for help he learned that he had also been expelled from Local 142. He later filed charges with the NLRB against the company, but the two-year legal struggle yielded only a settlement of $23,000 and no employment. During this time Kusley lost his $50,000 truck and his home in East Gary.

"I'm not sorry for anything that happened in 1967," Kusley reflected long afterward. "I only regret the bad rap I got for the settlement from the guys I'd worked with and fought beside. That hurt more than anything . . .

"It would be kinda hard for me to figure out whether we could've licked the Teamsters in an all-out war. But ya just can't underestimate a fellow who hauls steel; he's a pretty tough cookie. The problem was makin' him realize that the union is more afraid of him than he is of the union. I think we could've whipped the union in a fight if we had just showed some resistance. But there were some guys in our movement who just wanted to break from the union—and the failure of the 1967 protest gave them that chance.''[1]

Several days after the wildcat strike was settled the dissidents' leadership met in Cleveland to form the Steel Haulers Committee. Berkman took charge of its activities from the outset, although it was decided there would be no chairman. Suspicious of Parkhurst's domination, through Berkman, Paul Dietsch and Bill Hill led a majority of the committee to another meeting in Pittsburgh on November 5, and on that day the small group formed the Fraternal Association of Steel Haulers. FASH's purpose was to promote a spirit of cooperation among steel haulers; to exchange information about conditions in the industry; and to advise its members of their rights as individuals, union members, and businessmen. Although these were the stated reasons for FASH's existence, its underlying function, according to Paul Dietsch, was to ''free the steel haulers from the Teamsters and create a new union.'' But FASH had to move slowly and convince some of its own members that this was the right course to take.

Parkhurst, however, yielded to FASH and scrapped his idea of forming Steelmasters. He also, through *Overdrive*-Roadmasters, absorbed the $50,000 worth of legal bills for the protest. ''I wanted FASH to work, and all of us remained good friends. I continued to give them money, good press in *Overdrive*, and they even kept Berkman as their attorney.''

Forty-one-year-old Bill Hill was elected chairman of FASH. An imposing figure at six-foot-three, 230 pounds, mustachioed and with black, slicked-back hair, Hill had a powerful voice and a bearing that could intimidate an adversary if his size did not.

After four years in the Coast Guard, Hill had returned to his home on Pittsburgh's North Side and taken a series of jobs—gravedigger; bread, cement, and dump truck driver—all of which he hated. In 1958 he bought his first steel hauling rig, and within nine years he had earned four rigs and hired three other truckers. His small business operated east to Boston and as far west as New Mexico.

In late August 1967, while waiting fourteen hours to be unloaded in a Buffalo steel mill, Hill learned about the wildcat strike in Gary from other long-haul drivers who had just pulled in from there.

"I knew that those of us who drove our own trucks had problems with the government, the union, management, and everyone else," he says with a half-smile. "Christ, we had so many problems that it's amazing we survived at all. But the tough part is what happens to your family—the impact all these problems has on them. I'm one of the lucky ones. I have a great wife whom I care for very much, and she's been able to understand; and we were able to cope with that lousy routine.

"Don't get me wrong, I loved being an owner-operator for all the reasons any owner-operator would give you: the freedom, the pride of ownership, the self-reliance, and all of that. But there was something about that day in Buffalo when we got the word about the protest in Gary. I mean, we were sitting there, waiting to get our trucks unloaded—fourteen hours! And I know a lot of drivers who've spent twenty-six, thirty, even more hours detention time. Figure that out in weeks, months, and years. That's thousands of hours of wasted time that we weren't getting paid for. And Jimmy Hoffa, the president of our union, supported this system. You just come to a point where you have to say, 'Stop!' And that day for me came in Buffalo."

After deadheading back to Pittsburgh, Hill attended a protest meeting of several hundred steel haulers in nearby Glenville. A fight between two drivers led to a free-for-all, and like John Wayne in a western saloon, Hill got in his licks, handling two and three men at a time. Then, like a skilled diplomat, he climbed on a table above the fray.

"Listen to me, motherfuckers! Cut this shit out! We got business to discuss!"

"Who the fuck are you, pal?" shouted one driver from the floor.

"Step up on this table, asshole, and I'll show you who I am!"

Hill's intricate negotiations completed, the fighting ceased. Later he was selected as one of the leaders of the wildcat strike in Pennsylvania.

When negotiations were held in Pittsburgh, the focus of the strike shifted there, and Hill's role became more prominent. It was principally Hill, working with Parkhurst, who led the separatist forces that toppled Kusley as the leader of the protest. "I remember when I first saw Bill Kusley. Everyone was talking. 'Hey, did ya hear, Kusley's comin' to town!' Man, I wanted to see this guy who was raising all this hell in Gary.

"Anyway, he came to this meeting we had in somebody's basement, and I've never seen so many guns and pistols in my life. Somebody even had a machine gun. Well, I saw this little guy walk in, and I couldn't believe it when someone told me that he was Kusley.

"He was a fighter, sure. But he lost his perspective on the strike. He felt that the union could be reformed by working inside the union. A lot of us didn't believe it and wanted out. And because more of us didn't think he was right, we got rid of him."

Soon after he became chairman of FASH, Hill sold all his trucks and devoted full time to the organization, taking a considerable cut in pay.

After the strike the Teamsters agreed to meet with the rebel representatives to discuss a variety of grievances from steel haulers around the country. Fitzsimmons refused to meet with the group himself but selected a committee to deal with the complaints. The FASH leaders were merely going through the motions until they could form their own collective bargaining unit and split from the Teamsters. They just couldn't take the talks too seriously. When they saw Sawochka and Kagel sit down at the bargaining table across from them, they knew that the union wasn't taking the negotiations too seriously either.

As expected, the talks between the union and FASH broke down after two meetings.

Learning lessons from the 1967 wildcat strike was no easy chore, but the shutdown's remaining leaders agreed that there were two key points. First, the National Master Freight Agreement and its steel addendum affected nearly everyone who hauled for the industry. Since steel haulers were all in the same boat—with very few separate local contracts to confuse their common concerns—a national united front was essential. Second, neither the government nor the carriers was the front-line enemy. Rather—as the wildcat strike showed—their unyielding, unscrupulous opponent was the Teamsters Union, which had both the money and the muscle to lobby in Washington and to enforce contracts negotiated with management. The union rarely did either for the steel haulers and owner-operators.

Although the wildcat strike was a failure in the short run, it inspired many truckers to recognize the common enemy and to try to break from its ranks or beat it from within. But everyone knew it would be an uphill battle all the way.

11 Rebellion in Detroit

Although few steel haulers or union dissidents aligned themselves with the Black Panthers or the antiwar activists, a good case could be made that their directors of propaganda all went to the same school. For instance, one piece of Teamster reform literature read:

> The time has come for all brothers and sisters in the Teamsters Union to unite and stand up for their rights. Working together, we can demand good contracts and enforcement of those contracts. We are the sleeping giant . . .

Depending upon the issues of the day and the targets of the members' scorn, rebel movements among general and special commodities haulers and handlers usually came and went with the predictability of solar eclipses. The Motor Truck Steel Haulers Association of the late 1940s, in Michigan, Ohio, and Pennsylvania, made few dents in Hoffa's long-time position on the status of owner-operators. Later, such groups as the Steel Haulers Organization of Cleveland existed primarily to protest government regulations which they claimed impeded their membership's ability to make a living. Mike Parkhurst's ITA and Roadmasters were service-oriented groups, offering information and discounts to owner-operators. But when *Overdrive*-Roadmasters got involved in direct action politics in the 1967 wildcat strike, it became a natural ally of FASH, which grew directly out of the strike.

Some drivers think the 1967 revolt would never have occurred had Hoffa not been in jail. In fact, Bill Kusley, the mastermind of the protest, had planned the rebellion since 1964—after Hoffa negotiated the first National Master Freight Agreement. Although there were advantages in dealing with Fitzsimmons, who was much less pugnacious than Hoffa, the rebels knew that Fitzsimmons would use the same weapons against them that Hoffa would have used.

Hoffa had been inept when big Dominic Abata formed the Democratic Union Organizing Committee in Chicago's Local 777 in 1959 and organized a full-scale cabdrivers' rebellion in 1961. And Hoffa was equally powerless in Cincinnati when honest joint council president James Luken marched out of the IBT with Local 98 in tow, thumbing his nose at the Teamster boss.

The Voice, the legendary reform group of Philadelphia's Local 107, had come within a handful of votes of taking the entire local out of the Teamsters, and in the end Hoffa had to buy support with promises to raise pension benefits.

Even in Detroit, after the first year of hearings by the Senate Rackets Committee, Hoffa so feared a rank-and-file uprising in his own back yard that he took $58,000 from the union treasury and bought everyone in the local a Teamsters' jacket. That was more than any other candidate had ever given the membership, so Hoffa easily bought that election too.

Problems with the union, with employers, and with government regulation of some matters and inaction on others were monumental for the Teamster rank and file. Confronting these obstacles without large sums of independent money caused most reform groups to fade or disband between crises. Sometimes the old faces returned, but age, fatigue, and union reprisals usually took their toll. The next crop of rebel leaders was likely to be those who had recently been disappointed with the handling of their personal problems. In most cases joining a dissident movement grew out of desperation or desire for revenge rather than a personal commitment against the union's general policies and practices. Some took jobs with the union after a stint in the rebel army; some of these were told to infiltrate and spy. But most rank-and-file Teamsters simply weighed the possible loss of job or even life after joining a rebel organization, shrugged, and did nothing.

A major problem for each wave of dissidents was the lack of continuity. There was no way to learn from the mistakes and pitfalls of earlier rebel ventures. Group after group, with different names and acronyms, searched for their own unique identities, throwing away yesterday's rule book and writing their own. Rebels like Abata, Hill,

Kusley, Luken, Parkhurst, and the members of The Voice were the exceptions, not the rule.

In Detroit, the home of Hoffa and Fitzsimmons, opposition was unheard of until quiet Melvin Angel started protesting, and no one would have paid attention to Angel if Hoffa hadn't beaten him up.

In the early 1960s the Detroit press was filled with stories about all the beatings Angel had taken and the fact that he had both lost his job and been blackballed from the union—all because he dared to defy Jimmy Hoffa, who had completely lost his cool.

In late 1962, while appearing before Joint Council 43 with a charge that Hoffa had abused his constitutional authority, Angel was standing outside the hearing room during a recess and overheard a reporter ask Hoffa a question.

Pointing to Angel across the hall, Hoffa snapped, ''You'll have to ask him. Why, that guy has been offered job after job . . . ''

''That's a damn lie!'' Angel shouted.

Whirling around with a hard stare, clenching his fists and ready to brawl, Hoffa yelled back, ''Brother, don't you start that lyin' stuff with me, or you're in trouble.''[1]

Crazy Mel Angel walked up to Hoffa and went nose-to-nose with him. The spectators watched Hoffa. But to everyone's surprise, Hoffa just walked away. Maybe he'd learned his lesson from past experience. Lucky Mel Angel. Crazy Mel Angel. The Angel with the brass balls.

Because of Angel's dismissal from the union, he wasn't permitted to run for president of Local 299. When he appealed to the executive board for reconsideration, Angel was ruled off the ballot by Hoffa, the president of the local; appealing to Joint Council 43, also headed by Hoffa, Angel was again refused. Angel proceeded to petition the Michigan Conference of Teamsters, the Central States Drivers Council, the Central Conference of Teamsters, and the international's general exectuive board.

''No matter where I went, Hoffa was president.''

Angel threw his support to another car hauler, Ira D. Cooke, Jr., hoping to engineer some sort of upset.

Ira Cooke was a two-fisted, hard drinking hillbilly who could quote long passages from the Bible. Never accused of being an intellectual, Cooke was easy pickings for Hoffa, who decided he'd have some fun by challenging Cooke to a debate at Cobo Hall. Thinking that no one would take the debate seriously enough to show up, both contestants were awed when three thousand rank-and-file Teamsters filed into the large hall and waited to be entertained.

"Ira started out all right," an anti-Hoffa spectator remembers, "but then Hoffa began this long oratory about a piece of labor legislation called the Martin Bill. Well, after Hoffa got finished with a pretty impressive presentation, he turned to Cooke and asked what he thought about the bill.

"Ira was pretty embarrassed and just kind of shuffled around on the stage. So Hoffa accused him of not knowing what it was. When Ira still didn't say anything, Hoffa really started rubbing it in and said that Cooke didn't know how to spell 'Martin.' Everyone in the place was cracking up, even us guys who wanted Ira to look good.

"But then Ira pulls a pack of matches out of his pocket that says, 'Martin's Gas Station.'

" 'Ah kin too spell it, Jimmy: M-A-R-T-I-N.'

"Hoffa was right. If Ira hadn't had that book of matches, he'd never have been able to spell it."

As three thousand Teamsters held their sides with laughter, Cooke remarked, "Now, I know what Dan'l felt like when he was thrown to the lions."

Although everyone had a great time and elected Hoffa by ten to one, it was the last time the Detroit rebels were laughed at. From that point on, everything the dissidents did and wanted to do was deadly serious.

The man who turned the rebel force around in Detroit was a thirty-one-year-old trade unionist, sharp and articulate: Larry McHenry, a native of West Virginia. A former film hauler for Theater Trucking Services, owned and operated by the Fitzsimmons family, McHenry became a rebel after losing his job with the company. Taunted by Hoffa in those early days when he attended union meetings with a borrowed pair of shoes but plenty to say, McHenry was told more than once by Hoffa to "go home and take a bath."

"At first," McHenry says, "I was just another guy, standing on a soapbox waving a flag. But I was a truckdriver and I paid union dues. So I was the third party of a contract, and I worked under the provisions of that contract. And I obeyed the rules; so I thought everyone else should."

When McHenry started speaking out at union meetings, most of those in attendance placed him in the Cooke-Angel category, stupid or crazy. But McHenry was neither, and he knew how to take good advice.

"If you're gonna lock horns with me, Larry," Hoffa once told him, "you better start educating yourself."

McHenry got a copy of the Landrum-Griffin Act and literally

memorized it. With little formal education, McHenry began using the labor reform law as a foundation, frequently citing specific portions and challenging the union's leadership on that basis.

Before the local elections in 1962, McHenry tried to talk a militant steward from a nearby trucking barn, Merchants Forwarding Company, into running for trustee. Andy Provenzino had already had several run-ins with Hoffa and had a reputation as a sincere union man who was willing to attack the president publicly in union meetings.

Hoffa once dragged Provenzino into his office after a meeting and told him, ''Look, I've got all the problems I can handle in Washington and everywhere else right now. Get off my back, will you? I'll take care of your problems. I know these officers aren't always doing their jobs. Give me a little time—a year.'' Provenzino reciprocated Hoffa's respect, telling friends, ''One thing about Jimmy, he knew how to treat you like a man, especially if you didn't let him bully you.''

So Provenzino decided not to run for trustee against the Hoffa slate and gave Hoffa the year to make his changes. Provenzino waited. Nothing.

Finally, in 1964, when Hoffa had been convicted in Chattanooga and was on trial in Chicago, Provenzino joined McHenry to found the Teamsters Betterment League. Their issues were the usual ones: the need for better hospitalization, grievance procedure reform, election of business agents and stewards, more pay and job security, better working conditions, union democracy, a credit union, social and recreational programs, and generally a change from the ''gangster image'' of the union.

The following year Provenzino, then president of TBL, and Charles Collins, another dissident, ran for Local 299 secretary-treasurer and trustee, respectively. A month before the election, Rolland Mc-Master—then secretary-treasurer but ordered by Hoffa to withdraw from the race in favor of Dave Johnson—sent a squad into TBL's headquarters, a rented storeroom, ''to smash this hall and inflict mayhem on any TBL member who tried to stop us,'' according to a signed statement from one of his men. The squad broke up a TBL meeting by fighting, throwing bottles, and kicking in the windows.

Although Provenzino and Collins were soundly defeated by the Hoffa slate, they didn't give up. Nor did McHenry, who was ineligible to run for office in 1965 because he had lost his job. The rebels had plans for the future.

Having by now accused McHenry of being an *agent provocateur* for the AFL-CIO and Robert Kennedy, Hoffa blamed him for the new round of dissent in Local 299. "If you keep fucking with me," he told McHenry, "I'll have you standing on the corner, starving."

"I'd be willing to sell apples, Jimmy, just so I could sell them to Teamster members who would listen to what I had to say about you."

But Hoffa never put McHenry on the corner, and he was in jail in 1968, when the rebels wound up for a second assault on Local 299's leadership. Hoffa would be running for reelection from prison.

In April 1968, McMaster's probation period ended, and he was summoned to Washington along with Johnson and the Local 299 executive board. During the meeting Johnson says Fitzsimmons told him, "I'm going to put Mac in charge of the local union. He will have nothing to do with your affairs as secretary-treasurer. We got to put Mac back to work somewhere."

"Well, I offered him a job as a business agent," Johnson responded.

"This is the way it will be. Mac will run the local."

"Okay, sure, Fitz. But don't let him interfere with my job; tell him to stay out of my problems."

The change in command did not go unnoticed by the Teamsters Betterment League, but most of the membership simply wrote off the switch from Johnson to McMaster as a theatrical technique Fitzsimmons was using to show that he was his own man and not just Hoffa's puppet.

Reinforcing the members' belief that Fitzsimmons, although showing independence, remained a strong Hoffa man was his repeated statement at union meetings: "If Jimmy walked in here right now, I'd say, 'Here's the keys, Jimmy! They're waiting for you when you get back.'"

Crude in its organization and approach, TBL wasn't in shape to challenge Fitzsimmons, but with McMaster, a convicted labor extortionist, back in power, their chief issue against the union had been handed to them. Fitzsimmons was happy that he had his top aide back home again and praised him in the May edition of the *299 News*:

> Brother McMaster is no stranger to Local 299 members. His work on behalf of this union and its members over nearly 30 years is well documented. Because of his experience and dedication to service, your local union executive board turned to him to fill this need in your local union. We wish Brother McMaster the best of success in this challenging position.

Soon after Fitzsimmons appointed McMaster, a little poem, written by an anonymous lyricist and sung to the tune of ''McNamara's Band,'' circulated in Detroit:

> Oh, my name is Frank Fitzsimmons,
> And I'm the leader of this band;
> 299's my local,
> The most corrupt one in the land.
> We steal from drivers and warehousemen,
> We laugh and have a ball;
> And to make it even better,
> We do it in their union hall.

With the Fitzsimmons-McMaster issue well defined, the rebel leaders had to plot their strategy to exploit it in the best possible way.

No two men were ever more different in the way they lived and the way they carried their causes than Provenzino and McHenry. Well-groomed Provenzino was happy being a truckdriver, drinking and brawling with the boys. The father of seven, Provenzino was a big brother to anyone who fought for what he believed, especially if he believed in Teamster reform. He was a natural leader, perhaps the only person in Detroit who could have held the dissidents together. And he would never instruct someone to do something he wouldn't do himself.

Soon after TBL was formed, Provenzino was struck and injured by a hit-and-run driver who was never caught. He knew then that the game he was playing was for keeps. He liked to tell the rebels a story about when he was a kid in the old neighborhood. There was a bully on the block who was notorious for telling the youngest boy in their gang to go get the boy's sister for him. Like the other kids in the neighborhood, both the little boy and his sister were afraid of the bully. When the sister appeared the bully would sexually abuse her. Provenzino was afraid of the bully too, but one day, when he told the little boy to get his sister, Provenzino told the bully to leave the kid alone.

''I can whip you,'' said the bully.

''You haven't done it.''

''I can whip you . . . ''

''No, you can't.''

The bully walked away from Provenzino and never bothered the little boy or his sister again.

Provenzino used the little story effectively with his rebels, portraying the Teamsters Union in the role of the bully and the rebels as young

Provenzino. "They haven't licked us, because they can't. We're the rank and file; and they're more afraid of us than we are of them."

After many of the rebels, including Provenzino, lost their jobs because of their activities, they saw themselves with nothing else to lose but their lives.

"You never overtax any one person," Provenzino told his supporters. "The ones who are stronger or who have a little more have to make up for the shortcomings of the others. Everyone makes their contribution. And that's the way we operate."

"Andy was a man of enormous stature," says a dissident leader from Ohio. "McHenry wasn't in the same category as Provenzino."

McHenry, though a family man with eleven children, was an absolute loner, incapable of leading any number greater than one—himself. And at times people wondered whether he could handle that. Complex, cunning, sometimes cruel, he admits that he is a "stubborn Irishman" who allows few people to get close to him. McHenry's bitter passion was revenge against anyone who crossed him, say several of his associates.

"I've been playing with a short deck all my life," he says, scowling. "I'm not concerned about what's said about me. I got over that kind of bullshit years ago. Hoffa taught me that lesson: to get a thick skin in this business."

His suspicious nature cost him much of the support he needed in Local 299, but he was respected for his sincerity and his willingness to defy Hoffa and the Teamsters when doing so was far from fashionable.

McHenry thought the way to reform was by filing lawsuits and challenging union officials one-on-one over constitutional matters at union meetings. "If we were going to run people for office, I told them to go after the weak spots, those that were more vulnerable than others. I didn't want to go slate against slate. That was Andy's way of doing things."

Five foot seven and a trim 170 pounds, McHenry could whip the daylights out of a man twice his size. His broken-knuckled, stubby-fingered hands had fought many battles, probably for many reasons. He was a fierce debater, extremely intelligent but hot-tempered. His tone and disposition repelled many who wanted to like him.

Somehow, though, he was a survivor. As rebels came and went, McHenry was still standing, battling away. Some felt the reason for his survival was an unknown connection in Local 299. Some rebels thought he had an "open sesame" touch with someone at the union hall.

Richard Fitzsimmons, one of Frank's sons and a business agent in Local 299 since 1958, says that he and McHenry were friends from the early 1950s, when they used to drive together for Theater Trucking, run by the Fitzsimmons family.

Frank Fitzsimmons' old friend, Rolland McMaster, was able to swing a job for McHenry at Transamerican Freight Lines while he was a leader of the rebel force, hoping that McHenry would back off him.

"I don't try to put a halo around McMaster's head," McHenry says. "But I'll say one thing about him—and we've had a lot of disagreements—he's never bullshitted me once. He might have said some things I didn't want to hear and told me the way things were going to be. But he didn't bullshit me, telling me one thing then stabbing me in the back, like Hoffa did."

During the time that Hoffa was accusing McMaster of feeding information to the government, McHenry was in fact a regular visitor to Detroit's federal building. He was "an overt complainer," says Tom McKeon, who was a special Justice Department attorney under Robert Kennedy in Detroit. "He came into the bureau office and made allegations of improprieties against Hoffa, both unethical and illegal. There was nothing anonymous about it; he never tried to conceal anything. But he was a regular, like a turnstile. Within any given year he was in at least a couple of dozen times."

One of Hoffa's close confidants explains that Hoffa suspected that his enemies inside the local were using McHenry as their go-between with the government. Hoffa called him "a goddamn stool pigeon."

"Sure," McHenry comments. "Hoffa called me all those things, but I wasn't a middleman for anybody. If I had a complaint about the way Hoffa was running things, I went to the government. That's what it's there for."

In 1968, McMaster, the new leader of Local 299, was TBL's greatest challenge. What they thought of him is summed up in a thoughtful character sketch by one of the dissidents: "McMaster is absolutely aware of what's happening around him. He might not be in absolute control, but he stays alert. Normally, his control is casual; he is not normally abrupt or candid; maybe it's his nature. Although he can be goaded into losing his temper, he is not afraid of God, man, or beast and that makes him dangerous. But he'd be even more dangerous if he could control his temper like Hoffa, who was smarter than McMaster. McMaster knew it and didn't like it. Everyone knows that

McMaster is capable of having me or anybody else killed or even doing it himself. He is definitely a man who watches out for and can take care of himself.''

Not long after McMaster took control of the local, the dissidents changed their group's name to Unity Committee 299. Provenzino announced their intention of running a full slate of candidates in the December 1968 election; against McHenry's wishes, every office was to be challenged. The platform was primarily anti-McMaster:

> Was it a wise choice that our Vice President Frank Fitzsimmons made by appointing Rolland McMaster (with the approval of the 299 executive board) as Administrative Assistant to the Vice President of Local 299, or did he cram it down our throat with the members can go to hell attitude?
>   Look at the record.

The specifics of McMaster's conviction as a labor extortionist were spelled out on the fliers.

Passing out literature during a meeting of steel haulers at the union hall, McHenry and Provenzino were ordered by McMaster, who was chairing the meeting, to leave. The dissidents refused, and McMaster had three business agents remove them. Provenzino and McHenry filed charges with the Department of Justice which accused McMaster and the three business agents of ''violence.'' The charges were later dismissed, but it was a rap that McMaster, recently off probation, didn't need.

A month before the election, the Unity Committee distributed another newsletter:

> The part-time Vice President Frank Fitzsimmons made his appearance at the local cartage meeting on October 9, 1968. We would like to ask why? Was it because he wanted to be with the membership of 299? Was it because he had to be here to hold McMasters [sic] hand? Was it to see with his own eyes the sorry state our local is in under the leadership of Rolland McMasters and his stooges? . . . Why have you made Dave Johnson a puppet to McMasters? . . . If you don't feel Dave is qualified, why did you dump McMaster and run Dave for secretary-treasurer in 1965? . . . Did Hoffa endorse the executive board decision to make McMasters the Administrative Assistant to Fitzsimmons?

The dissidents were asking serious questions whose answers were a closely guarded secret.

McMaster turned to Fitzsimmons for more authority in the local—which meant control over the local's money. Fitzsimmons called a meeting at the Pontchartrain Hotel to discuss the situation with McMaster and Johnson; Richard Fitzsimmons was also at the meeting.

"I can't run that damn local as long as Dave has got hold of the purse strings, and he won't give me any money. I can't do a goddamn thing," McMaster shouted. "Get him outta here, Fitz!"

"Dave, why don't you resign?" Fitzsimmons asked.

"You go to hell, both of you!" Johnson retorted. "I'm not going to resign; why should I resign?"

Fitzsimmons repeated his demands for Johnson's resignation, even offering him a job in Washington as the IBT's safety inspector.

"Nope. I don't want to go to Washington. I'll stay right where I'm at. I'll stay in Detroit."

Nevertheless, Johnson's powers were greatly curtailed as McMaster took most of the financial power in the local. Johnson became in effect his bookkeeper.

With the election near, Jimmy Hoffa was campaigning from prison for reelection. Provenzino was put at the top of the Unity slate. Through an alliance with the dissident car haulers group in Detroit, the Mutual Automobile Transporters Educational Society, its president and vice president were running on UC's slate for trustee and vice president. McMaster's stranglehold over Detroit's 2000 steel haulers prevented them from getting anyone on the slate, even though Jim Leavitt was an active member of the Unity Committee. Leavitt, like Provenzino, had been fired for his politics after the 1967 revolt; unlike Provenzino, Leavitt had stopped paying his union dues.

UC handbills were passed out all over Detroit. One of the activists, Bernard Jakubus, was distributing literature in front of Local 299 when he was savagely attacked and stomped by Michael Bane, the son of Joseph Bane, president of Local 614 in Pontiac. Magazines and newspapers around the country carried a picture of Bane kicking the defenseless Jakubus, who was lying on the ground still clutching his handbills. Local authorities charged Bane with simple assault; the Unity Committee filed complaints with the Justice Department and Bane was arrested under the Landrum-Griffin Act for "impeding free and open elections." The "stomping of Jake," symbolizing the

Teamsters' suppression of dissent, moved many union members to become involved in reform. One of these men was Don Clemmenson, a quiet but articulate steel hauler.

Clemmenson, who had been hauling steel since 1948, was so distressed by the beating that he felt he must take action. "I couldn't call myself a man if I didn't." A reformed alcoholic and born-again Christian, Clemmenson, twice married and divorced, with a couple of kids, remembers how his fellow truckers once came to his aid when he needed them. About to be fired from a job, he was called for a company hearing. When everything looked hopeless, in stormed the entire night shift, and because of the strong showing for him, Clemmenson was reinstated.

Clemmenson decided after Jakubus' beating that he was going to vote against Jimmy Hoffa for the first time, a very courageous step for a Detroit Teamster to take. "It was like voting against Robin Hood, the guy who got us good salaries from management."

Clemmenson remembers the day well. "I got rid of my truck and went down to the hall to vote. I drove around the hall four times, telling myself that every parking space I saw wasn't big enough. The fact of the matter was that I was scared to death. I was there, and I was going to do it. Finally, I pulled my car in a space and just sat there. I tried to get out of the car, and my legs went out from beneath me. Frankly, I was so frightened that my legs wouldn't hold me up, and I knew it wasn't just my imagination. Fear does funny things to a person."

Dragging himself into the Local 299 hall, looking around hoping no one would see him, Clemmenson walked up to a long folding table with a dark-haired woman sitting behind it, handling both registration and the ballots. "As soon as she looked at me, I knew that she knew I wasn't going to vote for Hoffa. In this quiet panic I was trying to deal with, I expected her to push a button or something, and then twenty goons would bust through a door, and carry me away."

He was cold and shaking, but he glanced over at a driver he recognized from Youngstown Cartage who had also come to vote. He was just as scared as Clemmenson, and they drew some strength from each other.

Clemmenson walked slowly into the private booth, and "while I was standing there, I kept wondering if I was doing the right thing voting against Jimmy Hoffa. But it was at that point that I realized that we had all been conditioned to think just like that. We'd been taught that being anti-Jimmy was being anti-manhood. So I caught myself and voted for Andy Provenzino.

"When I left the booth and started to put my vote in the ballot box, a big, fat, cigar-smoking guy had appeared and was just standing there. But I couldn't look at him, even though I knew that he was looking at me."

Clemmenson left the hall and walked up to one of the dissidents passing out campaign literature in the street to tell him that he wanted to get involved. Clemmenson was taken to Provenzino, who was also passing out fliers.

"I want to get involved," Clemmenson said again.

"Welcome, motherfucker!" Provenzino said, laughing. "I hope the hell you know what you're getting involved in!"

Since Hoffa was running for president from prison; and Fitzsimmons was an absentee acting president running for reelection as vice president; and McMaster, an ex-convict, was running the local as an unelected official, the rebels seemed to have pretty good odds. But the Unity slate was defeated five to one.

Conceding the presence of irregularities in the election and in the subsequent ballot counting, the Labor Department reported that the union's violations "would not have affected the outcome of the election." Power failures, for instance, had occurred while the ballots were being counted. Perhaps the investigators were right: union old-timers may have thought Provenzino and his crew honest but not necessarily capable of running the local. But it was also true that of the twenty-three people responsible for supervising the election, only two were selected by the rebels. Senator Robert Griffin of Michigan criticized the Labor Department for not providing impartial supervision.

Badly beaten, the dissidents regrouped and assaulted McMaster on a new front. A 637-acre piece of land south of Ann Arbor, fifty miles west of Detroit, had been bought for use as a Local 299 recreation area. Stating that the property cost $800,000, McMaster received approval for the purchase at a membership meeting. The dissidents, however, got hold of the deed to the area—Saline Valley Farms—and learned that it had been bought before the ratification. At that time the land was appraised at only $483,788, leaving a difference of $316,212 from the purchase price. In addition, the rebels learned that McMaster was going to let a farmer who lived on the land continue using 350 acres of the property, leaving less than 300 for the recreation area.

In promoting the project, McMaster wrote to the membership, "Our members can't afford a swimming pool, tennis courts, a golf club and they are even finding it difficult to find places to take their families in the parks. It is our obligation to our members to provide such facilities and we can do it at minimal cost as a union organization."

What was not included among the photographs of beauty queens on a sunny beach was the fact that the area—literally a swamp—would cost the members a dues increase of $1.50 a month and an additional 50 cents a month for "various other administrative expenses."

Local 299 went all out for the consecration of the recreation area in mid-1969. Bowing politely and shuffling his feet in humility, McMaster apologized to the large turnout because the area was "still in the rough." Then he yielded to guest speaker Frank Fitzsimmons, who called the project "another milestone in the history of the local union. . . . One of the crises of the cities is that parks and recreation areas are so limited and expensive that city budgets more often than not cannot afford such a luxury," he went on. "The new recreation area at Saline, Michigan, is local union 299's answer to that problem, at least for the membership of Local 299 and their families."

Although rank-and-file reaction to Saline was unsurprised—"Someone's making a bundle off of us again"—most would have been surprised to know just how much McMaster had made.

As Saline's president, McMaster appointed his friend, businessman John R. Ferris, to administer the recreation area. Unknown to the rebels, in advance of the purchase of Saline, McMaster knew that the land was stocked with valuable black walnut trees. He authorized Ferris, at the union's expense, to cut the timber down and sell it at a substantial profit. McMaster says he put all the profits from the black walnut trees back into the Local 299 treasury. Johnson denies it: "He never put anything back in; he never gave me any money for that."

"Everything I did was approved by Fitzsimmons and the Local 299 executive board," says McMaster. Not true, says Johnson. "He broke the treasury; he was juggling bank accounts and everything else."

While the Hoffa-Johnson forces complained among themselves, McMaster instituted other innovations: a credit union, a shop stewards' council, a retirees' organization, a political action force, and a $52,000 switchboard in the union hall. He set up a training program for shop stewards and a "school" for business agents in Miami, Florida. He called the new face of Local 299 "Operation Upgrade," and he said he hoped to become active in family guidance and legal aid.

In May 1969, during a regular meeting, the dissidents challenged McMaster's ''reforms'' as personal moneymaking ventures. They further challenged the $2.00 per month dues increase that had accompanied them. Rebel leaders attacked McMaster from the floor with such intensity that even more passive members present began standing up and criticizing him as well. Losing complete control of the proceedings, McMaster simply adjourned the meeting and walked away from the podium. The dissidents then issued another newsletter:

> Those of you who attended [the May meeting] or attempted to attend this meeting, know first-hand the low regard in which your opinions are held by your Executive Board and Rolland McMaster. . . . The position taken by these people indicates that they regard the majority as being the Executive Board and Rolland McMaster, rather than 18,000 rank-and-file members.
>
> They proved this once more when the May 28, 1968 meeting was adjourned by Chairman McMaster, violating both the rights of the majority in attendance and the International Constitution and Local By-Laws in their entirety.

The rebels picketed the union hall on June 7 and showed up in force for the next regular meeting.

An old trick Hoffa used to pull during meetings was to load up the front rows on one side of the aisle with his goons and henchmen. When Hoffa made a proposal, his men would shout almost in unison, ''We're with you, Jimmy—a hundred percent!'' As a result of the blatantly planned response, the rebels began calling those front rows salted down with goons the ''Amen Corner.''

When McMaster took over after Hoffa and Johnson, he kept to the tradition, stocking the Amen Corner with his own boys. But because he was now being harassed with wailing screams of ''Amen, Brother McMaster! Amen!'' during meetings, the Amen Corner decided to get tough.

As Provenzino walked into the union hall for the June meeting, McMaster henchman Don Deters, an ex-Marine who studied labor relations at the University of Detroit, applied his education to his work by shoving Provenzino against the wall, trying to provoke a fight. Knowing that others would jump in and take their licks, Provenzino refused to tangle with Deters. He shoved his way through the crowd to take his seat at the meeting. What was supposed to happen, according to a statement from one of the goons, was that one of the Amen boys would pull a gun while the lights were intentionally turned off. With the room dark, he "was supposed to shoot holes in a portrait of Jimmy Hoffa, which adorns the front wall, and throw the pistol among the group of dissidents, who always sit together at the meetings for self-protection."

For some reason which was not explained, the scheme never came off. Presumably it was planned to discredit Provenzino, whose popularity among the rank and file was growing.

McMaster was obsessively overreacting to the threat of the rebel forces, as Hoffa had before him. Although the reformers had relatively little power and even less money, McMaster gave them strength by paying as much attention to them as he did. As McMaster perceived the battle, it was the dissidents versus his personal vanity.

In sheer desperation McMaster sent a letter with the heading "The Truth About the Plot to Take Over Local 299" to every member of the local. It was probably the longest letter that ever went out under the Local 299 letterhead.

THIS IS A WARNING!

This is a call for the responsible members of Local 299 to be alert to the dangers that are facing you and your union and, for that matter, your future personal welfare.

A small group of dissatisfied members of Local 299 are making a power grab to seize control of YOUR union.

Their method is to break up our meetings and smear our officers in order to deceive you to support them so they can run the local for their own purposes.

This is the same danger that is causing so much trouble in our college campuses and disrupting our whole way of life.

And, strangely, the dangers come from a small minority who are acting in an irresponsible, destructive and sometimes lawless manner to destroy the democratic procedures which have governed our way of life through centuries of progress. . . .

They have decided that they will set Local 299 policy and to Hell with the rest of the nearly 20,000 members. They have decided their word will be law, even though the members of Local 299 voted against them, 5 to 1, in the election of officers.

THIS IS THEIR GAME

After setting the stage with their attempts to bust up meetings, they approach the officers with resolutions cleverly written to seize control of the local. . . .

We can stop these disgruntled people from using the tactics of Stalin and

Hitler to achieve their purposes if the responsible members will stand up and refuse to let these radicals take over. . . .

It appears that the unrest on the campuses, the dissident voices in our union halls and the other demonstrations are all part of a world-wide movement. . . .

At our meeting in Detroit—or in upstate union halls—the protestors stand up and utter the same protests, almost as though they had the words written out for them.

They sound much like those of the Communists, only instead of trying to build a political ideology these are people trying to build their own interests. . . .

Let us know you are with us. Here's how:

1. —Make sure that all the men on your job and as many of your friends in Local 299 as possible read this.

2. —Let your Steward and Business Agent know you are with the Administration.

3. —Get the other men on your job to support the program of the administration. Get as many as possible to attend the meetings, to make certain we outnumber this mere handful who are bent on destructive tactics.

In this way we'll be able to save all the good things of Local 299.

The dissidents' next flier was of more modest length:

It would be fun to take their trash and refute it, point by point. But it would be also time consuming and costly. For now, let's just evaluate it on the basis of what is behind this publication *now*, at this particular time.

First off—and let's not kid ourselves on this—McMaster and his pack of Jackals base their every action in running *your* Local on one simple belief of *theirs*: ''The membership of Local 299 is stupid; they will believe and accept anything we want them to do. . . .

Blaming local violence on ''the professional workings of the Mc-Master Task Force—the Cobo Hall goon squad and the 'apprentice goons' '' from area barns—the dissidents accused McMaster of signaling his henchmen to disrupt meetings when the majority were not buying his programs.

Two new ''rank-and-file'' groups surfaced about that time, both supporting McMaster and his administration. The ''Investigating Committee'' and the ''Rank-and-File Committee for Progress'' issued several pieces of literature along the lines of: ''There are those among us who would like to wreck all of our programs, but the great majority of Local 299 members are interested in building an organization—not tearing it down.'' Because none of the ''rank-and-file'' members of these committees was ever identified, the members of the Unity Committee believed that no such groups existed.

The genuine rebel groups began to coordinate their work through a new magazine, *Teammate*, the brainchild of Roscoe McGehee, president of MATES, the rebel car hauler group in Detroit. With little support and less money, McGehee and a young writer named Wesley Hills managed to get the publication out. McGehee solicited help from the Fraternal Association of Concerned Teamsters of the Gary-Chicago vicinity and from national FASH, which promised to buy 7000 copies of each issue in return for having its newsletter, *Satellite*, printed. McGehee then approached Provenzino for support. With the proviso that *Teammate*'s editorial policy would be Teamster reform, Provenzino supported it, but McGehee was concerned about its becoming too political. In any case, Provenzino refused to become financially involved because FASH was participating. Most of what he knew about the rebel steel haulers' group was what Jim Leavitt, who had had bad experiences with the FASH leadership, had told him. Provenzino was angry when Don Clemmenson lent $1000 to get the magazine started.

FASH's alliance with the car haulers and with the Unity Committee, which was principally city cartage drivers, caused a serious split within the UC, and Larry McHenry resigned. McHenry hated FASH and refused to support it or *Teammate*: ''I knew that *Teammate* was blowing things way out of proportion, using dirt journalism, and taking things out of context, just to make a buck,'' McHenry explained. ''There were enough sincere people who had problems which they wanted solved that I didn't think they should be used as the vehicle for the *Teammate* owners to make a buck.''

McHenry's associates in the rebel movement felt otherwise. ''When Larry quit the Unity Committee,'' one explains, ''he began to show his true colors.''

Indeed, as soon as McHenry left the protest group he formed an alliance with Rolland McMaster, who promptly reported in the *299 News*: ''Now, we learn that they are squabbling among themselves. They are criticizing their own leaders.''

In September 1969 the first issue of *Teammate* was distributed. In its twenty-four glossy, *Overdrive*-like pages each participating group had a section of its own. There was also a piece giving results of the dissidents' investigation of Saline Valley Farms. Another feature in the first issue, "The Mister McMister Coloring Book," portrayed its hero standing in the dark while dumping election ballots down a toilet. The cartoon obviously referred to the several blackouts during the 1968 local election, and in case there was doubt, the cartoonist, Walt Lane, made a glass eye quite visible.

"There was a lot of discussion before publication that we were going a little bit overboard with our attacks on McMaster," a Unity Committee member recalls. "I mean, you just can't take a guy like him too lightly." During the week that *Teammate* was being passed out among the truckers and warehousemen, Don Davis, one of McMaster's most trusted organizers in the Central Conference, got into a fight with Tom Gwilt in Gary. Gwilt was now Indiana chapter president and national secretary of FASH, and he had written the FASH articles in *Teammate*. A few days after the fight, while he was attending a FASH meeting in Pittsburgh, Gwilt's home was bombed.

The Central Conference organizer was registered in a hotel a few blocks from the scene, and Gwilt says, "There isn't a doubt in my mind the organizer did it, and he was ordered to do it by McMaster because of my relationship with FASH and *Teammate* magazine."

FASH had just ended a membership drive and had two thousand new members, 75 percent of them card-carrying Teamsters. The week before the blast, Gwilt had given a speech in Gary to IBT officials and steel hauling executives. Bluntly defying the assembly, Gwilt said that the union and the industry would "have no choice in the future but to reckon with FASH."

"The meeting had been called by McMaster," he explains, "and I saw the look on his face when I started talking about FASH competing with the Teamsters. He walked up to me after it was over and said, 'You boys aren't interested in anything else but starting your own union, right?' I just smiled and walked away."

Commenting on the bombing of Gwilt's home, McMaster said that the incident was a result of "internal dissension" among the rebels. "They advocate blowing up things and setting fires. They are fighting among themselves—this is the result."[2] Davis himself says he knew nothing about the bombing until he "read it in the papers."

Soon after the Gwilt bombing, Frank Kiltzke, vice president of the Indiana chapter of FASH and another outspoken critic of the union leadership, was shot at from two passing cars and barely escaped injury. Neither the bombing nor the shooting incident was ever solved by the local police or the FBI.

Kiltzke, a brave and honest owner-operator, took a few men down to the Local 142 union hall in Gary, where they cornered its secretary-treasurer, Donald Sawochka, alone.

"I told Sawochka that the cars that ran me off the road and opened fire on me were loaded with his men," Kiltzke remarks. "Then we blamed him for also being involved in the bombing of Tom's home. He knocked us flat when he told us, 'McMaster did that, and I promise you boys that he'll get his.' "

The second issue of *Teammate*, released in October, had twice as many pages as the first and was twice as much in demand. Along with the sections by FACT, FASH, MATES, and the Unity Committee, there was a special report on the bombing of Gwilt's home that indirectly accused McMaster of ordering it. Also included was a report by Ralph Nader's consumer group on the lack of highway safety for truckers. (The report and an accompanying questionnaire were both reprinted in the December issue of *Overdrive*.) In addition, the Local 299 dissidents published their legal brief in which Unity Committee members asked for an injunction against the dues increase which was going toward the purchase of Saline Valley Farms.

On the lighter side, "Mr. McMister" was back—a comic strip, a half-page of "Mister McMister" jokes, and the clincher, a full-page advertisement for the "Mister McMister Doll": "It Walks! It Talks! Take it home, feed it money, and marvel at the way it picks your pocket, steals the food off your table, and the clothes off your back . . . Just like the real thing!"

Copies of the first two issues of *Teammate* were circulated throughout the country. As dissidents in other cities read about the problems of the rebels in Detroit, Unity Committees were formed in Indianapolis and Cleveland and discussed in other areas. As McGehee and his colleagues had hoped, the magazine had a tremendous impact.

In fact it had to be stopped. At 12:16 A.M. on November 2, before the third issue was completed, the offices of *Teammate* were bombed. Firemen arrived to battle the fire and a second bomb went off twenty minutes later, severely injuring several of the firefighters. Like the Gwilt bombing, the *Teammate* incident was never solved. The police reported that "professionals" were responsible.

Although the Unity Committee newsletter reported the day after the blast that "*Teammate* magazine will continue to publish: 'They' have frightened no one," the publisher and editor of the publication *were* frightened, and after one final issue was distributed in January, *Teammate* was closed down.

The same newsletter announced a mass demonstration in front of the union hall at noon on Sunday, November 9. By the day of the protest, the word had reached nearly every rank-and-file member that the demonstration would be the final showdown between the rebels and the goons in Detroit. Because of the large number of union legbreakers also expected to attend, most of the 18,000 rank-and-file members of Local 299 decided to stay home, open a can of beer, and watch the Sunday football game on television. Although the blackout of the Detroit Lions–Atlanta Falcons game, which was being played at home, was annoying, cussing at Joe Namath and the Jets was bound to be more fun than going down to the union hall to get beaten up.

As the roars from the fans in Tiger Stadium filled the crisp autumn air, three blocks away, where the cheers were still audible, twenty-seven rebels marched up and down Trumbull Avenue protesting the bombing of *Teammate*.

Badly outnumbered by the enforcers cluttering the street in front of the union hall, the dissidents clutched their picket signs—''Down with Dictatorship! Let's Take the Hood Out of Brotherhood!''—anticipating a frontal assault.

The police arrived on the scene, expecting trouble, and one police officer was overheard saying to McMaster, ''Well, Mac, you want us to move 'em out?''

''No, no. It's a free country; this is just freedom of expression.''

While the steel haulers met in the union hall for their regular Sunday meeting, and tardy football fans drove up Trumbull to the stadium, Provenzino—carrying a bullhorn—was being interviewed by a newsman. As Angelo Ellis, a local rebel, walked up to Provenzino, Ellis was grabbed by a local business agent and knocked to the sidewalk.

''All hell broke loose after Angelo got hit,'' Don Clemmenson says, shaking his head. ''Those next five minutes seemed to last for hours. And there were wives and kids there, too.''

Swinging their picket signs to defend themselves against the onslaught of goons, the rebels tried to hold off the wild free-for-all. Although it was ten minutes before the police could contain the brawl, the only person arrested was Ellis, who had been badly injured; he was charged with disorderly conduct.

There was a brief, futile protest over the arrest, and then Unity Committee members noticed a familiar face with an unfamiliar smile on it. Larry McHenry was standing behind a fence near the union hall with the McMaster goons.

The opposition of their union, the companies, and the local police department, as well as the apathy of Local 299's rank and file, hurt the rebels, but McHenry's betrayal was the proverbial unkindest cut of all.

"The publicity and notoriety had gone to Andy's head," is McHenry's explanation. "His ego hurt what he was trying to do. People used to say, including Hoffa, that Andy was Charlie McCarthy and I was Edgar Bergen, pulling the strings. But when we split, he proved it by getting into areas where he had to think for himself, and he found he couldn't handle it."

McHenry, whether thinking for himself or working for McMaster, unilaterally incorporated the name "Unity Committee," registering it with the state of Michigan. Thus with McHenry as the sole owner of "Unity Committee, Inc.," the dissidents were no longer permitted to use it as the name of their organization.

"After we had split earlier," McHenry says, "they were using the names 'Unity Committee' and 'National Unity Committees' as part of the *Teammate* format. I told them then that if incorporating the name of the organization was what I had to do to stop them, then I'd do it."

Using a legal fund which had been raised through a series of raffles to fight the Saline Valley Farms project and the Local 299 dues increase, Provenzino obtained a temporary restraining order forbidding McHenry's corporation from going into operation. McHenry then wrote an "Open Letter":

> By the actions of sincere people and myself, Unity Committee 299, was on December 12, 1969, legally and properly registered as a Non-Profit Corporation. . . . I did intend to publish under the name of the Non-Profit Corporation, however, I was served with a temporary restraining order issued out of the Wayne County Circuit Court. This order was obtained through the efforts of and at the request of Andrew V. Provenzino.
>
> I understand now, that Provenzino has instituted what he refers to as a "Legal Fund" and that members have contributed freely from their wages and are now being asked to go further by selling and buying raffle tickets to raise additional "Legal Funds."
>
> I ask this question; are the members and the general public being asked to finance a beneficial reform program in the Teamster's Union or are they unknowingly furthering Provenzino's own personal ambitions?

As the court ruled against McHenry and allowed the Detroit rebels to keep their name, they began organizing against the Teamsters' contract proposals for the 1970 National Master Freight Agreement.

More trouble was on the road.

12 Tremors and Explosions— and a Week in the Life of a Steel Hauler

Some have lived to tell that before an earthquake struck their community there was a long, continuous humming sound, warning of imminent disaster. Dredging itself up from the earth's depths, the hum became a soft rumble, then louder and louder until the ground began to shake.

The steel haulers had heard that ominous rising hum when they embarrassed the Teamsters Union during the 1967 protest. With the formation of FASH in its aftermath, and the publication of *Teammate*, the hum became a rumble, and it grew louder and more ominous with the bombing of *Teammate* and of Tom Gwilt's home.

In pursuit of their own union, the FASH leadership knew they had to convince a skeptical rank-and-file membership that they could not win within the present system. They had to create their own. And before that could happen, FASH had to prove that it had exhausted all existing channels in its efforts to change the Teamsters Union.

"So we contacted Frank Fitzsimmons and asked him if he'd sit down and talk with us about our problems," FASH leader Bill Hill explains. "He said no, just as we expected, but he told us he'd form a committee to deal with us—and we expected that, too. The committee, as expected, didn't do us any good, so we went back to Fitzsimmons and said we wanted to talk with someone who had decision-making powers.

"So, just as we thought he'd do, he put us in touch with his 'steel hauling expert,' Rolland McMaster.''

Hill and three other FASH leaders—Gwilt, Mike Boano, and Paul Dietsch—had two meetings with McMaster. They told him they wanted five steel hauling locals around the country, the authority to select their own leaders and the right to ratify their own contracts.

"You're crazy," McMaster told them. "These owner-operators are nothing but a bunch of whores."

"Well, Mac," said Dietsch, "I guess it takes one to know one."

As the FASH representatives laughed, McMaster chuckled too, looking at the table, then around the room, then at Dietsch.

Smiling that McMaster smile, the steel hauling expert asked, "Dietsch, how old are you?"

"Forty. Why?"

"Well, with your attitude," McMaster said slowly, with his most horrifying stare, "you might never reach forty-one."

Hummmmmmmmmmmm.

The ground began to explode on October 28, 1969.

"There was a wildcat strike going on in Youngstown," as Hill tells the story. "FASH was protesting the firing of one of our members from the Stony Trucking Company on October 17. Because Stony received most of its business from the local Republic Steel Company, we set up a picket line at Republic, at the 'Stop Five' security gate on Poland Avenue. We had already had some trouble there—somebody said a union goon had shown up with a gun or something—but we knew that more trouble was coming."

FASH was also on strike at B & P Motor Freight in Pittsburgh, protesting the firing of two steel haulers in Gary who had refused to accept an unsafe load, but Hill pulled his men off that picket line and took them to Youngstown. As the FASH protesters drove into town on the 28th, there were strong rumors that the Teamsters were planning a major confrontation.

John Angelo, Youngstown Local 377's president, announced on television news that he would run FASH out of the city "even if I have to bring a hundred men into town to do it." Angelo was warring with FASH national treasurer Mike Boano, who held him responsible for the bomb planted on Boano's front lawn the year before. "FASH was a pretty young organization at the time," Boano says. "But it had been around long enough that some of these personality conflicts could develop. Because of my position as president of Youngstown FASH, I had some of my own, including Angelo. Anything that happened was caused by the fact that he didn't like me or the organization."

Angelo assembled a squad of 120 Teamster business agents and hired thugs, piled them into fifty cars, and started for Youngstown. En route they stopped in Boardman, at the edge of Youngstown, and patronized local sporting goods stores, buying baseball bats and golf clubs for those who hadn't come prepared.

FASH members weren't exactly sitting around the picket line singing country and western songs. Word had been relayed several hours in advance that Angelo and his goons were heading their way, armed and dangerous. Equipped with ball bats, blackjacks, and a few handguns, the rebels waited.

"It's hard to explain the atmosphere before Angelo arrived. We were euphoric," one of the FASH men says. "I know how terrible that might sound, but it was a collective feeling of fear with a kind of gallantry—like we were going to fight for something we knew was right. I mean, we knew that this was going to be it. I had a gun, and I had every intention of using it if I had to."

Leaving Boardman, the Teamsters drove into Youngstown and parked in a lot next to the Stony Trucking Company. The Youngstown Police Department was waiting for Angelo and his men, but instead of trying to disperse them to avoid a bloodbath, the police escorted the convoy to Republic's Stop 5 gate.

Outnumbered two to one, the rebels got ready for the big clash as Angelo's lead car and a procession of others preceded the trucks which were going to try to break the picket line. Wire mesh covered the Teamsters' car windows and the passengers were wearing steel helmets. Angelo stopped his car just short of the strikers, and he and the other union men grabbed their bats and clubs and started walking toward the picket line, hoping the protesters would back down. They didn't; they advanced, and someone threw a rock that hit Angelo in the head.

"When they saw we had come out to meet them," FASH striker Bob Trent remembers, "they went back into their cars and started pulling out pistols and carbines. When they opened fire on us, those of us who didn't have guns started throwing rocks, and then someone threw a firebomb into Angelo's car. All hell broke out after that; it was war. One of our guys was the first to get hit by the gunfire. And the police were nowhere to be found."

In the midst of the fighting the Teamsters pulled out an awesome-looking machine gun, mounted it on a tripod, and began firing into the crowd. Then the machine gunner was reportedly gunned down by a striker, and after the ball bats broke and gun chambers went empty, both sides were reduced to hand-to-hand combat. Unlike movie brawls, in which two men take twenty solid punches each after breaking chairs and bottles over each other's skull, the battle at Stop 5 was decided by who could get up after one, maybe two, blows to the head.

The fighting went on for half an hour before the police returned and tear-gassed the FASH contingent. Six FASH men were arrested at the scene; several of Angelo's men were picked up later.

The Teamsters, with a two-to-one edge in manpower, had been unable to get more than two trucks into Republic Steel. Humiliated, Angelo and his goons ordered the rest of them to retreat; FASH had won the worst labor battle since the 1930s.

Miraculously, only one man was killed, an Angelo henchman from Cleveland. Eight were seriously wounded and had to be hospitalized; dozens of others were treated and released or went home and let their wives patch them up.

"We knew then," Hill says, "that there was absolutely no reason for us to stay in the Teamsters any longer. And three months later we announced that we were going to form our own union."

In early December, Bill Presser indirectly endorsed Bill Hill's decision in a telegram to Youngstown Local 377: "All present active members of Teamsters Local 377 who hold membership in FASH must make a determination in which organization they will hold membership or face disciplinary charges under the International Constitution."

Hill, Dietsch, and FASH official Peter Yerace agree that later on, when they talked to Presser about the Stop 5 violence, he told them bluntly, "I was against what happened to your men in Youngstown. But it was that goddamn McMaster, it was his idea from the beginning to start the trouble."

It was McMaster, appointed by Frank Fitzsimmons, who headed the union's official inquiry into the bloody shoot-out. Federal investigators used his final report as a source of information in seeking grand jury indictments. When the grand jury finished its work on the "FASH Shoot-Out" it indicted thirteen participants, including Angelo and Boano, on riot and possession of dangerous weapons charges. All received suspended sentences and fines of $1000 or less.

McMaster had his hands full of dissent and dissenters, and he probably made no distinction between his hometown Unity Committee, which wanted to take over the Teamsters and reform it, and FASH, whose announced goal was a new union. As both Local 299 chief executive officer and director of organizers for special commodities haulers in the Central Conference, he was expected to keep the lid on rebellion in both kingdoms. And McMaster knew that when negotiations for the 1970 National Master Freight Agreement and its steel addendum began in January, the rebel forces would be on the line with all the strength they could muster.

One opponent with special strength was Jim Leavitt, a Local 299 member who had been a leader in Gary in the 1967 wildcat strike and was a major force in the Detroit Unity Committee. Tough, with equal proportions of personal integrity and determination, Leavitt had been a trucker for twenty-three years.

Although he had no high school diploma, he was considered a thoughtful man who expounded a militant conservatism on such topics as human dignity and human rights; he insisted that everyone was entitled to both. He was only fifteen when World War II ended but he had idolized the ''Willies and Joes,'' the GIs who fought overseas. He couldn't understand how a guy who had been shot at daily could come home after the war, join the Teamsters, and allow ''some sleazy Mafia son of a bitch who didn't go to war'' to corrupt his union.

''After Guadalcanal, what the hell else can happen to you?''

Leavitt's decision to become a rebel was simply a matter of ''putting ass where mouth is,'' and he resented the fact that reform groups did not receive large swells of support from the rank and file.

Typically, as a steel hauler, on Sunday night at 10:00 P.M. Leavitt pulled his rig out of his Detroit trucking terminal and headed for Chicago with a load of steel. Arriving at 6:00 A.M., he was already tired of driving, watching the endless chops of straight white paint in the middle of the highway. Receiving operations wouldn't begin until seven, so he catnapped for an hour and dreamed of fishing on the Upper Peninsula. He was ninth in line to be unloaded, behind the railroad cars and other priority loads. Awakened abruptly by loud noises on the loading platform, he felt barely rested after his 300-mile haul.

The understaffed checking crew finally unloaded his cargo at 1:30 P.M. and he drove his empty flatbed to Gary, an hour's run. After billing and logging the day's work, he and the other drivers hung around his company's terminal until about 5:00 P.M. After Leavitt's number was called, he headed for Gary's U.S. Steel Plant at 8:00 P.M. to pick up a load to be delivered in Cleveland. Before arriving at the plant, he stopped and ate dinner—fried chicken, mashed potatoes, and green beans—and drank a cup of coffee, hot and black. Arriving at U.S.

Steel a half-hour early, he found that trucks were already backed up; it would be another long wait until they loaded him.

Seven hours later he billed out and wanted to catch some sleep, but his load was three thousand pounds over Indiana's gross allowance. He had to get into Ohio, where the weight limit was higher, before daylight.

Once over the state line early Tuesday morning, Leavitt crashed for a couple of hours in his truck. The short rest made him feel strung out, but he had a rule about the use of bennies: he didn't start eating them until he was ready to drop. After breakfast at a truck stop off exit 5 of the Ohio Turnpike, he headed, full throttle, for Cleveland.

At 4:00 P.M. he pulled into the lot of the consignee and was unloaded within an hour. Again he wanted to sleep but was told by his dispatcher to deadhead to Ironton, in southern Ohio. He had to drive seventy more miles before he could rest. Storming down Interstate 71, he was groggy. The billboards along the highway—hotels, motels, gas and oil products, service stations, restaurants, diners—passed by faster and faster. Then suddenly he didn't see them at all; he was driving in a long dark tunnel. Tunnel vision is one of the hallucinations of the long-distance driver; sometimes one also sees horses, trees, and barns.

Somehow Leavitt caught himself and pulled his rig over to the side of the road. He was relieved; other drivers hadn't been so lucky. He remembered the countless times he'd seen tractor-trailers on their sides with wheels spinning, windshields smashed, and drivers dead. He curled up in his rig, threw an extra jacket over himself, and slept.

Early Wednesday morning he was awakened by the motors and wind gushes of fast-moving forty-footers swooping by. He cleaned up and ate the baloney sandwich his wife had made two days ago. Out of coffee, he stopped at a small roadside café outside Columbus. As he got out of his cab he noticed that his front tire was low. Shaking his head, he walked around the back of his trailer and discovered that a taillight was malfunctioning. He jogged into the little restaurant, gulped some coffee and filled his thermos, and went back out to repair his truck. Because he was in a hurry, he decided that the tire had to wait until he got to Ironton. Other truckers helped him fix the back light and he was on the road again. At 8:30 A.M. he arrived in Ironton, but there were no trucks there and all the loads were gone. He was too late, so he tore down his tire and repaired it. After an eight-hour wait, he got a load for Effingham, Illinois, and had to be at Armco Steel Company in

Ashland, Kentucky, to pick it up at 7:00 P.M. After washing up and eating, he drove to the steel mill.

Again the loading crew was slow. Even though there were only two trucks in front of him, he didn't get out for several hours. ''There isn't much to do when you're waiting except study the company's bulletin board. I could probably recite every company notice in the Midwest ·from memory.''

Loaded up, Leavitt returned to Ironton to check out, then traveled west to Cincinnati, where he stopped for coffee. By 6:00 A.M. Thursday he was in Indianapolis, fueling up and eating breakfast. On the way to Effingham, near Terre Haute, a cap came off the tire on his tag axle. Leavitt lost another half-hour replacing it with a spare. But by busting ass he made his delivery in Effingham on schedule and was able to sleep for forty minutes before his truck was unloaded. When he called his company and asked where he should go next, he was told to drive empty into Gary. At the end of the six-hour trip it was 10:30 P.M. and too late for loading. He checked into a small truckers' motel. No work, but at least he'd get to stretch out in a bed.

On Friday, after he'd had six hours' sleep, the desk clerk called to wake him up; it was 7:00 A.M. and the company dispatcher had phoned the motel to roust his drivers out of bed. Everyone was to be at the terminal by eight o'clock. Because he stopped to eat breakfast Leavitt was a half-hour late, but he snagged a load to Detroit from McCook, Illinois. In McCook he learned that the steel hadn't come in from the shipper. Another wait.

Finally loaded up, he fought through the Chicago rush-hour traffic and arrived at his Gary terminal at 7:00 P.M. He scaled in but his trailer axle was overloaded by 2100 pounds, so he and a friend had to unchain and untarp the load to shift the steel and remove the extra burden on the axle. The operation took two and a half hours. Leavitt ate supper and was headed for Detroit by 11:00 P.M.

Before dawn Saturday morning Leavitt was driving in a downpour, almost into Kalamazoo, when the generator failed. Leavitt crawled under his rig to remove it, then caught a ride with a freight hauler to the nearest truck stop. A mechanic told him that the generator couldn't be repaired, but if Leavitt could wait a couple of hours he'd help him find a new one. Drenched and helpless, Leavitt had no choice.

At 7:00 A.M., he and the mechanic got in the mechanic's car and began ''the great generator hunt.'' After stopping at four places they finally found a generator that would fit. Leavitt returned to the truck stop with the mechanic and hitched a ride with an over-the-road driver heading in the direction of the disabled truck. Dropped off, he crawled back under the truck and replaced the generator.

It was still raining but not so hard. He arrived in Detroit with his load at 2:30 P.M. He wanted to wait until Monday to unload, but his Detroit terminal needed empty trailers and the dispatcher had arranged for the consignee to accept delivery immediately. Forced to postpone his weekly reunion with his family for a few more hours, Leavitt drove to the steel mill and unloaded, then was put on the list for a haul on Monday.

Leavitt got home on Sunday at 1:00 A.M. His children, who hadn't seen him in a week, were in bed. His wife, Dorothy, who had waited up, gently helped him get out of his soaked and grimy work clothes, then kept the kids quiet while he slept late into the afternoon. He had to start driving again the next morning.

While Jim Leavitt and thousands of other truckers were on the road, representatives of their union and of management were meeting in Chicago, hammering out the 1970 National Master Freight Agreement.

"Some drivers are pretty naïve, thinking that the conditions of the industry are going to get better," Leavitt said. "I just hope the contract doesn't make them worse."

Leavitt had had his present job only since January 1970. It was rugged work, but at least it was a job. He had been fired after the 1967 wildcat strike, ostensibly for refusing to give his company his new unlisted telephone number. He had protested that while he was out working or organizing his wife was at home receiving threatening calls. He had changed his number and wanted to keep it secret.

Newspapers called Leavitt's firing "political" and "blatant discrimination," since the rebels had been assured by both management and their union that there would be no reprisals. Leavitt filed a grievance with the Teamsters and charges with the National Labor Relations Board. He lost both cases and also his $27,000 rig when he couldn't meet the payments. He was blackballed from the industry and blacklisted by his own union; employers were told not to hire him.

Patrick Owens, a labor writer for the *Detroit Free Press*, wrote an article about Leavitt's dilemma with his company and the Teamsters

Union. Soon after it was published Owens wrote to Leavitt indicating that members of the Teamsters Betterment League wanted to meet with him. Leavitt did talk with TBL's leaders, Andy Provenzino and Larry McHenry, whom he had seen before, when they were "removed" from a steel haulers' meeting on McMasters's orders.

Provenzino and McHenry wanted Leavitt to join the TBL and run as a candidate on their reform ticket. But Leavitt was no longer a "member in good standing" because he had fallen behind on his union dues too, after he lost his job. He couldn't run for office, but he liked what the dissidents were saying and committed himself to the cause.

During the 1968 election campaign he and the other rebels founded the Unity Committee 299 which replaced TBL. Although they were soundly stomped in the election, their activities created near-havoc among the local's incumbents. Rolland McMaster, as the unelected chief executive officer of Local 299, became the dissidents' number-one target. Street propaganda from UC appeared almost daily, attacking his criminal record and his financial activities. McMaster responded with his goon squads and by calling the rebels "Communists."

The Unity Committee did not know at the time that Hoffa was also furious at McMaster's appointment, but by 1970 the dissidents sensed what insiders already knew: there was growing enmity between Hoffa and Fitzsimmons. Instead of repeating, "Here's the keys, Jimmy! They're waiting for you when you get back!" Fitzsimmons was now saying, in effect, Hoffa doesn't have as many friends around here as he may think.

Fitzsimmons had been acting IBT and Local 299 president for nearly three years and had grown comfortable with his new power and prestige. With his unpretentious, grandfatherly manner he had acquired the respect of politicians and other labor leaders. And through such gestures as marching with civil rights leaders in the funeral procession for Dr. Martin Luther King, Fitzsimmons gained points in the liberal community.

Perhaps one of the greatest surprises of Fitzsimmons' young administration was his alliance with UAW president Walter Reuther after the UAW stormed out of the AFL-CIO in July 1968. Later that month Reuther and Fitzsimmons met in Chicago and laid the groundwork for the Alliance for Labor Action.

Since the ALA drew strength from the nation's two largest labor unions—the two-million-member Teamsters and the 1.6-million-member United Auto Workers—it had the potential to rival the AFL-

CIO. And everyone knew that the widely admired Reuther wouldn't have given Jimmy Hoffa the time of day: when Reuther was shot in 1948, and Hoffa's old mob ally Santo Perrone was implicated, the police detective handling the case was also linked to Perrone. After bungling the case and being dismissed from the department, the detective was promptly given an organizer's job with the Detroit Teamsters.

Formally created in May 1969, in Washington, the ALA functioned effectively for a year. Then in May 1970, Reuther and his wife were killed in a plane crash. "America has lost one of its great citizens," Fitzsimmons said appropriately. "Organized labor has lost a great champion. I have lost a dear and personal friend."

Reuther's assistant, Leonard Woodcock, became heir to both the leadership of the UAW and the co-leadership of the ALA. Woodcock was not as enthusiastic about the Teamster-UAW alliance as his predecessor had been; he allowed the ALA to die a few years later. Woodcock did, however, remain friendly enough with Fitzsimmons to borrow $25 million from the Central States Pension Fund when the UAW's resources were depleted by a long strike against General Motors.

A mild-mannered man with many friends, Fitzsimmons was a breath of fresh air to the Teamster brass. The first few years of his tenure were a welcome contrast to the turbulence of the years 1957 to 1967, when Hoffa was running the IBT. Local union autonomy was brought back to the Teamsters as Fitzsimmons instituted a program of decentralization within the union. IBT vice presidents and local union officials had never had such freedom. Viewed as the IBT's new enlightened despot, a president who allowed the members of the IBT general executive board to function almost entirely on their own within their separate jurisdictions, Fitzsimmons began to receive quiet encouragement to remain general president permanently. The thought of tyrant Hoffa returning as chief administrator had become distasteful to many Teamster leaders.

To retain power, however, Fitzsimmons had to wrest control over Local 299 away from Hoffa. Even though McMaster was running the show for Fitzsimmons' side, Hoffa still had the backing of the rank and file. He knew of Fitzsimmons' ambitions and, via Dave Johnson, ordered his supporters to counter on the local level to protect his hometown sanctuary.

While Fitzsimmons continued to publicly pledge his devotion to Hoffa, and Hoffa, through his prison visitors, expressed pleasant thoughts about Fitzsimmons, Johnson and McMaster were quietly battling it out.

The strategy of grass-roots warfare had merits for both sides. It provided for some common-ground agreements, such as union contracts, and gave each side the opportunity for preliminary sparring before knockout punches were delivered. Because each faction was uncertain of the other's strength, wooing supporters was the primary consideration. And the business agents and stewards were the key to the local; both Hoffa and Fitzsimmons expected their respective business agents to get and keep the support of the stewards, the closest union representatives to the rank and file.

The rank-and-file Teamsters in Local 299 increasingly found themselves in the middle of the cold war between Hoffa and Fitzsimmons. With the leadership concentrating on union politics, members who filed grievances against their employers learned not to expect much help. The best they could hope for was that their local union would not hurt them. Even important grievances were not favorably resolved unless the member had connections with someone in the union hall or the officials had a grudge against the company involved. Generally, the members were forced to make the best deals they could with their employers.

Jim Leavitt and the Unity Committee charged into the midst of the power struggle, further complicating the already dangerous situation in Detroit. They viewed their conflict as a holy war in defense of the exploited membership. Although they had concluded that both sides of the power struggle were undesirable as rulers, they recognized their own manpower and financial limitations. To obtain any union concessions toward reform, they had to favor one side over the other.

Because of Fitzsimmons' support of the autocratic McMaster, the rebels decided to provide secretary-treasurer Johnson—and thus Hoffa—with a backhanded mandate. In their March 18, 1970, newsletter the dissidents reported that during a private meeting in which Fitzsimmons was asked to remove McMaster from office, Fitzsimmons retorted, ''I don't give a damn what the members want. I'm the boss of this union, and I'll make the decisions in this local.'' On April 6, 1970, the dissidents suggested:

Unity Committee 299 would ask the membership to demand that Dave Johnson be the chairman at our meetings. He may not be much better than McMaster, but he is an elected officer of this local. Let's let Fitzsimmons know that if he wants garbage like McMaster around to take him to Washington. Mac is not fit to be in the same local with us. Is he fit for anything?

Fitzsimmons was concerned. He knew that the siege against Mc-Master by the Unity Committee and FASH was gathering an enormous amount of support from the quiet rank-and-file member who just punched his timecard and did his day's work. McMaster's criminal record for taking payoffs from employers was well known among the membership, and it was a specific target in lunchroom discussions of ''reform,'' generally a forbidden word among the rank and file.

Fitzsimmons also knew that the bitterness against union officials and employers was growing to mammoth proportions while both were at the bargaining table in Chicago drawing up the 1970 National Master Freight Agreement. Fitzsimmons had prepared the membership for the worst, telling them at meetings that they should expect ''to tighten their belts.'' Rank-and-file cynicism grew, and there were cries from the ranks that the negotiations were artificial and predictable. The union had asked for a $3.00 per hour raise over three years, but sure enough, the demand was soon reduced to $1.10.

There were scattered protests around the country. In Indianapolis several goons from Local 135 ganged up on an elderly rebel, James Allison, who was handing out leaflets attacking the contract, and beat him so badly that he died soon afterward.

The Unity Committee hit the streets with a barrage of literature predicting a sellout contract and discussing the possibility of a wildcat strike. The dissidents knew that if they struck they would feel the wrath of the system as well as the union. City mayors and state governors, their political campaigns dependent upon the contributions of business and organized labor, could be expected to use all their emergency powers. The police and quite possibly the National Guard would be called upon.

Andy Provenzino, leader of the Unity Committee, was ready to take the risk and pressed hard for the strike.

Jim Leavitt was Provenzino's right-hand man—a role he knew well from the 1967 wildcat strike. ''My personal ego had nothing to do with any of these matters,'' Leavitt says. ''There was a job to be done in 1967 and again in 1970, and the two men who were leading these protests were men I admired and trusted. I was proud to serve under Kusley and Provenzino.''

In his role as ''acting secretary'' Leavitt helped to formulate strategy and handled most of the work on the Unity Committee newsletter. Like Provenzino and Kusley, he was a hard-liner. And unlike FASH, the Unity Committee wanted ''reform, not decertification''; it opposed any suggestion of leaving the Teamsters Union. Provenzino wanted to lead the first successful rank-and-file revolt in Detroit, and do it in the home local of Jimmy Hoffa and Frank Fitzsimmons.

Word came in early April that the union's $1.10 ''compromise'' had been approved by management—two days after the contract's March 31 deadline—without major changes in such fringe benefits as sick leave. The owner-operator steel haulers were raped again, forced to accept terms which constituted an actual reduction in pay. The dissidents called the agreement a travesty, a sweetheart contract at best, and rank-and-file anger increased with the news that Chicago Teamster Locals 705 and 710 and the Chicago Independent Truck Drivers Union had rejected the low bid and were holding out for $1.85 per hour through their independent bargaining procedures. As in 1967 the Chicago employers locked out their employees, who then went on strike. Wildcat strikes elsewhere began at once.

The union bosses had made what appeared to be a dramatic gamble. They were challenging the membership to the showdown everyone in truck stops throughout the country was anticipating. Since the contract was considered ratified unless two-thirds of the total membership voted against it, the agreement was as strike-proof as the previous one.

McMaster informed the Local 299 membership that the contract would be discussed on Wednesday, April 8, during the city cartage drivers' regularly scheduled meeting. On the sixth the Unity Committee began distributing a newsletter:

> Unity Committee 299 declares loud and clear, WE DO NOT TRUST OR CONDONE the action of Fitzsimmons, Rolland McMaster, and the rest of the scum that keeps selling the membership down the river. These are professional sell-out artists. They would sell their soul for a shilling.

On the morning of the eighth, Leavitt unloaded his truck in Detroit and drove to his terminal to find that all employees had been locked out by management. Detroit steel hauler William Anderson told him that FASH had ordered another national wildcat strike, and in response the National Steel Carriers Association, representing seventy-six member companies, had locked everyone out. Leavitt called Provenzino to give him the news, and they met to plot their strategy for the meeting that night.

By 7:00 P.M. the union hall was packed with irate Teamsters and arguments and fist fights were erupting all over the room. But for once the rank and file outnumbered the goons and the Amen Corner that always nodded its approval of McMaster's ramblings. McMaster and Johnson sat on the stage; they were fidgeting, worried, and for the first time in a long while they were on the same side.

Andy Provenzino was sitting down front, watching the two distressed Teamster leaders and laughing.

Outside the union building a small bonfire of Teamster contract proposals burned while Leavitt distributed the Unity Committee's April 6 newsletter. A union business agent surrounded by some of his tough friends walked up to him.

"Who the hell are you?"

"Jim Leavitt. I'm a steel hauler. What about it?"

The business agent said nothing.

Leavitt handed him a newsletter and quickly tried to get into the hall. But he couldn't get in; the place was too jammed.

For nearly a half-hour McMaster and Johnson had been trying to bring the meeting to order. Provenzino went up to the platform.

"This is ridiculous, Mac. If you need me, I'm available."

"I need you," McMaster replied desperately, and he announced to the angry members that their leader, Andy Provenzino, had something to say.

The crowd quieted down as Provenzino shoved his way up to the microphone, and the word spread quickly: "Provenzino got offered a job, like his buddy McHenry; he's going to sell us out."

Once on the podium, Provenzino looked solemn, concerned. Then, looking back at a smiling McMaster nodding to him to proceed, Provenzino shot his clenched fist high into the air and cried, "I SAY WE STRIKE!"

Bedlam erupted from the ranks. The meeting was out of control for good.

Burly truckers raced onto the stage and surrounded McMaster and Johnson. "Well, what the hell you two guys gonna do for us?"

McMaster looked at an equally helpless Johnson and murmured, "Anything you boys want." It meant the strike would be union-sanctioned, no matter how reluctantly.

Jubilant, the membership raced out of Local 299. Unity Committee dissidents met briefly and decided to establish their first picket line at Central Transport, a trucking company nearby.

Two hours later Dave Johnson appeared on a Detroit television program and informed viewers that the truckers' protest constituted a wildcat strike; the demonstration, he said, was being carried on without the support of Local 299 or the IBT. Fitzsimmons sent telegrams to three hundred locals around the country urging the membership to return to work.

Betrayed, Provenzino, Leavitt, and the other UC leaders were far from giving up. They spent the rest of the night as a floating picket squad, moving from company to company, encouraging drivers and warehousemen to man picket lines at their own barns. To their surprise and pleasure the membership greeted them with, "Hey, this is *our* strike—the rank and file!" Provenzino said to Leavitt, "They've been educated. And with all of them knowing that it's their thing, the strike is going to last a lot longer."

For the first time the quiet Detroit rank-and-filer was standing up en masse, defying the bosses of the system. Some merely refused to drive or load; others were cursing, carrying picket signs, and throwing bricks.

McMaster's goon squads were out in force, and there was talk on the grapevine that there might be an attempt on Provenzino's life for his defiance at the city cartage meeting. Provenzino sent his family to stay with relatives and Leavitt decided to sleep at Provenzino's house for the duration.

On the third night of the strike Leavitt and four other members of the Unity Committee were meeting at their informal headquarters, Andrew's Bar, on the near West Side. Burned out, Provenzino had gone home to bed an hour before. While the other rebels drank and talked, a 350-pound goon with a shaved, scarred head walked into the bar and asked who was in charge.

Silence.

"I said, who's in charge here?"

"Who the fuck made you straw boss around here?" shouted a Unity Committee member.

As the words tumbled out, fifty or so legbreakers crowded into Andrew's. Those in the bar who weren't Unity Committee members quickly split.

One dissident was in the telephone booth talking to a friend when the bar was invaded. Leavitt whispered to him through the crack in the door, ''Get some help! We're being inundated over here!''

The goons had the five rebels completely surrounded as Leavitt walked over to a friend at the bar. Local 299 business agent Don Deters came into the room and walked up to Leavitt, shoving his chest in the rebel's face. As in a B movie, Deters said casually, ''You look kinda thirsty. You want a beer, pal?''

Leavitt stared at the bar saying nothing.

A local cop entered the room. ''I understand there's a disturbance here.'' Thinking that his friend in the phone booth had called the police, Leavitt muttered under his breath, ''We're saved!''

As one of the dissidents tried to speak, he was immediately surrounded by goons. A Local 299 business agent smiled and said, ''There's no trouble here, officer.''

After the cop left, six business agents knocked down and beat the rebel who had tried to speak. Leavitt and the others were pinned against the bar and could do nothing. With the bloodied rebel lying on the floor, Deters pointed to Leavitt and said, ''End the strike now!'' He and the fifty other goons left quickly—five minutes before the cop returned with additional men.

The strike went on for eight days, and Fitzsimmons made no move toward conciliation. On April 15 Provenzino called a rally for 11:00 A.M.

Throughout the strike, the Unity Committee had been both spark plug and communications center for the protest. The press had been down on the wildcatters since the strike began, calling them troublemakers and worse. They had struggled against three court injunctions and innumerable violent attacks.

Leavitt was tired; he overslept and missed the demonstration.

Across town, Provenzino and some five hundred rank-and-file Teamsters met on a vacant lot at Twelfth and Bagley, near Tiger Stadium. Provenzino was at the peak of his moral indignation against the Teamsters' leadership. Waving his arms and gesturing, he spoke in a yell to the massive turnout of truckers and dock loaders. At last they had caught the fever Provenzino had been trying to pass on to them for five years.

''We are one! We are united! We got to push scum like McMaster out of our union!'' The responding cheers were heard for blocks as curious secretaries, insurance agents, and attorneys in nearby office buildings stared from their windows.

"They are going to listen to us!" Provenzino shouted. "We're going down there right now and tell them what we think of them!"

Thunderous cheers. Provenzino led the five hundred rank-and-file members for a mile, through the streets of Detroit, to the union hall on Trumbull Avenue.

When Provenzino and the other rebels had a few beers at Andrew's the names of the local Teamster officials often ran together: Hoffa-Fitzsimmons-Johnson-McMaster. So they usually referred to everyone as "the union hall," the symbol of all the leaders' tyranny. When only the hard-core militants were left at the end of meeting-drinking sessions, the conversation usually drifted to "the clean sweep": invading the union hall, breaking down its doors, booting every officer into the street, and taking over Local 299. The dissidents agreed, though, that they would need "at least a couple of hundred people to do it," and they thought it a pipe dream when they woke up sober the next morning.

Now five hundred angry Teamsters were marching up Trumbull. People walking beside Provenzino heard him repeating, "Clean sweep! Clean sweep day! This is going to be clean sweep day!"

As Provenzino and his troops approached the union hall they were greeted with roars and applause. Another three hundred protesters were already at Local 299.

"Eight hundred rank-and-file Teamsters have converged on 299," the police reported.

Jeering and catcalling, Provenzino and the men shouted for Mc-Master. "We want him! Send him out here!" But word spread quickly that McMaster had already left town and was in Washington with Fitzsimmons. There was confusion and indecision. The dissidents had staged this demonstration primarily because of McMaster, who would have been lynched had he appeared. Now they couldn't have him. "Damn, that bastard has double-crossed us again!"

Suddenly, in the midst of the chaos, someone threw a brick through the glass door of the Michigan Teamsters' Health and Welfare Building, across the street from Local 299.

"Let's go upstairs and have a meeting before there's trouble!" shouted a rank-and-filer. Several members opened the shattered glass door of the building and began marching in.

Provenzino had no choice but to follow the membership. The glass had been broken deliberately to avoid a confrontation; the membership was thinking clearly enough to know that a physical takeover of Local 299 would bring the whole weight of Fitzsimmons and the IBT down on the rebels.

There would be no "clean sweep" today.

Once inside the big meeting hall of the health and welfare building, Provenzino admitted the press, took the podium, and again began to articulate the strikers' demands. While speaking he noticed that no union representatives were present, so he sent one of his men over to Local 299 to invite a spokesman.

The man who responded to Provenzino's invitation was Robert Holmes, international vice president and president of Detroit's Teamsters Local 337.

"I told the strikers that no matter what they wanted me to say, the situation was cut and dried," says Holmes. "They were illegally on strike and that there was nothing I could do. The next move was up to them."

As Holmes spoke, Leavitt walked into the room and asked to be recognized.

"All this garbage we're listening to now is just to get you to waver and get you back to work," Leavitt heatedly told the audience. "When you end the strike, you're playing in their ball park. So we have to stay out in order to get what we want. Those of us who stuck our necks out will have them chopped off. They won't do it immediately; they'll wait until it's all over with. I know; I've been here before."

After Leavitt spoke a striker across the hall shouted, "By God, we've given them our message. Let's go back to work!" The Teamster was booed down, and so was everyone else who suggested ending the strike.

Provenzino asked that McMaster be fired as Fitzsimmons' administrative assistant of Local 299. There was great spontaneous applause from the crowd.

"I didn't hire Mr. McMaster, and I can't fire him," Holmes told the rebels. "But I'll go to Mr. Fitzsimmons, and tell him what you said. I can't tell him what to do, he's my boss, too."[1]

The meeting went on for three hours, with Provenzino and the rank and file making their demands and Holmes talking fast for the union. Provenzino asked for a vote on whether the men should go back to work. He was certain they'd stay out. But, surprisingly, the ranks apparently accepted the promises and explanations of Bobby Holmes; they voted to end the wildcat strike. The rest of the country was to follow suit within two weeks.

A few hours after the strike was over, Dorothy Leavitt was putting her two children to bed in their cracker-box home on the West Side. Smelling a foul odor from the kitchen side of the house, something like sulfur burning, she and her eleven-year-old daughter, Babe, walked hand-in-hand into the kitchen and closed the window where the stench was pouring in. Dorothy glanced at the clock on the wall and thought it was pretty late for the sewers to be backing up and causing the horrible smell. She and Babe turned and went into the living room, but the smell was there too.

Across town, Jim Leavitt and the other members of the Unity Comittee sat in the Tip-Top Café consoling each other. They knew they had lost the strike; the men simply weren't willing to stay out long enough. And it probably wasn't just Holmes's promises; rank-and-file Teamsters had food to buy and rent to pay, and very few could stay out for long with no strike benefits coming in.

"I could have ranted and raved, but it would've accomplished nothing," Provenzino said thoughtfully.

But the conversation came alive when the defeated rebels began discussing the impact of their strike. Unity committees had sprung up all over the country, and leaders of the new groups were asking the Detroit dissidents for help and advice. And although the wildcatting had ended in Detroit, it was still going strong in several parts of the Central States region and on the West Coast. In Chicago the two IBT locals and the independent CITDU were still holding out. By early May, because of their determination, management was to raise its counteroffer to $1.65 an hour over three years. Fitzsimmons' master contract was reopened and Teamsters in the rest of the country got the benefit of the Chicago settlement.

"The 1970 wildcats proved two major things," Leavitt says. "First, they showed that Fitzsimmons was cozier with management than Hoffa ever was during negotiations, which the membership could not respect. And second, it proved that as a result of the Chicago Teamsters and the wildcat strikes, the entire rank and file benefited when wages were renegotiated and increased."

Although the Detroit rebels had quit early, they had proved that the dissident movement could grow: they had almost succeeded in the home local of both Hoffa and Fitzsimmons.

As the Unity Committee members talked, somebody told Leavitt that he had a telephone call from his brother.

"Jim, I hate to tell you this, but your home was bombed tonight."

"What?"

"Don't worry, Dorothy and the kids are okay."

"Is it bad?"

"It's a mess."

"I'll be home as quick as I can."

Stunned, Leavitt leaned up against the pay phone on the wall. Then he ran back to his table and told his friends, "They bombed my house! I can't understand it! The strike is over! And they already won!"

Provenzino and the others took Leavitt home. In the car he kept repeating, "The strike is over! The strike is over!"

"Who could've done it, Jim?"

"Them!" Leavitt responded angrily. "They did it—McMaster!"

Fearing a second attack, the rebels parked several blocks from Leavitt's home and ran to the scene.

A crowd of neighbors and passersby was milling around in the street, on the sidewalk, and on the lawn, staring at the bombed-out house. Whining police cars and fire trucks were scattered throughout the area.

With the police cars' red lights throbbing in his sweaty face, Leavitt found his wife. She was dazed, possessed by a quiet delirium, but she and the two children were miraculously unharmed. They had been blown clear of the flying debris by the force of the blast, which had been caused by three sticks of dynamite set on long fuses under the kitchen window. Nevertheless, much of the Leavitt home was destroyed.

The police investigation immediately turned up a lead. A neighbor had seen a lone man in a yellow car screeching away from the kitchen side of Leavitt's house a few minutes before the blast.

"This was not just a warning," a policeman told Leavitt. "Whoever did this knew you weren't at home and your wife and children were. He was trying to kill someone. You don't use three sticks of dynamite just to throw a scare into someone."

Within minutes after Leavitt arrived, his telephone, still in working order, rang. One of the rebels answered the phone and talked to the caller, former Unity Committee member Larry McHenry. When the rebel told McHenry about the bombing incident, McHenry curtly replied, "Yeah, I heard. Do they know who did it?"

Outside his charred home, Leavitt repeated to the press that he assumed that McMaster had ordered the bombing—and that one of his goons had carried it out—in retaliation for his activities as a rebel Teamster. With his eyes tearing from the smoke, and the veins on his neck standing out because of his rage, Leavitt denounced the Teamster leadership, including both Hoffa and Fitzsimmons.

The next day McMaster offered a $5000 reward for information leading to the arrest and conviction of the person responsible for the bombing.

Leavitt wrote in his personal journal:

Considering the character of our enemy—of which we were and are fully aware—it must have been a form of insanity that forced frail beings like us to override our fears and confusion, to put aside our sense of responsibility to our families, our own pleasures and security, and openly challenge perhaps the most ruthless, powerful group of social criminals this country has ever known . . . Thus I reject entirely any position that entails anything less than an absolute and complete repudiation of the present Teamster leadership.

June 2, 1967. The most exciting moment of the protest was the appearance of two dozen Local 142 business agents with blackjacks dangling from their back pockets. Bill Kusley (holding picket sign) is confronted by business agent Jake Abshire. (Leavitt Collection)

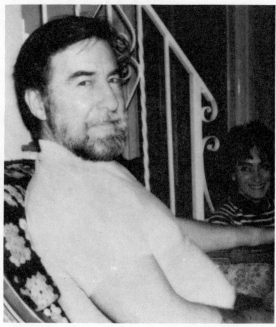

One opponent with special strength was Jim Leavitt, a Local 299 member who had been a leader in Gary in the 1967 wildcat strike and was a major force in the Detroit Unity Committee. Tough, with equal proportions of integrity and determination, Leavitt had been a trucker for twenty-three years. Jim Leavitt and his wife Dorothy. (Leavitt Collection)

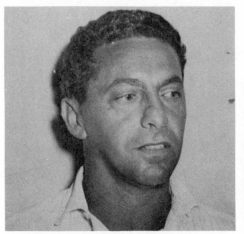

Andy Provenzino was a big brother to anyone who fought for what he believed, especially if he believed in Teamster reform. He was a natural leader, perhaps the only person in Detroit who could have held the dissidents together. (*Detroit News*)

The ''stomping of Jake,'' symbolizing the Teamsters' suppression of dissent, moved many members of the IBT to become involved in reform. Detroit Unity Committee member Bernard Jakubus is stomped by Michael Bane, an official of Local 614, on November 12, 1968. (UPI)

"When they opened fire on us, those of us who didn't have guns started throwing rocks, and then someone threw a firebomb into Angelo's car. All hell broke out after that; it was war." The FASH shoot-out on October 28, 1969. (*Overdrive*)

As the roars from the fans in Tiger Stadium filled the crisp autumn air, three blocks away, where wild cheers were still audible, twenty-seven rebels marched up and down Trumbull Avenue protesting the bombing of *Teammate*. (*Overdrive*)

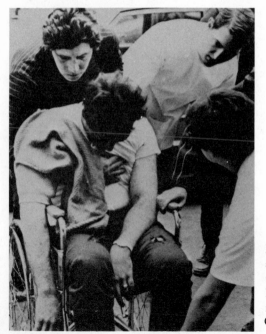

In the midst of the fighting, the Teamsters pulled out an awesome-looking machine gun, mounted it on a tripod, and began firing into the crowd . . . Miraculously, only one man was killed, an Angelo henchman from Cleveland, twenty-one-year-old John J. Gorslie, October 28, 1969. (Wide World)

Local 299 officers, 1970. (Standing left to right) Ralph Proctor, Ernest Rumsby, Rolland McMaster, Gene Page, Frank Fitzsimmons, Francis Russell, Dave Johnson, Martin Haggerty, Don Taber, (unidentified), George Roxburgh, Joe Thomas. (Front row, left to right) Earl Grayhek, Tony Sciarrotta, Steve Riddle, Richard Fitzsimmons, Donald Deters. (Johnson Collection)

Presentation of Hoffa portrait during the stewards' Christmas banquet in 1969. (Standing left to right) Rolland McMaster, Robert Holmes, Dave Johnson, James P. Hoffa, Josephine Hoffa. (Seated) Frank Fitzsimmons. (Johnson Collection)

As the top dog in jail, Galante provided the best protection against prison violence and homosexuality. Hoffa needed protection from both. Further, Galante's boss had gone to Arizona and made alliances with Hoffa's friends, Carlos Marcello and Santos Trafficante. For all these reasons, Hoffa alligned himself with Galante. (Wide World)

In September 1967, a month after the Hoffa-Provenzano incident, William Bufalino, Hoffa's long-time friend and attorney, broke off his relationship with the Teamster leader and quickly became a supporter of Frank Fitzsimmons. (*Detroit News*)

On July 17, 1972, meeting at La Costa Country Club in Southern California, the Teamsters general executive board gave Nixon its enthusiastic endorsement. After that the seventeen board members traveled to San Clemente, where they delivered the news in person and posed with Nixon for photographs. Frank Fitzsimmons introduces Ray Schoessling of Chicago to the President. Robert Holmes awaits his turn. (Wide World)

Forty-one-year-old Bill Hill was elected chairman of FASH. An imposing figure at six foot three, 230 pounds, mustachioed and with black, slicked-back hair, Hill had a powerful voice and a bearing that could intimidate an adversary if his size did not. Hill discusses the independents' demands on January 24, 1974. (FASH Collection)

Mike Parkhurst wrote several stories in his *Overdrive* on the theme of a sweetheart relationship between the government and the transnational oil companies. By October 1973 he was advocating a national truckers' shutdown. Parkhurst talks to reporters at the "Battle of Breezewood," in February 1974, during the shutdown. (*Overdrive*)

Pete Camarata left the convention center, alone at first. Then several colleagues in the rebel army joined him and walked him to his car behind the building. Had it not been for the small crowd surrounding him, Camarata would have been killed right then. Camarata (right) with TDU national secretary Ken Paff. (Jesse Epstein)

Led by Arthur Fox of PROD, angry dissidents filed charges with the IBT. In essence, according to Fox, the general executive board had "violated their fiduciary trust by dipping into the Teamsters general fund to make the contribution to, the Nixon campaign. Arthur Fox stands outside the Labor Department in 1976. (PROD Collection)

"I knew if I swung the election to Otto, then all the violence would start up again," Dave Johnson says. "And if that happened, Frank Fitzsimmons would have his excuse to impose the trusteeship. So I decided to back Bob Lins as a compromise candidate." Lins (left) and Johnson at a reception in July 1976 (Johnson Collection)

A block from the dark stadium, Dick Fitzsimmons eased back in his chair in Nemo's bar. "I was with three fellows," he says, "and I got up to leave and was on my way to my car when I saw it explode." Richard Fitzsimmons, September 1974. (*Detroit News*)

Frank Fitzsimmons appears before a Senate subcommittee in November 1977, answering questions about the purchase of insurance contracts with union trust funds. (Wide World)

Rolland McMaster's appearance before the Hoffa grand jury on December 4, 1975, was directly related to the testimony earlier that morning of top executives of the Detroit terminal of the Gateway Transportation Company. (*Detroit News*)

Ironically, the impetus for union reform and the concern about organized crime that developed in the 1970s was a result of the disappearance of Jimmy Hoffa. In the last known photograph of Hoffa, taken on July 24, 1975, he is wearing the same clothes he wore when he vanished six days later. (Tony Spina)

13 Averting the North-South Mob War

On a cold winter day, while freezing gusts swept off Lake Erie and smashed into the already frigid city, Teamster old-timers stood, bundled up, in front of Local 299, watching flames and smoke rise in the distance from an old three-story red-brick building. Although now only a warehouse, its accidental burning brought grief for those who could remember the good old days—when Local 299 was struggling and barely had enough money to pay its bills. Those were the days when everyone was together, whether just drinking beer or busting heads, when Rolland McMaster, Frank Fitzsimmons, Dave Johnson, and, a little later, Jimmy Hoffa were young rebels trying to clean up their union and fight the good fight against recalcitrant employers.

That shoddy building, 299's first headquarters, had heard great leaders speak of needed reforms and had seen lasting friendships made in the process. Its fiery demise in 1970 was symbolic of what had happened to those men and what could be expected to happen in the future.

Again, as in the past, organized crime was the determining factor in their relationships.

Some suspected that the mob had also been a factor when, on June 6, 1968, after winning the important California presidential primary, Senator Robert Kennedy was murdered in the Ambassador Hotel in Los Angeles. The assassin was Sirhan Sirhan, a former "hot walker" for the Santa Anita racetrack. "Through a friend at the track, Frank Donnarauma [a suspected New Jersey organized crime associate], Sirhan, hoping to become a jockey, got a job on a horse ranch in

Corona, California,'' says William Turner, a former FBI agent and co-author of *The Assassination of Robert F. Kennedy*.[1]

"Donnarauma and Sirhan were apparently very close and Donnarauma's name appeared throughout Sirhan's notebooks, which were later seized by the police. He wrote much of this material while he was under a series of mysterious hypnotic states, and at the time he shot Bobby Kennedy, he was quite possibly under hypnosis.''

With John and Robert Kennedy both gone, the threat against the underworld from the highest levels of government was virtually ended.

By 1967 Joseph Bonanno was permanently established in Arizona. He had made alliances with both Carlos Marcello and Santos Trafficante. Murders, illnesses, and a concentrated investigation by government agents had forced some leadership changes among the top five crime families in New York, including the Bonanno clan, which was hard pressed to find a permanent leader in the East as the Banana Wars continued. The most qualified man for that job was sitting in G Block at Lewisburg Penitentiary: Carmine Galante.

Still fiercely loyal to Bonanno, Galante blamed Gambino and Genovese for most of the underworld's problems, and he spent his cell time plotting a big comeback and revenge for their gang war against Joe Bonanno.

"He ought to be out of jail soon,'' wrote Vincent Teresa, the Boston mobster turned government informant, "'and if he is, the New York mobs are in for real trouble. He hated Vito Genovese while he was alive. To him, Genovese was a pimp, two-faced, a man you could never trust. But the man he hated most was Carlo Gambino. 'When I get out,' he used to say bitterly, 'I'll make Carlo Gambino shit in the middle of Times Square.' ''[2]

One of Galante's few friends in G Block was Jimmy Hoffa, "'a pretty decent guy, really,'' Teresa reported.

He was treated good at the prison because of Lillo [Galante], but he didn't get or ask for special privileges. He was in maximum security because he wanted to be. He was afraid of the blacks. He didn't want to get involved with them. He stayed in a cell right across the hall from me. He was well-protected, and you couldn't have got him out of there with dynamite. . . . He'd go to work at 8 A.M., take an hour for lunch, and be finished by 2 P.M. I'll say this for Jimmy. He helped many a guy who was ready to be paroled. They wouldn't have made it but for him. He'd send word out to union officials he knew, and they'd provide a job for the guy, put him to work on a truck or a loading platform.[3]

One of those Hoffa helped was a former member of the FBI's "Ten Most Wanted" list, Edward Edwards. A convicted bank robber and prison escape artist, Edwards had arrived at Lewisburg five months before Hoffa. Although he was not a local heavy like Galante and some of the other talent in G Block, Edwards got to know Hoffa, whom he remembered as "talking tough but always having a good word for everyone and always keeping himself in shape."

Edwards says, "The first time I met Hoffa was while we were going through the chow line, and he was lost. Everyone was looking at him, saying 'There's Hoffa! There's Hoffa!' He had his tray and was looking around to sit somewhere. So I introduced myself and asked him to join me. I kinda felt sorry for him, because I knew that this was something new for him . . . We just talked about the institution, the food, and prison policies. He wasn't the kind of guy you asked a lot of questions to. If he wanted you to know something, he'd tell you."

Through Hoffa, Edwards met another union official serving time at Lewisburg, former IBT vice president and Genovese captain Anthony Provenzano, who, before going to jail, was reelected and was receiving salaries as president of both Local 560 in Union City and New Jersey's Joint Council 73.

According to Edwards, Hoffa told him privately that he and Provenzano had personal problems. "It's just that he's become a sore spot with me," said Hoffa. "In 1959, when the Teamsters had the monitors supervising the union, I was told to suspend him. But I didn't. That was one of the biggest mistakes I've ever made. That guy is nuts."

Edwards didn't push the discussion further, but in August 1967 he was present when the situation seemed to come to a head. "I was sitting at a table in the chow hall across from Hoffa, and Provenzano was sitting to my right and Hoffa's left. They were talking between themselves, and I was talking to a friend of mine who was walking by. All of a sudden I heard chairs screeching, and both Hoffa and Provenzano got up and squared off. It was obvious that Hoffa was the aggressor, but no punches landed.

"So I tried to step in between the two men, but they were pretty hot and were just ignoring me. I grabbed Hoffa around the waist and pushed him back while I tried to tell them to cool it, because guards were all over the place."

Edwards says that as Provenzano backed off he was pointing at Hoffa and shouting, "Old man! Yours is coming! You know, it's coming one of these days . . . You're going to belong to me!"

Edwards added that Hoffa never told him the reason for the fight and he never asked, but he knew that Provenzano had at least one similar scene with Galante.

In September 1967, a month after the Hoffa-Provenzano incident, William Bufalino, Hoffa's long-time friend and attorney, broke off his relationship with the Teamster leader and quickly became a supporter of Frank Fitzsimmons.

"I went to see him every week until we came to the point that every time he was dissatisfied with something, he had to have somebody to blame," Bufalino says. "Whatever he had in his mind, if he wanted to squawk about something, he'd always pick on Bill Bufalino."

Hoffa's friendship with Galante and his changing attitude toward his old allies, especially Provenzano and Bufalino, helped erode his support within the Teamsters Union. Salvatore Provenzano was an acting IBT vice president under Fitzsimmons, in the absence of his brother, and thus Hoffa's undiplomatic move jeopardized much of his East Coast support, especially in New Jersey and New York, where the Provenzanos wielded enormous power.

Word of Hoffa's relationship with Galante passed quickly, and it put Hoffa in deep trouble with the remnants of the other mob families in New York. Carlo Gambino, fully aware of Galante's feelings toward him, was more and more relying on the support of Pennsylvania crime figure Russell Bufalino, William Bufalino's cousin, who was now a top adviser for the ailing Genovese family, of which Provenzano was a member. And since Provenzano and William Bufalino were related by marriage to the Giacalone and Meli mob families in Detroit, Hoffa's gangster support in his own hometown was also being neutralized.

By the end of 1967, Fitzsimmons, McMaster, Provenzano, William Bufalino, and all the people close to them had turned against Hoffa. It is quite likely that the new "hands off Hoffa" attitude was based primarily on the need for an alliance against Hoffa's vindictiveness.

"By that time Jimmy knew that he was being sold out," Dave Johnson says. "He knew that McMaster was trying to loosen his grip on Local 299 and that Fitz was taking away his support on the international level . . . I don't know that much about Jimmy's mob connections, but it was obvious that some of them, especially the guys in New York, had already come over to Fitzsimmons' side. All I knew was that Jimmy was upset about all of it. And he was sending messages back to Detroit that he was going to come back and get even. He said that by being in jail, he was learning who his friends really were."

Since Hoffa had gone to prison, only a handful of underworld figures had remained loyal to him; Marcello and Trafficante were the most important of these. With Hoffa playing ball with Galante at Lewisburg, and Bonanno forming a southern triumvirate with his two counterparts, Hoffa's support was centralized geographically. The crime families in New Jersey, New York, and Pennsylvania—forming a northern coalition and influenced by Detroit's Joseph Zerilli—had begun supporting Fitzsimmons soon after Hoffa went to jail and had ceased trying to free him.

The problems of this situation were obvious. If Hoffa was released from prison and resumed his duties as IBT general president, what would happen?

Theoretically, a nationwide mob war could have exploded out of the Banana Wars, which were still going on in New York. The northern mob was willing to fight to keep its extensive interests in the Teamsters Union, and the southern crime leaders, whose armies were bigger and stronger, were bound to retaliate, trying to claim portions of the union's funds for themselves.

At the center of this tense but quiet drama were Jimmy Hoffa and Richard Nixon.

According to one of Hoffa's closest confidants, the Teamster leadership was well aware of the fact that in 1960 Vice President Nixon had intervened on Hoffa's behalf to quash the Sun Valley indictment. Thus they naturally suspected that if Nixon became President, he would arrange for Hoffa's release. ''If Fitzsimmons and the other high Teamster officials had seriously wanted Jimmy out of jail in 1969, then their best bet was to elect Nixon.''

Instead, the IBT general executive board—which by now was in almost total opposition to a Hoffa comeback—voted overwhelmingly to support Hubert Humphrey. Had Robert Kennedy been the Democratic candidate, as seemed so likely in the spring, the IBT leadership would have been impelled to go with Nixon; their anti-Hoffa sentiments would have been overbalanced by the syndicate's fear and hatred of Kennedy. But now the cozy relationship between Nixon and the Teamsters that had begun in 1960 was put aside, at least for the moment.

After his remarkable political comeback, the ''new Nixon'' quickly fulfilled one of his campaign promises: to restore ''law and order'' in America by appointing an attorney general who could handle the job.

Having selected his Wall Street law partner, John Mitchell, as his crime-busting head of the Justice Department, Nixon balanced his administration by bringing aboard Murray Chotiner as a presidential adviser. An astute political trickster, Chotiner had numerous known connections with the underworld, particularly in the South and among the Marcello clan. With Mitchell and Chotiner, Nixon began a short-lived war against the underworld.

Nixon, according to Ed Partin, had received a favor from Marcello during the same month that the Sun Valley charges against Hoffa were dropped. Partin says that he witnessed the passing of a suitcase stuffed with $500,000 from Marcello to Hoffa, and that among those present during this meeting was Irving Davidson, a close friend of Marcello.

Davidson now says, "I know Marcello very well. I know him to this very day. He no more knew Hoffa than a bag of beans at that time . . . I don't think he knew him at all . . . I don't think he met him until a couple of years . . . I don't know if he ever met him. I know a couple of years or a year before Hoffa was going to jail, people went down to see Marcello to see if he could help him [Hoffa] with this Partin guy. And he [Marcello] told them all to go to hell, including me.

". . . I asked him [Marcello] about Partin once. I said, 'Who's this guy, Partin, from your backyard here in Baton Rouge?' He said, 'I know him; it's none of my business; and I'm not messing in any of your goddamn Teamsters. I don't want to have anything to do with it, and don't ask me about it.' "

However, *Life* magazine reported in 1966 that Marcello was involved with attempts to keep Hoffa out of jail, and that he recruited the governor of Louisiana's administrative assistant to help the cause. Marcello's telephone records indicated that Marcello had called the governor's aide on his private line at the capitol several times between June 1966 and March 1967, and that the aide served as an "intermediary in the efforts to bribe Edward G. Partin." Marcello, *Life* continued, had also been in contact with Santos Trafficante.[4] Trafficante, who had been involved in the Castro assassination plots, tried no less than three times to bribe Partin into changing his testimony. On all three occasions, Partin says he was approached by Trafficante's attorney, Frank Ragano, who had also represented Hoffa.

Both Marcello and Trafficante survived Nixon's "war against organized crime" rather well. Trafficante came through the Nixon years with an unblemished record, while Marcello had serious legal problems only once. Indicted for assaulting an FBI agent two years before Nixon took office, Marcello, in 1969, was found guilty and sentenced to two years in prison. But the trial judge, citing the mobster's "poor health," reduced the sentence to six months in a prison hospital after U.S. Supreme Court Justice Hugo Black tried to intervene on his behalf.

Chotiner and Marcello's friend Davidson had become friends, and both were active in the "Free Hoffa" movement. So when Nixon was elected, the chiefs of the southern organized crime alliance were confident that Hoffa would be released.

In 1969, the first year of the Nixon Administration, Chotiner told Davidson that Hoffa would be out of jail by Thanksgiving with a presidential pardon, and that approval had come "directly from the Oval Office." Davidson flew to Detroit to give the Hoffa family the good news.

Others got the word as well, and such talk so infuriated Walter Sheridan, the man most responsible for Hoffa's downfall, that he called his journalist friend Clark Mollenhoff, who had accepted a job as a special assistant to Nixon.

"It's all set for the Nixon Administration to spring Jimmy Hoffa," Sheridan said angrily. " . . . I'm told Murray Chotiner is handling it with the Las Vegas mob. John Mitchell and John Ehrlichman [Assistant to the President for Domestic Affairs] have something to do with it, and I'm told that it has been cleared with Nixon." [5]

When Mollenhoff inquired around, an Ehrlichman assistant told him, "Mr. Ehrlichman says you should not concern yourself with the Hoffa matter. He is handling it himself with John Mitchell." Later, during a brief telephone conversation, Ehrlichman informed Mollenhoff, "The President does not want you in this. It is highly sensitive. John Mitchell and I have it under control." [6]

But Thanksgiving came and went, and Hoffa was still in jail. What happened?

Davidson explains that Chotiner told him that the President's special counsel, Charles Colson, had persuaded Nixon to scuttle the idea. "Fitzsimmons was one of the few labor leaders supporting Nixon, and Colson wanted to keep that support," Davidson says.

This is not a very convincing reason.

Fitzsimmons and Nixon were not close in 1969, primarily because of the IBT's support of Hubert Humphrey the previous year. But Hoffa, through his supporters, had backed Nixon, who was certainly intelligent and political enough to understand that Hoffa could be more valuable to him than Fitzsimmons. Why then wasn't Hoffa released in 1969?

A more likely explanation for Nixon's eleventh-hour decision not to pardon Hoffa at that time was that John Mitchell, not Charles Colson, had persuaded him not to.

"It was generally known at the White House that Mitchell had been friends with Frank Fitzsimmons for some time and had been meeting with him fairly regularly after Nixon was elected in November 1968," says a former member of Nixon's legal staff. "Mitchell had the kind of clout with the President that if he wanted Hoffa out of jail, he would have been out—no matter what Colson or anyone else said . . .

"There was no reason back then for anyone to have a lot of confidence in the fact that Fitzsimmons was going to be a firm supporter of the President. They never even met each other until late 1970. But whatever Fitzsimmons said to the attorney general, you can bet that it was something big. Hoffa was supposed to be out in 1969."

It is quite possible that Fitzsimmons, during his sessions with Mitchell, openly discussed Hoffa's friendship with Galante at Lewisburg and the dangerous situation brewing between the northern and southern crime families. If this was the case, Mitchell must have clearly understood the implications of Hoffa's release: a nationwide, full-scale war could break out within the criminal syndicate. That was something the Attorney General and the "law and order" Nixon Administration had to worry about.

Biding his time, Mitchell could have decided to keep Hoffa in jail and told Fitzsimmons to unify his forces as lawfully as possible. One indication of the mob's cooperation came within three weeks after Nixon's inauguration, when the Banana Wars ended in New York, on February 6, 1969, with the murder of one of the major renegades of the Bonanno family. The Bonannos' victory—and subsequent peace—was further insured when Genovese died suddenly in an Atlanta prison a few days later.

The decision to keep Hoffa in prison had averted the North-South crime war.

Now union funds had to be redistributed to the South, to show good faith. But who could be the trusted middleman to make sure everyone got his fair share? It had to be someone in a neutral geographic location, someone away from the mob politics of New Jersey, New York, and Pennsylvania; and of Arizona, Florida, and Louisiana. Someone whom both the North and the South trusted.

Allen Dorfman of Chicago was the perfect choice.

Designated as "special consultant" and in control of the Central States pension and welfare funds before Hoffa went to jail, Dorfman was also well connected with the National Crime Syndicate. He had been a Hoffa supporter until February 1969. Now he had to be neutral while appeasing everyone involved.

An opportunity to display his neutrality came on February 8, two days after the end of the Banana Wars. On that day the second highest ranking IBT official, secretary-treasurer John English, died.

Hoffa, still president of the Teamsters, sent word from behind bars to caretaker Frank E. Fitzsimmons:
  "Name Harold Gibbons [as English's successor]."
  Fitzsimmons sent word back, "I can't."
  Why not?
  The Chicago Capone gang, it turned out, had another candidate. Its conduit to the Teamsters, Paul Dorfman, an old friend and business associate of Hoffa's, had called Fitzsimmons.
  "You know the deal!" Paul Dorfman barked.
  His memory refreshed, Fitzsimmons named the Capone gang's designee, a regional Teamster official from Chicago, Tom Flynn.[7]

The fact that the Dorfmans had become mediators among the various crime organizations on behalf of the Teamsters makes it much easier to understand why Fitzsimmons actually took orders from them. The most effective way to undermine Hoffa was to buy off his supporters, and the largest reservoir of Teamster money was the $628 million Central States Fund, which the Dorfmans controlled.

In a series of articles published by the *Oakland Tribune* in the fall of 1969, Gene Ayres and Jeff Morgan analyzed the tremendous power Allen Dorfman wielded over the Teamsters and the pension fund.

"Without Dorfman's approval, you may as well forget about getting a loan," Ayres and Morgan wrote. ". . . Dorfman, according to federal investigators, is the one man who can flatly say yes or no to an application for a loan from the huge pension fund . . . 'And now,' a source said, 'Frank [Fitzsimmons] hardly makes a move related to financial matters without consulting Dorfman.' "[8]

In their attempts to woo away Hoffa's chief support, Dorfman and the Teamsters lent millions to the southern underworld and its associates. For instance, over half of a $13.5 million loan granted to Irving Davidson and a partner for the promotion of a California real estate project was received after the Hoffa-Fitzsimmons split. And Trafficante attorney Frank Ragano participated in a real estate deal in Florida that involved an $11 million loan from the Central States Fund—again, over half of it received after the Hoffa-Fitzsimmons war began. Subsequently both Davidson and Ragano were indicted and convicted for crimes related to their pension fund loans, Davidson for bankruptcy fraud and Ragano for income tax evasion.

Another Hoffa mob ally, Morris Dalitz, received $27 million in 1969–70 for expansion of his La Costa Country Club in Southern California. Beginning in 1964, Hoffa had given Dalitz $19 million for the resort as well as $24 million for his Las Vegas casino interests. Although Dalitz continued to live at the Regency Apartments in Las Vegas, he had now moved his operations to California, selling the Desert Inn to Howard Hughes.[9] Hughes, another former friend of Hoffa, assumed responsibility for an $8.1 million Teamster pension fund loan when he purchased the Landmark Hotel in July 1969.

Meanwhile the union leadership drove around with ''Free Hoffa'' bumper stickers on their cars. So did the rank and file: the amiable Fitzsimmons was still unable to win their devotion. Even some of the Teamster rebels sported the bumper stickers, perhaps out of sentiment, perhaps out of a perception that any change of leadership might give them a new chance at reform. The heat was off Fitzsimmons, but if Hoffa came back the government would be watching the union and its treasury again.

Although the national dissident movement expanded in the wake of the 1970 wildcat strike, its situation in Detroit was not unlike the burned-out rubble of Jim Leavitt's home. The membership received few, if any, of the concessions they demanded. Those they did receive were cosmetic, rhetoric from union leaders who had made their careers by lying to the rank and file. McMaster was still Fitzsimmons' administrative assistant in Local 299 and his director of organizers in the Central Conference. The steel haulers were forced to accept the revenue reduction McMaster negotiated in the steel addendum to the 1970 national contract.

The Detroit rebels were badly weakened by their failure to hold the rank and file on strike and had quite realistic fears of reprisals against everyone who had participated. Exhausted, the militants mourned the overnight loss of the momentum which had taken them five years to build, while the rank-and-filer who had had his first taste of battling the system vowed that it was his last. Some felt the Unity Commitee had gone too far with the protest and jeopardized the job security of everybody who wildcatted in Local 299; others thought the rebel leaders had backed down to the Teamster leadership by not carrying out the long-awaited ''clean sweep'' of the union hall.

Andy Provenzino, still tough and defiant, was a marked man, avoided even by some who had been close friends. He would continue to challenge the union and management at meetings and during elections, but he had little membership support.

The Detroit Teamsters went back to work on April 16, 1970, and began to mend their fences with their bosses. Nationally, an impressive coalition of young union rebels was carrying on what they had started. The young Turks were responsible for the small pockets of wildcatting that still existed after the Detroit strike. In Ohio, Governor James A. Rhodes called out the National Guard. When the wildcatters finally went back to work, he sent the same tired guardsmen to Kent State University, where students were demonstrating against Nixon's Cambodian invasion. On May 4 the National Guard opened fire into the crowd of students, leaving four dead and ten wounded.

Three months before the wildcat strike began, FASH had announced that its executive board had voted to file petitions with the National Labor Relations Board in an effort to become the steel haulers' collective bargaining agent, the Fraternal Association of Special Haulers. The NLRB refused to set an immediate hearing, and when the Teamsters' ridiculously inadequate steel addendum was announced, the bitter FASH leadership was the first group to call for a national shutdown on April 5.

But the steel haulers' portion of the wildcat strike became more divisive than profitable when key FASH officials—Daryl Duncan, who had tried to break the 1967 protest, and Mike Boano, FASH's national treasurer—met secretly with Fitzsimmons in Washington during the strike and then announced their departure from the movement. Subsequently they led FASH renegades in Michigan and Ohio against the national FASH leadership and successfully broke the wildcat strike on April 16, the day after the Unity Committee capitulated.

Crediting Boano and Duncan for ''tearing FASH apart,'' McMaster wrote in the June 1970 edition of *299 News*:

> There have been several outbreaks of violence during the long strike, with steel haulers literally attempting to destroy each other's equipment. At times the FASH members took up guns and were shooting at each other.

The internal split that has developed within the FASH organization is similar to the rift within Unity Committee in Detroit and other dissident groups around the country, much of it developing as members realize that the Teamster contract is pretty good and they are being deprived of pay checks by unauthorized strikes led by FASH.

The young FASH organization was nearly wrecked by the Boano-Duncan split, and local FASH chapters began to sever their ties with the national leadership. The most common reason was that they disagreed with the FASH decision to break with the Teamsters.

"I feel this in my heart," says Boano, "Why should I create something worse than what I am trying to rectify [the Teamsters Union]? I didn't want to start a labor organization. I believe we have a good labor organization, just some of the people in it should be removed. And I don't believe it's feasible to do what they [FASH] are trying to do . . . I don't think they know what they're doing . . . I directed or instructed the people to sign [the NLRB petition], with never the intention of going through [with it], just use it as sort of a wedge to try to get a good contract out of the Teamsters."[10]

But Boano's intentions and motives look different to FASH leader Bill Hill. "As to his wanting to leave the Teamsters, we knew that Boano would never go along with it. From the very beginning, all Mike wanted was a job with the Teamsters."

Soon after Boano broke the 1970 strike, he became an organizer on the staff of Robert Cassidy, secretary-treasurer of the Ohio Conference of Teamsters. Boano and Cassidy had been arrested together on riot charges after the FASH shoot-out in Youngstown. But at that time Boano and Cassidy were on opposite sides.

In his prison cell at Lewisburg, Hoffa was receiving his own reports about the dissidents' activities. During the 1970 strike he was a mute cheerleader for the rebel forces because they were making Fitzsimmons look inept. Hoffa recognized too that his rival's brazen support of McMaster was self-defeating. Even though the rebels had suffered major losses in Detroit, they were still united with a majority of the Local 299 rank and file in their attitude toward McMaster. And that dislike of him carried up to the man who had put him in charge. It would be unwise to support the rebels openly, because it would look like a betrayal of his former friends, Teamster officials who were being harassed by the reform movement. Hoffa decided instead to capitilize on a specific rebel issue: Rolland McMaster.

Using McMaster as his primary attack point, Hoffa relayed a message to local secretary-treasurer Dave Johnson to take care of McMaster. "He was really upset about a lot of things Mac had done in 299," Johnson says. "He didn't like the way he was spending money for things like the recreation center at Saline."

McMaster learned almost immediately that Hoffa had put the machinery in motion to grind away what little respect he had left after the strike, and he responded in kind. He wrote to Hoffa warning him to "stay out of union politics" and the affairs of Local 299. He further suggested that Hoffa "leave the country" when he got out of jail. The arrogant tone of the letter so infuriated Hoffa that he ordered Johnson and his other supporters to quit playing games and "get McMaster out" of Local 299.

Hoffa had suspected that he was slowly being betrayed. Now, with McMaster's threatening letter in his possession, Hoffa had proof of what he considered treachery in his home local. It was that letter, and the reactions to it, which touched off the open war between Hoffa and Fitzsimmons.

McMaster and Fitzsimmons made the first move by summoning Donald Davis, a massive 350-pound organizer for the Central Conference, to come to Detroit as McMaster's top assistant on the spot. Violence was nothing new to Davis; he had been arrested at least eight times for strongarm crimes, and he was generally viewed as the kind of guy who would slap a paper boy around for throwing the morning edition in the bushes. That characterization was unfair, but he was a tough man who was useful when push came to shove on a picket line. By the end of 1970, however, he was to walk into—and be run out of—one of the most savage power struggles in the history of the American labor movement. He would be one of its first casualties.

Davis had attended the University of Missouri and become a popular business agent with Teamsters Local 135 in Indianapolis, appointed by Loran Robbins, whom Davis and McMaster supported for the local's presidency. Davis's best friend was the newly elected vice president of Local 135, Lloyd Hicks.

From the time the Robbins-Hicks administration assumed control in 1966, internal fighting plagued Local 135. The stronger faction was led by Robbins, the other by Hicks. Davis sided with his friend, and the two men proceeded to lay plans for Robbins's overthrow. But when Robbins's soldiers learned of the conspiracy, violence broke out between the factions.

In the midst of bombings and shootings by both sides, McMaster tried to neutralize the opposition by offering Hicks a job as a Central Conference organizer. Hicks flatly refused the job, still thinking he could whip Robbins. But later, after he and Davis had been defeated, Hicks accepted a McMaster offer and became recording secretary of Local 390, in Miami. The local's president was an old man who was terminally ill, and McMaster promised that when the old man died, Hicks would assume control.

With his friend gone, Davis continued to fight Robbins in Indianapolis. In another effort to get Davis off the scene, W. R. "Dick" Dininger, a Local 135 business agent who was Robbins's assistant and a close friend of McMaster, asked McMaster to give Davis the Central Conference organizer's position Hicks had refused.

In July 1970, the day after Davis's arrest for firebombing a truck owned by a company McMaster and Davis were trying to organize in Moline, Illinois, Fitzsimmons telephoned McMaster and told him to bring Davis to Detroit to help organize nonunion companies there. According to both Davis and McMaster, Fitzsimmons wanted to increase Local 299's membership from 19,000 to 25,000 before the next election, scheduled for November 1971. The wildcat strike had severely undercut Fitzsimmons' respect and he wanted to minimize the impact by bringing some new voters into the fold. Fitzsimmons and McMaster also needed some additional muscle in their battle with the loyal forces behind Hoffa and Johnson.

Davis, who had pled guilty to a lesser charge after his firebombing arrest and received a suspended sentence, quickly proved to be an asset to the Fitzsimmons-McMaster team. As Davis organized more companies, Fitzsimmons scored more points in his bid to unseat Hoffa. More members meant more money and more power.

"The Hoffa-Johnson people were really upset about Don's success," McMaster says. "He was doing a good job and making them look bad."

Some insiders thought that such competition was healthy for the local because it enlarged the union. But the undercover conflict would have less happy results later on.

Meanwhile McMaster, Davis, and company found time to relax a bit that summer, and McMaster's eleemosynary activities were duly recorded in the *Local 299 News*. In August he was pictured on the front page, shovel in hand, breaking ground for the $150,000

Olympic-size ''Jimmy Hoffa Swimming Pool'' at the Saline recreation center. Hoffa's response to this honor is unfortunately not on record, nor is his opinion of the subsequent Labor Day ''Mardi Gras'' at Saline, at which Ftizsimmons spoke feelingly about the IBT president-in-exile. With thousands of rank-and-file members and their families present, Fitzsimmons said that the ''great shame is that James R. Hoffa languishes in a federal prison as a political prisoner. . . . He sits in Lewisburg, Pennsylvania, this Labor Day, in a maximum security prison, serving a maximum sentence for an alleged offense, his first, while murderers, rapists, embezzlers, dope pushers, racketeers, petty thieves, and those who make it unsafe to walk the streets of America, run free on bond and bail, and most will never be brought to trial.''

Fitzsimmons concluded his talk with an appeal to the membership to write President Nixon and ask for Hoffa's release. He knew it would make no difference.

The September issue of the *299 News*, which featured Fitzsimmons' remarks, also carried some 130 photographs of the picnic: the talent show; the horseshoe-pitching contest; the be-boppers ''battle of the bands''; the big softball games; a mini-bike parade; the raffle for, among other prizes, a 1970 Buick, snowmobile, color television, and refrigerator. Josephine Hoffa and McMaster greeted the winners of the canoe race at the finish point, the ''McMaster Bridge.'' And, of course, there was the ''Miss Local 299'' contest, judged by William Bufalino with Richard Fitzsimmons happily handling the Bert Parks trip as master of ceremonies. The crowd roared and applauded when big ol' McMaster, red-faced and embarrassed, presented the winner with a trophy, then wrapped a sash around her shoulder and waist and gave her a little peck on the cheek after the ordeal.

McMaster, who chaired the day's festivities, even tried to win his old organizing partner's support away from Hoffa by naming the center's baseball diamond the ''Dave Johnson Athletic Field.''

Generally speaking, in 1970 no one worked harder to unify Local 299—its membership and officers—than Rolland McMaster.

''You have to give Mac credit for that,'' says one of his long-time allies. ''He wanted everyone to get along, and he wanted peace in Detroit. Even if he did skim a little bit here and there, like at the rec center, he was still sincere in trying to bring everyone together. And Dave Johnson used to be one of his best friends. And I'll tell you, it tore out Mac's guts to be fighting him, because he still liked and respected Dave. But McMaster was trying to tell everyone, in his own way, 'Hey, you people can have everything you had under Hoffa and more if you'll just support me and Fitz.' ''

In October, celebrations behind it, Local 299 was in a crucial organizing struggle against the Cam Chemical Company. When the company refused to negotiate, Fitzsimmons ordered McMaster and Davis to strike Cam Chemical for union recognition. Another McMaster organizer, Al Ouelette, originally appointed by Dave Johnson, helped Davis run the picket line.

Davis says, ''One day while I was with another company, Ouelette got a call from Johnson, who ordered him to allow trucks to cross the picket line. What could Al do? Dave was one of his bosses. So Al let the trucks pass, and it caused the strike to break.

''When I got to the Cam picket line and Al told me what happened, I got really mad. So I called McMaster, and he told me to reestablish the picket line. We organized the company after about a six-week strike—no help from Dave Johnson.''

During a Local 299 executive board meeting McMaster confronted Johnson and accused him of accepting a payoff from the company to break the strike. Fiercely defending himself, Johnson responded that he had merely complied with the county sheriff's writ of replevin, ordering recovery of a shipment of goods which had been placed on Cam Chemical's loading platform. Although no one believed that Johnson actually took a bribe from the company, matters weren't helped when McMaster discovered that the owner of Cam Chemical was a Masonic lodge brother of Johnson's. Thus Johnson and Hoffa became the bad guys of the Cam Chemical dispute. Everyone on the board knew that both a personal favor and union politics were involved in Johnson's decision to break the strike, and many, even among the Hoffa-Johnson supporters, were upset about it.

Taking advantage of the situation, Fitzsimmons and McMaster served up another ace with their November 1970 issue of the *299 News*. Adorning 20 percent of the front page was a photograph of McMaster with the governor of Michigan. The only other picture on the front page was one of Fitzsimmons.

In the same month McMaster sent the membership a six-page pamphlet entitled ''Progress, Like Time, Stands Still for No Man: A Report to the Members.'' Like the title, the whole publication was a not too subtle put-down of Jimmy Hoffa and a tribute to the ''progress'' Fitzsimmons and McMaster had achieved since Hoffa went to prison.

McMaster praised the local's stewards in an overt effort to gain their support:

> As most Teamsters know, there is no hidden secret to strong, hard-hitting "bread and butter" unionism. Its source is an open book. It comes from rank and file unity on the job, mutual confidence in each other, and determined collective efforts to achieve a better life for all. This means courage, "guts," and determination are things that are not negotiated in union contracts, but must come from the collective will of a group of union members to achieve as much security and dignity on the job as they possibly can.
>
> At the center of this effort on the job is the Steward.

The whole back page of the booklet was an announcement for the "Teamsters Local 299 1970 Stewards' Banquet." Frank Fitzsimmons, of course, was to be the guest speaker, but McMaster would introduce the stewards, business agents, and distinguished guests.

The Cam Chemical affair not only added to bad feelings between Johnson and McMaster. It strained relations between Johnson and the membership.

Trying to repair that situation, Johnson phoned a Unity Committee member, Peter Karagozian, and suggested they get together.

"Johnson called me and asked me to meet him," Karagozian remembers. "So I brought Provenzino with me. He came over to our table, and he said, 'Pete, I don't think Jimmy is going to be out of jail soon, and Fitz is going to stay in Washington and not run for Local 299 president. I was wondering if you would support me. It's going to be a struggle between me and Mac.' I told Johnson—and Andy agreed—that we'd support him; he was the best man for the job."

Defending his alliance with the dissidents, Johnson says, "Both Karagozian and Provenzino were hard workers. I had no problems asking for their help." But the implications were obvious. Johnson was actively soliciting the support of the rebels, McMaster's biggest enemies.

Hoffa and Johnson had realized that in future dealings with Fitzsimmons, McMaster, and Davis they had to be more tactful and less direct. Rebel support would be helpful, but there must be a way to rally the rank and file.

Like most Teamster organizers then, Don Davis paid his day-to-day organizing expenses out of his own pocket and submitted expense reports and receipts to the local office for reimbursement. Dave Johnson was the man who reimbursed Davis, and the local was then reimbursed by the Central Conference of Teamsters, which was headed by Harold Gibbons.

In the midst of Davis's organizing successes Johnson began to hold back on his expense money, which consequently restricted his activities. On several occasions McMaster had to lend Davis money so that he could do his job. By mid-December the Central Conference—via Local 299—owed Davis nearly $2000 in back expenses, and his pay checks were held up too. McMaster talked to Johnson about it with no result, so on December 15, not wanting to bother McMaster again, Davis went to see Johnson himself.

At Johnson's suggestion they met alone in McMaster's office.

As the two men sat down to talk, Davis in a chair and Johnson on the couch across the room, Davis asked about his expense money and why he wasn't receiving it. Johnson immediately began to question several of the expenditures, claiming that they hadn't been authorized by anyone but McMaster.

As Davis describes the scene, he said, ''Why the hell are you asking me about all this shit now, Dave, when it was approved by Fitzsimmons and Gibbons a long time ago?''

''Because I say it wasn't authorized, and I want you to reimburse the local five hundred and forty-eight dollars.''

''That's crazy, Dave! You owe me over two thousand in expenses right now; plus I haven't got my pay check in over four weeks.''

''Listen, Don, I can't pay you because the local's broke [because of the Saline Valley purchase], and we haven't received any money from the Central Conference.''

''The Central Conference check is in. I saw it this morning; your secretary showed it to me.''

''It's not in.''

''You're a liar, Dave!''

''You're a liar! Anyway, you shouldn't need any money considering how much you're stealing from the expense account.''

''You're a fucking liar!''

Johnson jumped off the couch and took a wild punch, which missed. Regaining his balance quickly, he grabbed the younger and tougher Davis, who shoved his attacker against a wall radiator. As he crashed into the wall Johnson stumbled, hitting his head on a table and knocking off a pottery ashtray, which fell to the floor and broke. Johnson had a small head cut and a bruised hip from the fall. He got to his feet, picked up a chair and hurled it at Davis, who floored Johnson with a hard right hand and grabbed him around the neck, yelling, ''You'd better cut this out! This is stupid!''

''I'll have you killed for this, motherfucker!''

''While you're having me killed, Dave, give me my expense money!''

Hearing the commotion, a Local 299 business agent, Joe Thomas, pounded on the door and asked what was the matter. Johnson came out, with blood flowing from the head cut, and told Thomas, ''Call the police. I'm going to get my gun!''

As Davis ran out to look for McMaster, and word traveled around the union hall, the general assumption was that Davis had intentionally and maliciously lured an unwitting and defenseless Johnson—still tough but sixty-two years old—into McMaster's office and then beat the hell out of him. Everyone also assumed that McMaster had ordered Davis to do it. Seeing the office staff's reaction, Johnson realized that this could be his opportunity to sink McMaster.

So, being pragmatic, he decided not to confuse the situation with the facts. He simply sat tight and waited for things to happen.

Out of breath after a dead sprint from the union hall, Davis found McMaster holding grievance hearings at the Fort Shelby Hotel. McMaster had already heard the details of the fight from his secretary and he shook his head in distress as he saw his frantic organizer.

''Honest to God, Mac, I didn't start it,'' Davis panted. ''He did.''

''No matter what happened, we're in big trouble, Don. I just talked to Fitz, and he says to get you out of town until things cool down. Half of Detroit is going to be gunning for both of us.''

By that time Johnson's supporters had torn Davis's car to pieces in the Local 299 parking lot, and Davis had to be flown back to his home in Indianapolis on a private plane. Within a few weeks he had lost his job. McMaster simply explained to him that he was a ''political casualty'' of the war between Hoffa and Fitzsimmons.

The Johnson-Davis fight triggered renewed demands for Mc-Master's ouster, and what sealed his fate was the fact that the fight had occurred in McMaster's own office. The Detroit newspapers reported that the incident was the result of the power struggle between Johnson and McMaster, not Hoffa and Fitzsimmons, and Davis was never asked, by any reporter, to give his side of the story.

Johnson told the sympathetic press that McMaster's organizer had repeatedly kicked him and beat him with the cheap clay ashtray, but he never filed assault charges against Davis. Nevertheless, Davis voluntarily took a lie detector test in Indianapolis which indicated that he was indeed telling the truth—that Johnson had thrown the first punch.

Jimmy Clift, vice president of Robert Holmes's Local 337, summed up nearly everyone's sentiments at a membership meeting on the day of the fight. ''Are we going to oust that son of a bitch over at Local 299?'' and Holmes, as chairman of Detroit's Joint Council 43, called a joint council meeting to consider Clift's dramatic question.

On December 21, the night before the joint council meeting, Fitzsimmons attended a Local 299 staff meeting that McMaster had called. Local officers and business agents, most of them loyal to Fitzsimmons and McMaster, were present too. Neither Johnson nor Otto Wendell, the local's recording secretary, showed up. A private set of minutes for the meeting was kept by a participant.

Early on the agenda was an announcement that Chuck O'Brien's mother, Sylvia Pagano Paris, had died and members of the staff were invited to attend the wake. The stewards' Christmas dinner was discussed, and the publication and distribution of the Labor Day ''Mardi Gras'' commemorative booklet. Then to the ''reason why we are here.''

Calling the situation ''a dangerous thing,'' Fitzsimmons asked to hear what had happened on the day of the fight. ''I don't want to condemn anyone until I know the whole story.''

A badly shaken McMaster explained that he had had breakfast with Davis and others on the morning of the fifteenth. ''Davis just mentioned in passing that he was on his way to the union hall. I thought nothing of it.''

Piecing the story together from Davis's version, McMaster emphasized that Johnson had provoked the fight by taking the first punch. ''I personally think that there is a conspiracy to weaken 299, Fitz . . . This whole thing is on me; it's concerning me!

''My wife called me and she was hysterical. She said that Jimmy Clift was calling and threatening me. She had to leave the house . . .

''Here's the strange part of it,'' McMaster went on explaining. ''I got a call Friday that Johnson had accepted a call from Provenzino and Dave told him that he wanted some help to get me out of control.''

''The rebels are going to try to make a martyr out of Dave Johnson,'' Fitzsimmons said. ''As far as we're concerned, nothing happened. Nobody should talk about it. There are fellows like Mr. Clift who want to make statements. We don't. Everything should be just routine.''

Sensing that Fitzsimmons was evading the real issue, McMaster insisted, ''Now, I'm going to tell you this, Fitz: I didn't generate this problem. I didn't have a goddamn thing to do with it, and I don't like people like Clift participating in our affairs.

''Fitz, you offered me a better job than this. But I'll tell you right now, as it is going, this local is going to be ruined. Decide now whether you want me to go. You have some goddamn good men here and only two handicaps: Dave Johnson and Otto Wendell. Make up your mind on what's going on.''

With all eyes upon him, Fitzsimmons paused momentarily and said, ''I would like everyone to stay around here and work.'' McMaster still had Fitzsimmons' support.

McMaster turned to the staff members and barked, ''Okay, we have a joint council meeting tomorrow. Be united, and don't be afraid if we get into a tussle. It'll be an open fight.'' Then, seeing negative looks on several faces, McMaster slowed down and said, ''I have to ask you fellows how much trouble you want to get into; mine is personal. We took an oath together, and I want to know if any one of you doesn't want to support me.''

After a moment of tense silence, George Roxburgh replied, ''I don't think we can go in there and do this.''

Another trustee, Ralph Proctor, claimed to be ''neutral.'' Then, staring at Fitzsimmons, Roxburgh said, ''Let Frank Fitzsimmons do what he is going to do. We'll go along with him.''

The staff nodded agreement with Roxburgh and the pressure fell back onto Fitzsimmons. He was facing a major mutiny if he made the wrong decision.

The meeting broke up and Fitzsimmons asked McMaster if he needed a ride home. During the drive to Wixom, Fitzsimmons made his decision.

On December 22, Joint Council 43, composed of the thirteen Teamster locals in and around Detroit, met, with Fitzsimmons present, to decide whether McMaster should be barred from Local 299.

''There were about 150 delegates present at the meeting,'' says Holmes, who presided. ''Everyone thought that we were going to have to carry McMaster out swinging, because everyone was going to vote to throw him out. There was never any question of that. Jimmy Clift had made sure of it.''

But the anticipated battle never took place. McMaster told the delegates that both he and Don Davis had been framed but at the same time he graciously and calmly stepped down as the chief executive officer of Local 299.

Hoffa's plan to knock McMaster out of power in Local 299 was accomplished, and also according to plan, Fitzsimmons was correspondingly weakened. The executive board promptly appointed Johnson to fill the vacancy.

''Everything that happened to me was all caused by Jimmy's behind the scenes chopping me up,'' is McMaster's view. ''I wasn't going to forget this deal.''

On December 23, the day after the joint council meeting, Fitzsimmons returned to Washington and went to the White House to be introduced to President Nixon. William Usery, then a federal mediator, and presidential special counsel Charles Colson were also present. It was the first time a Teamster president had been invited to the White House since the days of Dave Beck.

Fitzsimmons' newfound friendship with Nixon seemed to ease the pain of his tremendous setback in Detroit. It was a loss from which he and McMaster never recovered—until the murder of Jimmy Hoffa fifty-five months later.

14 "Free Hoffa!"

On January 18, 1971, Washington columnist Jack Anderson disclosed details, then unconfirmed, of the CIA-underworld plots to assassinate Fidel Castro. Anderson reported that CIA officials James O'Connell and William Harvey had contracted with gangster John Rosselli to coordinate the murder. Asserting that the strategy was to kill Castro before the scheduled Bay of Pigs invasion in mid-April 1961, Anderson discussed intricate facts about poison pills being passed to Rosselli by the CIA on March 13, 1961, during a meeting with O'Connell at the Fontainebleau Hotel in Miami.

The respected journalist went on to offer a chilling theory that some of the principals in the Castro plots might have subsequently become involved in the planning and execution of the assassination of President Kennedy.

Although the source for Anderson's story was Rosselli, the central figure in the conspiracy, this early account did not mention others who were probably involved in the plans: Santos Trafficante, Russell Bufalino, and Jimmy Hoffa. Two other Trafficante-Bufalino-Hoffa associates, who also participated in the conspiracy to subvert the Cuban government, weren't mentioned either. One of them, Salvatore Granello, had been found three months earlier stuffed into the trunk of a car and shot four times in the head. The other, James Plumeri, was brutally slaughtered several months later, in 1971.

Somehow it was a bad omen for the imprisoned Hoffa at a time when things in Detroit seemed a bit more cheerful for him.

In Detroit that January, distinguishing Hoffa-Johnson supporters from those of Fitzsimmons-McMaster was easy. The Hoffa people were smiling, even laughing. Fitzsimmons lamented the loss of McMaster in Detroit but made him an international general organizer. McMaster was still in the Central Conference of Teamsters, still responsible for the steel haulers and owner-operators. But his promotion and a raise of $8000 a year did not keep him from smarting over his loss of power in Local 299. And with Fitzsimmons' loss of prestige, rank-and-file support for Hoffa increased.

Although Fitzsimmons could not at the moment challenge the Hoffa forces in Detroit, he remained well entrenched in the IBT. There were rumors that Hoffa might be paroled from prison sometime before the IBT convention in July 1971, and the thirteen other vice presidents, secure in their baronies, didn't need Hoffa returning to centralize the union again. Fitzsimmons, quietly confident, knew that he had taken care of that through the President and the attorney general.

On January 11, Fitzsimmons' partisans were smiling again. Hoffa had lost his Supreme Court appeal for the overturn of his pension fraud conviction in Chicago. Facing an extra five years in jail, in addition to the eight he was already serving, Hoffa was far from sure of getting out in time for the convention.

Hoffa had just been implicated in another pension fraud scandal in the trial of David Wenger, an auditor indicted in 1968 for conspiracy and bribery after he tried to obtain millions of dollars in loans from the Central States Pension Fund. Organized crime figures in Florida, New Jersey, and New York were also involved in the scheme. Herbert Itkin, a slim, gentle undercover agent for both the FBI and the CIA, had revealed that Wenger had served as Hoffa's bag man. Itkin had worked in the pension fund for six years, feeding the feds for five. He explained that loans in the East and Southeast were channeled through Wenger, while the rest of the country dealt with Allen Dorfman until Dorfman took over the whole show, and he testified that a mandatory 10 percent kickback was demanded on Hoffa's behalf for numerous loans from the fund. He quoted Wenger as insisting on getting half of the 10 percent on such ''deals'' in return for avoiding ''headaches'' (labor troubles) with Hoffa. Asked under cross-examination whether Hoffa was ''supposed to get a piece of whatever deals [were] made,'' Itkin snapped, ''I said Wenger said [Hoffa] had to get a piece. He told me he wasn't getting as much as Wenger promised.''

''Who told you?'' asked the defense attorney.

''Hoffa,'' Itkin replied.

In spite of Itkin's revelations—which led to six convictions—the

"Free Hoffa" movement plodded along. The Michigan Building Trades Council, for example, collected 250,000 signatures asking for Hoffa's release, claiming that he had been subjected to "cruel and inhuman punishment" while in prison. The petitions were given to Senator Norris Cotton of New Hampshire, who presented them to White House special counsel John Dean. They were widely publicized by one of Cotton's strongest supporters, William Loeb, publisher of the state's *Manchester Union Leader*. From 1963 to 1965 the *Union Leader* had received $2,082,656 in loans from the Central States Pension Fund. Lobbying heavily for a Hoffa pardon from Nixon—whom Loeb had helped capture 80 percent of the vote in the 1968 New Hampshire primary—the newspaper actively sought, but never received, a signed confession from Ed Partin that he had perjured himself during Hoffa's jury-tampering trial.

While Loeb and others handled the publicity, Carlos Marcello kept the heat on Partin, whose federal protection had been relaxed since his testimony sent Hoffa to prison. Via D'Alton Smith, a powerful businessman who was Marcello's son-in-law, Marcello tried to help his friend Hoffa by forcing Partin to sign an affidavit admitting that he had lied after being coerced to do so by the government's "get Hoffa" squad.

Since the Chattanooga trial Partin had been harassed with trumped-up charges of restraint of trade and extortion, but he was still the head of Local 5 in Baton Rouge. He was told that his legal problems would end once he decided to cooperate with Marcello. One of Smith's employees, Audie Murphy—the most decorated soldier of World War II—obtained a thirty-one-page deposition from Partin in which he allegedly recanted his testimony. Partin would not recant, but he hoped that giving Murphy some sort of statement would get some of the pressure off him.

"I gave 'em nothing," he says. "Sure, I said some words, and they wrote them down. But they were accusing me of doing everything, including being involved in the Kennedy assassination. So I just told them what they wanted to hear and refused to sign anything."

Although Partin's signature was not on the document, the several witnesses who were present while he made his statement tried to make hay out of it anyway. But when the document was given to Morris Shenker for Parole Board consideration in March, Shenker wisely refused to submit it.

During the Parole Board's review the panel asked for a ruling on whether it could grant a parole to Hoffa but restrict his future union activities. The Justice Department replied that neither of Hoffa's convictions was covered under the Taft-Hartley Act or the Landrum-Griffin Act as grounds for barring an official from union affairs. The board rejected Hoffa's request for parole—the second since October 1970—but gave him ninety days to appeal for review.

Desperate, the team went back to work on Partin. D'Alton Smith and Audie Murphy again tried to squeeze an affidavit out of him. This time their ploy was to get Partin to meet with a man named Gordon McLendon, the owner of radio station KLIF, in Dallas. McLendon was one of the ''close friends'' whom Jack Ruby listed for the Warren Commission in 1964. Ruby had been in touch with KLIF on the evening of November 22, 1963, posing as a reporter and helping the station set up interviews about the assassination, as well as during the afternoon and evening of November 23, the night before he shot Oswald.

''But when it came down to doing business, McLendon wasn't involved,'' Partin says. ''Instead I was dealing with Audie Murphy, Arthur Egan from the *Manchester Union Leader,* and McLendon's brother-in-law, Lester May,'' a former U.S. attorney in Dallas.

The three men got another unsigned, worthless statement from Partin, and that was all. Partin was in terrible trouble and wasn't sure how he would get out of his frame-ups, but in the years after the Kennedy assassinations he was even less likely than before to repent his testimony against Hoffa. The Parole Board decision would stand.

Fitzsimmons, now a shoo-in for the general presidency, wrote in the *299 News* that he was ''deeply saddened'' by the Parole Board's verdict. ''It has been my fondest wish for more than four years now that Jimmy would be back with us.'' Johnson, Hoffa's loyal caretaker, simply said that he was ''surprised and disappointed.'' Some Hoffa supporters, burly truckers though they were, cried when they heard that Jimmy wouldn't be getting out after all.

Down to five members, the Unity Committee was too preoccupied with its own problems to worry about Hoffa's. Out of jobs and in danger of losing their union membership, the five remaining dissidents had filed a complaint in court demanding that they not be punished for their political activities in the union.

With Provenzino and the others struggling for personal survival and McMaster apparently out of Local 299 politics, Larry McHenry rejoined the rebel movement. Turning his bitterness toward Johnson, accusing him of misusing union funds, taking bribes, and fixing elections, McHenry published his charges in the *Watchdog Bulletin*, his one-man newsletter. He continued to work on McMaster's behalf, and rebels and union officials alike suspected that he was really on McMaster's payroll, especially when he attacked Johnson. McHenry maintains that "as a rebel, I only attacked who was standing up front, no matter who it was."

As McHenry's attacks on Hoffa and Johnson continued, Provenzino took time out from his own problems to write an open letter to the IBT general executive board: "Let's end the honeymoon with the Mafia and the carriers, and return to the principles of honest trade unionism. What say? As of this date, and despite all information you may have, the principal officer of Local 299, Dave Johnson, does not endorse Frank E. Fitzsimmons as a candidate for the office of General President of the IBT."

Detroit unionists viewed Provenzino's letter as an expression of independence from McHenry and his *Watchdog Bulletin*, and of the dissident community's continued support of the Hoffa-Johnson forces.

The May issue of the *Watchdog Bulletin*, headlined, "MCHENRY WINS," informed Detroit Teamsters that McHenry had won permission from union attorneys James P. Hoffa and David Uelmen to examine the financial records of Local 299 from 1968 to 1970. In another *Watchdog* he wrote that after a previous attempt to obtain the documents from Johnson and Otto Wendell he had been jumped and badly beaten in the local's parking lot, and he named the men he said had done it.

"I walked out of the 2741 Trumbull union hall front door to the back of the parking lot where I had parked my sister's car which I had used that day. Then they got me—three of Hoffa's goons—right beside the car."

McHenry further claimed that the beating took place immediately after he had talked to Wendell, who had refused to give him the information he was demanding. After insisting that the Local 299 officials had ordered him silenced, he accused Johnson of responsibility for the McMaster-inspired Saline Valley fiasco.

Two of the men who allegedly beat up McHenry were later found murdered; one of them had been killed by the third person supposedly involved in the attack. And within six months of the attack on McHenry, Wendell's barn was destroyed by an arsonist: "I lost livestock and farm equipment during the fire at my place in Fowlerville,'' Wendell said. ''I can't mention any names, but I knew that the guy who did it was a local rebel who thought I had him beaten up a few months before the fire.''

McHenry wrote in the *Watchdog,* ''What happened to Otto Wendell's barn? It burned down. Now we are certainly sorry that it happened and we want to convey our sympathy for this costly and unfortunate catastrophe to one of our Executive Board, but . . . If Joint Council 43's money, that comes from our dues goes into putting a new barn on Otto's farm, that is a gross misuse of funds . . . ''

At a party sometime later McHenry took credit for the firebombing in front of several witnesses. Questioned about that evening, McHenry shrugs off his conversation as ''big talk which meant nothing.''

The Local 299 recreation center had deteriorated since Johnson became president. The ''Jimmy Hoffa Swimming Pool'' was surrounded with barbed wire, and weeds had engulfed a children's train and its tracks. Johnson had repeatedly said, ''We can't afford the rec center!'' He also said that the local union was in poor financial shape because of the expense of maintaining the area. With McMaster out, Johnson was the ideal target to bear the responsibility for conditions at Saline. It was such a volatile issue among the rank and file, who would be voting for delegates to the IBT convention, that even Provenzino and the Unity Committee decided to support McHenry's investigation of Johnson. They allowed their names to be used in the *Watchdog Bulletin*, which led to charges that the dissidents, including Provenzino, were playing up to McMaster.

Nevertheless, and in spite of some favorable publicity, for once, the dissidents failed to capture a single seat among Local 299's sixteen-member delegation to the convention. Of the sixty-six people who ran, Provenzino finished twentieth and McHenry fifty-second.

Although the rebel movement in Detroit was almost nonexistent, Unity Committees continued to emerge and grow elsewhere, protesting the corruption within the IBT, especially its pension fund. Gearing up to try to overthrow both Hoffa and Fitzsimmons at the convention, the rebels, calling themselves the Teamsters United Unity Committees of America, searched for a leader who could challenge the Teamsters' high command in July.

Considering his background, Don Vestal of Tennessee was an unlikely Teamster to be found in the dissident movement. The deep lines in his weatherbeaten face told some of the tale of Vestal's rough-

and-tumble past in the Teamsters Union. Yet the spark in his eyes remained and the fire in his soul blazed; Vestal was ready for another battle and the scars he knew would accompany it. Perhaps he felt that, having survived Hoffa's orders to have him killed as a government informant in 1960, he could take on anything else the Teamsters had to offer.

Vestal had been Hoffa's friend and adviser from the mid-1940s to 1960. At that time Hoffa had tried to throw the Nashville local into trusteeship, but Vestal whipped him in the courts and remained in control of Nashville's Local 327.

"After Hoffa was convicted for pension fraud in Chicago, he was desperate, using his union office to influence people to force witnesses against him to change their testimonies," Vestal says. "He told me, through some of his middlemen, that my local wouldn't get any strike benefits or any other kind of help from the IBT unless I helped him get an affidavit from Partin saying that he had lied on the witness stand. To sweeten the pie for me, I was offered $10,000 cash. I was also told that I could write my own ticket in the union if I helped Jimmy.

"When I refused, Hoffa tried again to throw me into trusteeship."

After Hoffa was imprisoned Fitzsimmons took up the work of doing Vestal in. Finally, in March 1971, Fitzsimmons ordered Local 327 into trusteeship, and Vestal filed suit again.

While the case was being heard in federal court, there was a wild shoot-out at Vestal's Nashville home. "About a week or so before the shooting, I had been working late and forgot to put out the light in my office when I left. So, thinking I was still there, my secretary-treasurer, who had been meeting with Fitzsimmons, gave the key to my office to a couple of business agents. They came into my office, saw I wasn't there, and started shooting the place up anyway."

When the two gunmen were caught, the police told Vestal that they had been sent by the secretary-treasurer. Vestal tried to find him and couldn't, so he fired him by telegram. "When he found out about it he called me on the telephone and told me that he was coming over with three men to kill me. I told that bastard to come on.

"When they got there, they had brought five rifles and three handguns with them and started to open fire into my house. My wife was really scared so she called the police. But my son and I and a friend of mine also had our .38 pistols, so we went out on the lawn and shot at 'em as they were driving away."

Vestal and his two volunteers shot out the tires of the fleeing automobile. The assailants climbed out of their car, still firing, and were running down the street when the police got there.

The four gunmen were arrested but the local district attorney refused to prosecute. Three days after their arrest, Fitzsimmons hired two of the four, including the dismissed secretary-treasurer, as IBT organizers.

While Vestal and the goons shot it out in Nashville, Hoffa was hoping for a miracle. He tried to get a release on grounds that his wife was dying of a heart attack, and that request was denied also, but he was given a six-day furlough. In early April he went to California, unguarded, saw his wife in a San Francisco hospital, and met with several union officials, including Fitzsimmons, Bob Holmes, and Dave Johnson. He then met secretly at the Hilton Hotel with White House special counsel Charles Colson and presidential adviser Murray Chotiner.

"Hoffa said that he was told by those two guys that the President would release him from prison if he resigned all his union offices before the IBT convention in July," one of Hoffa's assistants remembers. "They also told him that they wanted him to support Fitz to take his place." But Hoffa refused to commit himself, still hoping that he would be freed through a presidential pardon.

In early May Hoffa asked a federal judge in Chicago to allow his two sentences to run concurrently, which would make him eligible for another, immediate parole review. The request was denied, and two days later Fitzsimmons would only say, "I will run for the presidency if Hoffa is not available."

With almost all hope lost, Hoffa sent his son, James P. Hoffa, to see Will Wilson, the head of the Justice Department's Criminal Division.

"It was my thirtieth birthday, May 19, and I went in and told Wilson that my dad was willing to resign as president of the Teamsters in return for his release from prison," young Hoffa recalls. "There was no deal made at that point; Wilson said that he didn't have the power to make it. But he told me to come back and see him in a few weeks."

Hoffa's son, a former All-State linebacker, had graduated from the University of Michigan Law School in 1967 and run unsuccessfully for the State House that same year. As other alliances were undermined, James P. was becoming his father's most trusted confidant and legal adviser.

Young Hoffa's next assignment was a trip to Louisiana for another try at persuading Ed Partin to change his testimony. When that failed he met with Wilson again and told him that his father would not seek reelection: "The deal was set. Wilson told me that my dad would be paroled by the end of the summer."

On June 3, 1971, James P. Hoffa joined Fitzsimmons in a press conference at which Fitzsimmons, pledging undying devotion to Hoffa, announced that Hoffa would not run for reelection as IBT president and would support Fitzsimmons as his successor. The coup had been four years in the making. Surely nothing could stop it between now and July.

What almost stopped it was the last thing Fitzsimmons or Jimmy Hoffa or anyone else expected—a suit on behalf of the Teamster rank and file which asked for an injunction against the convention, charging that Hoffa had illegally delegated his power to Fitzsimmons when he went to jail. Don Vestal, the plaintiff, contended that Fitzsimmons was merely the IBT general vice president and as such was not constitutionally qualified to call the convention.[1] Several hundred rank-and-file members of the United Unity Committees of America traveled to Washington from all parts of the country to demonstrate in support of the suit.

Filed in Washington on June 21, just fifteen days before the opening of the IBT convention in Miami Beach, the suit presented a new problem for Fitzsimmons and the Teamsters. They knew that the convention could be legally held only if Hoffa resigned as president, so that Fitzsimmons, as general vice president, would have the authority to call the convention.

An hour after Vestal's suit was docketed, Fitzsimmons called a special meeting of the IBT general executive board at the convention site, the Playboy Plaza Hotel in Miami Beach. All the members of the board except Hoffa were present, but James P. Hoffa brought word from Lewisburg.

In his message of resignation Hoffa did not mention Fitzsimmons by name. He simply said: "Under the Constitution, the General Vice President takes over my duties and position subject to election in July of 1971. At such time, I hope the delegates will give him the honour of being elected to the General Presidency of the great International Union." Immediately after Hoffa's statement was read to the vice presidents, Fitzsimmons was sworn in by secretary-treasurer Tom Flynn as general president of the IBT.

Fitzsimmons then called in the press to announce Hoffa's resignation, and a moment later in strolled the President of the United States. Nixon sat down next to the new president of the Teamsters Union and said, ''My door is always open to President Fitzsimmons, and that is the way it should be.''

There was a brief picture-taking session; then Nixon and the executive board retired to a private meeting room which was closed to the public and the press.

The newspapers of June 22 were bitter reading for Hoffa, alone in his prison cell. That day he followed up his resignation as president by resigning his positions as director of the Central Conference of Teamsters, chairman of the Central States Drivers Council, and president of both the Michigan Conference and Joint Council 43. The most painful step was giving up the presidency of Local 299, but he did it ''so that they would have no more excuses to refuse my parole . . . Maybe that was the hardest job of all; I had been head for so long of that local, which was my starting place so many, many years ago.''[2]

On June 30, six days before the convention, U.S. District Judge June Green refused to order an injunction which would stop it, as Vestal had asked. Instead she ruled that the IBT must become a ''more democratic organization'' and that its officers must rewrite the union's constitution, giving the rank and file an opportunity to vote on this new constitution.[3] The union appealed, and the case died when the dissidents failed to come up with the money to contest the matter.

At a press conference a reporter suggested that Don Vestal run against Fitzsimmons at the convention; the new dissident leader smiled and announced his candidacy, and he went to Miami Beach prepared to follow through on a campaign. But he knew the chances were slim, and when some of his East Coast supporters urged him to ''resign from the race—we've got too much against us with the President of the United States supporting Fitz,'' Vestal withdrew in favor of Theodore Daley, secretary-treasurer of New York Local 445, a pro-Hoffa man who had already announced his candidacy.

For four days, July 5 to 8, 2100 delegates to the IBT convention enjoyed themselves, soaking up the praise bestowed upon them by President Nixon, in a ''Dear Frank'' letter; Secretary of Labor James Hodgson; Senator Harrison Williams, Jr.; United Auto Workers president Leonard Woodcock; former IBT general president and former convict Dave Beck; Josephine Hoffa, who had recovered from her heart attack; Hoffa's son James P.; an archbishop, priests, rabbis, ministers;

and assorted other labor leaders and politicians. Resolutions were passed on ecology; an end to the Vietnam War; and permanent jobs in the union for Hoffa's wife and son. A dues increase for the membership was voted, as well as hefty raises for the members of the general executive board, the union's trustees, and the IBT general organizers. Fitzsimmons and each member of the general executive board, including a newly added fifteenth vice president, were elected by acclamation. Both Carlos Marcello and Santos Trafficante were able to swing vice presidential slots for their associates, Roy Williams and Joe Morgan. In addition, Salvatore Provenzano officially replaced his brother Anthony.

Neither the press nor the delegates paid much attention to the passage of "Resolution No. 8," a general executive board resolution regarding the "problem of special commodity riders." The convention empowered the board to "adopt and place into effect an extensive and intensive program to root out the employers who may be engaged in violations of the Special Commodity Riders [addenda] . . . " Few of the Teamster delegates realized that the vaguely worded resolution gave the executive board carte blanche to destroy the union leadership's most troublesome enemies, the owner-operator truckers and the Fraternal Association of Steel Haulers, which represented many of them. Perhaps not even the executive board members who drafted it realized that the proposal added yet another safeguard against any attempt by Hoffa to regain power in the union.

When the convention adjourned, Don Vestal went back to Nashville in discouragement. A week later Fitzsimmons, now the fully empowered general president, put Vestal's Nashville local into trusteeship and, this time, the courts refused to overrule.

Out of a job and angry, Vestal met with eighty union rebels from sixteen states on July 25–26 in Toledo, Ohio. From this meeting came a new grass-roots organization, Teamsters United Rank-and-File, which included members of the various Unity Committees; two California groups, the 500 at 50 Committee and the Fifth Wheel; Philadelphia's The Voice; and FASH, among others. The reformers met again in Denver on September 25–26 to formulate structure and by-laws.

"The main purpose of the organization was to run TURF slates against union incumbents who were abusing their authority in their locals," Vestal explains. "Also, we were trying to clean up corruption in the Central States Pension Fund while bringing democracy to the Teamsters Union."

With Grover "Curly" Best as president and Vestal as executive director, TURF at once began an ambitious organizing campaign, and by the end of 1971 nearly fifteen strong TURF chapters had been established.

Litigation, however, was equally important to TURF. In late 1971, when the general executive board voted to give Hoffa a $1.7 million lump-sum pension, Vestal filed a suit charging that if Hoffa received his pension in such a manner and other union officials received theirs under the same formula, then no money would remain in the Teamsters Affiliates Pension Fund, reserved for Teamster office holders and, as Vestal says, "invested in blue-chip stocks." Though he eventually lost the case, Vestal managed to hold up payment of Hoffa's pension for a couple of years.

To complement the Hoffa pension suit, and to follow up on the July 14th indictment of Allen Dorfman on kickback charges, Vestal's son, Gerald, also an IBT member, filed suit for an accounting of the Central States Fund. In his claim to the court, Gerald Vestal wrote:

The pension fund has been mismanaged by the defendants, making loans without reference to the risks involved but rather on the basis of friendship, graft, and payoffs to the defendants, their business associates and others. The pension plan has formed an open bank to members of the gambling syndicate and has specialized in lending money on substandard risks, without obtaining sufficient credit information, with insufficient collateral, and has been forced to charge off countless millions of dollars of bad loans.

Through a motion of discovery the Vestals won access to the pension fund's secret ledger of loans. The information within was devastating. Reporting total assets of $917.9 million, the records disclosed that the fund had plowed hundreds of millions of dollars into loans that were not merely unwise but often fraudulent.

A subsequent audit by Price Waterhouse & Company yielded further revelations, such as the fact that 89 percent of the fund was committed to real estate loans, when most similar pension funds do not put more than 5 percent into such ventures. Nor were these loans on prime real estate; they often involved second or third mortgages. Some 36.5 percent of the real estate loans were in default, and in other cases they were being paid back only through additional loans.

As Jon Kwitny of the *Wall Street Journal* summed up the audit information:

Through such loans . . . the fund has passed millions of dollars to companies identified with Mafia members and their cronies. It has also lent millions of dollars to employers of teamsters; and according to . . . rank-and-file teamsters, the union has sometimes deserted members' interests in favor of the employer-borrowers.[4]

"The thing that's absolutely frightening," according to a Justice Department official, "is that through the Central States Pension Fund, the mob, quite literally, has complete access to nearly a billion dollars in union funds."

Even with their hard-won confirmation of the Central States Fund's financial cheats, TURF was in effect throwing rocks and sticks at the well-oiled IBT machine. Massive support from the rank and file or from the federal government was not forthcoming, and TURF could not keep up the pace—in its organizing or its litigation. Vestal himself had to withdraw from his organizing activities or face personal financial ruin, and with him gone, arguments and defections began. The most damaging blow was the resignation of their first vice president, Andrew Suckart of Cleveland. His TURF colleagues didn't know that in June 1971, Suckart had pled guilty to possession of 98 bars of nickel stolen from an interstate shipment the previous year, and had been put on probation. He resigned from TURF in January and soon afterward took a job with William Presser. TURF was no longer effective, and Teamster dissidents were ill prepared for the next union crisis, which would come with negotiations for the 1973 master contract.

Again as in the past, the rank and file became spectators to the activities within their union. Although several Unity Committees in larger cities survived the fall of TURF, their leaders too were walled off from participation—a situation somewhat like that of Jimmy Hoffa, who was still stuffing mattresses in Lewisburg. In July 1971 his hopes of release had brightened when the Parole Board agreed to another hearing on August 20. But the Parole Board hammered away at Hoffa's lump-sum pension, the IBT salaries of his wife and son, and his connections with organized crime. As in the previous two hearings, the board voted unanimously to reject Hoffa's appeal for probation. Feeling betrayed, Hoffa loyalists blasted the Justice Department and the Nixon Administration for keeping Hoffa in jail. Continuing his charade, Fitzsimmons too criticized the Parole Board's decision. On Labor Day at Saline Valley Farms he called for Nixon to pardon Hoffa.

As Fitzsimmons spoke, Detroit Teamsters were still upset about the latest bombing. Four sticks of dynamite had been placed under James Clift's car in the driveway of his Farmington home. Clift claimed that he had no enemies, but everyone knew he had been the leader of the anti-McMaster delegation the winter before. McMaster says that Clift at first blamed him but then became "very friendly to me." It was the second act of violence against a known enemy of McMaster since his departure from Local 299; it followed by three months the firebombing of Otto Wendell's barn. The pattern of violence that was beginning to take shape clearly showed that Hoffa's relinquishment of power had not brought peace to Local 299.

It had, however, opened up five key union posts besides the presidency. Harold Gibbons became head of the Central Conference of Teamsters; newly elected IBT vice president Roy Williams of Kansas City was named chairman of the Central States Drivers Council; Robert Holmes became president of both the Michigan Conference of Teamsters and Joint Council 43; and Dave Johnson was elected by the local executive board to succeed Hoffa as interim president of Local 299.

Nearly sixty-four, Johnson wasn't eager to remain in union politics. Since his brawl with Don Davis in December he had started carrying a gun and had hired a former policeman, Mike Raggish, as a bodyguard. But because Hoffa had not been released from prison by fall, Johnson swallowed hard and made plans to run for the local presidency. Fitzsimmons, with his prestige still low in Detroit, didn't give much consideration to challenging the popular Johnson. He settled for running for reelection as Local 299's vice president, the post he had held since 1946.

Surprisingly, McMaster didn't follow his boss's lead. Instead, he tossed his blackjack into the ring and had himself nominated for president. Only one member stood up to challenge his qualifications—Peter Karagozian. An archenemy of Larry McHenry, Karagozian had been a candidate for Local 299 trustee on the Unity Committee's slate in 1968; he knew as well as anyone how McMaster operated.

"Fitz was chairing the nominations meeting, and Johnson and McMaster had been nominated for president," Karagozian says. "I got up after McMaster's name had been brought up and told the membership, 'I'd like to protest the nomination of Rolland Mc-Master.' "

"Oh, why?" asked Fitzsimmons.

"The way I look at it, this man was not only indicted but convicted on thirty-two separate counts of extortion. Now I can understand the government framing a person on a single charge, but he was convicted on all thirty-two counts. The man was found guilty of selling out the members and taking money for labor peace. I don't think he has the moral conviction or is fit to run the local."

As he sat down after his speech, Karagozian glanced over and met the well-known McMaster stare. "A few weeks later," he says, "I got up one morning and my eight-year-old son came up to me. 'Daddy, did you leave a box on the porch?' I said, 'What kind of box?' So he explained what the box looked like. I got up and went out to the porch. I opened the box and pulled away the plastic wrapping.

"Well, I've seen movies but that was the first time I'd ever seen it in real life. Fifteen sticks of dynamite! They kind of looked like those cigars you buy in a test tube. I just looked at it; I couldn't believe it."

Karagozian gently placed the dynamite in his car, drove to a pay phone, and called the FBI and the Detroit police.

"They told me something must have gone wrong that it didn't explode—or else it was some kind of a message."

Johnson was angry at McMaster's nomination too. He told Fitzsimmons to "get McMaster out of this race; you ain't gonna do to me what you're doing to Jimmy." Fitzsimmons made no move, however, and to solidify support Johnson changed the Christmas stewards' banquet from late to early December, before the election, and gave the local's business agents a $100 a week raise.

Larry McHenry backed McMaster and Fitzsimmons, which gave Detroit Teamsters the impression that the Unity Committee was also supporting them. In response Pete Karagozian wrote in a flyer which was passed out to the membership, "Sometime in the future, you will probably read their [the rebels'] so-called 'Watchdog Bulletin' supporting Rolland McMaster for President of Local 299 to run against Dave Johnson. They hope to obtain a job if McMaster is elected or run with him on a slate. This is the real intent, and they are trying to cause harassment for Dave Johnson for this purpose only."

Soon after the flyer went out, Provenzino announced his candidacy for president, hoping to defeat Johnson, McMaster, and Robert Lins, now a local business agent and also an announced candidate. Fitzsimmons' only competition for vice president was business agent Earl Grayhek, who withdrew, and Jim Leavitt, the Unity Committee leader.

Leavitt was declared ineligible to run against Fitzsimmons because of a technicality, and when Leavitt sought to retrieve his right to run, his appeal had to be sent to the IBT's general president, who was, of course, Fitzsimmons. In the end, Fitzsimmons ran unopposed. McHenry ran for trustee on McMaster's ticket.

Before the election, however, McMaster succumbed to pressure from Johnson, via Fitzsimmons, and withdrew from the race. McHenry wrote in his *Watchdog Bulletin*, ''The Watchdog was very sorry to see Rolland McMaster withdraw as a candidate for President. Although we did not always agree with McMaster on every issue, we did not know how good we had it with him until he was gone. We know 'Mac's' heart is with 299, but apparently General President Fitzsimmons feels he needs McMaster more than we need him here.''

With only 4500 out of 20,000 elegible members voting, the election, held December 2–4, was no-contest. Johnson, busing voters from their trucking terminals to the polling area, whipped Provenzino by five to one, and McHenry was beaten four to one. Otto Wendell was secretary-treasurer, Richard Fitzsimmons recording secretary, and Ralph Proctor, George Roxburgh, and Don Taber were trustees.

With Hoffa's local in Detroit still safe from Fitzsimmons, ''Bring Jimmy home before Christmas!'' was the battle cry among Local 299's rank and file. The wheels were in motion—Hoffa applied for executive clemency in mid-December.

Hoffa's major enemy had meantime spent the fall of 1971 strengthening his friendships at the White House. Although most labor leaders opposed the Nixon Administration's wage and price controls, Fitzsimmons was more pragmatic. When Nixon announced that the freeze would end on November 13, Fitzsimmons, in the *299 News*, diplomatically called for the elimination of inequities that hurt wage earners if ''Phase II'' of the President's economic policy went into effect after that date. If Phase II was declared, then it ''should make the industrial sector offer up the same sacrifices as the working man is making now. If inequities are not eliminated, the plan is doomed to failure. The nation cannot afford a failure at this junction in its economic history.'' As a result, in late October, Nixon appointed Fitzsimmons to the Phase II Pay Board. Although most of the five-member panel contended that the inequities remained, Fitzsimmons nevertheless supported the President's program.

''[Fitzsimmons] is the only one who will stand up to George

Meany,'' presidential adviser Charles Colson told a reporter, and he added that Fitzsimmons would remain on the Pay Board regardless of how its other four members felt about him.

The Nixon Administration sincerely appreciated Fitzsimmons' support, and did not intend to jeopardize it, but by December Hoffa was no longer a threat to Fitzsimmons. The mob factions of North and South had been appeased and were again getting their fair share of the IBT's funds and sharing in its leadership on the general executive board. There was no reason to keep Hoffa in jail any longer.

On December 23 the President signed the papers that freed Hoffa from prison, citing his wife's health as the reason. However, with Hoffa's enemies influencing Nixon, via Charles Colson and John Dean, a proviso was added to Hoffa's commutation that barred him from union activities until March 6, 1980, when he would be sixty-seven years old.

Released from jail on the same day as Hoffa, along with 250 other recipients of presidential clemency, was Calvin Kovens, a co-defendent with Hoffa in the Chicago pension fraud trial. Well connected with the White House and with organized crime in Florida, Kovens received his early release through the efforts of Colson; Senator George Smathers of Florida; and Bébé Rebozo. In a telephone call to Colson, Smathers told him he thought the administration should intervene to "expedite" Kovens's parole. Smathers told Colson, who secretly taped the conversation: "It involves a case of a man by the name of Calvin Kovens. He was convicted about [1964] for having borrowed money from the Teamsters Union and he borrowed more than he actually spent and the allegations were generally that they had made a kickback of some kind to Hoffa and he was one of the victims of Bobby Kennedy.''

Smathers also told Colson that Rebozo agreed with him that the Nixon Administration should help Kovens by speeding up his parole. At that point Colson asked John Dean for help in a December memo that described the matter as ''too hot for me to handle.'' It was handled, however, and after Kovens was paroled he contributed $30,000 to the Committee to Re-elect the President.

At the same time that Colson, Dean, and other Nixon aides were handling the Hoffa and Kovens releases, Colson was interceding in yet another Teamster case. In the third episode Colson agreed to intervene in a Justice Department investigation of Teamsters Union associate Daniel Gagliardi and his close friend John Ardito, one of the more violent members of the Vito Genovese crime family. The Ardito-Gagliardi relationship was believed to be central to various Teamster–organized crime activities in the New York area.

Gagliardi was then on the verge of being indicted for various Teamster extortion activities in the New York–New Jersey area, along with Teamster official Samuel Tritto. In a memo to Colson of January 24, 1972, Colson's deputy, George Bell, stated, "I talked to Gagliardi who maintained complete ignorance and innocence regarding the Teamsters," but who nevertheless "asked that he be gotten off the hook."

At the bottom of the Bell-Colson memo, which also indicated that John Dean was being consulted on the case, Colson made the following handwritten notation: "*Watch for this*. Do *all* possible."[5]

Several days earlier Colson and his aide had obtained a summary of information on the Gagliardi-Tritto case from Henry Peterson, the Assistant Attorney General, who in turn had gotten the information from Charles Ruff, then with the Management and Labor Section of the Justice Department's Criminal Division. Ruff's summary, dated January 19, 1972, noted that "an indictment in this matter" was expected "sometime next month."

The indictment never came, and the case was dropped.

Wearing a baggy charcoal-gray suit, blue tie, brown shoes, and dark coat, Hoffa emerged from the gates of Lewisburg Penitentiary on December 23, having served four years, nine months and sixteen days of his thirteen-year sentence. He looked back at his fellow inmates and threw a clenched fist in the air. Swarming around Hoffa, reporters shouted their questions.

"You gonna run again, Jimmy?"

"I have no intention of returning to the Teamsters," Hoffa said as if reading from a script. "The leadership is in good hands. Frank Fitzsimmons is doing a good job."

"What about the . . . restrictions Nixon put on you, forbidding you from running for union office until 1980?"

His smile disappeared and he replied that he was unaware of any restrictions. He claimed that the document he had signed on December 22 made no mention of them.[6]

After telephoning his wife from a nearby motel, he headed to the nearest airport. There he was greeted by Fitzsimmons, who was waiting for him in a car. Fitzsimmons later described the scene:

"I didn't want to be at the gates when he got out, so I waited for him at the airport. He climbed into my car and we shook hands and I said, 'Well, what are you gonna do now?'

"He said, 'What do you mean?' So I told him I thought he ought to go home and spend Christmas with his family and then take Josephine on a tour of the South Seas for a couple of months and get readjusted, then come back and see what he wanted to do.

"He just looked at me and said, 'We'll see about that,' and I got out of the car."[7]

Hoffa then boarded a private plane and flew to Detroit, picked up his son, James P., and flew on to his daughter's home in St. Louis, where his wife was staying.

Hoffa was to be on probation until March 1973; his travel, associations, and jobs would be under rigid scrutiny. Any violation of his commutation provisions would put him behind bars again.

Word of Hoffa's release came to Detroit's Teamster leaders during a Christmas celebration at Carl's Chop House. Jubilant over the news, Jimmy Clift said, "With Jimmy out of jail, it's going to be the greatest Christmas present ever."

Dave Johnson remarked, "I'm glad [President Nixon] had the courage to do it. I'm very happy. I think President Nixon did us a great service."[8]

Spending a quiet Christmas with his family, Fitzsimmons had no immediate statement to make. The commutation restrictions were Fitzsimmons' Christmas present, and if more insurance against a Hoffa comeback was needed, it was available in "Resolution No. 8." Already in operation, the product of the IBT executive board's deliberations was the IBT's "Freight, Steel, and Special Commodities Division." While organizing nonunion truckers, selected members of the special organizing team would also function as operatives of a "Hoffa watch."

The head of the new "task force" was a man close to Fitzsimmons who understood the political situation of the Teamsters, both on the national level and in Detroit's Local 299. The man also hated Jimmy Hoffa. He was, of course, Rolland McMaster.

15 The McMaster Task Force and the Nixon Plumbers

Supposedly a response to contract violations by special commodities carriers, the IBT Freight, Steel, and Special Commodities Division was really a reaction to the activities of the Fraternal Association of Steel Haulers. When the National Labor Relations Board certified FASH as a bona fide labor union, the young organization wasted no time in beginning to woo new members. To attract truckers who were afraid to lose the benefits they'd built up in the IBT, FASH devised a pension plan superior to that of the Teamsters. There was no loss of credit for breaks-in-service and drivers could continue to work while receiving their retirement benefits. In addition, FASH offered ten options for pension settlement, including the lump-sum receipt of up to $39,000.

"We needed to build an incentive for truckers to leave the Teamsters and join us," says Bill Hill. "Plus a lot of these guys, because of their breaks-in-service, knew that they weren't going to get a Teamster pension anyway. Others were aware that they might lose their benefits just because they moved from one local to another."

FASH did become attractive to many drivers and it organized its first company—Tajon, Inc., of Mercer, Pennsylvania—in October 1970. After that its membership of owner-operators grew rapidly, and it filed forty more petitions to represent nonunion carriers as well as some already affiliated with the Teamsters Union.

"But in December 1970 there was a decision by the NLRB," Hill explains. "FASH was told that it could not raid Teamster locals until the contracts in effect had expired. That hurt us badly. And because of our limited funds, we had to become more selective in the companies we wanted to organize."

In spite of its financial situation, FASH stunned the Teamsters with a three-to-one victory in an election among the truckers who drove for and leased to the Pittsburgh-Philadelphia Transportation Company. And Teamster leaders who considered the PPT election a fluke were badly shaken when FASH organizers followed up with a six-to-one rout of the Teamsters at Tryon Trucking, in Pittsburgh. It is obvious why the leaders, meeting soon after the two defeats of June 1971, decided to set up a special organizing division, but there are varying explanations of why Rolland McMaster became its chief.

"We had an awful lot of unorganized truck drivers," Harold Gibbons says. "One of the big areas of nonunion operations was the steel haul. So we set up a legitimate program for steel hauling to deal with the problems we were having in that area. Weldon Mathis, Fitz's assistant, was supposed to be in charge of it. I objected to Mathis's taking it because he already had a full-time job and couldn't do justice to that kind of organizing campaign. You put in a guy who can devote all of his time to it. Frank argued with me, then turned to me and said, 'We'll make McMaster chairman of it.' "

At a subsequent meeting in Chicago the specifics of the program were developed. "It was McMaster's idea from the beginning," an Eastern Conference Teamster official says of that meeting. "He was heading up our campaigns with the steel haulers, especially in the Central States, and FASH was making him look mighty bad. I want to tell you, he was pretty fed up with those damn rebels after his experiences in Detroit. Anyway, he said that Bill Hill and FASH were kicking the hell out of us and he wanted our support for a project where he could get some men. Hell, everyone in the room knew what Mac was thinking . . . Give McMaster a handful of guys and he'll turn 'em into a goon squad in five minutes."

Another official adds, "Mac's philosophy [about companies that hire owner-operators] is 'Put 'em out of business; it's the same as organizing 'em.' "

But the traditional rough stuff of owner-operator organizing efforts—and the manpower needed for it—was going to be expensive. "So Mac told us that he wanted a few hundred bucks a week and some 'stealing money' too—that's what he called expense money," another leader recalls.

McMaster got the support he needed for the special organizing unit. Okayed by Fitzsimmons and the general executive board, it was concealed in "Resolution No. 8," which was approved at the 1971

IBT convention. During its next meeting—at the Rancho La Costa Country Club, in Carlsbad, California—the general executive board formally created the IBT Freight, Steel, and Special Commodities Division.

According to the unit's propaganda,

> There is much to be done; hundreds of nonunion trucking companies operate over the nation's highways engaging in rate-cutting, paying cheap wages to drivers and destroying the financial well-being of the trucking industry. The Teamsters know that a healthy trucking industry is a must and they have entrusted accomplishing that job to McMaster. His record for success is well-known.

In August 1971 the general executive board chartered a new local in Monroesville, Pennsylvania, to represent steel haulers exclusively. Claiming that Local 800 was merely a front for McMaster's shady activities, a former president of the local says, ''I didn't have to protect my men against the employers, I had to protect 'em against the International.''

At the same time McMaster began selecting his team of organizers—most of whom, he said later, were recommended by IBT officials. He also recruited several renegades from FASH who knew its leadership and operations. One former FASH officer, Mike Boano, became his assistant.

Although McMaster insists that he was unaware of their backgrounds, he hired several organizers with arrest records for crimes ranging from possession of stolen goods and assault to armed robbery, rape, and murder. Jack Robison, of Finleyville, Pennsylvania, was typical of the chosen crew. Mean-looking, brawny, and said to be an explosives expert, Robison had been convicted of grand larceny, drunk driving, breaking and entering (twice), and disorderly conduct (three times). He had been arrested for slugging a trucking executive in the mouth when he refused to sign a Teamster contract, and indicted for murder and acquitted on grounds of self-defense. Altogether he had been sentenced to a total of thirteen years in prison and had spent seven behind bars.

''Even if some of them were a little on the rough side,'' McMaster says, ''they behaved pretty well with me . . . I just asked if anyone had any police records, and everybody answered no.''

Nearly thirty people worked with the task force, though not all at the same time. All had the title ''IBT organizer'' and were provided with business cards that showed their jurisdiction as the "Central, Eastern, Southern, and Western Conferences of Teamsters." "I went in on one particular case at the Labor Board," one of them remembers, "and they asked me who I worked for. I told them the Eastern, Central, Southern, and Western Conferences. They said, 'You're an awfully goddamned busy man.' This is the image McMaster wanted us to have."

Organizers also received telephone, Standard Oil, American Express, Hertz Rent-A-Car, and Air Travel credit cards; $200 cash per month for car allowances; and full IBT pension, health, and welfare benefits: "When I said I wanted the job with the squad, I got a letter from McMaster telling me to be in Chicago on such-and-such a day. There I got a whole stack of credit cards and they told me, 'You're on your own, enjoy yourself while you're out there.' We lived on unlimited expenses . . . ."

Although agreeing that his men could place almost anything on the Teamsters' tab, McMaster remembers at least one exception: "I had one unusual thing happen—and the guy doesn't work for me any more. He bought a gun . . . I didn't exactly dump him. I sent him back where he came from. He had to pay us back, and he did pay us back. I don't know whether he kept the gun or not."

All expenses for the task force were channeled from the IBT to the Central Conference of Teamsters in the guise of "special organizing grants." Authorizations for expenditures were okayed by Fitzsimmons, general secretary-treasurer Murray W. Miller, and the directors of the Central Conference—Harold Gibbons until 1972 and Ray Schoessling from 1973 to 1975. According to sketchy reports submitted by the Central Conference to the Department of Labor, task force members averaged an annual salary of $18,000. Four "directors" or "crew chiefs" who coordinated the activities of the organizing teams were paid an average of $21,000 a year. Boano pulled down an additional $2000 as McMaster's right-hand man, and McMaster received his yearly wage as an IBT general organizer, $30,000.

When they were selected for the team, the organizers attended a one-week training program in Chicago during which they "would learn the contract and know what their job was in life," McMaster says. "I wanted them to know that there was no stealing going on and no corruption of any kind." One organizer, however, remembers the training program as "a first-class school for goons, where we learned the fundamentals of how to shake a trucking company down . . . We were taught the principles of terrorism and extortion.

''Here's something I learned . . . I'll tell you how to start a fire. It's very slick. There's no way you can tell. They'll take oxygen, and they'll find out where the boiler room is, say, in a warehouse, right? And they'll fill that son of a bitch up with about eight or ten bottles of oxygen. Eventually that oxygen is gonna find its way to that flame, and when it does, there's a flash. Oxygen don't burn, it just helps fire burn. And there's no smell, no trace, nobody knows what happened. There's nothing. Because after they load the place up with oxygen, they walk away from it. It's just a matter of a half-hour or so by the time the fresh air finally filters through the place, and you get a flash—bang!—that quick. The arson squad comes in and everybody. Dynamite leaves a smell. Very simple. They can't figure out how these fires start.''

Task force members were required to report to McMaster's office by telephone twice a day, and to submit written daily, weekly, and monthly reports via McMaster's long-time secretary, Sally Jones.

Typically, the task force would arrive without warning. A director and two or three organizers would seek out company drivers and owner-operators at such places as truck stops and delivery destinations. After explaining the benefits of becoming Teamsters the organizers would ask the drivers to sign union intent cards indicating a wish to join the union. ''Some drivers who refused to sign,'' a task force member remarks, ''would get their lights punched out.''

In one incident an Ohio driver was assaulted by two unidentified organizers when he refused to sign an intent card. One of them, holding a blowtorch, told the driver where the driver's eight-year-old son attended school, as well as the route he walked to and from classes. To emphasize that he meant business, the organizer then lit his own cigarette with the blowtorch.

The driver signed.

When a majority of drivers hauling for a carrier had signed the cards, task force representatives invited the employers to witness a card count and then to sign a recognition agreement designating the Teamsters as the employees' bargaining agent. The details of a labor contract were worked out later, if the employer signed the agreement.

If the company refused to grant recognition on the basis of intent cards, both sides prepared for an NLRB recognition election. The organizer continues, ''We'd go out campaigning and passing out stuff to the drivers telling them what to expect when they became members of the union. If the companies resisted us we threw up a picket line and shut 'em down. Hell, even if the drivers didn't want to be organized we set up an 'informational picket line.' We harassed 'em until they *wanted* to join the Teamsters.''

To avert long recognition strikes, the union and management often negotiated sweetheart contracts. ''McMaster and this big stupid goon showed up at my office one day during the strike and made me an offer I couldn't pass up,'' says the owner of an Illinois steel hauling outfit. ''They said their pension contribution demands were less than half of what I was paying for my men in an independent plan I'd set up. So I took it.''

To crack tougher nuts who refused to be threatened by strikes or bought off with sweetheart contracts, the task force intimidated the customers of companies under siege, hoping to add further economic pressure. One customer of Star Delivery of Canton, Illinois, claims that after he had refused to restrict his business with Star, sticks of dynamite were thrown over the fence surrounding its property. The customer promptly cut his business ties with Star Delivery.

If a company facing economic ruin still refused to either sign a Teamster contract or go out of business, it was subjected to shootings, beatings, arson, vandalism, and sabotage.

''From the beginning—I remember a few of us were talking about it—there was something not real right with the whole setup, you know what I mean?'' a task force member says thoughtfully. ''I mean, we were there, and we were working and all that, but it just seemed like we were going through the motions, like what we did didn't really mean anything, or even that we were fronting for something else.''

With McMaster on the road and Hoffa out of jail, Dave Johnson felt better about the situation in Detroit. He celebrated his old friend's release in an article for the *299 News* that called Nixon's commutation ''a most humanitarian move.'' Although many not connected with Teamster politics questioned the law-and-order President's rationale for releasing a convicted jury-tamperer and embezzler, elated Hoffa partisans were interested in only one thing: ''When's Jimmy coming back to the union?'' Everyone knew that Hoffa's parole would be up in March 1973 but that his commutation restrictions prevented his seeking union office until 1980. But ''Jimmy's first appearance in Detroit was at my New Year's Eve party,'' Johnson says, ''and the way he was politicking around that night, everyone, especially his enemies, knew he was going to fight those restrictions.''

At 3:53 A.M. on January 12, three weeks after Hoffa's release, pro-Hoffa business agent Gene Page's home was bombed. The front of the house was blasted away and the aluminum front door was thrown twenty feet inside the house. Page was not at home, but his wife was asleep on a couch near the front door. Somehow she escaped injury. The police investigated and told Page that a single stick of dynamite had been carefully planted and then detonated under the front steps.

The question had to be asked whether the bombing was Hoffa's welcome home present from some of his more ardent adversaries—a warning not to let returning to Teamster leadership cross his mind. Using a lowly business agent to get the point across was less risky than direct action against the legendary Hoffa. That would have been headline news, but the Page bombing was barely mentioned, even in Detroit.

Nevertheless, to union insiders the incident was extremely puzzling. No one could figure out who wanted to harm Page. Even Dave Johnson had difficulty piecing reasons together: ''Well, the only thing is that Gene Page and George Roxburgh [then a strong Hoffa supporter] worked closely together. When Roxy went on vacation he would ask Gene to handle his companies. When Gene went, he'd ask Roxy to handle his. As far as I know, Gene was a very loyal Hoffa man who didn't have many enemies. What they did was a surprise to everybody. It's not like he was the leader of something.''

Page himself was mum on the subject.

Federal investigators thought it possible that both Page and Roxburgh had made some enemies in the course of their ordinary union work. As business agents both men had working relationships with two steel hauling firms, Capitol Cartage and J&J Cartage, whose co-owners were first cousins and had ties with Detroit's organized crime families. Vincent A. Meli, nephew of Angelo Meli and brother-in-law of former Hoffa attorney William Bufalino, was the labor negotiator for J&J, which worked in concert with Capitol.

McMaster, as the IBT's steel hauling expert, outranked the Local 299 business agents in dealings with the two companies, which engaged in illicit practices such as overloading and rate cutting. Hauling tons of steel to the Ford Motor Company and Chrysler, among other places, the drivers, principally owner-operators, never complained.

"The government believed that the way these companies were able to by-pass both the law and their collective bargaining agreements was to force their owner-operators to declare themselves as independent companies subcontracting themselves to the steel hauling firms," a Detroit law enforcement official explains. "But even though there was skimming of profits [by the companies], none of the workers were filing grievances. So what could the union do?"

There were several reasons why union members failed to complain: some of the men were in the process of purchasing their rigs from the company; some were simply afraid to buck the system. "You know, this is a pretty frightening business," as one Capitol driver put it. "And it's run by some pretty powerful people whose names never appear on any official company documents. . . . I just mind my own business, just like any other smart driver. I've got a criminal record and I'm happy to be working. I don't want no trouble with anyone."

Detroit businessman John R. Ferris allegedly owned three of Capitol's tractors and trailers, and "Ferris," a federal agent says, "is a suspected front man for Teamster official Rolland McMaster."

As for J&J Cartage, George Roxburgh, formerly McMaster's assistant in Local 299 and a union trustee, says that he and Page had discovered that "J&J had held out on their pension and health and welfare employer contributions which had been negotiated in the [1970] contract while McMaster was administrative assistant. Because we thought that over $80,000 was owed, Dave Johnson appointed two business agents, Don Deters and Jim Morsette, to investigate our charges. We were right, and J&J paid their back debt in full."

There were many missing pieces in the puzzle of connections among Capitol, J&J, Ferris, Roxburgh, and the bombing of Gene Page's home. One possible piece came to light when Larry McHenry was drinking with friends one evening soon after the bombing. Three people listened to him blurt out that he knew who planted the dynamite at Page's home. "Who do you think did it?" he boasted. "Who do you think did the job on Page's house?"

"He did everything but come right out and say he did it," one of the witnesses recalls, "but I'll tell you this, when he knew what he had said, he clammed up real fast."

According to another of the three, "Larry is known for talking in codes. But that night he was coming across loud and clear. There was dead silence in that room. We just looked at him."

Six months after the Page bombing, Roxburgh was sitting in his car in front of his girl friend's house in Royal Oak. "We drove up in her circular driveway. Then, while we were sitting there talking, one car pulled up in back of me and another pulled alongside—that was a red car. I saw this guy in the red car up in the front seat fumbling around for something; there were three people in the car altogether, but all I could see were shadows. Then the guy in the front, fumbling around, pulled out a shotgun. The next thing I knew, bang! I was hit.''

At least two blasts crashed through the windshield on the driver's side of the 1972 Cadillac. Roxburgh was wounded in the head, arms, and chest.

"My eye actually came out of my head.'' Roxburgh winced recalling it. "I knew my girl wasn't hurt, but I was kind of delirious, and I ran to somebody's front door. Then some people made me lie down.''

Admitted to the hospital in critical condition, Roxburgh survived the experience but lost the sight of his right eye.

"I thought the attack was a result of my dealings with J&J,'' he says. "I wasn't going along with what was happening after I had checked their books and found that they weren't paying proper health and welfare and pension benefits. Some people told me that it might have been one of McMaster's men, since I refused to support him when he and Dave had their troubles just before Mac left the local. But I didn't believe it. You just don't throw all those years of friendship away like that.''

Soon after the Roxburgh shooting incident, former union dissident Larry McHenry became a member of the McMaster task force.

In March 1972, two weeks after the Page bombing and three months before Roxburgh was shot, Fitzsimmons delivered a stirring speech at a meeting of the Central States Drivers Council in Chicago. Attacking owner-operators, even those who were Teamsters, he announced that the IBT had implemented a program to halt "gypsies'' from hauling special commodities, particularly steel, over the highways: "We'll cross conference lines, if necessary, to organize these nonunion carriers.''

Soon afterward the McMaster task force moved into Elm Springs, Arkansas, to organize Willis Shaw Frozen Express, a nationwide food carrier owned by Del Monte. During the campaign telephone cables were cut, truck windshields were smashed, tires slashed, and moving trucks were fired upon.

"Two organizers went through the procedure of collecting the intent cards,'' one of the organizers remembers. "Then they approached Willis Shaw, and Shaw told them that they weren't interested. So the drivers took a strike vote and struck 'em. Then the company started checking the cards out. Maybe two-thirds of the cards were good; the rest of them were phonies out of the telephone books. McMaster got hostile about it, so he said, 'Let's stir up some shit down there. Let's get this thing moving. We want to get some trouble started!' "

Within hours of McMaster's statement a Teamster organizer was allegedly stabbed on the picket line by an elderly security guard who insisted that he was innocent and who was never prosecuted.

"McMaster used the stabbing as his reason for the violence—he called it 'revenge.' "

"I admit that Willis Shaw was a monster I couldn't control," McMaster says. "They started shooting at everybody down there. They shot at us, and they stuck a knife in one of my organizers. I didn't retaliate or order any retaliation at all."

When a recognition election was finally held, NLRB chairman Edward B. Miller wrote of it that he felt it took place "in an atmosphere of confusion, acts of violence and threats of violence such as to render impossible a rational, uncoerced choice by the employees."

The Willis Shaw campaign ended when the drivers voted against joining the union. The firm's mechanics had voted to become Teamsters, but after a meeting between McMaster and company executives, the task force mysteriously left without accepting the mechanics' membership.

Such instances became more frequent. On several occasions McMaster had carriers on their knees almost begging to be organized. Then, after a meeting with management, McMaster and his squad would simply walk away empty-handed.

The reason for McMaster's sudden withdrawals from organizing campaigns can best be explained by the timely appearance during violent episodes of a former Teamster business agent turned labor consultant. Richard Dininger, an old friend of McMaster's, had retired from the Teamsters after serving for nearly twenty years as a business agent for Indianapolis Local 135 and as a member of McMaster's IBT steel hauling grievance and negotiating committees. When the task force went into full swing, the handsome Don Ameche look-alike was a partner in an Indianapolis labor consulting firm, Labor Associates. When McMaster's men struck a company and the violence began, Dininger would make telephone calls to the firm's owner guaranteeing "labor peace"—for a price. The price for making the

Teamsters vanish varied according to the size of the company and the amount of violence already generated.

Dininger's first known offer for total labor peace in return for a payoff came during an organizing effort against the Eck Miller Transportation Company, in Owensboro, Kentucky. Within two weeks of the first appearance of the task force, twenty-six separate acts of violence had been recorded, including shootings, beatings, and sabotage. A Teamster organizer—not with the McMaster unit—was shot in the stomach but survived. "Bullets were flying everywhere," as Paul Jeffries, the company president, describes it. "It was a miracle that nobody got killed."

On July 15, 1973, in the midst of the violence, an anonymous telephone call was made to the local newspaper in Owensboro: "Something's gonna happen at Eck Miller"; and a few hours later two trucks parked in the company lot were badly damaged. One had been firebombed.

"A couple of things happened that didn't help me," is McMaster's comment on the Owensboro campaign. "This shooting match down there at Eck Miller did not help our organization. I had to answer some questions that I couldn't answer. That did not help. We do not need bad publicity. We try not to have bad publicity. After all, this whole labor picture has changed . . . We gotta present ourselves."

Richard Dininger telephoned Jeffries "four or five times" in the midst of the violence. Jeffries says that Dininger told him, "There was an easier way to do things"—for $10,000, after which Jeffries "could get rid of the Teamsters for good." The company president did not succumb to the blackmail offer, but he did finally receive "labor peace" by agreeing to drop several multimillion-dollar lawsuits against the union.

"I'd just hear reports and make a telephone call," Dininger says. "I told them that I could do something for them workwise. I'd say I'd like to represent them, to have their business." Although Dininger denies working in collusion with McMaster, it is clear that he did often make good on his promises of labor peace.

A spokesman for Anderson Freight Lines, in St. Cloud, Minnesota, admits that his company met Dininger's demands. Although he refuses to say how much money changed hands—saying only that it went to Dininger—he confirms that after the payment was made McMaster and his unit immediately abandoned the organizing campaign.

In Portsmouth, Ohio, Acme Cartage confirms that in return for an initial payment of $2500 and an additional $200 a month, both paid to Dininger, the company received a sweetheart contract providing for pension payments that were nearly $10 a week less than the national contract called for.

Noble Graham Transport, Inc., a small family-run steel and lumber hauler in Michigan's Upper Peninsula, was put on notice in November 1973 that the Teamsters intended to organize the company's thirty-five drivers. After some minor violence Dininger telephoned a company representative on January 29, 1974, two weeks after the Teamsters had filed a petition for an NLRB election. Introducing himself as a labor consultant, Dininger told the carrier that it might need his help because "the going could get rough," and he then offered to get the task force off Noble Graham's back by stopping the organizing drive, eliminating the election, and insuring that the company would never hear from the union again. He would deliver labor peace in return for $20,000 to $25,000, payable over a five-year period.

Dininger suggested meeting with company representatives at the Drake Hotel in Chicago, and the next day Mike Boano telephoned the firm. This and later conversations were recorded by the company.

"Who the hell is Dick Dininger?" the company spokesman demanded in the first conversation.

"The labor consultant," replied Boano.

"He claims to have some interest in this matter and would like to have," said the company man.

"Well, he represents quite a few of the carriers," Boano responded. "He is a pretty understanding gentleman."

Later in the conversation, while the two were discussing the NLRB election and disputes over the eligibility of some drivers, Boano asked, "What did the gentleman propose?"

"Which one?"

"The one you mentioned."

"Dininger?"

"Yeah."

"Well, he wanted to meet with us and talk in Chicago, and I don't think we're going to be able to get down there because of our own time schedule. He had some specific ideas relative to withdrawal of the [election] petition, and we are a bit reluctant to follow that course. He's not specific on the phone, and we don't think we can clear ourselves out of here to get with him. So, I don't know that that's going to go anywhere.''

''Uh-huh,'' said Boano. ''Well, I do know he's reliable and he can usually substantiate his claims. I have had quite a few dealings with him—he represents companies.''

The day after that, Dininger called the Noble Graham official again: ''I'm going to be in Chicago tomorrow and Friday, at the Rodeway Inn, just about ten minutes from the airport there.''

''We think that we'll just stick with a lawyer and not hire any more management consultants at this point in time.''

''Well, I think you're making a mistake. Let me explain it a little why I think so. I just figured up the health and welfare and pension alone for the next five years is $431,000, and that's not counting what might be negotiated two years from now, you know.''

''Yeah, yeah,'' said the company official.

''And, ah, that's a little bit of money right there in itself. So, if you care to pursue it any further, why that's up to you.''

Noble Graham held out. Its drivers had refused to man the picket lines at the company, and on March 2 they voted against joining the Teamsters. Larry McHenry claims that he stayed on after the union left. ''There were still drivers who did want to join the union,'' McHenry says, ''so they came to me, and I carried the thing [the organizing drive] on as a cost to myself.''

While the McMaster task force roamed the country, shaking down employers and threatening violence to those who didn't give in, rumors filtered through to union insiders that McMaster's men were behind the four acts of violence against known Hoffa loyalists—Otto Wendell, James Clift, Gene Page, and George Roxburgh.

''Hoffa was aware of McMaster's goon squad,'' according to Johnson, ''and he was concerned about it.''

In February 1972, appearing on ABC's ''Issues and Answers,'' Hoffa had said he would not violate the restrictions on his commutation. Two weeks later, in an interview with a UPI reporter in Miami Beach, he announced that he would seek the presidency of the union in 1980, when he would be sixty-seven years old. Praising Fitzsimmons, Hoffa said the union was in good hands. ''The contracts have been excellent. The membership has increased and he has done an excellent job.''

The façade of friendship and peace continued.

On February 29, Fitzsimmons lost his number-one money handler, Allen Dorfman, who was convicted in New York of taking a $55,000 kickback from a recipient of a pension fund loan. Although he resigned from his job as the Central States Pension Fund's special consultant, Dorfman was permitted to remain in control of the union's Central States Health and Welfare Fund while his conviction was on appeal, and to hand pick his successor to the pension fund.

More bad publicity came to the Central States Fund when NBC News correspondent Edwin Newman televised an award-winning documentary, "Pensions: The Broken Promise," on September 12.

" . . . it's common practice for a man to be forced to transfer from one local to another every time he changes jobs . . ." Newman explained. "A teamster must have twenty years of membership in one local to draw a pension. His pension rights are not portable. He cannot take them with him from one local to another. A lot of drivers don't know that until it's time for them to retire. And when they do find out, they can't understand why it should be so."

The next public blow came when Ralph Nader and Kate Blackwell, with the help of Karen Ferguson, an attorney with Nader's Public Interest Research Group, wrote *You and Your Pension*, an excellent evaluation of modern pension funds. The authors described the problems rank-and-file members had in collecting from the Central States Pension Fund and told the story of perhaps the most famous pension case, that of Stanley Flowers, an Ohio trucker.

> Some employees have taken their cases to the courts. Stanley Flowers, a fifty-eight-year-old truck driver of Richfield, Ohio, has filed suit against the Teamsters' Central States, Southeast and Southwest Area[s] Pension Fund, which he says has denied him a pension on the basis of faulty record keeping. Mr. Flowers applied for benefits in January 1971. His records showed he had thirty years of service under the pension plan, which would make him eligible for a $300-a-month benefit under the plan's early retirement provision. In August 1971, Teamsters Local 407 of Cleveland, Ohio, denied his application, claiming that Flowers was short two years of qualifying. Flowers' suit charges that the union "has carried out a willful and malicious plan to deprive persons entitled to their pensions . . . by refusing to pay and continuing to request information of the applicant until he either dies or gives up attempting to collect." He is asking $6000 in back payments and 1 million dollars as "punishment" to prevent the union from continuing the alleged practices.[1]

Flowers, who later recovered his pension—but only as part of an out-of-court settlement—had been a member of TURF, the rank-and-file reform group organized by Don Vestal after the 1971 IBT convention. At the time of his lawsuit he said, ''I'm fighting for every Teamster in the country.''

While Teamster rank-and-file members fought for their pensions and future security, the only trustee of the Central States Fund to be convicted of misusing his authority and the only Teamster ever to receive a $1.7 million lump-sum pension relaxed at his beautiful Miami Beach apartment in the Blair House, built with the help of more than $2 million in pension fund loans.

Hoffa could afford to take it easy and soak up the Florida sun. The flood of criticism in newspapers and magazines and on radio and television was Fitzsimmons' headache now, not a problem for the man who had created the problem in the first place. Short-memoried people and rank-and-file members willing to forgive yearned for Jimmy's return.

Hoffa thought he had plenty of time, and he meant to use it well. Dave Johnson, although longing for retirement, remained faithful as ever, and pledged to stay on as president of Local 299. But he very much wished for a resolution to Hoffa's legal dilemma. Since Johnson had been elected only in December 1971, Hoffa had three years to wheel and deal with the courts, the union, and the mob before the next local election. And if he was still unable to take over the presidency, he had a fall-back plan.

''After the restrictions were overturned,'' Johnson says, ''then I would appoint Hoffa to a key post in Local 299, as a business agent. He'd be easily elected a delegate to the 1976 convention. And you know it's from those delegates that the general president has to be elected.''

Obsessed with his return to power, Hoffa lived for the moment when the chair would call for nominations for IBT president. Johnson thinks he must have dreamed of the commotion and applause swelling louder and louder as the chanting, ''Hoffa! Hoffa! Hoffa!'' grew in equal proportion. Union officials and rank-and-file members would stand on their seats, tears streaming down their faces.

''Jimmy's back! Things are gonna be awright!''

The recurring dream, the omnipresent dream, the dream of Hoffa obsessed. And the dream alternated with moods of impatience and anxiety. He began to tell Johnson, ''Time is running out. We just don't have as much time as I thought.''

And as time quickly passed, Hoffa realized that his only link to the throne of the Teamsters Union was one man—Dave Johnson. The problem was that others knew it too.

Johnson himself had been under pressure for a long time, but that spring and summer it became different, and much worse. First came the anonymous phone calls. ''My wife and I were getting these damn calls all the time. They'd call at two and three in the morning, and we'd answer, and they'd just go, 'Ha, ha, ha, ha, ha,' then hang up. That's when I started to think seriously about getting out of all this stuff. But Jimmy wouldn't let me—he had his dream.''

Johnson knew that more trouble was on the way, and it came in October 1972, when shotgun blasts rang in the night, smashing the windows of his office in the union hall. Buckshot was scattered all over the room and glass covered his desk when he came to work the next day. Like other Hoffa supporters he knew that more was to come. First a business agent, then a trustee, now the president—three Hoffa supporters attacked since Hoffa was released from jail, and two others earlier. There was no doubt: each was a warning to Jimmy Hoffa.

Suspicion fell again on Don Davis, who, at the initiative of the Labor Department, had been indicted a month before the shooting spree for allegedly embezzling $1000 from Local 299. But word spread quickly that McMaster, instead of defending his former organizer, had testified against him to the grand jury. Davis was later acquitted on that charge and cleared, through civil suits of his own, of the charge of beating Johnson, but meantime he allowed himself to draw the Local 299 Hoffa supporters' wrath away from McMaster.

''It wasn't easy for me, but I was still in Indianapolis when all that stuff was going on against the Hoffa people,'' Davis says. ''But McMaster told me that if I took the heat for him, then he'd give me the information I needed to win my lawsuits . . . He kept good on his word, and my lawyer and I had it arranged with Mac so that we'd meet with this 299 business agent who was close to him on the corner of Twelve-Mile and Telegraph roads in Bloomfield Township, where this business agent would pass these secret documents to us.''

For Hoffa watchers, an event that overshadowed Johnson's and Davis's troubles was the publication that fall of Walter Sheridan's book. The former head of the ''get Hoffa squad'' had spent seventeen of his forty-seven years living through the events and accumulating the material which he documented in *The Fall and Rise of Jimmy Hoffa*. Based primarily on information obtained through transcripts of government hearings and Hoffa's trials, his work exposed the political tentacles Hoffa had grown during his rough-and-tumble climb to power. Budd Schulberg wrote in the introduction:

> In this painstaking book, Sheridan faces up to the reality that, after all the convictions and sensational disclosures, corruption flows on. George Jackson rotted in jail for nearly a decade for heisting $70. Jimmy Hoffa cops a million, bribes juries, runs with the most dangerous gangsters in America and, thanks to the intervention of his good friend Dick Nixon, does an easy five . . .
>
> The enemy within seems to grow stronger every day. Whether or not a Jack Anderson, a Ralph Nader, a Walter Sheridan can arouse our people from their complacency is the question on which the future course of America may depend.[2]

In fact, the complacency extended all the way to the White House, where Nixon, so recently Hoffa's "good friend," was more and more Fitzsimmons' good friend too. It was a case of "where the power resides," and the power of the IBT now resided with Fitzsimmons.

Nixon's and Fitzsimmons' mutual support in the wage and price control program was followed by the Nixon Administration's interference to stop a Justice Department investigation of Fitzsimmons' son Richard, who was accused of allowing his wife and children to use a union credit card for the purchase of $1500 worth of gasoline for their automobiles. "Any information pertaining to investigations of either the misuse of Teamster funds or illegal activities of Teamster officials is frowned on by Washington," according to the Illinois Legislative Commission, which was investigating connections between the White House, the Teamsters, and organized crime.[3]

Nixon appointed the elder Fitzsimmons to the Federal Communications Satellite Corporation and his wife became a member of the Advisory Committee on the Arts for the John F. Kennedy Performing Arts Center. And although Fitzsimmons had previously called for an immediate end to the Indochina war, in the spring of 1972 he praised Nixon's order to mine Haiphong Harbor as a spirited gesture that would bring "peace with honor."

In May the *Seattle Post-Intelligencer* charged that former Teamster president Dave Beck had received a moratorium on his debt of $1.3

million in back taxes as part of the administration's "deal" to maintain Teamster support for the President's economic and military policies: "Beck's tax break was negotiated by John B. Connally, who resigned suddenly [May 16] as Secretary of the Treasury after the [*Post-Intelligencer*] began delving into administration links with the Teamsters."⁴

In return for such favors the Teamsters' help in Nixon's reelection campaign was actively solicited. "One source close to the Teamsters claimed the union had raised more than $750,000 for Nixon, most of it in cash," Jack Anderson wrote. "Much of the money came from Las Vegas gambling lords whose casinos were financed by the Teamsters' pension fund," according to one of Anderson's sources. "Another source close to the President told us the amount was smaller. But all sources agreed that a huge cash collection was turned over to . . . Attorney General John Mitchell, on behalf of the Teamsters, by crime-connected Allen Dorfman."⁵

According to *Newsday* reporter Russell Sackett, Dorfman had actually flashed a receipt for $100,000 from Mitchell in front of several people during his trial in New York. "The witnesses described the receipt as a standard form (the kind available in any stationery store)," wrote Sackett. "The witnesses said that the receipt was not made out to anyone and did not state for what purpose. It was, however, in the amount of $100,000 and bore the signature of 'John Mitchell,' the witnesses said."⁶

There is no documentary evidence that money was channeled from the Teamsters Union into the presidential campaign funds, but union officials made large personal contributions through Fitzsimmons—who himself reported $4000. Other contributors were Salvatore Provenzano and William Bufalino.

"Fitzsimmons was saying that only about fifty or sixty thousand were contributed to the Nixon campaign in 1972," says Harold Gibbons, "but I know that Hoffa was saying privately that it was more like a million bucks . . . Frankly, I didn't know who was telling the truth."

Gibbons has reason to know other aspects of the 1972 campaign in exact figures. On June 12 Charles Colson sent John Dean an "eyes only" memorandum about a former Hoffa aide who was supporting antiwar activities as well as the presidential candidacy of George McGovern:

I have received a well informed tip that there are income tax discrepancies involving the returns of Harold J. Gibbons, a Vice President of the Teamsters Union in St. Louis. This has come to me on very, very good authority.

Gibbons, you should know, is an all out enemy, a McGovernite, ardently anti-Nixon. He is one of the 3 labor leaders who were recently invited to Hanoi.

Please see if this one can be started on at once and if there is an informer's fee, let me know. There is a good cause at which it can be donated.

According to a Justice Department official, the source for the information was "almost certainly" Frank Fitzsimmons.

"It was a horrible time for all of us," says Gibbons, who later lost his position as director of the Central Conference because of his politics. "It symbolized the worst kind of abuses of power by both the White House and the union. Because of my support for McGovern, the National Labor for Peace organization, and Jimmy Hoffa, I became a marked man."

As "enemies lists" were compiled in the White House, the thought of Nixon running against the third Kennedy caused stutters and stammers among the usually quite articulate members of the President's staff. Colson selected E. Howard Hunt, a former CIA official who had been a key political coordinator for the Bay of Pigs invasion, as the head of a special "plumbers unit" responsible for digging up information to use against the "enemies."

Senator Edward Kennedy was among the important targets of the special undercover squad, and Frank Fitzsimmons was apparently heavily relied upon to procure some "damaging" material, or "dirt," which could be used against the senator.

According to federal investigators, Hunt met Fitzsimmons at least once and was told by Colson that the Teamster president was providing "derogatory information" about Kennedy. Hunt told the investigators that Colson said the material came from Teamster sources in Las Vegas. "Colson had told Hunt that Fitzsimmons and his boys could really deliver the dirt on Kennedy," says a Justice Department official. Hunt spoke of Fitzsimmons telling Colson that the specific "dirt" he could provide on Kennedy had come from "a couple of Vegas show girls" who had passed details on to various Teamster sources. Hunt reportedly told the government that Colson was greatly interested in Fitzsimmons' information because it was "of a sexual nature."

"It was the same old Colson bullshit about how 'we've got the inside dirt on Kennedy,' says a federal investigator. "It was the usual Teamster crap—probably invented by Fitzsimmons to try and ingratiate himself with the White House even more."

Another government agent remarks, "This was the same trash that Colson tried to peddle about . . . other Nixon enemies . . . He always claimed to have the hot poop to smear these guys, but all he ever came up with was a bunch of rumors—or clips from the *National Enquirer*."

Hunt claimed to his questioners that Colson never did give him the "secret" Teamster information which had been scheduled for public release.

On June 20, the day the White House cover-up of the Watergate burglary began, and a very busy day in the Oval Office, Nixon placed a long-distance call to New York IBT vice president Joseph Trerotola, an associate of Anthony Provenzano. Interestingly enough, just fifty-three minutes earlier the President and H. R. Haldeman had had their first detailed discussion of the cover-up, which was recorded on the tape with the famous eighteen-minute gap. The President's call to Trerotola, at 1:38 P.M., lasted only a minute. Soon afterward Nixon called Colson, who came to the Oval Office at once for a seventy-minute discussion. The meeting was followed by two telephone conversations between the President and Colson later that evening. The significance of the Nixon-Trerotola call remains unknown; apparently that part of the June 20 tape was not subpoenaed for review by the Watergate prosecutors.

On July 17, 1972, meeting at La Costa, the IBT general executive board gave Nixon the enthusiastic endorsement of the Teamsters Union. After that, the seventeen board members traveled thirty-five miles up the coast to San Clemente, where they delivered the news in person and posed with Nixon for photographs.

Fitzsimmons wrote in the *299 News*:

This year we have somewhere to go. For the first time, the Republican Party plank has made an honest, outright appeal to working Americans . . . The choice is clear, and every vote counts. The biggest weapon the American worker has to protect himself and his country is the ballot. This year we are going to use it to reject the extremism of George McGovern, and to re-elect a great American—President Richard Nixon.[7]

Soon after Nixon won the November election and gave the

American people "four more years" of law and order, the President offered the cabinet post of Secretary of Labor to gun-toting Peter Brennan, president of the Building and Construction Trades Council of Greater New York. Brennan had been recommended by Fitzsimmons.

"There were several allegations before Brennan's confirmation that he was closely associated with members of the criminal syndicate," a Justice Department official says. "In fact, one of his closest friends and predecessor as head of the New York Trades Council was actively pursued during the McClellan Committee hearings by Bobby Kennedy. Kennedy publicly charged that Brennan's buddy had shaken down a New York racetrack.

"Another fellow who was close to Brennan had also been convicted of labor racketeering. It might not sound like much—and, of course, all these union officials have friends who have operated on both sides of the law—but Brennan actually took this bird to the White House with him in the spring of 1970 to show their support for Nixon's Vietnam policy."

On December 20, 1972, Nixon commuted the sentence of Angelo DeCarlo, a killer who had been imprisoned for extortion. DeCarlo was a top rackets figure in New Jersey and a captain in the Genovese crime family. His loanshark office had been monitored by the Justice Department from 1961 to 1965, and investigators had heard him discuss several murders as well as his gambling operations. He had served only two years of a twelve-year sentence when his petition for executive clemency, on grounds that he was ill with cancer, traveled a direct path from the Justice Department's pardon attorney, Lawrence Traylor, to Attorney General Richard Kleindienst, John Mitchell's successor.

"This Gyp DeCarlo," one Justice Department official said immediately after the pardon, "he is a very bad guy, with a history of political connections in New Jersey all laid out on public records. I can see where the pardon attorney might have forwarded it as a routine terminal illness case; but from there on, someone just had to give that thing a push."

The man who provided the push was Murray Chotiner.

On February 10–11, 1973, three months after Nixon trounced McGovern, two meetings were held simultaneously on the grounds of La Costa. One of the meetings was among Fitzsimmons; Allen Dorfman, who entered prison the following month for his kickback conviction in New York; California mob figure Peter Milano, a former member of the Cleveland syndicate with La Costa owner Morris Dalitz; and reputed members of the Chicago underworld, including Anthony Accardo and Lou Rosanova. The Teamsters and the mobsters met first on February 8 at the Ambassador Hotel, in Palm Springs, where Fitzsimmons had been invited to play golf in the Bob Hope Desert Classic. Then they moved to La Costa the following day for the final four days of talks. Government wiretaps on a Los Angeles underworld front, People's Industrial Consultants, disclosed that at least one purpose of the meeting was to plot a massive fraud scheme in which money from a Teamsters' health and welfare fund was to be channeled into People's Industrial Consultants. Later Rosanova was heard by federal agents bragging that he had ''made a deal with Fitzsimmons to share future kickbacks.'' Another organized crime figure who was at the meeting said, ''The deal with the Teamsters is set.'' He described ''the deal'' as involving a 7 percent commission—on a $1 billion per year health and welfare business—for the California mob, with the boys in Chicago taking 3 percent of the kickback. According to other FBI data, in a conversation with Milano, Fitzsimmons gave his personal approval to the multimillion-dollar swindle.

Fitzsimmons claimed during a television interview that his only purpose for being at La Costa in early February 1973 was to play golf. ''[A] fellow by the name of Lou Rosanova just came by up the stairs from being out on the practice range. Well, knowing Lou as far as a man is concerned for a number of years, shook hands, said hello and what not . . .''[8]

On February 9, after meeting with the President at San Clemente, Haldeman, Ehrlichman, and presidential counsels John Dean and Richard Moore drove south to La Costa and met at Haldeman's villa. The Senate Select Committee investigating the Watergate affair had been set up only a few days before, and according to Dean, the purpose of the meeting—''12 to 14 hours of discussion''—was ''to deal with this committee's investigation of Watergate.''[9]

Two former Nixon aides, who were later implicated in various Watergate-related areas, confirm that the La Costa meetings were regarded as ''very strange'' even by other members of the Nixon staff. One says, ''It was no secret to us that the meetings were going on in a setting which obviously had the Secret Service, FBI, and Justice people climbing the wall . . . I say it was no secret. What I still don't know is if it was no accident.''

Another former Nixon assistant, who was later convicted of Watergate crimes, adds, ''It's just another one of these untouched areas which no one's ever gone into . . . Our Apalachin was being held at the same time and same place as their Apalachin . . . It's just another one of these strange Mafia things. And don't think some of us aren't as intrigued by it as you are. . . .

''I can tell you one specific thing I know for a fact. Word came down from Haldeman to the Secret Service to make sure the agents for that trip kept their mouths shut—about the appearance of impropriety of these [meetings] being held in the midst of Fitzsimmons' Apalachin affair. The agents and a couple of other officials knew all about it and knew how rotten it looked. There were obviously a lot of red flags.''

Although there is no evidence of a meeting between representatives of the two high-level conspiracies, Nixon invited Fitzsimmons to meet him at the marine air station near the Western White House and accompany him on the Air Force One flight back to Washington. Fitzsimmons accepted and they flew back together on February 12.

Soon after their return to the capital, according to reports by Denny Walsh for the *New York Times* and by *Los Angeles Times* reporters Bill Hazlett and Jack Nelson, Attorney General Kleindienst refused to authorize continuation of electronic surveillance on People's Industrial Consultants. Assistant Attorney General Henry Peterson merely stated that ''prior electronic interceptions were unproductive in obtaining evidence in the case.''

With the Justice Department's decision, the investigation ended abruptly. There were no indictments.

On March 10 presidential special counsel Charles Colson left the White House and joined his former law partner, Charles Morin, whom Nixon had named as the first chairman of the fifteen-member National Commission on Gambling Policy. Subsequently, when Fitzsimmons failed to persuade long-time IBT attorney Edward Bennett Williams, who was representing the Democratic Party in the Watergate bugging case, to back off from his attack on the Nixon Administration, the Teamsters fired Williams and gave the $100,000-a-year business to Colson and Morin.

Later in March, John Dean told the President that a million dollars in hush money would be needed to silence the Watergate conspirators, and Nixon quickly responded, ''We could get that . . . You could get a million dollars. You could get it in cash. I know where it could be gotten.'' Dean mentioned that laundering money is ''the sort of thing Mafia people can do,'' to which the President replied, ''Maybe it takes a gang to do that.''[10]

In April, Arthur Egan, a senior reporter on the *Manchester Union Leader*, wrote that Fitzsimmons and the mob had secretly paid more than a million dollars in cash to Nixon in return for the restrictions which Nixon placed on Hoffa's commutation and for other favors the Nixon Administration could provide. Six hundred thousand, Egan charged, was given by Fitzsimmons in two equal installments, which were added to an earlier payoff of $175,000 which Fitzsimmons had collected from various Teamster officials, including organizers and members of the IBT executive board. Another $400,000 had gone to Nixon, via the mob's Las Vegas gambling interests, for short-circuiting various Teamster-Mafia investigations. The go-between for the complicated arrangement was Murray Chotiner; and Watergate conspirators Gordon Liddy and Howard Hunt made the necessary trips to Las Vegas to pick up the cash, according to Egan.

In response to Egan's accusation that he ''had at times doubled as the White House 'fixer' [and] gave birth to the idea of the political espionage teams,''[11] Chotiner sued for libel and the *Union Leader* retracted the story later on.

However, the Senate Select Committee found that Chotiner had indeed initiated at least two spying efforts for the White House, using the code name ''Chapman's Friend.'' The secret ''Chapman'' reports submitted by Chotiner were read only by Mitchell, Haldeman, and some of Haldeman's personal staff. Second, Egan's allegation that Hunt and Liddy had made secret trips to Las Vegas was confirmed on May 22 by James McCord and again with the disclosure of the tape in which Ehrlichman told Nixon that both Hunt and Liddy had gone to Las Vegas for covert purposes. Third, Ehrlichman's personal notes on the day Egan's article appeared indicate such concern over the matter that Ehrlichman, Haldeman, and the President had a meeting to discuss its implications; unfortunately the meeting was aboard Air Force One and was not recorded. Fourth, during an executive session of the Senate Committee in May 1974, Haldeman's deputy, Lawrence Higby, confirmed the existence of a secret fund—which had been confirmed to him by Haldeman—containing $400,000. In June 1974 the *Washington Post* reported:

> President Nixon told his White House chief of staff, H. R. (Bob) Haldeman, that money from a secret fund would be available for Haldeman's legal

defense in the Watergate case, according to accounts of secret testimony given to the Senate Watergate Committee.

The President told Haldeman that the money was being kept by Charles G. "Bebe" Rebozo, the source said, and included as much as $400,000. . . .

The information was supplied to the Senate Committee last month by Lawrence M. Higby, who previously was one of Haldeman's chief assistants in the White House . . .

According to accounts of Higby's testimony, the President made the offer to Haldeman about April 30, 1973, the day Haldeman resigned from the White House staff.[12]

Later, *Time* magazine stated that a Las Vegas mob-Nixon payoff of a million dollars was being investigated by the Justice Department: "According to a secret FBI report, the $1 million was intended as a payoff for the Administration's cooperation in preventing Jimmy Hoffa from wresting the union presidency from Frank Fitzsimmons, a staunch Nixon supporter."[13] According to *Time*, government investigators had named Fitzsimmons and Provenzano as the key Teamsters involved in the scheme.

"Provenzano and his muscleman, Salvatore Briguglio, ordered in early January 1973 that $500,000 in cash be delivered to a White House courier in Las Vegas," *Time* reported.

Provenzano allegedly told an associate he had collected the money at Fitzsimmons' request and that another $500,000 had been provided for Nixon—also on Fitzsimmons' orders—by Allen Dorfman, a convicted Chicago insurance racketeer and adviser to the Teamsters Union pension fund. Provenzano was quoted as further saying that the cash had been requested by White House aide Charles Colson, who handled the Administration's relations with the Teamsters.[14]

Although the FBI called the information "solid," Salvatore Briguglio, one of those named in the report, denied it. "I wish the hell I had access to $500,000. I wouldn't give it to fucking Nixon or anybody else.

"We didn't care who got in as general president—Fitzsimmons or Hoffa. I'm just a business agent in New Jersey. Why the hell would I get involved in these things?"

A short, slim man who wore glasses and spoke with a heavy New Jersey accent, Briguglio did not look like a muscleman, but he had been convicted of extortion and had taken a rap for Salvatore Provenzano when he was indicted for his alleged role in a counterfeiting ring. After Briguglio pled guilty the charges against Provenzano were dropped. Two other defendants in the case disappeared before the trial.

Jimmy Hoffa kept in close touch with developments in the White House-Teamster-mob relationship. He learned about the Las Vegas payoff from his good friend Irving Davidson, the Washington public relations man, who had broken with Chotiner when the latter became a Fitzsimmons supporter. According to three of Hoffa's closest associates during the Watergate period, he was quietly supporting the probe and asking them to cooperate with it.

"Jimmy was really red-assed about the whole thing between Fitz and Nixon," Dave Johnson says. "He knew that his only chance to get back into the union was for Nixon to fall on his face. So he pitched in and helped him do just that. But openly, he told us to 'get along with 'em. We just don't need no damn trouble yet.' "

Not yet ready to start open warfare between himself and Fitzsimmons, Hoffa testified under oath, in a deposition taken for Egan in connection with Chotiner's libel suit, that a single person was responsible for the restrictions placed on his commutation.

"I blame one man . . . Charles Colson," Hoffa declared on October 2, 1973.

Calling Fitzsimmons "a highly respected labor leader . . . well regarded inside and outside the Teamsters Union," Colson, in his deposition for Egan, refused to respond specifically to Hoffa's accusation:

Question: Were you personally involved in any transaction that related to the release of Mr. Hoffa on commutation of sentence or otherwise?

Colson: I was asked at one point in 1971 to give advice with respect to the commutation of Mr. Hoffa, which I did.

Question: By whom were you asked?

Colson: By the President.

Question: In other words, the President on his initiative came to you and said, "What should we do about Jim Hoffa?"

Colson: Well, I'm not going to characterize my discussions with the President, but I would say he didn't exactly come to me. I talked to the President every day, and this was an area on which at one point I was asked for my opinion.

When asked what advice he gave the President, Colson, claiming attorney-client privilege, responded, "I'm not going to go into the question of what I advised or did not advise the President with respect to this particular matter.'' He did, however, admit that he had discussed the Hoffa case with Fitzsimmons before the White House commuted the sentence.

Later, questioned on the subject by the Senate Watergate Committee during a closed session, Colson invoked the Fifth Amendment.

With the heavy enemies he had, it was obvious to Hoffa that he needed allies wherever he could make them. And surprisingly enough his long-time enemies, the dissidents and the owner-operator truckers, were likely candidates for recruitment into his army. They needed friends as much as he did.

16 Rebel Hoffa and the 1974 Shutdown

When he was president of the Teamsters, the only thing Jimmy Hoffa did for owner-operators was add to their difficulties. Threatened by their numbers (approximately 100,000 in the 1970s), independence, and potential power, Hoffa viewed them as incentive workers, ready to scab on Teamster-authorized strikes. He gave as little help as possible even to those who were members of the union, refusing to negotiate a profit for their equipment "because it complicates the bargaining process." Many owner-operators felt that the union's consistent policy toward them was to "organize, control, then rape." And Hoffa's policy was fully shared by his successor, Frank Fitzsimmons.

But by the end of 1973 Hoffa's situation was very different. In desperate need of allies, he found them where he could, and the events of the time brought some unlikely coalitions.

Since FASH set up its collective bargaining organization in 1970, testimony about the miserable conditions of owner-operators and of the Teamsters' failure to protect these drivers had filled pages of NLRB hearings. "It was discovered that steel haulers were vastly underpaid for their work while the Teamsters turned their backs on contract violations by management," says Bill Hill. "The Teamsters and the carriers had about forty lawyers [at the hearings] to our one," but in spite of that, "specific companies were singled out for their continued exploitation of their drivers and publicly reprimanded by the government."

The Fifth Wheel, in Oakland, California, outlined the financial problems of the owner-operator trucker:

If the union doesn't get to the owner-operator, the employer will. Not all employers are out to completely shaft the owner-operator, but you can bet they'll never come out on the short end of the deal. They either pay percentage or mileage; either way they can't lose. They take 25% to 35% of the load (which is the usual percentage). It doesn't matter how little the load pays, or if the cost of lumpers [loaders] and fuel comes to more than the load pays, the broker still gets his 30% off the top. For example, the owner-operator picks up a load for Los Angeles, which at regular rate would pay about $290.00. The broker gives the owner-operator $150.00, which is standard to run L.A.

Someone had already made $140.00, which the owner-operator never knows about. This $140 is absorbed by the shipper or another broker (or in some cases several brokers). He then may have to pay $25 to get it loaded, drive to L.A. (about $25 for fuel), and if he has to pay lumpers in L.A., that could come to another $30. So he makes about $70, and if you figure wear and tear on the equipment, the owner-operator has not even made wages. No matter what kind of losing proposition it is for the owner-operator, the broker still gets 30% of the $150.

If the employer pays mileage, the usual mileage rate is about 29ᶜ to 35ᶜ a mile. It takes 21ᶜ a mile to operate a truck. That includes fuel, depreciation, wear and tear, and insurance. That leaves about 8ᶜ to 14ᶜ a mile, which is usually not up to union wages.

FASH was faced with additional problems as companies they tried to organize began to claim that their drivers were "independent contractors" and could not be unionized. Aetna Motor Freight, in Warren, Ohio, was among the first companies to use this means of keeping FASH out. FASH took the case to the NLRB and won a regional decision. The company then appealed to the Washington NLRB, which upheld the lower ruling.

"After the appellate decision Aetna was ordered to hold an election, sanctioned by the NLRB, among its company drivers who would choose between us and McMaster's Teamsters. Because there was a third choice on the ballot—'no union'—no one got a majority of the votes, but in a runoff between FASH and the Teamsters we beat them by a pretty good margin," Hill says.

"The company didn't want to sign a contract, and it went to court to prove that its drivers were independent contractors. The case went all the way to the U.S. Supreme Court, which refused to hear it, and we won each time."

The definition of "independent contractor" versus "employee" has always been a problem in the trucking industry. Many companies claim that their drivers have control over whether they accept a load or not. Owner-operators, however, insist that the choice between accepting a load and not working is really no choice at all.

"For instance, a customer might call Sears and Roebuck to put up some aluminum siding on his house. Well, it's not Sears employees who would come out to do the work," Bill Hill says. "It's some guy who has a siding company and is under contract with Sears to handle jobs. Now truckers aren't independent contractors in the same sense. The siding contractor who goes to Sears to subcontract does so willingly. If he wanted to go directly to a homeowner and make his best deal, he could do that as well. In trucking, a driver can't go to, say, U.S. Steel and ask for a load of steel to haul. He has to work for a carrier which has a permit from the ICC and haul under its authority. And this authority gives the carrier complete control over the owner-operator's equipment. So what we're saying is that anyone who is forced to work under these conditions for an authorized carrier should be able to bargain collectively."

Soon after the Aetna decision FASH had two serious setbacks, when NLRB rulings favored the contentions of Conley Motor Express of Pittsburgh and Fleet Transport of Tampa that their drivers were independent contractors. The Fleet decision was similar to that of Conley, which stated: "Owner-operators are free to make their own decisions as to whether they wish to accept any such offered load." Thus they could not be organized.

The matter was still far from settled, however, because the board decided to hear matters of this sort on a case-by-case basis, deciding each on its own merits.

The 1973 Arab embargo on oil shipments to the United States brought more problems for the owner-operators, as well as for the rest of the citizenry. On November 7, President Nixon delivered an address on the energy crisis in which he announced temporary cutbacks on the use of gas and oil. Among other proposals he suggested that states lower and strictly enforce highway speed limits and later he requested that gas stations be closed on Sundays.

The owner-operators complained strongly about the dwindling supply of diesel fuel. Truckers waited impatiently in longer and longer lines at gas pumps while the price of a gallon of fuel skyrocketed from 31 to 55 cents between May and December 1973. And the ten- or twenty-gallon fuel quotas placed on each customer who hauled a rig with a hundred-gallon capacity got him only from one truck stop to the next. Private motorists and company drivers—who were paid by the hour and in most cases were Teamsters—were also hard-pressed, but the owner-operators felt the energy shortage more than any other group. Because of federal regulations which prevented more than ten hours of driving per day, the drivers lost valuable time during their long delays for increasingly expensive gas. The closely monitored speed limits made it even more difficult to earn a decent daily income.

Mike Parkhurst wrote several stories in his *Overdrive* on the theme of a sweetheart relationship between the government and the transnational oil companies. By October he was advocating a national truckers' shutdown, and on November 30 he met in his Los Angeles office with several truckers from Indiana who were interested in the idea.

"Within twenty-four hours after the meeting I started getting telephone calls from all over the country from truckers who were asking, 'What's this I've been hearing about a shutdown?' " Parkhurst says. "I'd figured it would take at least a week or ten days before anything happened."

As word of a planned shutdown spread among the truckers, there was an immediate, crippling, spontaneous stoppage on December 3, when three owner-operators used their rigs to block traffic on I-84 at the state line between Connecticut and New York. The trucks remained stationary for nearly ninety minutes, clogging all traffic. News of the action traveled primarily by way of a relatively new medium of truckers' communication, the citizens' band radio. Using the three eastern truckers' CB handles, other drivers passed along the information about the shutdown incited by "Dopey Diesel," "Doggy Daddy," and "Bit Sissy."

The stoppage on the East Coast was an incentive for similar action later the same day, near Exit 43 of I-80, in Pennsylvania, when drivers stopped to help J. W. "River Rat" Edwards, who had run out of fuel and pulled off on the shoulder. Talking about the exploits of Dopey, Doggy, and Sissy, the truckers realized that the situation was ideal for their own dramatization of their problems. They quickly blocked traffic on one side of the highway. Other drivers soon joined them—educated by CB—and by the next day both sides of the interstate were closed.

While the squawk box chattered and the country music twanged, the truckers drank coffee—blond and sweet—exchanged road stories, or just lounged with their feet on the dashboard, thinking and talking about their cowboylike pasts, presents, and futures. Other motorists fumed over the delay caused by the protest, and the state police were sent to deal with these new American romanticists who insisted that their stand was for "a good greater than our own." Under threat of mass arrests and complicated legal problems, the drivers decided they had made their point and ended the shutdown.

As long-haul road jockeys heading west broadcast the news of the isolated blockades, others with their "ears on" staged a three-day shutdown on the turnpikes and surrounding interstate highways of Ohio and Pennsylvania. The police were not so lenient this time; they slapped the cuffs on many of the protesters and charged them with criminal obstruction of justice, a crime carrying a one-year prison sentence and a $2500 fine. In case the state troopers failed to end the blockades, the National Guard was on alert. Nevertheless, the idea of the "greater good" caught on, and further demonstrations were planned.

"I picked December 13 and 14 for the next shutdown because it couldn't be any closer to Christmas—I didn't want the truckers to be the villains for every delayed turkey or Christmas card," Parkhurst says. "At the same time, I knew that Congress was going on vacation, and it would have been stupid to have a protracted strike when the Congress wasn't in session—how could a law be passed?

"I wanted to use the first shutdown as a left jab to show the government that we were ready, willing, and able to do nasty things out there to get the attention of the public and the press to put pressure on Congress. So another two-day strike would show them that we meant business."

Without the authorization of Parkhurst, who had early established himself as the truckers' moral leader, River Rat Edwards—the protester who had run out of fuel in Pennsylvania—led a small group of owner-operators to Washington to see Secretary of Transportation Claude Brinegar. Soon after the meeting River Rat was taken to a high-powered CB transmitter maintained by the U.S. Coast Guard and urged those few still shut down to end the protest because their problems were now being dealt with by the government. In addition, River Rat, on his own initiative, called for a postponement of the scheduled December 13 protest.

On December 8, just after the first demonstrations, Frank Fitzsimmons met with President Nixon for an hour; the meeting was arranged by Charles Colson. William Simon, head of the new Federal

Energy Administration, later joined the session, which went on for another two hours. When the meeting ended Simon told the press, ''Mr. Fitzsimmons and I agreed very strongly that any action that would obstruct our highways really should be avoided at all costs.''

The President then turned to Fitzsimmons and said, ''Well, we got the blockades down, thanks to you.''

''Teamster members are loyal American citizens first and truck drivers secondly,'' Fitzsimmons responded with a smile.

Few among the general public realized at the time what the differences were between company drivers-Teamster members and the independent owner-operators over whom Fitzsimmons had no direct control.

''At the same time Nixon and Fitzsimmons were patting each other on the back I was holding a press conference of my own,'' Parkhurst says. ''One of the reporters in the audience told me what had happened at the White House. So I said, 'Neither Fitzsimmons nor Nixon has the power, respect, or ability to call off the truckers' shutdown. The only thing that will call it off is if they yield to our demands.' ''

Just before he made his statement, Parkhurst too had conferred with Secretary Brinegar. ''He wanted to feel me out to see whether I would yield, whether I could be manipulated. Then I said, 'It looks to me as though there's a conspiracy between the government and the oil companies.' With that he stood up, pounded his fist on the table, and said, 'I don't have to sit here and listen to that kind of crap.' ''

After his three-hour session with Brinegar, Parkhurst got in touch with owner-operator groups including FASH, the Mid-West Truckers Association of Springfield, Illinois, and the Associated Independent Owner-Operators of Southern California, and told them to pass the word that the December 13–14 shutdown was still on.

Knowing from experience that they would be arrested if blockades of public highways were resumed, the rebel organizations decided that the most effective way of handling the situation was to order the drivers to park their rigs at the pumps of roadside truck stops and refuse to let anyone be serviced. Many truck-stop owners, angry about their own fuel costs and shortages, closed their pumps voluntarily in a protest of their own.

As planned, the truckers' demonstration lasted for two days and ended at 12:01 A.M., December 15. Violence against the protesters and against other motorists was widely reported; the most serious incident was the bombing of a truck in Arkansas.

While the government's concern increased with rumors of a third shutdown, Parkhurst sent mailgrams to several truckers' groups— some of which had popped up only in December—calling for a secret "unity meeting" in Cleveland on January 4, 1974.

"Fifty-five of the seventy-three invitations I sent out came back with indications that they would attend the Cleveland meeting. When everyone arrived, I got them to sign a paper on which we agreed to certain principles, like demands for a fuel cost rollback. Then we decided to stage another shutdown on January 31. The reason for that date was that the mood of the truckers in December was that they were willing to stay shut down longer, and the feeling was, 'Let's do it again next month.' So psychologically the truckers were primed to shut down in January. But it would have been irresponsible to do it just as Congress came back from vacation on January 23 or 24, so I thought it would be a good idea to give them a week to work out some legislative proposals that we would give them.''

In an attempt to clarify for the public the distinctions between the two types of truckers, and to make plans for the proposed nationwide shutdown on January 31, Parkhurst invited representatives from the same groups that had attended the January 4 meeting to attend another in Washington, on January 23, at the Mayflower Hotel.

The night before the meeting Parkhurst and Bill Hill got into a brief argument about procedures for the following day. Parkhurst wanted to form a committee which would become active only when the government formed its own, with represenetives from Congress and the executive branch. He also insisted that the committee have no chairman. Hill disagreed. Parkhurst got his way, but only temporarily. The one thing both leaders agreed upon was that a young attorney affiliated with Ralph Nader's Public Citizen Litigation Group, Arthur Fox, was to preside over the festivities the next day.

Fox, a University of Virginia Law School graduate and a former attorney for the NLRB, was the head of the Professional Drivers Council for Safety and Health (PROD), which had grown out of Nader's Professional Drivers Conference held on October 2, 1971, in Washington. It had become fully operational in the spring of 1972, when the talented Fox took over. Earlier, however, the Nader group had published *The Interstate Commerce Omission*, written by Robert Fellmeth. The highly detailed, well-documented, and extremely critical 1970 study blasted the regulatory commission for its unresponsive attitude toward both truckers and the general public.

The independent owner-operators' leaders trusted and respected Nader; thus Arthur Fox of PROD was the logical choice to moderate their organizational meeting.

"I tried to stay out of this pissing contest between Hill and Parkhurst," Fox says, "especially since PROD was a Teamster reform group which primarily represented drivers who used company-owned equipment and were Teamster members, not independent owner-operators. But I thought, like the rest of them, that the differences between them should be clearly articulated. They hadn't been previously. And the independents had some very serious problems.

"Parkhurst was pretty militant, and he wanted to shut down the country until it fell to its knees screaming. Hill was maybe a little more sympathetic to the average joe who owned a truck and had that monthly mortgage payment to make. Hill wanted to shut down, no doubt about that, but he wanted to end it as quickly as possible with as much as they could get."

The January 23 meeting began at nine o'clock and went on all morning. Stressing to the truckers that their protest should be geared to inform the public of their problems, keeping the focus on the oil companies, Fox suggested that the group form a Truckers Unity Committee to be the independents' spokesman if and when, as Parkhurst had suggested, the government formed its own committee. The drivers, representing nineteen different organizations, selected a six-member committee to deal with the government. To Parkhurst's dismay, Hill was selected chairman.

The next day, as the towering Hill stepped in front of the television cameras to read the committee's statement announcing the January 31 shutdown, Fitzsimmons was appealing to America's truckers to ignore the protest and continue to haul. Hoots and catcalls greeted Fitzsimmons' television appearance while Hill boomed out the independents' demands for a rollback on gas and diesel prices to the levels of May 1973, and for a public audit of the transnational oil companies.

Hill's tone was firm, but dissension was already in evidence. In Akron, Ohio, militant truckers who had attended the January 23 meeting decided not to wait until January 31. They shut down a week early, and drivers in other areas began to shut down early too. Both Hill and Parkhurst had warned that a disjointed demonstration could get somebody hurt, and sure enough, a trucker was killed in Allentown, Pennsylvania, when a rock through his windshield made him lose control of his rig.

On the eve of the scheduled protest, presidential special assistant William J. Usery made a last-minute effort to head off a nationwide shutdown. Usery and others in the White House continued to credit Fitzsimmons for negotiating on behalf of the truckers; the leaders of the unity committee mocked Usery's inadequate proposals and held to their plans.

Then, "several hours before the shutdown began," Hill recalls, "Governor Milton Shapp [of Pennsylvania] called and asked me to meet him at the Pittsburgh airport. So a bunch of us went out there to see what he had to say. He pleaded with us through the evening, trying to get us to call a forty-five-day moratorium until the government had a chance to consider our problems. Really, though, Shapp was the only one around, besides us, who thought we could really pull it off."

Hill refused to postpone the demonstration but told Shapp that he could help by getting the White House involved and arranging a meeting between the truckers and various officials in Washington.

Parkhurst objected to Hill's handling of the conference with Shapp. "How were we going to get anything from the government if we were talking about negotiations before the shutdown even started? Anyway, you don't negotiate with governors. First you shut down, stay shut down, and you'll get what you want. I wanted legislative action on the books before we went back to work."

The peaceful highways became a national nightmare as blockades went up and guerrilla warfare erupted in the darkness on the night of January 31. Independents parked their rigs at truck stops from coast to coast. As in 1967, 1970, and December 1973, the 1974 shutdown was accompanied by shootings, beatings, and bombings. Rocks were thrown at those who tried to keep hauling—if their tires hadn't already been slashed by vandals. One driver returning from a rebel meeting was nearly killed when a sawed-off steel beam tumbled from a viaduct and fell on his truck.

"An act of God," claimed a police officer. "Yeah," the shaken driver responded, "if God is a member of the Teamsters Union."

In the chaos it was difficult for the police to find out who was responsible for the violence. The rebel forces were blamed for most of the trouble, but in fact Teamster goon squads accounted for much of the damage, especially in Ohio and Pennsylvania. Teamster-paid strongarm specialists stormed into the national FASH headquarters in Pittsburgh and wrecked its offices.

"Tom Fagin [president of Teamster Joint Council 40, in Pittsburgh] held a big meeting of Teamsters to talk about the shutdown," said Hill. "So I anticipated trouble. I told a bunch of our guys to go to our office with their guns. But when I actually got word that the Teamster goons were coming, I decided I didn't want another shoot-out like in 1969, so I told everyone to get the hell out of the office and let 'em have it."

"We monitored the offenses committed on both sides," says prosecutor Blair Griffith, the U.S. Attorney in Pittsburgh. "And the Teamsters were the number-one problem. We criticized the FBI for not moving quickly enough against these activities, and we were even critical of Attorney General Saxbe for overheating the situation. He was, quite frankly, beating his breast, making promises that couldn't be delivered about our law enforcement capabilities."

Fitzsimmons closed his eyes to Teamster-instigated violence and accused the dissidents of "acts of murder, violence and intimidation." Members of the McMaster task force—who had tried to organize many of the owner-operators involved—certainly contributed to the latter two.

Harry Budzynski, Titus McCue, and Jack Robison, all from the Pittsburgh area, were arrested for breaking the windshields and smashing the radiators of two shut-down trucks. The police picked up the trail of McMaster's men and followed them to a hotel in a suburb of Pittsburgh, a prearranged rendezvous point where they shared a room registered in Robison's name. Search warrant in hand, the officers explored the organizers' cars and found a small arsenal of rumble gear: a bent tire iron, a slingshot with a bag of fifty marbles, a broken ax handle with a double-bladed head, and a loaded .38-caliber revolver. The cops confiscated the weaponry and took the three organizers into custody, but the search warrant was found to be faulty and the case was thrown out of court. The owner of one of the annihilated trucks, a FASH member, then filed suit against McMaster's men in civil court and collected several thousand dollars in damages.

Like the Teamsters, the oil companies had their own hired guns. Armed members of the Hell's Angels motorcycle gang were paid by Sohio, a subsidiary of the Standard Oil Company, to escort tanker trucks leaving Refiners Transport in Cleveland, according to Parkhurst.

Bellied-up and jackknifed eighteen-wheelers littered the roads all over the country. In New York the Holland Tunnel was blockaded and in Pennsylvania a bridge on the turnpike was bombed. Leaders from *Overdrive* were shot at while holding Teamster goons at bay during the "Battle of Breezewood," just off the turnpike. A driver hammering down through Delaware was shot and killed.

The drivers' trucks became personal fortresses. Door handles were removed so that assailants couldn't pull drivers out into the streets for beatings; windshields were taped to prevent injuries from flying glass. Drivers carried baseball bats, shivs, and guns.

The National Guard was called out in eight states; food shortages were widespread and there were more than a hundred thousand layoffs. Two Chrysler plants alone had to tell 5500 employees to stay home. The massive shutdown achieved what was intended: a recognition of the importance of owner-operators and their problems as well as acute realization of the energy crisis.

Fitzsimmons again looked inept and helpless as members of longshoremen's unions and others honored the independents' strike. Although nearly half the population supported the truckers' protest, according to a Lou Harris poll, the Teamster leader claimed that the shutdown was merely a "publicity stunt for private profit" and ordered trucks driven by Teamster members to travel in convoys or be police escorted. Independent and union owner-operators both attacked him on radio, television, and in the newspapers.

The government strayed from Fitzsimmons momentarily and began doing business with the truckers. Early in the strike Governor Shapp had gotten Hill and the dissidents' committee a meeting with several administration and congressional leaders, including Usery and Senator Henry Jackson. On Sunday, February 3, the dissidents were scheduled to meet with thirty-six federal and state officials, but the plans for that meeting so infuriated Parkhurst that he bolted from the committee and telegraphed Hill that "if you insist on this publicity gimmick, you do so without my support. If you follow through on this meeting with the attendant publicity, then it will be obvious to us and our constituency what is really important to you." Parkhurst went on to say that the meeting was premature and a "sellout."

Fitzsimmons also deplored the meeting. He criticized the "actions of some government officials who kowtow to those who perpetrate violence and lawlessness against others to gain their goals."

Nevertheless, the talks began as planned, with Hill maintaining his hard approach. By now the dissidents had lengthened the list of concessions needed to end the shutdown; their most important demands were the Sunday sale of fuel, no reprisals against truckers participating in the protest, help for owner-operators from the Small Business Administration, uniform state truck and cargo weight limits, and a fuel-cost pass-through system to offset the rise in prices.

The February 3 meeting was unwieldy and inconclusive. The shutdown held out. The dissidents tried to break the impasse by talking directly with Simon, who had meantime appealed by telegram to the fifty governors to keep their states' trucks rolling no matter what the cost. Insisting that no price rollback on fuel could be negotiated because of the Arabs' stranglehold on the price of crude, Simon and Secretary of Labor Brennan refused to recognize the Truckers Unity Committee as the voice of the owner-operators. Instead they continued to deal with Fitzsimmons, who was still talking behind closed doors with Nixon and Colson. Simon, like Usery before him, gave Fitzsimmons public credit for his peacemaking efforts. It had become quite clear that the Nixon Administration was determined to make Fitzsimmons a national hero whether the protesters liked it or not.

In view of Simon's response, Hill and the unity committee redrafted their demands. This time they proposed that owner-operators must have all the fuel they needed at a price which could go no higher than a ceiling to be fixed within ninety days. In place of the price rollback which Simon had vetoed, Hill demanded an immediate surcharge on everything the truckers hauled. "But before our revisions were submitted to the government, Simon was already on the fucking television telling the world that the strike had been settled. So we told him and the rest of them to shove their settlement up their asses."

Simon indicated in his announcement of February 5 that the drivers had accepted a price freeze over fuel costs which would last until the end of February and the establishment of a truckers' "hot line," a toll-free number that drivers could call to air their grievances. These proposals were the sum total of the government's "concessions."

Governor Jimmy Carter of Georgia was "deeply sympathetic" with the problems of the truckers. "It's just a publicity stunt to make it appear that the administration is doing something for the truckers," he said. "The basic [energy] problem is not going to be solved by harassing the truckers."

The independents' rejection of Simon's proposals brought additional pressure from the administration. Attorney General Saxbe vowed to prosecute the dissidents. "A handful of truckers is not going to bring this country to its knees," he said.

While the truckers chuckled and elbowed each other over Saxbe's public statement, Usery made serious threats in private. "You guys don't understand what you're playing with," he told Hill and the committee. "You're not negotiating with an industry, you're negotiating with your government."

"He was shaking, and he was scared," Hill explains. "Then he told me that federal troops were ready to move in and wipe us out on orders of the President.

"At first I thought, 'Man, we got these guys scared.' Then I started reading into what was going on. Usery was scared to death of what that asshole in the White House was going to do. As the strike went on, public opinion started going against us, and some people were telling me that Nixon wanted to use it as an end run around his Watergate-bullshit problems.

"I knew then that Usery was shaking because he was scared for what Nixon might do to us."

At 12:01 A.M. on February 7, Usery and two Nixon aides went to the Mayflower to give Hill and the dissidents the government's final offer.

As described by Bill Hill, "I have this envelope," Usery warned. "Now I'm going to open this son of a bitch up. In this envelope is just about what you guys presented us in your last demands. But before you look at it, I want you to know that this is our final offer. I can't change one goddamn sentence; I can't change a comma; I can't make a capital P a little p. This is it.

"Now I'm going to leave the room. You guys read it. If you accept it—fine. But this is it."

"So we read the thing and it was exactly what the hell we wanted," Hill says. "At about two in the morning, after our lawyers checked it out, we called Usery back in. He said, 'Fine, now we're going to go downstairs and tell everyone that we're going back to work.'

"I said, 'Nope. No way. This has to be ratified by the independent truckers. We're not making the announcement to end the shutdown until it's been accepted.'"

Usery retorted angrily, "That's not the way we're going to do it!"

"Then piss on it! We're not takin' it!" shouted Hill.

The dissidents and the government officials argued for three hours. Finally Usery agreed to limit his television announcement to the fact that a tentative agreement had been reached.

"So we went downstairs and the son of a bitch pulled one of the worst goddamn things I'd ever seen. He went completely against all the things we had agreed to and announced that everyone could go back to work; he never announced anything about us going back and voting on it.''

As Usery finished speaking, Hill charged up to the microphone and shouted to the truckers to ''stay shut down until we come back to explain the agreement and take a vote.'' The truckers voted hastily, and within three days the trucks were rolling again—with a 6 percent surcharge which would be passed down from the certified carrier to the owner-operator who hauled for it.

Hill and most of the dissidents were elated.[1] Governor Shapp—who had been the independents' best friend and go-between during the whole shutdown—joined in the victory celebration. In his speech Shapp declared that because of Nixon's self-imposed isolation from the independents' representatives, martial law had barely been avoided; throughout the shutdown the President had failed ''to come to grips with reality.''

On Saturday, February 9, President Nixon addressed the nation to announce the end of the shutdown and to call its leaders ''desperados.'' ''I want to commend Frank Fitzsimmons,'' said the President, ''who leads the country's single largest union, the Teamsters, for his responsible actions during this period.''

In view of Nixon's Watergate problems at the time, his praise of Fitzsimmons meant little to the truckers and even less to Jimmy Hoffa, a behind-the-scenes participant in the drama.

On at least two occasions during the shutdown Hoffa tried to reach Hill, but Hill refused to talk to him: ''A couple of guys from Detroit said that Hoffa wanted to talk to me, and that they could arrange a meeting. It was hard to believe but they said Hoffa wanted to help us out. But, hell, the last thing we needed was getting that guy involved. So I told them to forget it.''

In a telephone call to *Overdrive* during the same period Hoffa told its executives that if he were president of the Teamsters he ''would be fighting on their [the independents'] side.'' It was an incredible statement for Hoffa to make, considering his long opposition to the owner-operators, but he went on to say that owner-operators were ''entitled to make a profit [for their equipment], and they're entitled to make a decent wage.''[2]

''Hoffa referred to the owner-operators as 'my boys,' '' Parkhurst says. ''He said that if he had been president of the union he would be supporting us. He gave us his full backing from his position. But we didn't publicize it because of his legal problems, and he didn't want to jeopardize his commutation either.''

The reason for Hoffa's remarkable turnabout was simple: the rebels offered Hoffa a means to attack his enemies in the Teamster high command. That was why Hoffa seemed to be going back to his roots as a young Detroit organizer, portraying himself again as the workingman's hero, the defender of the rank and file.

On his home ground Hoffa was more involved in the shutdown. He helped and advised the dissidents in Local 299 and the independent owner-operators.

''I was in contact with him two, three times a week,'' says Mitchell Miller, a leader of the Michigan protest. ''He thought what we were doing was a great thing.'' ''I talked to him frequently during the strike,'' adds William ''Red'' Anderson, another leader of the shutdown. ''He believed that we needed some help on the rate increases and he agreed that the owner-operators needed help. He was willing to help us, so we helped him . . . The whole thing was to make Fitzsimmons look bad.''

Rebel activities in Detroit had all the earmarks of pro-Hoffa rallies. In one instance over a hundred drivers congregated at a truck stop outside Detroit, chanting for Fitzsimmons' ouster. A dissident spokesman received resounding applause when he leaped to the front of the meeting, called Fitzsimmons a ''fat cat,'' and shouted, ''You all know Jimmy was one of us independents. If we could get him back here to handle it, then we could stop this thing in three or four days.''[3]

But stopping the shutdown wasn't what Hoffa wanted; he enjoyed seeing Fitzsimmons backed against the ropes. When word came on February 7 that Hill and the Truckers Unity Committee had settled the shutdown, Hoffa and the local rebel leaders decided not to end it in Detroit until all the other truckers in the country had gone back to work. When a vote was taken the back-to-work proposal was received with a chorus of boos and hisses and almost unanimous agreement to stay out.

That same afternoon, a Detroit Teamster official says, he was with one of McMaster's organizers who said that Hoffa's owner-operator supporters had to be taught a lesson. The organizer then showed the official several explosive devices in the trunk of his car.

Later that night Red Anderson's home was bombed.

''I was home when Red called me,'' Miller remembers, ''and we were talking on the telephone when the damn thing blew up. He said, 'Jesus Christ! My porch just blew up!' So I jumped in the car and went over there. I got there just before the cops did. The whole back end of his house had disappeared.''

''I had no problems with why it happened,'' Anderson says. ''There were certain forces in Detroit who didn't like me dealing with Hoffa. They knew he had offered jobs to me and a couple of others through Dave Johnson.''

Although Miller later became a business agent under Johnson, Anderson refused the job and instead worked on his new organization, Michigan Owner-Operators. But that group, composed chiefly of steel haulers, soon switched its loyalties from Hoffa to Rolland McMaster.

''After they bombed my home, I didn't want any more trouble,'' says Anderson. ''McMaster has been fair to me, and whether he did the job on my house or not, he's been good to me ever since.''

The energy crisis was as good a reason as any for the IBT to disband the McMaster task force before anyone found out that the organizing campaign was a smokescreen for efforts to get carriers to pay for labor peace. The project was halted on February 10, 1974. Spending over $1.3 million on its forty-eight-state exercise of terrorism, leaving sweetheart contracts in its wake, the task force organized only 750 new members at thirty-five companies during its twenty-two-month history.

In his official report to the IBT, McMaster claimed to have organized over twice as many Teamsters at fifty-four companies. But eleven of the firms had been organized some years before the task force was set up; at two others the union had lost recognition elections; and three companies were, and remained, nonunion. Of the thirty-five companies McMaster did organize, eleven soon went out of business.

Three months before the task force was officially disbanded, Mc-Master's nominal supervisor, Roy Williams, said in an interview with McMaster's task force publication, *Teamster-Owner-Driver*:

> The special division based in Chicago is doing an excellent job under McMaster . . . The special division is assisting the local union with special manpower and talents all directed toward the focus of organizing the particular company that is the target. New techniques, methods, and organizing procedures are always being used to accomplish the ultimate objectives which are union contracts. The [general] executive board is supporting this new division with every tool, and we already know from the scoreboard of victories that this division will be quite successful.

McMaster's "new techniques, methods, and organizing procedures" were really nothing more than the same old "bust their heads open and shake 'em down" philosophy. Those with some knowledge of the IBT would find it hard to believe that Fitzsimmons, Williams, and the board did not know how McMaster was operating.[4]

"We did hard work," McMaster says. "There was no skullduggery going on."

Although formally out of business, the McMaster task force would be resurrected within a few months, with selected members reunited in Detroit, to fight a different enemy. But before that occurred, the work of a brilliant young reporter gave the Teamsters more headaches. Jo Thomas, a former Nieman Fellow at Harvard and a star investigator for the *Detroit Free Press*, published a devastating seven-part series about Detroit trucking companies that were tied to organized crime.

Her eighteen-month investigation led to several indictments, including that of a Local 299 business agent; a Detroit underworld figure; and the co-owners of a local steel hauling outfit. Her articles detailed the "classic" case of a mob-operated company trying to force its competition out of business. Through her research she learned that two steel hauling companies, one of which was J&J Cartage, had been "squeezing out their competitors by cutting rates, overloading trucks, and shaking down drivers for funds to bribe county weighmasters, ignoring Teamster contracts with impunity, and intimidating employes and competitors alike.'"[5]

J&J's labor negotiator, Vincent A. Meli, was later indicted for extortion.

"Jo Thomas's work on the mob's connection with the Detroit steel hauling businesses was really well done," says Vince Piersante. "It showed how deeply entrenched organized crime has been in the industry since the 1930s, when Santo Perrone had control of the Detroit Stove Works and was hauling steel for it. Other Detroit crime families also got involved—the Polizzis, the Toccos, the Melis, and the Giacalones.

"While Priziola and Jimmy Quasarano were dealing in drugs and the Zerillis were into gambling, the smart money was into steel. It was potentially lucrative and gave a legitimate cover for some of their shadier activities.

"And with Rolland McMaster serving as the Teamsters' steel hauling expert throughout the Midwest, it has to make you think how involved he might be in all of this. In Watergate Washington, to solve the crime you followed the money; in Detroit, when investigating certain mob activities, you followed the steel.''

Following the steel, it was virtually undisputed that McMaster was the number one Teamster to deal with in the area of iron, steel, and other special commodities. The executive director of the National Steel Carriers Association—which represented nearly a hundred companies—was the former Local 299 legal counsel, George Gregory Mantho. According to federal agents, McMaster and Mantho at one time shared an apartment at 8200 East Jefferson Street in Detroit. Although McMaster vehemently denies that, he does admit that Mantho was a frequent houseguest.

When Mantho died in 1973, he was replaced as director of the National Steel Carriers Association by Robert Coopes, McMaster's personal attorney, who had represented him in legal proceedings at least three times. The employer chairman of the National Steel Carriers Association was William F. Wolff, president of Youngstown Cartage Company, who was convicted with McMaster in 1962 for sixty-four counts of labor extortion.

Not unexpectedly, McMaster claimed to be only ''distant friends'' with the racketeers who were trying to monopolize the Detroit steel hauling industry. This was the same Rolland McMaster who had once been ''the strongest arm behind Hoffa'' and, according to several Teamster officials, Hoffa's liaison with such crime figures as Santos Trafficante. McMaster's relationship with Trafficante and David Yaras was flourishing at the same time that Hoffa's associates, Trafficante and Giancana, were working with the CIA.

But in 1974, the close friendship between the two men long gone, McMaster saw Hoffa as just another rebel.

17 The Blank Check

The final, dramatic clash between Hoffa and Fitzsimmons had been foreshadowed in midsummer 1973, when Fitzsimmons suddenly resigned as vice president of Local 299, "to concentrate on my activities as general president of the Teamsters." The announcement caused considerable speculation that Fitzsimmons was simply broadening his power base to thwart Hoffa's comeback in Local 299. The executive board's prompt appointment of Fitzsimmons' son, Richard, to replace his father as the local's vice president encouraged such rumors. Local trustee Don Taber replaced Richard Fitzsimmons as recording secretary, and Taber, in turn, was succeeded by Hoffa's uncle, Steve Riddle.

"With my father being the general president, he just didn't think he could devote the necessary time to doing the job as vice president," says Dick Fitzsimmons. "So he resigned and I was elevated from recording secretary to vice president."

With his promotion Dick Fitzsimmons became next in line to succeed Dave Johnson as president of Local 299. Thus if Johnson retired on January 1, 1974, as he had said he would, young Fitzsimmons would immediately be moved up, blocking Hoffa from being appointed to a position in his old local.

"I had no choice," Johnson says. "Jimmy was in a jam, so I had to postpone my plans to retire. God, I really wanted to get out of there too. I knew the pressure was really going to be turned on to get me out."

Although McMaster had held no position in the local since December 1970, at the annual Local 299 stewards' Christmas luncheon in December 1973, Hoffa brought up McMaster's tenure in his keynote address. Refusing to name his target but leaving the clear impression that he was talking about McMaster, Hoffa shouted in his rambling, passionate speech, ''We've come a long way since 1932, and almost all the officers and agents of this union sitting here came in after Jimmy Hoffa; and he came into your house and brought with him Bobby Holmes, Frankie Collins, and Martin Haggerty. We're the only survivors today out of the original sixteen that started this great union in the city of Detroit, the state of Michigan. Oh, I indeed hear a lot of things about what some people did say, and I realize that certain people whisper, connive, scheme, lie, and have you believe they're responsible for this great organization as it is today . . .

''There are those today spouting off and mouthing off, concerning what they did for this union. And then when organizing they compromise our health and welfare and pension plans, because they believe it will create strikes, destroy the organization and their salaries [if they don't].

With pro forma praise for Fitzsimmons, Hoffa made his long-awaited announcement amid great applause, and quickly followed it up with another shot at McMaster.

''I can assure you that it is my hope and desire that I will lead the battle, and I will be a candidate for president [of Local 299] in 1974! And we will resurrect the spirit that built this union! We will resurrect the spirit that put our treasury over two million dollars that is now depleted for some unknown reason during that day-to-day operation—by no fault of our present officers! That individual who was not elected and was given your trust betrayed you on that accord!''

When McMaster heard of the speech he realized, of course, that he was the object of Hoffa's remarks and called the Hoffa house to protest. Hoffa refused to talk with him.

''Hoffa looked at the books and knew what happened,'' McMaster says. ''Look at the motions that were made and the records of the executive board. Everything I did was approved by them! I did the job! Jimmy didn't like too much progress unless he was the one that stamped it and put it out.''

Before Hoffa could legally run for president of Local 299 he had to rid himself of the restrictions placed upon his commutation. Guarding against directly attacking the President—who he still hoped would pardon him if all else failed—Hoffa continued to blame Colson, now general counsel of the IBT.

When John Dean testified before the Watergate Select Committee he indicated that it was John Mitchell, not Colson, who proposed and approved the restrictions, but on October 15, 1973, Hoffa obtained an affidavit from Mitchell:

I, John N. Mitchell, being duly sworn, depose and say:

1. That neither I, as Attorney General of the United States, nor, to my knowledge, any other official of the Department of Justice during my tenure as Attorney General initiated or suggested the inclusion of restrictions in the Presidential commutation of James R. Hoffa.

2. That President Richard M. Nixon did not initiate with or suggest to me nor, to my knowledge, did he initiate with or suggest to any other official of the Department of Justice during my tenure as Attorney General that restrictions on Mr. Hoffa's activities in the labor movement be a part of any Presidential commutation for Mr. Hoffa.

Hoffa continued to accuse Colson of being the actual go-between for the Teamster leadership and the White House, and he charged that Colson's payoff for keeping him out of union politics was the job as general counsel.

Attorney General Saxbe disputed Hoffa's version and said that the matter would have to be settled in court. He added that he had been the target of enormous pressure from congressmen and various Hoffa supporters to overturn the restrictions.

Saxbe himself had been under investigation earlier about the circumstances by which both he and Frank Fitzsimmons acquired stock in Bally Manufacturing Company, the largest producer of gambling machines in the country. Saxbe and the Teamster president owned six hundred and nine hundred shares, respectively, in the company which, government investigators claimed, was involved with several organized crime figures and had received a $12 million loan from the IBT's Central States Pension Fund. Saxbe, then a senator from Ohio, had acquired the securities in 1969; he liquidated his interest in the enterprise after the *Dayton Daily News* revealed the fact a year later. Saxbe said in 1974 that his quick action resulted from his suspicions that ''there might have been involvement of people of unsavory reputation . . . ''[1] Fitzsimmons kept his stock and said nothing.

Hoffa threw his first public barb at Fitzsimmons in February 1974, remarking that he was playing too much golf. Saying that if he were the IBT general president he would refuse his pay check, Hoffa announced that he was willing to return his $1.7 million lump-sum pension. He emphasized, however, that all his plans were meaningless unless he could regain an office in Local 299, which could serve as his springboard to the IBT convention in 1976, when the next Teamster president would be elected.

"Fitzsimmons is . . . traveling all over the country to every damn golf tournament there is, when being president of the Teamsters is an 18-hour-a-day job."

All Fitzsimmons had to say about Hoffa was, "Let him try to run. I'll take him on."[2]

On March 13, 1974, Hoffa filed suit against Nixon and Saxbe in U.S. District Court in Washington. The presiding judge was John H. Pratt, ex-Marine, war hero, graduate of Harvard Law School, and an appointee of President Lyndon Johnson. Stating that he was unaware of the restrictions barring him from union activity at the time he accepted the commutation, Hoffa charged that the condition "barring participation in the management of labor organizations . . . " was a "selective, discriminatory and unprecedented act of the Executive, done for impermissible and illegal purposes" that "originated and derived from no regular clemency procedure but was caused to be added to said commutation by Charles Colson, Special Counsel to the President, pursuant to an agreement and conspiracy" by Colson and Fitzsimmons.

"I'm positively sure that he had a hand in it," Hoffa said of Colson in a television interview, "and I'm positively sure that he was the architect of the language . . . He did it to ingratiate himself with Fitzsimmons. And in doing so got the job of representing the Teamsters. And Fitz did it, through Colson, to be able to keep the presidency of the international union."

Fitzsimmons (videotaped separately) responded, "There is no truth whatsoever. And as far as Jimmy Hoffa is concerned when he makes that statement, he knows he's a damn liar. He accuses Chuck Colson and me of creating them restrictions. I didn't know nothing about them restrictions, didn't know anything about 'em until I read it in the newspapers."

And Colson too claimed that the charge was false: "The accusation has been made that Fitzsimmons and I cooked this up, some conspiracy, to keep Hoffa from coming back into the Teamsters. That's just plain malarkey . . . Fitzsimmons and I never discussed the restrictions on Hoffa's commutation. I advised Mr. Fitzsimmons I think the day before Hoffa was to be released that he was going to be

released under the conditions that seemed to be in the best interest of
the labor movement and the country at the time. I never told him what,
what those restrictions were.''³

As Hoffa filed his civil suit, Dave Johnson, as president of Local
299, sent him a letter formally offering him a position as a local
business agent with a minimum salary of $15,000. Hoffa hoped that if
the court found in his favor he would be permitted to accept the job; it
would be necessary in order to be eligible for the presidential elections
at the next IBT convention.

Hoffa was joined as plaintiff in his suit by several dissident Team-
sters, including steel haulers and Detroit shutdown leaders Mitch
Miller and William R. Klann and former Local 299 Unity Committee
members Pete Karagozian and Andrew Pellerito. Four anti-
Fitzsimmons locals on the East Coast also joined Hoffa: Local 445 in
Yonkers, New York, headed by Ted Daley; Local 676 in Collingwood,
New Jersey, lead by John P. Greeley; and Locals 1 and 326 in
Philadelphia and Wilmington, Delaware, respectively, both heavily
influenced by Frank Sheeran, president of Local 326. Sheeran, a long-
time friend of Hoffa, had been charged with murder in 1967 but
acquitted on grounds that the court failed to give him a speedy trial. He
had said in 1973, ''I'll be a Hoffa man till the day they pat my face
with a shovel and steal my cuff links.''

Dissident Teamster Karagozian says, ''Jimmy and I had met
through Dave Johnson. I had talked with Hoffa several times, and he
told me he'd done his time and was going straight. Then he said he
wanted to clean up the whole mess in the union. Later he called me and
asked me to be a co-plaintiff in his lawsuit. I told him that I'd be glad to
support him. I said that I personally felt that until his restrictions were
lifted I didn't feel that I could really nominate, vote, or help to elect
who I wanted in Local 299. Andy Pellerito and I were good friends, so I
brought him in on the suit as well.''

Because of Hoffa's strange alliances with the owner-operator
truckers and the Teamster dissidents, his enemies tried to dismiss him
as just another rebel leader, a rank-and-file member throwing rocks.
There was no reason for Fitzsimmons and the IBT general executive
board to treat Hoffa any differently from the way they treated Andy
Provenzino, and Mel Angel before him.

Fitzsimmons finally and openly split with Hoffa by firing Josephine
Hoffa from her $40,000-a-year post as the head of the IBT women's
DRIVE committee and James Hoffa from his $30,000-a-year position

as a counsel for the IBT. Both firings occurred on May 8, the day before the House Judiciary Committee began reviewing its staff's investigation into the possible impeachment of President Nixon.

The war was out in the open. Hoffa had slapped Fitzsimmons across the face with his glove and Fitzsimmons returned the challenge, saying publicly that Hoffa shouldn't be allowed to reappear in the labor movement.

In June, at a testimonial dinner in Cleveland for William Presser, Fitzsimmons began receiving powerful public support from the IBT general executive board. Its members swarmed around Fitzsimmons before the banquet, and Presser said in his speech, "Wherever he goes, I'll be one step behind him." When reporters asked whether his support would remain even if Hoffa ran, Presser snapped, "No matter who runs against him."[4]

On June 13, on a WXYZ-TV talk show, Hoffa struck back. "I understand from reliable sources in the international union," he said coolly, "that Fitzsimmons is seeing a psychiatrist twice a week. That's why he's making the statement [about] the man who took him off a truck, taught him all he knows about organized labor . . . then hand-picked him for the president of the international union."

As for Dick Fitzsimmons, he was a "nice boy" and Hoffa had "known him since he was born, but some people have that [drinking] problem. Anyone who wants to go down to the London Chop House and various places to see young Fitz become an actor instead of a representative of the trade union will realize that problem."

A few days later Dave Johnson announced that he would seek reelection as the president of Local 299 and continue to serve as Hoffa's caretaker until the commutation restrictions were overturned. "It was probably the roughest decision I ever had to make," Johnson thinks. "Christ, I knew that Jimmy's enemies were going to come down on me. 'Get Dave Johnson out of the way, and you'll have Jimmy Hoffa out too!' "

"I don't care whether Dave Johnson quits, jumps off a building, or runs for the head of the Methodist Church," Frank Fitzsimmons shouted angrily. "My son could beat either [Johnson or Hoffa] or both together."[5]

Weary from his thirty-four years of union battles in Local 299, Johnson swallowed hard and got ready to tough out one more campaign.

Soon after Johnson's announcement, a former member of the McMaster task force received a telephone call from McMaster, who asked him to come to Detroit for a special project. The organizer remembers the call well: ''The main thing was: don't let Jimmy into 299. If he gets into 299, that makes him eligible [to run for IBT president]. So the main thing was: stop him. The international tried all the legal things in the courts and everything . . . The main fight, though, came out of Detroit. The idea was [to] keep Dave Johnson out. If Hoffa would have come in, he [Johnson] was going to resign, turn the power over to Hoffa, which would have made him the [local's] principal officer, a delegate to the convention in '76. And when it came to nomination, he would stand up and say, 'I'm challenging you, Frank, for my old job.' . . . This is why Fitzsimmons gave McMaster a 'blank check.' When I say a 'blank check,' I don't physically mean a check. I mean, 'Whatever it costs to do it, you do it.'

''McMaster called me and asked, 'Are you working? You want to come to Detroit? . . . I got a project going. We got unlimited money to upset Dave Johnson and disrupt that whole goddamn operation . . . You come on up and live in Detroit, and it'll be like old times [on the task force]. Unlimited expenses, and I'll take care of your wages. There's no ceiling on it, but we gotta succeed.' That's the way he put it to me.''

That organizer refused to go and so did several others who were asked. But the organizer names former colleagues who did join up with McMaster: Larry McHenry, the former dissident; Jack Robison, the violent ex-convict and reputed Pennsylvania bomber; and Jim Shaw, of Eddyville, Kentucky, a big, good-looking bruiser whom McMaster had hired as an organizer during the violent campaign against the Eck Miller Transportation Company. Federal officials have confirmed that the three men were in Detroit and working for McMaster during the summer of 1974.

In July, Jim Drinkhall of *Overdrive*, who in the 1970s had become the indefatigable investigator of the Teamsters that Walter Sheridan was in the 1950s and 60s, wrote a surprisingly naïve story, ''Hoffa—The Question Is Not '*Will* He Come Back?' It's '*When?*' '' Citing a national survey of rank-and-file Teamsters that indicated that Hoffa could beat Fitzsimmons in a referendum with 83 percent of the total vote, the respected journalist virtually absolved the ex-Teamster leader of his crimes against the union and society.

Some of the foes of Hoffa—and that certainly must include Fitzsimmons, now—will be quick to point out that Hoffa is not just a strong labor leader, he's also an ex-convict, having spent several years in prison for a collection of crimes that included mail fraud and swindling membership money.

Some of those same foes will drag out the history books, dust them off, and throw a searching spotlight on some of the many deals Hoffa got involved in, such as the car hauling company, and the virtual giveaway of millions of dollars for investments handled by very shady characters . . .

But it is not easy, nor is it fair, to dismiss a man like Jimmy Hoffa. Though many criminal acts can be laid at his feet, and others strongly alleged, the complex person who is Hoffa is unquestionably one of the ablest labor leaders this country has produced.[6]

"He was a guy making a comeback," Drinkhall explains. "The only reason the piece seemed to be favorable was that he really had been out of and back in the union business. So he wouldn't have been doing the same things he'd done before. What the hell could you say about him that was bad? Also, at that time there wasn't really anyone strong enough to challenge Fitzsimmons. Really, I wouldn't have supported either of those two fellows had the circumstances been different, but looking at it as a reporter, Hoffa was a more effective union leader than Fitzsimmons. As to whether the magazine would've supported Hoffa, my guess would be yes, it would."

McMaster, who had continued as an IBT general organizer after the task force officially disbanded in February, was still, in theory, working under IBT vice president Roy Williams. Through the Kansas City Joint Council 41, which he controlled, Williams received a $54,000 "organizing grant" from the Central Conference of Teamsters and another $41,538 for unspecified purposes, both in 1974.

Williams, a short, broad man with a flat face and ever present sunglasses, has refused to discuss the grants or his relationship with McMaster. A close associate of various underworld figures in the Midwest and of Marcello in the South, and a former Hoffa supporter, Williams has twice been indicted for embezzling union funds. He was acquitted in the first trial after a key witness was shotgunned to death; the second indictment, in 1972, was dismissed by a judge who cited procedural errors during the investigation. In early 1974 he was indicted for falsifying union records, but that charge too was aborted by the government.

When McMaster's task force was set up, five of Williams' henchmen had been appointed to it, three of them in the key "director" positions. None of Williams' men, however was involved in the "blank check" scheme to stop Hoffa in Detroit.

On July 7, at 3:20 A.M., while Johnson was on vacation in Florida, his forty-five-foot Elco cabin cruiser was blown out of the water behind his home on Grosse Ile, near Detroit. The twenty-four-year-old yacht, "Big Mac," valued at $25,000, was insured for only $15,000.

"My son-in-law called me in Florida and told me my boat had been bombed. I grabbed the next plane and went home. When I got there the FBI and the state police were all over the place, making their examinations. They asked me what I thought it was, so I told 'em, 'Someone bombed the boat!' They said they thought it was a gas explosion. So I asked how the gas got on the boat; I didn't leave any in its tanks or on board. The fire marshal finally agreed that the boat had been bombed."

Because Grosse Ile really is an island, with toll bridges as the only way on and off, the authorities theorized that if the boat had been bombed the assailants probably used a speedboat to do the job and then headed out toward Lake Erie.

Within a week of the bombing, according to a Detroit federal attorney, a government informant named one of the bombers as "a guy named Jack Robison from Pennsylvania," but because of lack of evidence the U.S. attorney's office decided against proceeding with criminal prosecution. No one investigating the case knew about Robison's relationship with McMaster.

Robison admits that McMaster asked him to come to Detroit "to do some work for him" but denies having anything to do with the bombing of Johnson's boat. "Hell," he says, "I didn't even know the guy."

While the McMaster task force was being reorganized, President Nixon's mounting problems continued to affect the Teamster leaders' maneuvers. Remaining in the shadows as the fate of the man who had so affected his own was being determined, Hoffa publicly defended Nixon, still hoping for a last-minute pardon if Nixon had to leave the White House—Hoffa's only recourse at the moment if the courts denied his petition. While he anxiously awaited both decisions, he must have smiled privately when, on June 3, Charles Colson pled guilty to obstruction of justice in a case that grew out of the burglary of Dr. Daniel Ellsberg's psychiatrist's office after Ellsberg released the Pentagon Papers. But while awaiting sentencing, Colson perhaps felt some pleasure and some vindication when Judge Pratt decided on July 19 that the President had acted within his powers when he placed the conditions on Hoffa's release from prison.

Defeated again in the courts, Hoffa scrambled for alternatives. He was still determined to become president of Local 299 in the December election. Because his best judgment told him that Nixon would not pardon him now, Hoffa cheered the impeachment proponents in private. If Vice President Gerald Ford, whom Hoffa had known for many years as a congressman from Michigan, became President, he might well consider a full pardon.

Hoffa publicly called the House Judiciary Committee's hearings "absolutely ridiculous" and described the Watergate break-in as "a second-rate burglary . . . blown . . . out of proportion."[7] But in private "Jimmy was happy as hell when the Supreme Court told Nixon he had to give up those tapes," Johnson remembers. "He called me up and said, 'Well, Dave, it looks like Nixon's out and we're in!' "

Fitzsimmons and the IBT general executive board did everything they could to prevent Nixon's departure. They contributed $25,000 from the union's general fund to Rabbi Baruch Korff's National Citizens' Committee for Fairness to the Presidency, and issued public statements claiming that the contribution was "not political" but "for good government."

Led by Arthur Fox of PROD, angry dissidents filed charges with the IBT. In essence, according to Fox, the brief contended that the general executive board had "violated their fiduciary trust by dipping into the Teamsters general fund to make the contribution. It was a classic case of the International Union abusing its membership," Fox explains. "Fitzsimmons had actually said that he didn't care whether the members supported the contribution or not. He was going to deliver it and take it right out of the general fund—which was composed of the rank and file's dues money checked off from their pay checks. If the union was going to pull a stunt like that, then they should've taken the money out of the political DRIVE fund, which was made up of voluntary contributions. It was a bald political action no matter what Fitzsimmons said—just another example of the union buying immunity from the Nixon Administration."

The publicity that PROD's charges received forced the general executive board to permit three rank-and-file members—Gordon McKinley of Akron, Ohio; Lincoln Merrill of Winston-Salem, North Carolina; and Larry Mueller of New Carlisle, Ohio—to present their case at a board meeting in Washington.

"We were scared to death," says McKinley, who like the other two was a PROD member. "But we'd had it with everything they were pulling over on us all the time. It wasn't fair, so we made our stand."

Noble as that stand was, the general executive board was unimpressed when Mueller, the group's spokesman, asked that "the $25,000 be returned to the treasury, or we want the two men who made the contribution—Frank Fitzsimmons and Murray Miller—to face federal criminal charges."

The board quietly dismissed the charges and neither PROD nor the dissidents had the money to take the case to court.

During the final months of the Nixon Administration, General Alexander Haig, the White House chief of staff, conducted a secret investigation into "whether Nixon had ever been mixed up in organized crime." A special investigator for the Army Criminal Investigation Command was assigned to the project.

According to the *Washington Star*:

" . . . Haig wanted some things checked out on the President.

"It involved [John] Caulfield and [Anthony] Ulasewicz . . . Haig wanted to know whether Caulfield and Ulasewicz had been to the Far East and carried back any money for Nixon. He also wanted to know whether Nixon had ever been mixed up with organized crime . . .

"I never could find that Caulfield and Ulasewicz had gone to the Far East," [said the Army investigator] "but in my verbal reports to [the CIC chief] I pointed out that in those days an American didn't need a passport to get into Vietnam . . .

"I concluded that they probably had gone to Vietnam, and I considered there were strong indications of a history of Nixon connections with money from organized crime."[8]

Having ordered the investigation, and presumably having received the investigator's report that "there were strong indications" of Nixon's having ties with the underworld, General Haig, as far as is known, pursued the matter no further, but it may have been one of the things that helped bring about Haig's literal takeover of the White House during Nixon's last days.

A former Nixon aide, not privy to the Haig investigation, says that one of his associates in the White House mentioned to him sometime "during the impeachment summer" that "someone high up, maybe Haig," was interested in Nixon's possible "organized crime involvements." That conversation involved "a massive payoff" from those in "Army service club scandals in Vietnam," during 1969 or 1970. The aide says that the service club ripoffs "involved the Mafia and millions of dollars," and that the main focus of the interest by "someone high up" in the White House was on whether "the top Mafia guy" who ran "all these things in Southeast Asia" had made payoffs to Nixon. The crime figure, he says, was "the one who was apparently known as the so-called mastermind or architect of the Southeast Asian drug trade . . . who was very powerful and very well known as a mob leader . . . "

According to government narcotics experts, the central figure in the Indochina–Golden Triangle narcotics traffic was Santos Trafficante, who had established the route in the mid-1960s through his connections with the French Corsican underworld.

"The whole goddamn thing is too frightening to think about," says a Justice Department official. "We're talking about the President of the United States . . . a man who pardoned organized crime figures after millions were spent by the government putting them away, a guy who's had these connections since he was a congressman in the 1940s.

"I guess the real shame is that we'll never know the whole story; it'll never come out."

The House of Representatives had scheduled Nixon's impeachment trial for the third week in August, but it never began. Instead, Haig quietly orchestrated the release of the damning June 23, 1972, tape transcripts, in which Nixon was heard discussing the Watergate cover-up, and this forced the President to give in and resign on August 9, 1974.

As the American public awoke from its "national nightmare," President Gerald Ford unpretentiously assumed office. With the rest of the country, Jimmy Hoffa looked forward to brighter days ahead.

At the moment, however, things were still fairly gloomy for him. There was no stunned silence in the streets of Detroit when Richard Fitzsimmons formally announced on August 20 that he would run for president of Local 299 whether Hoffa was a candidate or not. As vice president after his father's resignation, young Fitzsimmons had taken it for granted that he was being groomed for the presidency by both his father and Dave Johnson. "But Johnson wasn't a man of his word," Fitzsimmons says. "He indicated that he'd support me for president and then he didn't. He said he was going to retire and not run at all, then he changed his mind."

A clean-cut Navy veteran with a boyish face and short wavy hair,

Richard Fitzsimmons had started his union career driving a truck for Detroit's Theater Trucking Services with his good friend, former dissident and McMaster organizer Larry McHenry. "Larry and I were friends. We went to school together and later worked together, too. He's a person with a commitment. Just because I didn't agree with McHenry's beliefs about the union didn't mean we couldn't still be friends."

When Jimmy Hoffa made him an organizer for the Michigan Conference of Teamsters in 1957, Richard Fitzsimmons led a drive against low wages and poor working conditions that resulted in his negotiation of the area's first office workers' Teamster contract. Impressed, Hoffa appointed him a Local 299 business agent in 1958, and he was soon representing most of the dock workers in the area who loaded and unloaded over-the-road freight. By the time Dick Fitzsimmons became vice president, at the age of forty-four, Frank Fitzsimmons was building his forces against Hoffa's anticipated try for a comeback.

Considering all that had happened, Dick Fitzsimmons' announcement came as no surprise at all. It was his selection of Rolland McMaster as a vice presidential running mate that nearly shook the local apart.

Johnson says, "Christ! I couldn't believe it. Mac was finished with this local politically, and we had all had it with him. I gave Dick more credit than that. We knew that McMaster was just trying to take over Local 299 again."

But "there was no problem in selecting Mac," according to Dick Fitzsimmons, "because of his experience. If a man can do a job, that's all that matters to me. And Mac has certainly been around awhile."

"Sure, I wanted to run and be closer to my local union," McMaster says. "I've always just wanted to help the boys in Local 299. Dick made a good selection; he knew I was sincere."

Dave Johnson got busier, and after chairing consecutive meetings of four hundred car haulers, seventy-five over-the-road drivers, and two hundred steel haulers, he announced that he had unanimous support from the members in attendance. "It looks like they want me," he proclaimed. "I'm running, and I'll have rank-and-file members on my slate."

Dick Fitzsimmons disputed Johnson's estimate: "That's a damn lie. Only about forty-five steel haulers attended that meeting, twenty-eight over-the-road drivers, and about the same number of haulaway drivers.

And anyway, I have the support of 85 percent of the business agents in Local 299, and they represent 90 percent of the membership.''[9]

In mid-September, Johnson used his authority as president to fire three local business agents loyal to his opponents. ''I called them insubordinate and I got rid of them for refusing to follow my orders,'' Johnson says.

''He did it for purely political purposes,'' according to Dick Fitzsimmons.

The business agents agree with Fitzsimmons. ''We had just gotten back from a summer seminar with Joint Council 43,'' says Ray Banks, one of the three. ''I saw I got a telegram, and it was from Dave Johnson. He told me I was fired—no reason or anything.'' Another, Jim Morisette, thinks that ''the reason was: back when Johnson announced that he wasn't going to run for reelection as president of Local 299, Dick Fitzsimmons, as the vice president, decided to run. So Dick passed out pledge cards backing his own candidacy. I liked and respected Fitzsimmons, just like I liked and respected Johnson. All of us did. But Johnson said he wasn't running, so we signed the pledge cards. Dave didn't put in the telegram his reasons why we were fired, but when we went to see him he accused us of not being loyal to him.''

Another Local 299 officer thinks the decision to fire the three men was not Johnson's idea at all, that it was Hoffa who decided to purge the local of those who weren't completely supporting his comeback. ''Dave had no taste for that dirty work,'' he says. ''Jimmy put him up to it. The business agents are really important in a union election. If they're not on your side, you ain't gonna win.''

Led by McMaster and Dick Fitzsimmons, on September 16 two hundred pickets demonstrated in front of the union hall shouting for reinstatement of the business agents and removal of Johnson. Robert Holmes, the Detroit international vice president, at once began negotiating with both Johnson and young Fitzsimmons, trying to arrange a peace settlement before Local 299's pattern of violence was renewed. Insisting that all the problems of the local revolved around McMaster's ambition to take control again, Johnson told Holmes that he was willing to call a truce with young Fitzsimmons but only if McMaster was abandoned as his running mate.

''I had no problem with that,'' Holmes says. ''I told both Dick Fitzsimmons and Dave Johnson that McMaster was bad news and shouldn't be in there anyway. So I told both of them to stay in touch, and we'd work the situation out—without McMaster.''

Within minutes after Holmes talked with Johnson and Fitzsimmons, Holmes's wife was getting telephone calls warning that her husband and the rest of his family would die if he did not stay out of the affairs of Local 299. Mrs. Holmes, almost in hysterics, called her husband, and he ran across the street to the demonstration in front of Local 299 and charged up to McMaster. His voice shaking with rage, the usually calm Teamster leader told McMaster that he would ''blow the heads off'' the people behind the calls if he found out who they were. Mc-Master, angry at the implication that he was responsible, shouted back, ''Go fuck yourself,'' and walked away.

Holmes was furious but not frightened at the threats against him and his family, and he continued trying to mediate between the Johnson and Fitzsimmons factions. As he saw it, it was his job: ''I was the only international vice president in Detroit. Fitz was in Washington and his son and Dave Johnson were directly involved in the matter. Mc-Master's goons were running all around, so what the hell could I do? I tried to negotiate a settlement that would be favorable to as many people as possible.''

Two days after the demonstration, McMaster tried to humiliate Johnson by stacking four Local 299 meetings—of the local's city cartage drivers, steel haulers, car haulers, and over-the-road drivers—and disrupting them. At the city cartage meeting, where the disruptions were the most serious, Johnson had to be escorted to his car after a forced adjournment.

As Johnson remembers it, ''There was a gang of McMaster's hoodlums there in the front row making all kinds of accusations, saying that I had no right to discharge the business agents. So I read the by-laws to them which said that anyone could be discharged by the president without recourse of any hearings. I told them that if my business agents didn't follow orders, I'd fire them.

''Then McMaster got up and started challenging me, and the others started howling about it. It got scary, so a bunch of my members ganged around me and walked me to my car.''

''I got up after Dave made some sort of goofy ruling,'' is Mc-Master's recollection. ''I told him, 'Just a minute, Mr. Chairman . . .' and I went through it and made a good explanation. Because some of the men clapped, he got upset about it. They were booing him and everything. And then some member stood up and said, 'Bullshit! When McMaster was here, this shit didn't go on.' So Dave said that the meeting was adjourned . . .

''The way we'd disrupt a meeting—if we really wanted to—would be to start a brawl and hurt people. That didn't happen at that meeting.''

Larry McHenry insists, ''That meeting was Johnson's fault. He tried to follow the procedure that when you get questioned strenuously in front of the membership on an issue, the best thing to do is adjourn the meeting. He had a bad habit of telling this group one thing and that group something else. At that particular meeting, a bunch of those groups were all there at the same time.''

A week later, George Roxburgh, who was still recovering from his gunshot wounds, began receiving threatening telephone calls in which he was warned to stop using farm equipment from the Saline recreation area on his own farm. The day the calls began three head of Black Angus cattle were stolen from the farm. ''I swear, I never used any of the local's farm equipment,'' Roxburgh says. ''The local backed me up on that. I was a Hoffa-Johnson supporter, and the opposition was trying to embarrass me. That and shooting me wasn't enough either. They had to steal three of my calves.''

Later that day, after the cattle rustling incident, Holmes proposed to Johnson and Dick Fitzsimmons that they get together a coalition ticket with an equal number of Johnson and Fitzsimmons supporters, in lieu of a bitterly contested election. ''We had to do something,'' he explains. ''Things were getting out of hand, and I didn't want to see someone get killed next. So I told Dave, 'Why disrupt the whole election if I can get Dick Fitzsimmons to call off his men from running against the pro-Hoffa people? We can have a coalition slate.' ''

Johnson agreed with Holmes: ''I told Bobby it was all right with me as long as McMaster wasn't involved. Anyway, I knew the local couldn't afford to spend $67,000 to run the election. And with the violence getting so bad, I was sure, too, that someone was going to get hurt.''

Dick Fitzsimmons wasn't prepared to consent to the Holmes compromise that quickly. ''I had committed myself to other people, like McMaster,'' he says, ''and I owed them an explanation . . . McMaster told me I'd be very foolish to drop him from the ticket. He thought I should run [for president]. He told me, 'You're too naïve with people. You listen to people—they say something to you—and you take it as their word. But their word isn't worth a damn.' And this came out to be true.''

''It was no big thing,'' according to McMaster. ''I was just asked to step aside for the good of the local. It wasn't a bad deal for me, and I still had my job with the international.''

After meeting with Frank Fitzsimmons in Washington, Holmes, Johnson, and Dick Fitzsimmons agreed on the coalition slate: Johnson as president; Dick Fitzsimmons as vice president; Otto Wendell as secretary-treasurer; Don Taber as recording secretary; and George Roxburgh, Earl Grayhek, and Robert Lins as trustees.

Conspicuously absent from the ticket was Frank Fitzsimmons himself, who had run in every previous Local 299 election since 1946. Instead of brawling in Detroit with everyone else that fall, Fitzsimmons relaxed in California, where the Frank Fitzsimmons Invitational Golf Tournament was held, October 9–12, at La Costa Country Club.

''The event is billed as a charity affair: officials of the Teamsters Union and the trucking industry pay $200 each to play in the three-day [sic] match,'' Jim Drinkhall wrote in *Overdrive*,

> with the proceeds then given to Little City Foundation, which operates a school for mentally retarded children in Palatine, Illinois. This Foundation was established in 1959 by the late Paul (Red) Dorfman, a labor racketeer. Dorfman is generally credited with being the person who introduced Jimmy Hoffa to the syndicate.
>
> The participants . . . are representatives of what the gathering is really about; namely, a hodge-podge of respectability and corruption, ranging from top financial managers and show business personalities to organized crime figures and convicted felons. The important point is that those involved continue their associations even in the midst of federal investigations, grand jury probes and indictments.[10]

Morris Dalitz teed off in the first fivesome with his honored guests: Fitzsimmons; the president of Gateway Transportation Company; a Las Vegas casino operator; and Allen Dorfman.

Dorfman was perhaps the most prominent of the more than twenty Teamster associates who were under indictment at the time. Released from prison in December 1973 after being convicted for obtaining a $55,000 kickback on a Central States Pension Fund loan, Dorfman had been indicted again in 1974 for defrauding the fund of $1.4 million. It was Jim Drinkhall who had exposed the alleged crime when he came across Dorfman's newest enterprise on a visit to La Costa.

''I happened to be at La Costa one day, checking things out there,'' Drinkhall says. ''And at the airport that serves La Costa, Palomar [in San Diego], I noticed Dorfman's jet there, and it was just taking off. So

I was talking to the control tower people, and I asked the guy where the plane was going. He said, 'Deming, New Mexico.'

"I figured, 'What the hell would he go to Deming for? Then I got ahold of one of Dorfman's phone bills and noticed, among other calls, a lot of calls to Deming. And then it struck me what was in Deming. I remembered that old pension fund loan, then it was just a matter of record checking."

Remembering that between 1959 and 1969 the Central States Pension Fund had lent more than $4.5 million to a rubber toy company in Deming, Drinkhall uncovered the fact that none of these loans had been repaid, and that the fund had subsequently taken over the firm. But in 1971, Irwin Weiner, the Chicago bail bondsman and organized crime associate who was a friend of Jack Ruby, had purchased 100 percent of the stock in the company and received another $1.4 million loan from the fund—with a mere $7000 deposit.[11]

Weiner was indicted with Dorfman, along with two pension fund trustees and three Chicago underworld figures. "There was no scam going on in Deming," Weiner says. "My attorney, Albert Jenner, was concerned about the fact that a government witness in the trial had been killed, but I told him that we were innocent men and had nothing to do with it. He believed me."

The government witness, Daniel Seifert, was preparing to testify against one of the gangland defendants. Jon Kwitny wrote of his murder in the *Wall Street Journal*:

> . . . on the morning of September 27, 1974, Mr. Seifert . . . entered his office at International Fiberglas Co. in a Chicago suburb, accompanied by his wife and son. Two men in ski masks, surprised to see the entire family, shoved the wife and son into a lavatory and shot Mr. Seifert. But he fled into a hallway. There he encountered another man, with a shotgun, and turned to flee again. A buckshot blast ripped away the back of his head, But Mr. Seifert continued into the Fiberglas plant. The two men in ski masks chased him, firing and yelling to the startled employees to 'Hit the deck!' They did. But Mr. Seifert managed to run out a back door. There he encountered another man with a shotgun, who fired at him point-blank. None of the witnesses has come forward with a good identification of the killers.[12]

Dorfman, Weiner and the others were eventually acquitted.

Two weeks after the murder, while the Teamsters and their friends were blasting out of sand traps at the Frank Fitzsimmons Invitational Golf Tournament, Jimmy Hoffa was still trying to amass grass-roots support for his comeback. That fall he had begun speaking to various groups around the country—from Teamsters to prison reformers—trying to make new friends and keep his name in the spotlight. Six days after the tournament ended, Hoffa was the keynote speaker at a testimonial dinner for his friend Frank Sheeran, in Delaware.

When he wasn't on the lecture circuit Hoffa was winning friends and plotting strategy in Detroit, where Dave Johnson's meetings continued to be disrupted and threats of further violence hovered over Local 299 like an ominous cloud. It was unlikely that the U.S. Court of Appeals would decide Hoffa's case before Local 299's December election, but Hoffa and his attorneys made an elaborate, seemingly desperate plan which they hoped would avoid any legal hassles with the government.

The plan was that Hoffa would allow his name to be placed in nomination in November, and then in December, after winning the election, he would name Johnson to serve in his place. Campaigning was to be handled entirely by his supporters; thus Hoffa would, he and the lawyers hoped, be technically in compliance with the conditions of his release. This scheme would doom the coalition slate, but Hoffa was ready to scuttle it and any other attempts at peacemaking to achieve his ends.

"Jimmy didn't think the appeals court was going to go with him," Johnson says. "So even if he lost that and the Supreme Court decision later on, he was ready to defy the Justice Department and run for Local 299 president anyway, whether in the 1974 election or after I appointed him a business agent and retired.

"Hoffa hoped that if the government ignored him while he took over Local 299, then he could become a delegate to the convention in 1976 and beat Fitzsimmons. He thought that with 1976 being an election year, no one running for President—especially his Michigan friend Gerald Ford—would risk losing the Teamster rank and file's votes by trying to stop him.

"But everything hinged on his taking over Local 299. Everything meant nothing if he couldn't do that."

There were shock waves throughout the IBT as word of Hoffa's intentions spread, and his adversaries began planning strong countermeasures. The first public reaction came from McMaster's camp, when Larry McHenry filed suit against Local 299. Using his own ejection from Local 299 as the basis for the suit, McHenry challenged Hoffa's right to run for office.

"Hoffa was made 'president emeritus,' which gave him life

membership and everything that went with it," McHenry says. "Why should he have any more rights than anyone else? Why should Hoffa be singled out for such privileges while I'm denied them?"

Although McHenry had worked "officially" only one day since leaving the McMaster task force in February 1974, he continued to pay his Local 299 dues. But there were many in the pro-Hoffa camp who saw this as the act of a troublemaker who enjoyed his assignments of disruption rather than the gesture of a loyal union man. "For two or three years solid, every meeting was disrupted by people agitated by McMaster, and McHenry was his number-one ringleader," said Otto Wendell. "Because McHenry hadn't worked in a few months, we denied him the right to speak at a meeting [in April 1974]. Later on, we refunded his dues and gave him his withdrawal card."

"I was also fighting that the local by-laws did not limit a person's activities if he was laid off," McHenry continues. "That is, unless his dues weren't paid. And mine were through December 1974."

"We just wanted to get the guy out of the way," says Johnson. "He was nothing but trouble. McHenry didn't want the coalition; he didn't want anything. He just wanted McMaster in there and all his other friends in office."

Calling McHenry's suit "frivolous" and "a form of harassment," Johnson says that his actions against McHenry were legal according to the union by-laws, and that after McHenry repeatedly refused to accept his dues refund and withdrawal card, the union hired a process server who finally forced them upon him.

But McHenry's litigation—filed three days before nominations for Local 299's offices were to open—was a blessing in disguise for Hoffa. Hoping to buy more time on the chance of either a favorable appellate court decision or a presidential pardon, Hoffa told Wendell—through Johnson—to postpone both the nominations and the elections until McHenry's suit was resolved. When Wendell postponed nominations until January 12, 1975, providing Hoffa with two additional months of precious time, it seemed that the tables were turned.

But while McHenry's suit was in the courts, a second wave of anti-Hoffa sentiment roared over Local 299 from another direction: Frank Fitzsimmons announced that he was prepared to use his powers as IBT general president to block Hoffa's attempt to gain control of Local 299—even if it meant throwing the local into trusteeship.

That announcement was followed by a warning in the press by a Justice Department official that the department was prepared to take legal action against Hoffa if he ran—which meant that he could be sent back to prison to complete his thirteen-year sentence.

Hoffa decided to continue challenging Fitzsimmons but not the government, and his recent setbacks were somewhat balanced by a bit of welcome publicity soon afterward, with an ABC-TV Close-Up presentation entitled ''Hoffa.'' On Saturday, November 30, 1974, ABC reporter Jim Kincaid centered the program on the Hoffa-Fitzsimmons feud.

> Hoffa: They took Fitzsimmons up to the mountains and showed him the valley and he bought the valley, and he forgot his friends . . . forgot where he came from. After forty years he forgot who took him off a truck and who put him into an executive position. And then he double-crossed me. It's very simple.
>
> Fitzsimmons [videotaped separately]: I've never forgot a friend in all my life. In fact, it's quite the opposite. If Mr. Hoffa will recount his activities against me, such as charges brought against me, charges that I double-crossed him. He knows in his heart he's a liar.

Kincaid's reportage on the Central States Pension Fund, the circumstances of Hoffa's commutation, and La Costa's underworld connections was excellent, although he, like many other members of the press, hung onto the post-Lewisburg portrayal of Hoffa. Kincaid called him a ''champion of the working man,'' and ABC's scenes of rank-and-filers reaching up and out to Hoffa—with that ''see me, feel me, touch me, heal me'' look—must have been nauseating to the thousands of honest, hard-working Teamsters who had been shaken down, cheated, beaten, and generally defrauded by cult hero Hoffa. ''It was one of those unfortunate 'lesser of two evils' situations,'' Kincaid says. ''I had known Hoffa for many years, and he seemed sincere in his desire to clean up the union. Sure Hoffa was a bad guy, but Fitzsimmons was much worse.''

Ten days after the ABC broadcast, U.S. District Judge Lawrence Gubow dismissed Larry McHenry's suit because he had ''failed to exhaust his reasonable intraunion remedies.'' Despite all the desperate efforts of both McMaster and Hoffa, the proposed Local 299 election coalition, remarkably enough, remained intact. This was not good news for Hoffa, and more unwelcome information was to come from a higher court.

Hearing the case of Army Sergeant Maurice I. Schick, the Supreme Court ruled that the President had the right to impose conditions of his choosing when commuting a prison sentence. Sgt. Schick had been sentenced to death for murder but President Eisenhower had commuted it to life imprisonment with the restriction that during his life term Schick would never be eligible for parole. The ever optimistic Hoffa forces argued that the difference between the two cases was that their man had been give a ''harsher sentence'' instead of a lighter one, and Hoffa claimed that the decision hadn't altered his plans to return to union office, but the Schick decision was a blow to his and his lawyers' hopes.

In a press interview Fitzsimmons called Hoffa ''nuts,'' and produced a signed note from him which read, ''I agree not to be in organized labor as an officer.'' The note, said Fitzsimmons, was written while Hoffa was in jail. Fitzsimmons predicted that Hoffa would never again run for IBT general president.[13]

In response Hoffa said he would return ''someday, somehow,'' and accused Fitzsimmons of intervening with President Ford to forestall a full pardon.[14]

Hoffa went swinging into 1975, while the clock ticked off the final moments of his battle-scarred life.

18 Living by the Sword

On the day Local 299 nominations opened, Rolland McMaster, in defiance of the arranged coalition, challenged Dave Johnson for the local presidency. He had almost a full slate of candidates, including former trustee Ralph Proctor, a casualty of the coalition slate when he was among those dropped from Richard Fitzsimmons' ticket. Another member of the McMaster slate was Larry McHenry, a candidate for trustee, defying a court decision that had ruled him ineligible for union activity. Even McHenry's girl friend was on the ticket, running for recording secretary.

"I noticed that I didn't get too warm a reception . . . when I was nominated," McMaster comments. "But Proctor and McHenry and the rest of 'em were going to run with or without me, so I thought I'd just lend 'em my support by running."

Johnson was furious, and he was most furious with Frank and Dick Fitzsimmons. Johnson sent Robert Holmes to tell Frank Fitzsimmons that he would "torpedo that goddamn coalition and close Dick Fitzsimmons out forever if McMaster was allowed to run. I also told two business agents who were running with McMaster that I'd fire them if they didn't pull out of the race. I told all the business agents to support the coalition or else they'd lose their jobs."

Again Holmes stepped into his role as mediator, holding a series of meetings between the Hoffa-Johnson forces and those of Fitzsimmons-McMaster. When the negotiations ended, Frank Fitzsimmons, through his son, backed down and asked McMaster to withdraw as a candidate. "Dick came up to me and said, 'I'd like to ask you a favor. We've got a coalition, and it can work pretty good.' He told me this with fifteen or twenty of my men standing there. So he asked me to pull out of the election,'' says McMaster.

Like the coalition which was created to prevent violence, the election, for the same reason, was held without the participation of Rolland McMaster. ''It was just another case where Hoffa was behind the scenes, chopping me up,'' he insists.

''I had thought that McMaster was going to be the hardest nut to crack, but I was wrong,'' Holmes says. ''Even though he withdrew with no problems, the men who were running on his slate refused to do likewise. Hell, all of us thought McMaster was behind them, but what could we do? He wanted us to come to him and ask if he'd help. He thought then we'd owe him.

''McMaster cooperated and ordered his men to take their names out of contention. But Larry McHenry still wanted to run for trustee and refused to drop out. It took Frank Fitzsimmons, personally, to step into the picture to get McHenry out. He just ruled that he was ineligible— period. That's it. McHenry was gone.''

As McHenry was taken kicking and screaming out of the election, all visible opposition to the coalition vanished. Johnson and the compromise ticket were officially declared elected—without an election.

No one had any illusions about who was calling the shots for Johnson in Local 299, and the invisible forces against the coalition were quietly at work.

''Hoffa used me as his tool,'' Johnson says. ''I'll admit it, no problem. I functioned independently as long as it didn't interfere with Jimmy's plans; then he told me what he wanted done. I wanted to retire and only stayed to help him. He had no hope of coming back as president of the international unless he had control of Local 299—no hope at all.''

''Hoffa had other problems too,'' remarks Michigan's organized crime expert, Vincent Piersante. ''Because of the mob's tremendous influence in the Teamsters Union, he had no chance of returning to power unless the mob okayed it. That is a fact of life.''

The fact that Frank Fitzsimmons and other top officials had been playing ball with the underworld was indisputable. The relationship that had developed since Hoffa went to prison in 1967 had insulated the Teamsters' new decentralized power structure from Hoffa's anticipated challenge. With millions in Central States Pension Fund money shoveled over to the mob and its associates, Hoffa's support had quickly deteriorated among his former underworld cronies, including even Carlos Marcello and Santos Trafficante.

The year 1974 had been a transitional year for the mob; things had happened quickly and confusingly.

That year Carmine Galante, Hoffa's friend from Lewisburg who was the underboss of the Bonanno crime family, was released from prison. Moving quickly but quietly, Galante came back into power through Philip Rastelli, who turned back the leadership of the Bonanno clan to Galante. (Bonanno was still in Arizona, still working closely with Marcello and Trafficante.) A former lieutenant to Galante in the Montreal drug connection, Rastelli had been serving as his forces' field marshal in the continuing war between the Bonanno family and the rest of the New York organized crime families. What had been a cold war with sporadic shooting incidents since the end of the ''Banana War'' in 1969 flared up again in January 1973, when Carlo Gambino's nephew was found murdered and half-buried in a garbage dump in New Jersey.

''When Rastelli stepped aside for Galante after Galante got out of jail in 1974, everyone expected the biggest mob war in history to break out,'' Ralph Salerno says. ''It was no secret that Galante hated Gambino with a passion and had sworn in prison to get even for the loss of prestige suffered by the Bonanno family.''

According to New York law enforcement officials, Galante, on probation, carefully began to reestablish his old narcotics contacts in Europe and the United States. He also came to terms with the black and Hispanic pushers who had taken on much of the dope trade in Harlem, and this was a further threat to Gambino.

Trying to avert the clash, Gambino used his influence in the Genovese crime family. Virtually leaderless, the Genovese clan had suffered through the 1970 imprisonment of Gerardo Catena and the July 1972 murder of Thomas Eboli, who had blown over $3 million of Gambino's money in an aborted dope deal. Subsequently Funzi Tieri, old and feeble, became Eboli's successor. To fill the vacuum left by Tieri's weakness, Gambino strengthened his allies' forces by proposing that the Genovese family give greater power to Meyer Lansky's associate, Vincent Alo, and eastern Pennsylvania–upstate New York crime boss Russell Bufalino.

It was a brilliant move. Gambino not only acquired the support of Lansky, he also developed stronger lines of communication to the Trafficante-Marcello-Bonanno criminal empire in the South through

Lansky's close association with these mobsters. No matter how indirect Gambino's relationship with Bonanno was, it was surely a sign of peace.

Seventy-two-year-old Russell Bufalino had, in 1974, taken over the kingdom of the late Steffano Maggadino in Buffalo. As the principle agitator of the split within the Bonanno family during the 1960s, Maggadino had also been targeted by Galante for retaliation. But Maggadino had died, and with Bufalino—a reputed heroin trafficker in the Montreal connection—as his replacement, Gambino hoped Galante would be appeased.

According to information provided by government informants, Galante did decide against immediate retaliation. "Any decision Galante made not to take on Gambino was primarily based on his decision to avoid a probation violation," Salerno thinks. "He didn't want to go back to jail. And every law enforcement agent in New York was watching his every move. The last thing he needed was to become involved in a gangland war."

Galante's wise decision not to fight was bad news for Jimmy Hoffa. According to government investigators, Hoffa was depending on Galante to help him recapture the IBT presidency.

"Hoffa had lost nearly all his friends in the mob," a Justice Department official explains. "Galante, his buddy from prison, was one of the few he had left. Even his old allies Marcello and Trafficante had, to all intents and purposes, gone over to Fitzsimmons' side. Pension fund loans had flowed in their direction, so they were happy. Hoffa knew he couldn't win the union presidency unless he had mob support, and Galante was his only hope.

"If Hoffa had any plans to say to Galante, 'Hey, it's you and me against the world!' he might as well've forgotten it," Salerno adds. "Galante might have done favors for Hoffa occasionally and even told him that he'd support his position when dealing with other mob guys, but Lillo Galante couldn't afford the trouble had he openly supported Hoffa. Anyway, Hoffa was out of power, and I question how important Galante thought Hoffa was. I'm certain Galante viewed him as a low priority."

Refusing to believe he could be locked out of the Teamsters Union, Hoffa continued to push. Since early 1974 he had been writing his autobiography, *Hoffa: The Real Story*, the latest in a series of "tell all" media gimmicks he had planned for release just before the 1976 IBT convention. Oscar Fraley, co-author of *The Untouchables*, was working with Hoffa on the book.

Was Hoffa prepared to tell all? It is doubtful that he could have done so without badly damaging himself, but Dave Johnson thought he was going to: ''Jimmy was ready to expose the fraud in the pension fund. He was going to clean it up when he got back in the union. He said that his book was going to be the first step.''

Whether Johnson is right or not, Hoffa's new role as crusading journalist was certainly an extension of the pragmatism he had exhibited through his temporary alliances with owner-operator truckers and the Teamster rebel community—not to mention his attempts to woo Carmine Galante. Hoffa used his newfound common cause with the dissidents as a means to bring the press over to his side as well.

Newsday's Russell Sackett, for instance, did Hoffa no harm with the publication of a five-part series in January 1975 which was as highly favorable to Hoffa as it was critical of Fitzsimmons. Although Sackett wrote that Hoffa was using his new post as executive director of the National Association of Justice, a prison reform group, as ''a purposeful forum and a means for at least staying in touch with some of his old pals from the labor movement and the underworld . . . '' the reporter clearly echoed the myths that Hoffa cooperated with the mob from a position of independence while Fitzsimmons sat in its pocket.

''That may have been the way it was before Hoffa went to jail,'' says a Detroit government agent, ''but if Galante or Lansky or any other gangster could have handed Hoffa the union, then there is little doubt that he would have been in their pocket as well. Our information shows that Hoffa wanted his job back so much it hurt, and he was willing to make a deal with anyone in order to get it.''

Fitzsimmons, however, wasn't the only serious enemy Hoffa had. According to his son James, there were others as well. ''Dad knew that regardless of whatever Fitzsimmons said or did, the number-one guy feeding him advice was Tony Provenzano,'' says young Hoffa. ''Tony Pro and my dad hadn't been friends for years, and during that period of time Provenzano went over to Fitzsimmons' corner.''

By the early 1970s the feud between Hoffa and Provenzano had intensified. During a Teamster meeting in Miami which both men attended after their release from jail, Provenzano ''threatened to pull my guts out or kidnap my children if I continue to attempt to return to the presidency of the Teamsters,'' Hoffa told New York Teamster rebel Dan Sullivan on May 5, 1974.

An official of Miami's Local 390, Lloyd Hicks, who had become a union dissident, boasted to friends before the Hoffa-Provenzano meeting that he was arranging to have the session secretly tape recorded.

Later that day, after Provenzano made his threat against Hoffa, Hicks was found dead, shot a dozen times. Neither his killers nor the tape recording were ever found.

Rolland McMaster denies that Hicks tried to monitor the Hoffa-Provenzano meeting. "He would have called me first," says McMaster, who had sent Hicks to Miami, and he writes off the murder as just "another Teamster squabble; one of those things that you can find out nothing."

Whatever the circumstances of Hicks's mysterious death, the relationship between Hoffa and Provenzano continued to deteriorate. In 1975 Provenzano was still a top official in the Genovese clan and was close to Russell Bufalino. As the co-host of the 1957 Apalachin Conference Bufalino had enormous status in the mob and got along well with his colleagues in the underworld, even Galante. William Bufalino, Russell's cousin, president of the Detroit Teamsters' jukebox local, had angrily split from Hoffa in 1967. Raffaele Quasarano and Peter Vitale, his partner in Central Sanitation Services, a garbage disposal plant, had chosen Fitzsimmons over Hoffa some time ago. Joseph Barbara, Jr., son of the other host of the 1957 mob summit, was associated with Quasarano.

In another overt sign of peace with the Detroit and Galante mobs, a New Jersey bank that Provenzano controlled made several loans to underworld leaders, including $25,000 to Galante. Law enforcement officials considered such accommodations with Galante a direct result of Bufalino's leadership in the Genovese family. Before the bank folded it also lent Central Sanitation Services $85,000 to buy a garbage disposal machine, according to investigative reporter Robert Windrem. Once a close friend of Hoffa—who had used his union position to protect the narcotics flow into Detroit—Quasarano was working with Galante, who was again in control of the French Corsicans' Montreal-Windsor-Detroit drug traffic. Neither Galante nor Quasarano really had any use for Hoffa out of power. It was strictly business.

Fretting over the fact that rival forces were stripping away his closest supporters, Hoffa countered by trying to use loyal middlemen to negotiate settlements. Among those he considered "loyalists" who were also close to such enemies as Anthony Provenzano was Frank Sheeran of Delaware, who, unknown to Hoffa, was also a close associate of Russell Bufalino.

"Jimmy was my friend," says Sheeran, who was a frequent visitor at Hoffa's Lake Orion home. "I thought he was great, and I had him speak at a banquet they threw for me at the end of '74 . . . I knew he and Tony had some problems, and I was happy to help . . . I did nothin' special . . . just carried messages.''

Sheeran was, knowingly or unknowingly, helped in his message carrying by another long-time Hoffa associate, Anthony Giacalone. Married to a cousin of Provenzano's, Giacalone was meeting and playing golf with Provenzano around the country.

Government investigators believe that at least one purpose of these meetings was to arrange a ''sitdown'' between Hoffa and Provenzano. But Salvatore Provenzano says that no such preparations were necessary. ''I'm telling you, Jimmy was calling Tony at his house. Now if they were warring, he wouldn't have been calling him . . . I was there when Jimmy called him. I saw letters Jimmy was writing to Tony.'' However, Salvatore Provenzano added that he could not produce these letters. ''I said Tony had them at home, but everything got burnt up when his home went up in flames.''

According to a Hoffa associate, Provenzano—who was under investigation in New Jersey for misusing a small East Coast Teamster pension fund—was upset because Hoffa was advocating the consolidation of these smaller funds into one large fund, modeled on the Central States Pension and Health and Welfare Funds.

James Hoffa says that in early 1975 ''Giacalone started tying to arrange a meeting between Provenzano and my dad. But Dad said that he wasn't ready yet, so he kept putting Giacalone off.''

Giacalone was under investigation by a Detroit federal grand jury for income tax fraud and bilking a Teamster hospitalization plan—both of which he was indicted for in the spring of 1975. The previous year he had barely escaped conviction for tax fraud when a key witness recanted his testimony. After a couple of earlier acquittals and the one in 1974, government prosecutors were hungry and rumors had spread among union and mob insiders in Detroit that taped conversations, recorded by the FBI, of Giacalone and his associates might be released in court. The recordings would have been extremely embarrassing to Hoffa and to his family as well, since they contained information about Mrs. Hoffa's secret love affair with Anthony Cimini.

A Michigan law enforcement official comments, ''Knowing that the family scandal hadn't been made public, Hoffa could deal with it. But there's no telling what he would've done had those tapes been made public. His pride couldn't have taken it.''

For Hoffa, other problems were building.

McMaster's top assistant, Larry McHenry, had moved into the Leland House, a hotel in downtown Detroit, a few days after the Local 299 coalition slate was accepted. Living rent free in room 601 while remaining unemployed, McHenry in return did ''odd jobs,'' as he puts it, for John R. Ferris, a suspected McMaster front man who was co-owner of the Leland. Ferris's partner was Detroit attorney Mayer Morganroth, one of McMaster's lawyers. Because of McMaster's close association with both Ferris and Morganroth, federal investigators have speculated that McMaster is a secret partner. Denying this, McMaster admits that he was trying to legalize gambling in Michigan and wanted the Leland House to receive the state's first gaming license.

''Anything Mr. McMaster did on behalf of the Leland House was done upon his own initiative,'' says Morganroth. ''He had no financial interest in the hotel. But even if he did, there would have been nothing illegal about it. He's a Teamster official, and there was no conflict of interest.'' Morganroth insists that he was unaware that McHenry was living at the Leland House. ''That was probably a decision made by Jack Ferris,'' he says. ''He ran the place and hired who he wanted. If he gave McHenry a free room or something, he didn't tell me about it.''

It was understandable that Mayer Morganroth had no time to worry about running the Detroit hotel. He had other things on his mind. According to an official in the Detroit Strike Force Against Organized Crime, ''Morganroth is under investigation for a $7 million loan from the Central States Pension Fund which was given to a private corporation in which he was a principal stockholder. We are looking into the possibility that a kickback was involved after the loan had been made.'' The official also indicates that Morganroth's ''personal business records and the records of companies in which he is a director have been subpoenaed by the grand jury in Detroit,'' and that Morganroth is being investigated in connection with the channeling of American mob money into Canada. But even with all his personal legal problems, Morganroth found time to represent McMaster when his second wife filed for a divorce in early 1975.

Two other former McMaster task force organizers, Jack Robison and Jim Shaw, frequently joined Larry McHenry at the Leland House. Robison, whom federal officials considered the leading suspect in the bombing of Dave Johnson's cabin cruiser, had gotten a job, via McMaster, as a driver for Lakeshore Trucking, in Pittsburgh, after turning down an offer from McMaster to put him to work at the Gateway Transportation Company, in Detroit. Formally employed nearly 300 miles away, Robison often hauled steel in Detroit on weekends and attended Local 299 meetings, which were again being disrupted. "McMaster and McHenry just asked me to come into town to go to those meetings. I never got paid for it, and I never caused no trouble," says Robison.

A youthful thirty-four-year-old image of McMaster, six-foot-five, 245-pound Jim Shaw first met the task force chief during the violent organizing campaign which struck Eck Miller Transportation Company in Owensboro, Kentucky, where Shaw was working as an owner-operator. A leader of a local dissident drivers' group, Shaw, with his rebel team, joined forces with McMaster and his organizing team and tried, but failed, to organize the company. Shaw's private automobile was riddled with bullets while it was parked in a vacant lot during the organizing effort, and it is still not known whether the attack was instigated by the firm in retaliation for the violence or merely staged for dramatic purposes by the Teamsters themselves.

An army veteran and former mechanical engineering student at the University of Maryland, Shaw impressed McMaster so much that he was immediately hired as an organizer in the Central Conference. Although his name never appeared on any reports submitted to the Labor Department—"I guess because I wasn't there long enough"— Shaw worked on several organizing campaigns in Michigan's Upper Peninsula. When the task force was disbanded he returned to Eck Miller, which had been sold to a new owner, and stayed with the company until June 1974, after which he began working for Liquid Transportation, in Louisville. Like Robison, Shaw came to Detroit on weekends "to work for McMaster" and to visit with his new friend, Larry McHenry, who took Shaw to Local 299 meetings.

Just before McMaster announced that he was a candidate for Local 299 president, Shaw left Louisville at McMaster's request and came to Detroit, where McMaster got him work hauling steel. Soon after Frank Fitzsimmons ordered McMaster to withdraw from the presidential contest, Shaw moved into room 620 of the Leland House, across the hall from McHenry. In return for his quarters Shaw worked part-time at the hotel. "I was a bouncer at the bars they had there."

Soon after McHenry and Shaw moved into the Leland House full time, and Robison began staying there on weekends, John Ferris became embroiled in a legal case involving the Interstate Motor Freight

System. As the top honcho in the Teamsters' iron, steel, and special commodities divisions, McMaster was still the man to see when a company wanted to extend its business, and he had given Interstate permission to haul steel into Detroit. He had also recommended Ferris and an associate as Interstate's agents in Detroit, according to an Interstate executive. But after several months Interstate complained that it was being cheated. According to the charges, Ferris and his partner had billed Interstate's customers under the names of their own three companies, concealing profits from Interstate. Consequently Interstate fired its two agents.

Claiming that they had invested in equipment and incurred debts for which Interstate was responsible, Ferris and his partner filed suit against Interstate for $3 million. The same attorney who filed McHenry's suit against Local 299 in November 1974 represented Ferris and his companies.

On February 3, 1975, after the trial had been postponed four times, the Interstate terminal in Murraysville, Pennsylvania, was bombed. The damage to the building—which was only six months old—totaled over $500,000. The figure would have been higher but the fire was contained in the portion of the building where the company's records were kept. An Interstate executive charged that the documents lost in the blast were to have been used as proof that Ferris and his partner had not operated in good faith. Subsequently Interstate surrendered and settled out of court with its former agents.

A former organizer for the McMaster task force, who claims to have known about the Interstate bombing in advance, says "The dynamite that was used for the job came from a construction site in Kittanning, Pennsylvania. Robison handled that one too and got $25,000 for it."

Without the former organizer's cooperation, federal investigators had already come to the same conclusion.

"Robison was a very busy man in Pennsylvania," says a government official in Pittsburgh. "We think he was responsible for more than just the Interstate bombing. He certainly had access to the tools of his trade. His son used to haul dynamite for a construction company just off Pennsylvania's Route 28, near Kittanning."

Although he took the Fifth Amendment during his grand jury appearance after the incident, Robison later insisted that he had nothing to do with the bombing. "I'm not sorry for anything I've ever done," he says. "So it's hard to believe that I could be accused of something like that. The Interstate thing is a bad rap."

McHenry, suspected of being an accomplice, was also called to testify at the grand jury hearing. He too took the Fifth.

''I wouldn't know how to light a fucking firecracker without blowing my damn fingers off,'' McHenry insists. '' . . . I had heard about the Interstate bombing six or eight months after it supposedly took place, but I wasn't aware of it when it happened.''

In Detroit, McMaster and his men were still bitter over the Local 299 coalition. Remarkably enough, it was working. People on both sides of the Hoffa-Fitzsimmons war were leaning over backward to avert any serious problems. To show good faith, Dave Johnson turned the day-to-day administration of the local over to union trustee Earl Grayhek, who had been on Dick Fitzsimmons' ticket.

''Everyone wanted peace around here and so did Dave,'' says the dapper, gray-haired Grayhek. ''But he was sick of the mess here in Detroit, so, more and more, he started taking off for Florida, where he was building a house for him and his wife when they retired. Because he was gone so much, he put me in charge. I ran the local.''

But just a little over a month after the coalition began functioning, Johnson—on Hoffa's orders—fired four pro-Fitzsimmons and McMaster business agents. ''They were plotting against me and my supporters,'' says Johnson. ''They were taking their orders from McMaster. Hell, one of them later admitted that to me. I told Jimmy, and he told me to get rid of 'em.''

Frank Fitzsimmons ordered Johnson and the other members of the Local 299 executive board to attend a meeting of the IBT general executive board in Miami. ''Fitz jumped all over me at the meeting for firing those four guys,'' says Johnson, ''and then the other vice presidents started doing the same thing to me, saying that I was taking my orders from Hoffa, and that peace was being jeopardized in Detroit because of it. So I just told them that it was the local business agents who were playing the politics and threatening the peace in Local 299.''

Johnson told the general executive board that anything that happened in Detroit was no concern of the international. Fitzsimmons and Johnson began shouting at each other, and the match ended only when Johnson stormed out of the room. As he left Fitzsimmons shrieked, ''Fuck you, Dave!''

The four firings became the main issue in the local. Meetings chaired by Johnson were again disrupted. The influx of McMaster's supporters—led by McHenry, Robison, and Shaw—increased, and their disruptions again brought early adjournments. Viewing the situation as McMaster's effort to force Fitzsimmons to throw Local 299 into trusteeship, Johnson packed union meetings with his own men.

"We knew that McMaster was bringing his goons into the meetings," Johnson says. "So what the hell could we do? Let Fitz put us under trusteeship? We fought back."

One tip-off that McMaster was bringing out-of-state troublemakers into Local 299 meetings came when a Hoffa loyalist spotted Robison's Cadillac, with its Pennsylvania license plates, parked in the union hall's lot. Prepared for trouble when the meeting started, Johnson's men quickly surrounded Robison and the others, who were badly outnumbered.

"It was really something," says Steve Riddle. "But rather than having bloodshed or a riot on his hands, Johnson adjourned the meeting. And the goons got escorted to their cars."

Indicating that both McMaster and McHenry had asked him to come to Detroit, Robison says, "I remember that meeting very well. They nearly killed me. Johnson had a pretty vicious crew up there."

"McMaster blamed Robison and his car for the fiasco," says a former McMaster task force organizer. "Then he told Robison to 'get rid of that goddamn car.'

"So a couple of weeks later, it happened."

On Sunday, April 6, in Pittsburgh, while it was parked on the property of the Lakeshore Trucking Company, trucker Jack Robison's Cadillac was bombed with four sticks of dynamite. Robison denies any knowledge of the circumstances of the blast but at the same time accuses FASH of being behind it. "I've been working against FASH for a lot of years. They probably bombed my car to get even with me."

McMaster agrees with Robison, blaming the reform group for the bombing, but according to a Justice Department official in Pittsburgh, the government had different ideas. McHenry was their top suspect in the bombing.

"I heard about it, but I don't know anything about it," McHenry says. "As a matter of fact, I thought that—considering Robison being who he is and working in the areas he is—it was probably FASH. They didn't like him."

Hearing that McMaster, McHenry, and Robison had said that FASH blew up Robison's car, FASH president William Hill laughed. "Ridiculous, absurd. We're plenty busy keeping our organization together, and the last thing we need is trouble with McMaster and his goons. It's nice, though, that they think we're so powerful.''

No matter what they said about the incident, McMaster, McHenry, and Robison promptly took the Fifth after being subpoenaed to appear before a federal grand jury investigating the bombing.

That spring agents for local law enforcement agencies in Michigan were investigating the use of stolen tractors and flatbed trailers which were being used illegally by area carriers. One such investigation concentrated on the operations of John Ferris and his partner, who were still litigating against Interstate. According to Michigan investigators, hot trailers were being used to haul loads of stolen steel coils. Drivers of the stolen trucks were paid as much as $1000 for each coil. One agent says, ''The owner of the stolen rig usually knew in advance that he was going to be ripped off. But he didn't care. He could collect the insurance benefits if the truck wasn't found. Plus he'd get a piece of the action for his trouble as well as his silence.''

In December 1975 one of Ferris's associates, Donald Wells, was indicted for, and pleaded guilty to, hauling stolen steel. Wells lived with McMaster at his 200-acre Wixom farm and was a partner of McMaster's brother-in-law, Stanton Barr, in a trucking company called Spot Leasing. Wells also owned a Time-D.C., Inc., terminal in suburban Detroit, and Jim Shaw worked for him.

On April 17, 1975, Shaw's new Kenworth truck, valued at $50,000, exploded and burned in the Time-D.C. terminal. The bombing was never solved but the truck was insured.

Soon afterward Shaw, through McMaster, got a job with the Detroit steel division of Gateway Transportation Company, which was headed by Stanton Barr. Shaw's former employer says he worked at Gateway ''for the next several months.''

In late May, an Indianapolis financier named Albert Lieberman came to Detroit to attend a meeting of people interested in investing in an office building to be built in Troy, Michigan. McMaster's associates say that he was upset that Lieberman was considering the investment, since McMaster thought Lieberman already owed him money from 1967, when McMaster was on probation from prison. That year, after putting $30,000 into a short-term Bahamian investment, Lieberman met McMaster through another $30,000 investor. Though McMaster was principally interested in real estate ventures, he persuaded

Lieberman to include him in the Bahamian enterprise, which included the purchase of South African diamonds. Just out of jail, and with a salary of only $22,500 before being sent to prison, McMaster came up with $150,000 for the diamond deal.

A couple of months after the money had been sent to the Bahamian broker, it became obvious that all the investors were going to be swindled. Two alleged business associates of Meyer Lansky had moved in and were heading for Europe with the cash. McMaster immediately blamed Lieberman for his bad fortune, accusing the financier of conspiracy with the Lansky people.

"McMaster demanded that I refund his money," Lieberman explains. "But how could I when I was taken too? So McMaster and his people tracked down the fellows who cheated us. And they got Morris Shenker as their attorney out of St. Louis."

Shenker had represented McMaster in appeals of his labor extortion conviction, so presumably the negotiations were friendlier than would normally be expected. According to Lieberman, McMaster recovered at least some of his $150,000. McMaster urged Lieberman to pay the remainder of the loss, claiming that the money he received from Shenker's clients had merely covered the expenses for finding them, but Lieberman refused.

Years passed without Lieberman's seeing or hearing from McMaster. Then, in the spring of 1975, after word had spread that Lieberman was considering investing in the Troy office building, federal investigators think he heard from McMaster again.

It was May 29. Lieberman and his wife had turned in early in their comfortable second-floor apartment. At about 2:30 A.M. the Liebermans and their daughter were awakened by a loud explosion that seemed to have come from their living room. Amidst screams from his wife and daughter, Lieberman groped through his dark, smoke-infested apartment, thinking that his furnace had exploded. As Lieberman moved slowly through the dense cloud, looking straight ahead, his wife and daughter close behind, he fell through a gaping hole, landing on the first floor in a pile of debris. He was bruised and cut up, and he had nearly lost an eye when he fell face first into a two-by-four with nails protruding from the wood.

After a quick trip to the hospital he came home to hear the police tell him that several sticks of dynamite at his front door had caused the explosion.

Several days after the blast which nearly cost him his life, Lieberman was sought out by John Ferris on McMaster's behalf. Ferris told Lieberman that for $50,000 McMaster was willing to forget his loss in the Bahamian diamond scheme. Again Lieberman refused to yield.

"Well, you know, we have some Italian friends whom I can get to do what I want," Ferris told Lieberman.

Although Ferris and his associate McMaster are known to have made threats of this kind, there is no record of their threatening Hoffa. Hoffa, however, in the last months of his life, became more and more "vicious in his descriptions of McMaster. I remember he was even starting to refer to him as 'that fucking one-eyed son of a bitch,' " says Peter Karagozian, the union dissident who became a Local 299 business agent under Johnson.

Hoffa—through Johnson—had been reciprocating the Detroit rebels' support. Like Karagozian, several leaders of both the old Local 299 Unity Committee and the 1974 owner-operators' shutdown had been appointed local business agents and elected company stewards with Hoffa's backing. Among them was steel hauler Mitch Miller, the dissidents' spokesman during the 1974 protest. These political appointments were made at the expense of the jobs of other local officials, like the four Johnson fired at Hoffa's direction, who were loyal to Fitzsimmons and McMaster.

The pro-Hoffa rebels, led by Karagozian and Miller, formed a group called How Old Friends Feel Active (HOFFA), which planned a series of $15 a plate dinners on Hoffa's behalf to be held at Detroit's beautiful Roma Hall. Peter Camarata, a member of HOFFA, says that the purpose of the banquets was "to raise money for Hoffa's comeback bid and to solicit petition signatures urging his return to power." HOFFA had the full support and cooperation of Dave Johnson.

Teamster leaders from other states participated in the pro-Hoffa movement too, including Frank Sheeran.

The Hoffa partisans held two dinners, with nearly 1500 people attending each, in the late spring and early summer of 1975, and were planning a third for the first week in August.

The guest of honor would never attend that August banquet.

At this desperate point Hoffa's only firm areas of support were the majority of the Local 299 executive board and the Detroit rebels. They were working together, wooing the national rank and file, sympathetic union officials, and influential politicians around the country. Hoping that a massive grass-roots campaign in Local 299 would provide the foundation to challenge Frank Fitzsimmons for the IBT general presidency in July 1976, Hoffa waited for word from the court of appeals.

"Jimmy and I were in almost daily touch with each other," says

Johnson. ''He was just trying to settle his business deals in a Pennsylvania coal mine and some other deals in New York. He didn't want any conflicts of interest standing in the way of coming back into the union. All the information he was getting was that the court of appeals was going to rule in his favor. He was really happy about that. And I was getting ready to retire and give him the local.''

Even if the court had denied Hoffa's appeal, there was still reason for optimism. President Ford sent up what looked very much like a trial balloon with his full pardon of Dave Beck in the spring of 1975, and Attorney General Edward Levi reportedly advised the President that the clause restricting Hoffa from union activity appeared to be illegal.

''Yep,'' says Johnson, ''Jimmy was coming back. He didn't think anything could stop him.''

Getting ready for a strong offensive against Fitzsimmons during negotiations for the 1976 National Master Freight Agreement—which would start in January—Hoffa became militant toward trucking management:

> I have been asked many times why I want to come back as general president of the Teamsters; why not sit back and take it easy?
> . . . I see one last big round of fights coming between labor and management. I've said consistently that no employer ever really accepts a union. They tolerate unions. The very minute they can get a pool of unemployment they'll challenge the unions and try to get back what they call management's prerogatives, meaning hire, fire, pay what you want. I've been saying that ever since I came out of prison.
> I'm convinced this war is going to take place and I want to be part of it. . . . And when it's over the unions will be a bigger part of this government than ever before.
> When war comes, Jimmy Hoffa wants to be right up front.
> And . . . you can bet on it because I'll be back.[1]

Hoffa's first big chance to prove his new status as a union reformer came on May 15, when he was questioned before a grand jury, under subpoena to answer questions about misuse of union funds for ''no-show'' jobs in Local 299 and in Pontiac Local 614. With the exception of a few routine questions, Hoffa took the Fifth on all others. ''And I'm damn proud of it,'' he told one reporter.

In his role of journalist Hoffa accused Frank Fitzsimmons of several criminal offenses, and of ''selling out to mobsters and letting known racketeers into the Teamsters.'' Specifically,

> I charge him with permitting underworld establishment of a union insurance scheme which in one year was a ripoff to the tune of $1,185,000 in the New York area alone and in which his own son, Don, participated on a national level . . . There will be more and more developments as time goes on and I get my hands on additional information.[2]

Considering his past performance as a union leader, it was laughable for Hoffa to make such criticisms of Fitzsimmons. Certainly not a reformer, Fitzsimmons still had to live with the criminal ties Hoffa had handed him. If Fitzsimmons had stood up to them, he surely wouldn't have been the IBT general president for long. Few men would have had the courage to step in and clean up; Fitzsimmons had been no different.

Still, Hoffa's accusations about the insurance scheme could not be ignored. Federal investigators had already begun their study of the matter, concentrating on the plan's mastermind, Louis Ostrer, a convicted insurance embezzler. Billed as a severance–fringe benefit arrangement, the Ostrer Plan had been sold to Local 295 in New York. According to an internal memorandum of the Justice Department,

> Ostrer is apparently one of the founders achieving this new fringe benefit as a wholly employer supported fringe in lieu of wage increases . . . However, the possible ''kicker'' in the scheme is that the insurance is absolutely uncancellable by anyone until the man [employee] dies or retires over age 65. Therefore, the insurance company has a guaranteed annual premium. Possibly Ostrer and his sham agents are thus able to negotiate higher fee kickbacks or remissions . . .

As Hoffa claimed in his autobiography, one of those ''sham agents'' was Frank Fitzsimmons' son Donald. A consultant to the program since 1971, Donald Fitzsimmons had previously worked as sales manager for Market Vending, the Detroit vending machine company run by Raffaele Quasarano and Peter Vitale. He was also on the payroll of Local 614, paid with a grant from the IBT—$2000 a month plus expenses and a car.

In February 1972, Ostrer and Donald Fitzsimmons approached Local 299 with the insurance plan during an executive board meeting called by Richard Fitzsimmons, recording secretary, upon the authority of his father.[3] Neither Dave Johnson nor secretary-treasurer Otto Wendell was present. When Wendell, a Hoffa supporter, heard about the proposed plan he wrote a letter—dated June 15, 1972—to Donald Fitzsimmons, asking for an actuarial review of the insurance company. Ignoring Wendell's and then Johnson's complaints, Dick Fitzsimmons proceeded to authorize payment of the first $5000 premium to Ostrer's company after the names of twenty-one union officials were allegedly forged on application cards.

Later, Dick Fitzsimmons and one of the four business agents Johnson had fired in 1975 were indicted by a federal grand jury in Detroit for embezzling the $5000 premium from Local 299. In December 1977, as Dick Fitzsimmons' trial approached, Wendell was found slumped in his car with two gunshot wounds in his side. He died before the trial. Fitzsimmons and his co-defendants were acquitted.

By bucking Ostrer and Fitzsimmons' family Hoffa had taken on much more than he may have bargained for. As a close associate of the Genovese and Lucchese crime families, Ostrer had been given the go-ahead to approach East Coast Teamster locals by Anthony Provenzano, and, in Detroit, the man "who helped design the plan," according to the Justice Department, was Rolland McMaster.

In mid-June 1975 there was a strange meeting at the Pontiac Airport, several miles north of Detroit. An airport employee described what he saw: "I was taking a break, just looking at who was coming in and out of the airport. It's not a real busy place. I remember watching a small private plane land and pull over near the terminal. Then I saw two men get off the plane and walk toward Rolland McMaster, who was sitting in a dark-colored Cadillac. I knew who McMaster was; he was always picking people up there.

"But the reason why I noticed it this particular time was that one of the two guys McMaster was picking up was Tony Provenzano from New Jersey. I've seen a lot of pictures of him. Later on, I told a few people that I saw them together.

"Another thing that I noticed was the car McMaster was driving. It was black, maybe brown, and I knew he owned a gold Cadillac. I figured he must have borrowed someone else's.

"Anyway, Provanzano and the other guy—who I didn't recognize—got into McMaster's car and drove off. I guess they came back about four hours later. Then they got out of McMaster's car and got back on their private plane and flew to Kansas City. Just before they got on the plane and while they were still talking to McMaster, I was close enough to hear them talking. I couldn't make out what they were saying, but I was absolutely certain that the one guy was Provenzano.''

Scoffing at the eyewitness's story, McMaster commented, ''Tony Provenzano and I are good friends; we've known each other for years, and that's no secret. We played golf together at the Frank Fitzsimmons Open at La Costa [in 1974]. I haven't seen him since. And, hell, I'm too busy to be picking up people at the airport.''

McMaster did, however, say that in June 1975 he frequently borrowed John Ferris's brown Cadillac and his brother-in-law's black Cadillac.

A few days after the alleged meeting between McMaster and Provenzano, a Local 299 business agent, Ralph Proctor, was roughed up outside the Brentwood Inn in nearby Melvindale. ''I just had lunch,'' Proctor says, ''and it was broad daylight, about two in the afternoon. As soon as I walked out the door—boom—I got it. Some guys jumped me from behind and knocked me unconscious. I never saw who they were.''

Proctor, who is pro-Fitzsimmons and McMaster, refuses to speculate why he was beaten, but says he called Johnson and accused him of having it done.

''Hell, I told him, 'If I wanted you taken care of, I would've done it myself,' '' Johnson says.

The alleged assault was the first act of violence against a Fitzsimmons-McMaster supporter. Asked about it, McMaster shrugged. ''I never could find the goddamn answer to it. We had that kind of crap happen. I put investigators on it, but they didn't find out anything.''

Was Proctor really beaten up? Or was the incident staged to portray retaliation by Hoffa partisans against a supporter of Frank Fitzsimmons? Or was it a ploy by a third force in the union, taking shots at both sides, to force Frank Fitzsimmons to throw the local into trusteeship?

About two weeks later, Thursday, July 10, on a warm, balmy, summer evening, traffic was flowing smoothly up and down Michigan Avenue in downtown Detroit. Nearby Tiger Stadium was empty; the Detroit Tigers were playing the Kansas City Royals in Kansas City. A block from the dark stadium Dick Fitzsimmons eased back in his chair in Nemo's Bar, tossing down a few drinks and rapping about the tough week he was having. "I was with three other fellows," he says, "and we were sitting in Nemo's . . . And I got up to leave and was on my way to my car when I saw it explode."

The sleek, white, elegant 1975 Lincoln Continental given to Fitzsimmons by Local 299 for his use as vice president had been reduced to a rubble heap: tires flat, all windows shattered, all four doors and the trunk flapping open, almost peeled off their sturdy hinges. Bent and blistered, like a burned piece of Plexiglas, the engine hood hung over the front of the car. Other parts of the automobile had been blown several hundred feet and caromed off the Tiger Stadium fence. Long after the local fire department watered down the blaze, the pungent smell of dynamite filled surrounding Michigan Avenue and the local establishments whose windows had been blown out from the blast. "It was quite a shocker at first," Fitzsimmons says. "Then I went with some friends up the street to get some coffee and talk it over."

As Detroit buzzed about the bombing and the press theorized about the motives behind it, a Local 299 secretary took an anonymous telephone warning that a bomb had been planted in the union hall.

"It was a crank call," Johnson explains, "but everyone was afraid for their own safety. I knew Jimmy and our people had nothing to do with it—there was no reason for it. So our executive board met, and we decided to institute a 'buddy system,' where our officers and business agents would travel in pairs. We also told everyone not to use union cars when going to beer gardens or when they were seeing women other than their wives."

It was a time for both factions to tread softly. Even the unshakable Jimmy Hoffa had to reflect on what was happening around him and who was behind it.

"I can't understand the damn thing, Jerry," Hoffa told reporter Jerry Stanecki during an interview for *Playboy*. "Dave Johnson's boat blown up—broad daylight. The Fitzsimmons kid's car—broad daylight. Ralph [Proctor] getting stomped by two guys—broad daylight. I just don't understand it . . . because it gets dark every night."[4] In his autobiography, however, Hoffa blamed the mysterious acts of violence on "some nut. A guy trying to start trouble. But everyone in the local knows who he is."[5]

"Rolland McMaster," says Johnson. "Hoffa was sure McMaster was behind all the violence. He repeated it over and over again to people he was close to. And he thought that Allen Caulder was the man who was actually carrying it out. He was a steward at one of the area trucking companies who got fired a few years ago. Anybody who gets fired at a trucking company—and after four or five times gets fired again—becomes a dissident. Caulder was no different, except he didn't join a group, like his buddy, Larry McHenry.''

Though stocky, rough-talking Caulder and McHenry were friends, having grown up together in Detroit, McHenry denies that either he or Caulder had anything to do with the violence. But he adds, ''If you want to talk about a guy with a reputation, there's a guy with a reputation.''

The investigation of Caulder's possible role in the Fitzsimmons bombing fizzled when Caulder provided the government with an iron-clad alibi: he had been in northern Michigan at the time of the explosion. But by that time federal agents had their lead and were soon sure who had bombed Dick Fitzsimmons' car. Their judgment was based on information provided by one informant which was corroborated by data provided by others. And instead of just one man involved in the actual placing of the explosives, there were two. A government spokesman has confirmed that the two top suspects are Larry McHenry and Jim Shaw.

''We're sure that they're the ones who did it,'' says a federal agent, ''even though it doesn't make sense why.''

''Me and Larry were bumming around together for some time,'' Shaw says. ''Then a couple of weeks after Dick Fitzsimmons' car was bombed, a couple of FBI agents came out to see me at work. I wasn't there any of the times they were, so I called their offices in Detroit and even went down there to see them. When I got there, they told me that they had enough evidence on me and Larry to bring us before a grand jury for bombing Fitzsimmons' car. I couldn't believe it.''

McHenry adds that he had reason to believe the government suspected him. ''The investigations of me and what I did with people like Jim Shaw were as a result of phone taps on my son's conversations.''

McHenry's nineteen-year-old son, Patrick McHenry, lived and worked at the Detroit Leland House like his father and Jim Shaw. According to Larry McHenry, his janitor son ''talked to a lot of people, and he tried to play the big wheel like his old man was into everything. And I would imagine that the reason for [the FBI's] inquisitiveness, their investigation, about me was based upon conversations overheard by wiretaps on the Leland House, where my son made his calls . . . there were tapes of Patrick's conversations, just like there were tapes of mine and Shaw's. They taped all the calls that went through the switchboard at the Leland House.''

Although the FBI confirmed that young McHenry had been talking openly about his father's activities, it denied that any wiretaps, court authorized or not, were used on the Leland House.

Within a week after Larry McHenry and Jim Shaw were interviewed by the FBI about the bombing of Fitzsimmons' car, Patrick McHenry was found dead in room 523 of the Leland House.

''The death certificate said, 'Death due to narcotic addiction,' '' says the dead boy's father. ''His body was found by his girl friend. She thought he'd od'd and tried to bring him to. She got help from a friend, and the friend came and got me [in room 601]. I went downstairs, and Patrick was laying dead on the floor.

''There was no foul play; my son was an addict. But the FBI said to my wife that our son knew too much about my extracurricular activities, and that's why he was taken out.''

A government official remarked that young McHenry had been injected with enough heroin ''to kill an elephant. If Patrick was murdered because of something he knew, we'd like to know what it was,'' he said.

On July 30, 1975, two days before Patrick McHenry's mysterious death, McMaster and his brother-in-law from Gateway's steel division met for breakfast near Detroit's Metropolitan Airport at 6:30 in the morning. Both men had reservations to fly to Chicago on American Airlines and had reserved a car to take them to Gary, where they were to attend a meeting of Gateway executives and union representatives in a restaurant. Donald Sawochka, who served with McMaster on the Teamsters' iron and steel negotiating and grievance committees, was the host of the Gateway meeting.

At the last minute, however, there was a sudden change of plans. ''I was going to fly in,'' says McMaster, ''but the way the flights are set up, when you leave Detroit at 8:00, you get to Chicago at 8:00—because of the one-hour difference in time. Then, once you get there, you end up thirty-five to fifty miles from the center of Chicago. So Stan [Barr] was going on the same flight. I said that I'd meet him at the Ramada Inn near the airport, and we could have breakfast. But when we got there, the sun was shining beautifully, so we decided to drive to Gary instead.''

On the drive to Gary, McMaster says, he and Barr got lost and couldn't find the restaurant where the meeting was. Using his telephone credit card, McMaster called long distance to Sawochka at the restaurant and asked for directions. ''We finally got there at about noon.''

Back in Detroit, things were happening quickly.

Hoffa's ''foster son,'' Charles O'Brien, had missed an early morning flight to Toronto, where he was to have attended a meeting with Robert Holmes, Pete Karagozian, and a Local 299 trustee. ''When we got to Toronto for our meeting, Holmes turned to me and Lins and asked us if we'd seen Chuckie,'' Karagozian remembers.

''Then I said, 'He knew about the goddamn meeting,' '' Holmes adds. '' 'I wonder where the hell he's at. He knew about this damn meeting.' ''

O'Brien's explanation is, ''I missed my plane; it's just that simple. I knew about the meeting and was ready to go to Canada, but I just missed my plane.''

Because he didn't catch his plane, O'Brien decided to go to his office in the Joint Council 43 building, across the street from Local 299. He was driven to work by Robert Holmes, Jr., who met him at an intersection on Telegraph Road. While in the area O'Brien was staying with friends in suburban Birmingham.

O'Brien's office was between those of Robert Holmes and Local 985 president William Bufalino. After an hour or so of paper shuffling and phone calling, a deliveryman appeared in the Teamster headquarters to drop off a twenty-pound salmon which had been sent to Holmes from a union vice president in Seattle.

''It was melting or something,'' says Bufalino, describing the packaged fish which was leaking through its plastic container. O'Brien decided to take the present to the Holmes household. O'Brien says that he called his friend Joseph Giacalone, the son of Detroit mobster Anthony Giacalone, to borrow his car, a 1975 maroon Mercury.

''Chuckie was in the process of moving to Florida,'' says Bufalino, ''and his car had been sent down. He didn't have a car.''

Preparing for his daughter's wedding, which was to be held in two days—on Friday, August 1—Bufalino had been entertaining a number of relatives who were in town for the wedding and staying at his house. Among those early arrivals was Bufalino's daughter's godfather, Russell Bufalino, who a year earlier had become a top figure in the

Genovese crime organization. The man driving Bufalino into town that morning, federal agents have confirmed, was Frank Sheeran of Delaware.

A respected and feared man, Russell Bufalino had achieved little public notoriety. In recent years the only press he had received was in a small piece, buried in the June 9, 1975, issue of *Time,* which simply reported, in a tongue-in-cheek manner, that Bufalino's help had been solicited and received by the Central Intelligence Agency for the Bay of Pigs invasion. Two associates of Bufalino, also named in the *Time* report as has having cooperated with the CIA—Salvatore Granello and James Plumeri, who were also close friends of Jimmy Hoffa—had been found murdered in 1970 and 1971.

That information had come to light as the result of a Senate investigation of the CIA-underworld plots to kill Castro, which was sparked by a March 10, 1975, article by Seymour Hersh in the *New York Times.* Senator Frank Church was the head of the Senate committee investigating the allegations.

The Church Committee learned that the CIA had obtained the services of Howard Hughes adviser Robert Maheu and gangster John Rosselli. Through Rosselli the CIA was introduced to Chicago mob leader Sam Giancana, who persuaded Santos Trafficante, the man with the Cuban contacts, to join the conspiracy.

Committee pressure immediately fell upon Maheu, who refused to say anything unless he was granted immunity from prosecution: "I knew from the beginning that I was going to be the fall guy if this ever came out, and I was ready to deny everything Rosselli and Giancana were going to tell the Committee." There is a strong implication in Maheu's statement that he believed one or both of the mobsters would admit their involvement in the Castro plot.

Although Rosselli testified, Giancana never had a chance to. On June 19, 1975, while cooking dinner in the kitchen of his Chicago mansion, he was shot six times in the face by an assailant who escaped without a trace.

Although Chicago investigators thought that the motive for Giancana's slaying was his demand for more of the syndicate's slot machine action in the Caribbean, former contract killer Charles Crimaldi and several Church Committee staff people had other theories.

Claiming that the mobsters involved with the CIA were responsible for Giancana's murder, Crimaldi told his biographer, John Kidner, an official of the Bureau of Narcotics, "Momo [Giancana] knew too much, and was ready to talk to the Senate investigating committee about the Chicago underworld's part in the CIA assassination plot against Fidel Castro . . . ''

''I told him [Crimaldi] that that would take some proving,'' Kidner wrote. ''He didn't bother to prove it, but replied: 'I don't need proof. I say he was hit by the CIA guy. He didn't pull the trigger himself. He used one of our guys [in the underworld]. An import.' ''[6]

The Giancana gunman turned government informant later claimed that Jimmy Hoffa had also participated in the plots. And at that time Hoffa's chief contact with Trafficante, according to Edward Partin, was Rolland McMaster, who had set up Teamster locals in Miami with the help of reputed Giancana executioner David Yaras.

According to Crimaldi, Hoffa had been the ''original liaison'' between the CIA and the underworld. He strongly implied that it was Hoffa who had brought in Russell Bufalino and his associates.

Crimaldi's statements would be impossible to take seriously if not for his previous activities as an informer for the Bureau of Narcotics. A former deputy director of the bureau, who used Crimaldi's information about the underworld's narcotics traffic in numerous successful prosecutions by the bureau, called the former syndicate figure ''absolutely reliable.''

Within a week after Giancana's death, Edward Partin, the key government witness against Hoffa in his 1964 jury-tampering trial, flew to Washington and met Senator McClellan.

''Friends of mine suggested that I go,'' says Partin. ''They wanted me to tell all I knew about Hoffa's involvement with the Mafia people who were trying to kill Castro. I thought that it was time the truth came out, and the Church Committee wanted to hear it.''

But for unknown reasons Partin was never called to testify in either open or closed session. And if Hoffa had intended to tell the committee what he knew, he never got the chance.

In Detroit on July 30, Chuck O'Brien dropped off the salmon and stayed at the Holmeses' until about one o'clock, visiting Holmes's wife and baby.

''When I got home from Canada,'' says Robert Holmes, ''my wife was complaining that the damn fish had leaked blood and slime all over the kitchen.''

While Mrs. Holmes mopped up the mess and O'Brien played with the baby, Jimmy Hoffa, twenty-five miles north at his cottage on

Lake Orion, prepared for an appointment with Anthony Giacalone at the Machus Red Fox restaurant, seven miles northwest of Detroit. An elegant restaurant and a favorite of Teamster officials, the Red Fox was not a place where Hoffa would take his mob associates, but it was a convenient rendezvous point. The meeting had been arranged three days earlier, after Giacalone had a series of sessions with Hoffa trying to convince him that he should meet with Anthony Provenzano, with whom Giacalone was in close telephone contact at the time. Vito Giacalone was also present during some of these meetings, and, according to federal investigators, so was Hoffa's old friend Louis Linteau, who served as go-between for Hoffa and Giacalone.

Two days before the scheduled "sitdown" among Hoffa, Giacalone, and Provenzano, Hoffa had spoken to IBT vice president Harold Gibbons, who later said he had learned that Hoffa "was talking to hoodlums, who were trying to get him to drop out of the race [for the IBT general presidency]."

Wearing a dark blue shirt and trousers and sun glasses, Hoffa climbed into his dark green 1974 Grand Ville Pontiac and headed for the Red Fox. As he pulled out of the driveway his wife noticed that he was uncommonly nervous. It was obvious that he would have preferred to stay home.

En route to the meeting Hoffa stopped to see Linteau at his airport limousine service. An amateur boxer in Canada for five years, Linteau had met the labor leader during the early 1940s. Later, after Hoffa named him a business agent in Pontiac Local 614, Linteau had been indicted for extortion along with Fitzsimmons and had gone to prison while Fitzsimmons went free.

"On the afternoon of July 30," Linteau says, "Hoffa came to see me, but I was out and missed him. He was a half-hour early. Jimmy knew some of the other employees and started talking to them."

One of those employees remembers that "Hoffa seemed kind of nervous about something. He just made small talk and said that he was meeting Giacalone [and] Tony Pro. . . . Before he left, he told us he was supposed to meet them at the Red Fox and wanted Louie to come. But Louie had already gone to lunch."

The two men whom Hoffa thought he was meeting had no intention of showing up; both have denied that any such meeting had been arranged. Giacalone was at a nearby health spa; Provenzano was in the Local 560 union hall in Union City, New Jersey, playing Greek rummy with several business agents.

Back on the road again, Hoffa proceeded directly to the Red Fox and parked in a shopping center lot next to the restaurant.

Meanwhile, as Bill Bufalino scurried about north of Detroit, picking up candy and nuts for his daughter's wedding on Friday, Frank Sheeran was driving his own car, heading for the Pontiac airfield, where McMaster had allegedly picked up Provenzano the month before.

Government investigators believe that Sheeran picked up three New Jersey men who had just flown in on a private plane. The four men then headed for the house where O'Brien was staying. The owner of the house and his wife were out, having a late lunch.

In Chicago, Rolland McMaster had concluded his business with the Gateway Transportation Company and had gone to the Central States Towers, the midwestern headquarters of the IBT, to see fellow IBT organizer Frank Murtha, the former administrator of the Central States Pension Fund, whom McMaster had already called for messages twice that day. Murtha says it was the first time he had seen or heard from McMaster in several months, and adds that he didn't see him again until several months later. "I can't tell much," says Murtha, "but I will say that it was rare when McMaster was here. He has an unmarked office with only a telephone and desk inside. Nothing else. The place is empty."

Murtha refused to say what he and McMaster had discussed, but McMaster didn't. "I remember we were talking about it . . . Hoffa's disappearance. I remember talking to Murtha about it."

Interestingly enough, Hoffa hadn't vanished then. But by 6:00 P.M. the following day, he had become "Missing Person #75–3425."

"Well, whenever it was," McMaster added, quickly correcting himself, "I do remember talking to him about it."

19 The Real Hoffa Legacy

Jimmy Hoffa had fallen off the face of the earth.

Frank Fitzsimmons expressed "shock and dismay" when he heard the first reports. He told Jack Crellin, labor editor of the *Detroit News,* "It is just unbelievable that anything like this could happen. Sure, Jim and I have had our disagreements, but something like this is, well, just insane . . . I just don't understand what is going on back there in Detroit. I was very irritated when I learned of the bombing of my son's car and now we have something like this."[1]

Dave Johnson, numb and scared, with four bruisers surrounding him, said dejectedly, "No, I don't think he's alive. I don't think he'll ever be found."

Rolland McMaster quipped, "If Hoffa was killed in broad daylight, even you reporters won't be safe."

From what government investigators were able to piece together, the disappearance was a three-act drama—the delivery of Hoffa to the scene of his death, the murder, and the disposal of the body—with different characters starring in each act.

Hoffa had slipped unseen into the Red Fox at about 2:30 P.M. and called his wife from the pay telephone on the lower level of the restaurant. He did not have to go through the dining room or the bar.

"Has Tony Giacalone called?" Hoffa asked.

"No," she replied.

"Well, if he calls, tell him I'm waiting for him."

Before stepping back outside into the hot July sun and acknowledging the greetings of a couple of pedestrians walking by, Hoffa called his friend and backup man, Louis Linteau, who had returned from lunch.

"Giacalone didn't show up," Linteau quoted an angry Hoffa as shouting. "I'm coming out there."

"That was the last time anybody heard from him," Linteau adds. "He never made it to my place, so I guess he was snatched before he got into this car. If he'd changed locations he would have called me."

As against Linteau's theory that Hoffa was "snatched," federal agents speculated that Hoffa was picked up by someone he trusted.

"If there was one man whom Hoffa would have trusted in a situation like this, it would have been Chuckie O'Brien," says a government investigator in Detroit. "O'Brien was not only Hoffa's 'foster son,' he was like a blood relative of Tony Giacalone's. Like Hoffa, Giacalone had had an affair with O'Brien's mother, and Chuckie even called him 'Uncle Tony.' "

Raised primarily by the Hoffa family from the age of six, O'Brien was generally considered by Teamster officials, underworld figures, and government agents to be Hoffa's real son.

Denying it, O'Brien insists, "I'm not a bastard. I've got a father. My mother was not some kind of goddamn prostitute; she was a saint . . . But if I had a father, I couldn't have asked for a better one [than Hoffa] . . . He was the only father I've ever had."

He spent most of his time in the Hoffa household until his first marriage, and he returned when he was divorced. In early 1974, flying on his own again, he was an organizer in the Teamsters' attempt to beat out the United Farm Workers in unionizing the California vineyard migrants. Living fast and spending lots of loot on the West Coast, O'Brien went badly into debt. When he returned to Detroit he borrowed money from Hoffa to invest in a condominium project that later defaulted—as O'Brien's loan from Hoffa also did. Trying to teach his reckless protégé a lesson, Hoffa cut the cord with him in the fall of 1974.

"Considering that Chuckie had done a lot of Jimmy's dirty work, like throwing around a lot of money with Marcello in Louisiana to get that guy [Ed Partin] to change his testimony, both Jimmy and Chuckie knew that their split was only temporary," says a close friend of the Hoffa family. "They cared for each other too much."

Regardless of how much affection there was between Hoffa and O'Brien, the young organizer did not at once straighten out, and Frank Fitzsimmons threatened to send him to Anchorage, Alaska. Pleading for reconsideration, O'Brien received it only after IBT vice president Robert Holmes intervened on his behalf, persuading Fitzsimmons to send him instead to the Southern Conference of Teamsters in Miami.

"O'Brien is a valuable man," Holmes explains, "even though he was wild and misbehaved a lot. He had been taught by the best, Jimmy Hoffa, and his talents were too good to waste. So I stepped in for both the good of the union and O'Brien."

Just six weeks before Hoffa vanished, O'Brien displayed some eagerness to accept responsibility when he married a woman from West Memphis, Arkansas, who had three children. They were planning to move to Florida, where O'Brien would start his new IBT job with the Southern Conference. Now, on July 30, he was running errands, trying to be a good union man.

According to his attorney, James Burdick, O'Brien was with the Holmes family no later than 1:00 P.M. "Chuck had only stopped by to drop off that bloody fish packed in dry ice, with the leaky plastic container," Burdick says. "It was pretty much a hello-goodbye thing. He stayed long enough to drop off the fish and play with the Holmeses' new baby." At about the same time O'Brien left the Holmeses' suburban house, Hoffa was leaving his cottage in Lake Orion for his afternoon meeting. "Because the fish blood and slime got all over the back seat of young Giacalone's car, O'Brien then went to a nearby car wash to get the stains wiped off," Burdick adds. "He used a Standard Oil credit card—issued to Local 299—to pay for the cleanup job."

"It was no fish story," O'Brien joked. "That damn fish ruined the upholstery in the back seat of the car. I went to the car wash to get it off. That's all. The car wasn't mine; I had borrowed it from Joey Giacalone. I was responsible."

The government seized Giacalone's car, charging that "O'Brien used the car to lure Jimmy Hoffa into a meeting with his abductors." Trained tracking dogs had detected Hoffa's scent in that same car.

"Now that's another lie," says William Bufalino, the last person to see O'Brien at the union hall. "Do you believe that? First of all, they'd never be able to ask a dog, the only dog they'd be able to ask is [Robert] Ozer [head of Detroit's Strike Force Against Organized Crime], and he'd tell them that the dogs smelled Hoffa in that car . . . Actually there was no blood; there was no Hoffa. There was a fish in the car."

"No matter how people like Bufalino deny it," a Michigan law enforcement official's theory is that "Hoffa was a sitting duck for O'Brien. He had plenty of time to pick up Hoffa and take him to the site where the meeting was supposed to be held with Giacalone and Provenzano. And Hoffa had no reason not to trust O'Brien with his life. His money—no; but his life—yes."

According to Burdick, after O'Brien left the car wash he drove to the Southfield Athletic Club, where he met Anthony Giacalone in the lobby at about 2:15. "O'Brien's kids' birthdays were coming up, and Giacalone wanted to give them their presents," Burdick says. "During the three-minute meeting Giacalone handed O'Brien an envelope with $100 in it—$50 for each kid . . .

"Now O'Brien volunteered this information to the FBI. If he was involved in some conspiracy to kill Hoffa with Giacalone, do you think that he would have freely admitted getting money from him just minutes before Hoffa disappeared?"

The government believes that O'Brien arrived at the Red Fox immediately after Hoffa's call to Linteau and drove him to the home of the friends O'Brien was staying with, a four-minute trip from the restaurant. Did Giacalone go with O'Brien to meet Hoffa? Government investigators think not. Giacalone's attorney claims he was with his client in his law offices—in the same building as the athletic club—from two-thirty to four that afternoon. However, the government is investigating the possibility that Giacalone's brother, Vito, was with O'Brien.

Although official reports conflict about whether O'Brien was alone when he picked up Hoffa, an eyewitness told the FBI that he (or she) had seen Hoffa climb into a maroon car driven by a man fitting O'Brien's description.

"I never did anything to hurt Jimmy Hoffa," O'Brien insists.

"We think that O'Brien should've amended that statement to say that he wouldn't have 'knowingly' done anything to hurt Hoffa," says a Detroit government official. "It is quite possible that O'Brien simply thought he was taking Hoffa to just another meeting. But even if that's true, O'Brien certainly became an accessory to the subsequent cover-up. He didn't tell us all he knew afterwards."

The government believes that the house in which O'Brien was staying was the site of Hoffa's murder—though O'Brien's hosts are under no suspicion—and that his killers had flown in earlier in the afternoon and been taken to the home by Frank Sheeran.

Months passed after Hoffa's abduction while government investigators and private citizens—after a $300,000 reward was offered by Hoffa's family and friends—searched through land fills, woods, waterways, and garbage disposals for Hoffa's body. Nothing turned up.

In the meantime Hoffa's pathetically self-serving autobiography, *Hoffa: The Real Story,* was published. "I *charge* [Frank Fitzsimmons] with making vast loans from the billion-dollar Teamster pension fund to known mobsters,''[2] Hoffa wrote about the $1.4 billion Central States Pension Fund, a major target of government investigators. The dramatic irony of Hoffa's disappearance and the accusations published in his book, along with the government's own continuing probes, glamorized the situation for the press. "Hoffa's legacy" was transformed from one of crime and corruption into one of reform.

The press helped extend the "legacy" into the growing Teamster dissident movement, too. Some rebels were flattered; others were not. That fall a dissident wrote in the union reform publication, *The L.A. Grapevine* of Los Angeles:

> To win under our present conditions, Hoffa would have had to do something he never attempted to do in the good old days—organize the rank-and-file of the union for a militant fight against the employers. Sometimes Hoffa did support rank-and-file militants, but this was usually when it was in his own interests to do so . . .
>
> Mostly, Hoffa disorganized us and built a bureaucratic machine.

Until Hoffa's death PROD had been the only reform group able and bold enough to launch and support a functioning national reform organization since TURF became inactive. Begun in late 1972 with the help of consumer advocate Ralph Nader, PROD had been a devoted proponent of solutions for the rank and file's most serious everyday problems: the union's lack of commitment to job security, safety, and health. Arthur Fox, the lawyer who was PROD's executive director, operating out of a cramped office near DuPont Circle in Washington, worked for fundamental changes within the union. His small staff was expanded two years later and included an administrator, twenty-three-year-old Michael deBlois, and a research director, John Sikorski. Dealing with the bread-and-butter issues—outlined in its 1975 "PROD Manifesto"—PROD also emphasized the criminal activities that some officials of the IBT practiced and condoned.

"All of us in PROD are dedicated trade unionists, and we believe in strong unions which work for and protect their membership," Fox explains. "But when you bottom-line the problems of the rank and file, they are, quite simply, the grievance machinery, the IBT constitution, and the local by-laws. Union reformers who try to change these union laws are up against tyrannical leaders, who, in reality, are accountable only to the IBT general president and the general executive board. Try to get these puppets out, and you face the wrath of the international. And even if you do succeed in winning an election or two, the IBT can easily arrange to have activists fired and to have their grievances dismissed—by the IBT's ability to trade deals with management and manipulate grievance panels. An honest aggressive official who can't win grievances won't get reelected. And even if you somehow get around all that, the IBT general president, under the constitution, can throw your local into trusteeship for eighteen months or redefine your jurisdiction to undermine your political constituency.''

PROD filed suits against the IBT for these oppressive tactics, and broadened its base to include investigations of pension and welfare fund fraud as well as organized crime's influence in the union. Before PROD took on these areas, Mike Parkhurst's *Overdrive* magazine, featuring the work of investigative editor Jim Drinkhall, had been virtually alone.

From the inception of PROD the more militant unionists had viewed it as merely an extension of Nader's Public Interest Research Groups, which were primarily concerned with lobbying and lawsuits. ''A lot of rank-and-file members wanted to do something directly with the membership, not just the legislators and the courts,'' says Robert Grant, founder of the Chicago group, Concerned Truckers for a Democratic Union. ''And PROD refused to do that, even though it had a national membership.''

''That is true, but only up to a point,'' according to Fox. ''Decisions affecting the trucking industry are made in Washington, and that's where we've been most effective, influencing those decisions on behalf of Teamsters. Because of the pressure we've placed on Congress, the National Labor Relations Board, and the courts, truckers are now safer while driving than ever before. We even went to court for a man who had been fired from his job for refusing to drive an unsafe rig. He refused to haul in that particular truck and was fired; and the union supported the company. In the end, after we won the case, the driver was not only reinstated in his job, he was also given nearly $39,000 in back pay. In addition, PROD chapters throughout the country are particularly active in their locals and in fighting for contract enforcement.''

Complementing PROD's litigation-education approach to union reform, a small group of militant rebel leaders met in Cleveland in mid-May 1975 to lay the groundwork for direct action. Dan La Botz, Laura

Hoge, Robert Grant, and his wife, Mary Grant, were all sincere hard-core activists from Chicago's CTDU; Mel Packard was the leader of the Concerned Rank-and-file Teamsters of Pittsburgh; Ken Paff edited a Cleveland underground newsletter, ''Membership Voice''; and Lester Williams was the former president of Cleveland's TURF Chapter. Paff was named national secretary, and Paff's home in Cleveland became its national headquarters.

''We wanted to go a step or two beyond what PROD was doing,'' Paff explains. ''We wanted to organize the rank and file into a strong force which could stand up against corrupt union officials, their big money and their goon squads, which were notorious for scaring potential reformers away from meetings because of the threat of physical danger. Since we thought that the membership would be more willing to respond to economic issues, our strategy became one of forcing the union into meeting our contract demands in the 1976 National Master Freight Agreement.''

The foundation set in Cleveland, the militants agreed to hold a second meeting in Chicago on August 16, and invited twenty-five seasoned activists from ten cities to attend. The new group took the name ''Teamsters for a Decent Contract'' and began working with PROD and other rebel organizations.

''The first thing we did was print up 20,000 brochures about our new organization,'' says Paff. ''In addition, we started passing around petitions, trying to pressure the union into pushing management for not only $1.00 per hour in wages already lost to inflation and $1.00 in 'new money' but a full, unlimited cost of living increase which rose with the cost of living index. The reaction to our proposals was so great that we had to print up an additional 150,000 brochures for members in over a hundred locals who were requesting them.

''And, frankly, the response was due more to our noneconomic issues than anything—like job security, improved working conditions, and a better grievance procedure.''

Assuming that neither PROD nor TDC would be any more successful than earlier reform movements like TURF and Local 299's Unity Committee, Frank Fitzsimmons and his union associates naturally went on with business as usual. In the fall of 1975, during the annual Frank Fitzsimmons Invitational Golf Tournament at La Costa Country Club, Fitzsimmons played a round of golf with former President Richard Nixon, who had emerged from his self-imposed exile to pay tribute to his Teamster friends. Among the other tournament players were Rolland McMaster and Anthony Provenzano, both by now top suspects in the Hoffa disappearance. Provenzano had been called before the Hoffa grand jury on September 8, 1975, along with his chief lieutenant, Salvatore Briguglio. McMaster and several of his men had been questioned by the FBI.

In late November, Provenzano's associates in New Jersey held a $100-a-plate dinner celebrating the end of his five-year suspension from union politics for his extortion conviction. During the dinner, which raised over $160,000 for a scholarship fund in the name of Provenzano's mother, Fitzsimmons made a speech praising Provenzano, and he later told reporters, ''I think Tony is a wonderful man, and if I decide I need an organizer or I need him, I'll appoint him.'' To no one's surprise, a week later Provenzano returned to Union City Local 560 as its secretary-treasurer. But his ability to stay out of trouble was short-lived.

The following morning, while Fitzsimmons was holding a rare press conference in Washington, there was a break in the Hoffa disappearance case. Anthony Provenzano's brother Nunzio, president of Local 560 and another ex-convict, was rousted out of bed by Strike Force agents who laid subpoenas on him and demanded access to the local's records and to a locked filing cabinet in the union hall used by business agent Salvatore Briguglio.

''[The government was] looking for two .38s with silencers,'' Briguglio explained. ''They came in, they didn't find any .38s with silencers; instead they found some papers with some numbers on them . . . They tried to accuse me of loan sharking.''

While federal agents rifled the union hall, other investigators converged on the Garden State Bank across the street, holding subpoenas for safe-deposit boxes rented by business agent Stephen Andretta and Briguglio's brother Gabriel, vice president of the Provenzano-controlled Local 84, in Fort Lee, New Jersey.

''This box I had only opened up two days prior,'' Andretta says. ''First time in my life I had opened a safety deposit box.'' He added that he had used the safe-deposit box only for his jewelry, two watches and two rings. On December 3, ''I go to the bank. I go around back. And there is an FBI agent, waiting for me by the doorway of the building. 'Hi ya, Steve. I want to talk to you. I'm special agent so-and-so.' I said, 'Listen, I'm very busy, I've got people waiting for me upstairs [in Local 560]. I just had to come to the bank.'

'' 'Do you mind if I come to the bank with you?'

" 'Come on, it's a free country.'

"We walked into the bank. As soon as we got to the back of the bank, forget about it—there were ten or twelve agents, prosecutors, U.S. attorneys, and they gave me these two subpoenas.''

According to Salvatore Briguglio, "Now, my brother Gabe has a safety deposit box in there. They got a subpoena for him. They go in and rifle it. You know what they found? A sock, an old sock with some old coins in there. That's all they found, so that's another blank. God knows what they were looking for—the bastards—what they expected to find in there.''

Government investigators in Detroit and Newark said they were looking for the weapon used to kill Jimmy Hoffa.

Robert Ozer, head of Detroit's Strike Force, announced later that day that the government knew who had murdered the former Teamster leader and said that they were going to be called before a grand jury in Detroit.

On December 4 reporters and TV cameramen crowded into the Detroit federal courthouse hoping to get a glimpse of Salvatore Briguglio, Gabriel Briguglio, and Thomas Andretta, a labor racketeer who was the brother of Stephen Andretta. Partitions had been set up to block the journalists' view as those subpoenaed marched in and out of the grand jury room pleading the Fifth Amendment. The barrier also prevented the press people from identifying Frank Sheeran, another alleged witness to Hoffa's murder. Sheeran and his alleged co-conspirators were all represented by attorney William Bufalino, who said that he was handling their cases for free. "If someday they have some money,'' Bufalino says, "they can pay me. If Hoffa were here right now, he'd say, 'Continue defending these people; they weren't the ones who did it . . .' ''[3]

The Justice Department later confirmed, after John Sikorski of PROD filed a complaint, that it was investigating Bufalino for a $1350 monthly retainer which he was allegedly receiving from Local 560 and that a grand jury had subpoenaed his financial records.

Bufalino also represented Rolland McMaster that day. "They told McMaster that he was a target of the investigation,'' says Bufalino, "and he asserted a constitutional privilege [the Fifth].''

Since July 1975 McMaster had been in trouble with the law only once. In late September, he and his friend and partner John Ferris were arrested for pistol whipping a Michigan barber who had given them the finger on I-75 near Bay City—after Ferris tried to drive him off the highway for refusing to yield the right of way. The whole incident was kid stuff, but the barber had to have twenty stitches. A few days after McMaster and Ferris had posted their $3000 bond—which McMaster peeled off a roll in his pocket at the time of their arraignment—the charges were dropped when Ferris passed a lie detector test: he said the barber had drawn a switchblade before Ferris and McMaster drew their guns.

The young barber was not charged but had learned his lesson: Never give the finger to Teamsters on the expressway.

McMaster's appearance before the Hoffa grand jury in December was directly related to the testimony earlier that morning of top executives of the Detroit terminal of the Gateway Transportation Company. The officials were asked to provide the grand jury with dispatch records for two weeks beginning on the day Hoffa vanished. One of those subpoenaed was McMaster's brother-in-law, Stanton Barr, who had been with him on the day of the murder.

"I had no idea why we were called," Barr says. "The government asked us for our records as well as information about any fifty-five-gallon oil drums which had been transported during that period of time."

Barr testified that when they returned from Chicago at about six o'clock on July 30, he had dropped McMaster off at his second home in Lathrup Village, near Twelve-Mile and Telegraph roads—a four-minute drive from the Red Fox restaurant. That evening, according to federal investigators, McMaster had dinner with John Ferris. McMaster denies this; Ferris refused to be interviewed.

Unemployed Larry McHenry and Jim Shaw, the driver for Gateway, who were still living at Ferris's Leland House, were both interviewed by the FBI several days after the disappearance. They were likely suspects because of their alleged roles in the bombing of Dick Fitzsimmons' union car on July 10.

Defending himself and his two organizers against any role in the Hoffa murder, McMaster explains, "Teamsters have professional ethics just like reporters. We don't shoot people and kill people." He theorizes that Hoffa "ran off to Brazil with a black go-go dancer" to escape continued "persecution" from the government. "I hired a soothsayer and asked her where Jimmy was. That's what she told me."

Stephen Andretta was also called to testify on December 4, after McMaster and Barr, because of an interesting conversation he was said to have had with Ralph Picardo, an inmate at Trenton State Prison. According to the government, Andretta, his brother Thomas, and a union accountant visited Picardo together in early August. Talking to him by telephone through the thick glass barrier, Stephen Andretta allegedly told Picardo the outline of the Hoffa disappearance. If this is true, it was a grave mistake. Soon after the conversation Picardo began talking to federal investigators.

Ralph Picardo had been in prison since May 1975, when he was convicted of pumping five bullets into the head of a loan-shark associate. A chubby, baby-faced man of thirty, Picardo was a driver for Anthony Provenzano and a business agent for Local 84 before buying his own nonunion trucking firm. He had been recruited by Salvatore Briguglio and Thomas Andretta. By way of background, Picardo told government officials that in December 1972 Salvatore Briguglio and Thomas Andretta had murdered a fellow loan shark, stuffed his body into a tree shredder, and buried the remains in a garbage dump under the Hackensack Bridge in Jersey City.

In addition, it was Picardo who was responsible for the Hoffa grand jury's questions about oil drums. He said Andretta told him that Hoffa's body had been stuffed into a fifty-five-gallon oil drum and taken—on a Gateway Transportation Company truck—to an unknown destination.

"They asked me about my visit to the prison," Andretta says of his grand jury session. "I was highly insulted . . . We never discussed anything about Hoffa with Picardo."

Stephen Andretta was given immunity from prosecution but still refused to talk about his alleged conversation with Picardo. He was sentenced to sixty-three days in Michigan's Milan Prison for contempt.

"They spent ten million dollars trying to throw Hoffa in jail," Andretta says bitterly. "And now they've spent a figure very close to it trying to find out what happened to him. And they're trying to get anybody involved in it, for whatever reason they want. They're very embarrassed. The more embarrassed they get, the more they delve into it. There's no end."

Government agents confirm that two secret internal reports, one in January 1976 and a thirty-eight-page one of February 15, 1977—both based on Picardo's information—expound the theory that Hoffa was asked to attend a "sitdown" with Provenzano by Detroit mobster Anthony Giacalone, Provenzano's relative. Waiting for Giacalone at the suburban restaurant, Hoffa was picked up by Chuck O'Brien, who took his passenger to his temporary residence, four minutes away from the restaurant. Waiting calmly at the house were Salvatore and Gabriel Briguglio and Thomas Andretta, who had flown in on a private plane. Frank Sheeran was also present, and Hoffa's murder was authorized by Russell Bufalino, who had given the contract to Provenzano. Picardo's information tallied with earlier investigations: Sheeran had driven Russell Bufalino to Detroit on the day Hoffa was killed.

"They were trying to put Russell Bufalino's name all over the grand jury transcript," William Bufalino says indignantly. "When Stephen Andretta was in there, they asked him, 'Do you know Russell Bufalino? Did he pay you not to testify against him? Do you know whether he was in Detroit? Do you know whether he saw Hoffa? . . . '

"In fact, I wanted to testify. I sent [Andretta] back in [the grand jury room] and said, 'If you're trying to drag Russell Bufalino's name into your record—let me tell you one thing. Ozer tried it before.' He went in to tell them . . . If they want to know the truth about Russell Bufalino—I sent [the government] a note [through Andretta]—'As soon as I get through, Mr. Bufalino, Bill Bufalino, wants to come in and testify.' They said that that's not permitted. What isn't permitted? To learn the truth? I asked them, 'Let me go in there and tell them about Russell Bufalino. I'll straighten the grand jury out, about what Russell is, the type of person he is. They'll have to listen to me for three days.'

"Do you know what? I never testified."

The Briguglio brothers and Thomas Andretta were among the business agents who claimed to have been playing Greek rummy at the Local 560 union hall with Provenzano. "It's the same as rummy," according to Provenzano's brother. "You knock everybody out, and when one man remains, he's the winner."

But Salvatore Briguglio said he didn't play cards very long. "I left earlier that day, because I had had an operation on my mouth the day before . . . It was the type of dental operation in which they cut me on the inside and outside. And they scraped my bone and sewed my mouth closed again. If anybody could do any traveling under those circumstances—and do what they claimed I've done—[he] would have to be Superman . . .

"I don't know anyone in the world who would want to hurt Jimmy. He wasn't a threat to anyone to my knowledge."

The motive for Hoffa's murder becomes explicit in the third act of the drama.

An Ohio syndicate figure, Leo Moceri, gave a friendly government agent some information about the disappearance. According to another internal FBI report, Moceri said a few days afterward that "Hoffa's

death was the same thing that happened to a man named Giancana,"
that both were killed because of the Church Committee's closed hearings on the CIA-underworld plots to murder Castro. After his second
meeting with the agent, and before the end of August, Moceri disappeared. His car was found at a motel in Fairlawn, Ohio. Some days later
his golf clubs were found in a river at the edge of Akron.

Charles Crimaldi, the underworld assassin turned government informant who told government investigators that mob leaders who planned
to murder Castro for the CIA had killed Sam Giancana, echoed the
same theme when he claimed to have "hard evidence" that the same
people had ordered that Hoffa be killed. Crimaldi believes the underworld was afraid that both Giancana and Hoffa had become so unpredictable that they might betray the long-standing secrets of the Castro
assassination plots.

According to John Kidner, "[Crimaldi] repeated over and over that
the body of James Hoffa would never be found . . . "[4] " 'Hoffa is now
a goddamn hub cap,' Crimaldi said. 'His body was crushed and
smelted.' "

Chuck O'Brien, oddly enough, made a similar remark several
months after the disappearance in front of several witnesses: "Hoffa is
now just a fender, being driven around by someone."

"O'Brien first made that statement to me in private," a Southern
Conference Teamster leader explains. "When we went back outside
where everyone was in the car, the subject was brought up again. I was
floored when he repeated it in front of everyone else."

If such a plan was made to dispose of Hoffa's body, the reasons for
the government's inquiries about Gateway Transportation and oil
drums become more clear, especially if Hoffa's body was transported as
the government says it was. Gateway executives, including McMaster's brother-in-law, were out of town on the day of the murder, and investigators do not imply that they took part in any conspiracy.

McMaster, who has been linked to the company as well as to Santos
Trafficante, says, "If I was involved in that [Hoffa] thing in any way,
shape, or form, I'd be heading for the hills." Similarly, Gateway driver
Jim Shaw, now a labor consultant for Transamerican Freight Lines,
denies any knowledge of Hoffa's whereabouts. "The only reason why I
was suspected of anything was because of my friendship with Larry
McHenry."

Soon after Hoffa vanished, McMaster was involved in a new organizing drive, even more ambitious than earlier Teamster campaigns, in

which McHenry and Shaw participated. It was formally proposed in August, when the IBT held its annual warehousemen's conference in Boston. Among those who attended was Chuck O'Brien, wearing a "Fitz in '76" campaign button. The three-day meeting was closed to the public and the press.

On the final day of the conference, IBT general organizer Jackie Presser, the son of Ohio Teamster leader William Presser, proposed a new Teamster organizing task force, the "Tri-State Energy Haulers Division" to unionize coal truckdrivers in Ohio, Pennsylvania, and West Virginia. Frank Fitzsimmons was not there for the presentation, so Presser outlined his ideas in a letter to him dated August 29, 1975:

> First, I am sure that we all basically agree that an energy division is an absolute necessity for the I.B.T. Secondly, according to the national geographical mine sections, it appears that Ohio and its surrounding states would be the logical place for us to start this energy division . . . At the present time, this committee is prepared to proceed with a prearranged program which first would permit us to establish headquarters, committee chairmen, organizing team captains, daily and weekly reports, as well as a conservative necessary financial structure.

Presser asked for a "revolving, operating budget of $250,000," as well as the support of the IBT, its Central and Eastern Conferences, and the three area joint councils in Cleveland, Ohio; Pittsburgh, Pennsylvania; and Charleston, West Virginia.

The new Teamster task force hoped that "by becoming a factor now, we most certainly would be getting our fair share of all future federally or state financed energy programs that would be forthcoming across this nation . . . In the ultimate end," Presser concluded, "we the IBT would be representing, properly, the members in the energy fields across this nation."

A five-man "survey team" had already conducted a "feasibility study" of the organizing effort. Among its members were two organizers for the United Mine Workers—both with arrest records for strong-arm activities—and three members of the old McMaster task force: Harry Budzynski, Titus McCue, and Jack Robison. As expected, the team concluded that there was a need for the proposed energy division.

The UMW's director of organization, Thomas Pysell, says that his union went along with Presser's plans because "We were faced with 1300 scab mines and 20,000 scab trucks. We didn't have the money and manpower to go after them alone. So with the Teamsters and us combining both our money and manpower, it was decided that we'd take the miners and they'd take the truckers. To show good faith, the Teamsters had six coal mines under contract that they turned over to us.''

But according to a Teamster official involved in the project, Presser and the IBT had their eyes on much bigger goals. ''The master plan is control,'' he says. ''We want to stake our claim in the future of the coal liquefication process, and, by heavily influencing the state of Alaska and its oil pipeline, we will have a tremendous voice in the usage of America's energy . . .

''The key to the organizing drive will be the trucks. If we are resisted by nonunion companies, then the trucks will be shut off in the mining areas, unable to enter or leave, until they negotiate with us.''

Two months after Presser's letter to Fitzsimmons, the IBT general executive board approved the proposal. The announcement of the new division appeared in the November 1975 issue of the *International Teamster:* ''After an exhaustive survey of nonunion coal haulers in a three-state area by a committee headed by General Organizer Jackie Presser, the General Executive Board gave approval to an extensive organizing campaign among these non-union drivers.'' That month Presser selected his first two organizers, both recommended by Mc-Master: Vic Everett, from Columbus Local 413, and Larry McHenry.

Because of internal problems the UMW fell behind on its commitment to the Teamsters and merely continued to respect the two unions' no-raiding pact, hoping the IBT would do the same.

Presser and the organizers moved first into the Wheeling, West Virginia, area, where they had targeted five nonunion companies for Teamster membership. In January 1976, Presser called a meeting with the coal hauling firms. One owner says that Presser told them, ''You can write your own tickets into this union.'' Presser said he didn't care how the companies handled the situation and added that he was going to organize ''the entire Ohio Valley, even if it takes a bloodbath to do it.''

Two months later, during the second meeting of the union-management group, Presser, according to another company president, threatened that companies which resisted ''will be destroyed,'' and repeated the threat of a ''bloodbath.''

One employer, the target of bomb threats during the campaign, said that his group was intimidated by Presser's tactics and hired a professional negotiator to draw up a contract which they hoped the Teamsters would accept. "All of us were really afraid of what might happen if we didn't cooperate."

Presser and the Teamsters promptly signed the agreement, which the employers considered "an extraordinarily weak contract. We couldn't believe that Presser, with only minor changes, had accepted our proposals . . . We, as employers, were permitted to determine our employees' seniority rights. We only had to pay $10 per week in health and welfare; and we didn't have to pay any pension benefits at all . . . Would I call it a sweetheart contract? No doubt about it. It definitely was."

A few weeks after that Presser suddenly resigned and handed the energy division over to the new head of the Central Conference of Teamsters, IBT vice president Roy Williams, and Williams's top lieutenant, Rolland McMaster. Since the energy division's personnel also came under Williams's control, organizer McHenry and his former boss, McMaster, were reunited.

With Jimmy Hoffa dead and new supporters seeking approval and favors, McMaster acquired power in Michigan that rivaled that of the state's IBT vice president, Robert Holmes. He had no title except that of IBT "roving" general organizer, but, working behind the scenes, he was rebuilding his Detroit base.

Weary of union politics and violence, Dave Johnson decided in early May that he was ready to retire on June 30. With Hoffa gone, there was no reason for him to hold onto the Local 299 presidency any longer.

The announcement came as no surprise to the local executive board. Everyone knew that Johnson had finished building his retirement home on the Peace River in southwestern Florida. He just wanted to get away, taking his wife, Anne, and his dog, Hubba Louie, with him. He wanted to eat trout for breakfast and oysters for lunch, then climb back on his beat-up twenty-two-foot boat and spend the rest of the afternoon looking for alligators, which were sprawling on the muddy beaches in the Florida sun. The old man didn't want to do his tightrope act any more.

"I knew that when I announced I was retiring the war was going to start all over again," Johnson says of that summer. "Not that it ever stopped, even after Jimmy disappeared. McMaster wanted to take control of the local under some guise—probably through Dick Fitzsimmons—and Fitz [Frank Fitzsimmons] was going to let him do it. I didn't want that to happen, but I didn't want to get involved. I wanted to be finished with it; get it behind me.''

No sooner had Johnson made his announcement than Richard Fitzsimmons—also to no one's surprise—let it be known that he wanted to succeed Johnson. But in view of the political atmosphere in Detroit, there was nothing automatic about the vice president filling a vacant presidency. Even though Hoffa was dead, there were still Hoffa supporters. He had become a martyr to thousands of honest working people—which was perhaps the most tragic result of his murder—and his followers were zealous. Loyal union insiders forgot the man who cheated and stole from his membership and remembered his belated alliances with union reformers when he wanted the presidency back. It was certainly the way the pragmatic Hoffa would have wanted to be remembered.

Trying to jump-shift Dick Fitzsimmons, Johnson approached local trustee Earl Grayhek, who had been running the local for Johnson since the coalition slate came in the year before, and asked if he would accept the presidency. ''There was a serious personality struggle going on around here,'' Grayhek says. ''It wasn't at all ideological. Basically, everyone's philosophy about unionism was the same. All of us had been officers, business agents, or stewards under Hoffa; we were all his students at one time or another. But the war between Hoffa and Fitzsimmons had become so bitter that the old friendships which went way back to the thirties had really gone to hell. It had become a 'them' and 'us' situation. And those of us who weren't directly involved in it tried to appease both sides. After Hoffa disappeared, we still had to choose—even those of us who wanted to get along with both sides. I had to make a tough choice, like the other fencewalkers did. But when it came to making it, I knew that Frank Fitzsimmons was the general president of this union, and I knew that I wasn't his choice for president of this local.''

But there were only two members of the Local 299 executive board who felt as Grayhek did—Dick Fitzsimmons and George Roxburgh. In 1976 Otto Wendell, Steve Riddle, and Bob Lins were still Hoffa loyalists. Wendell, the local's secretary-treasurer, decided to represent their interests and oppose young Fitzsimmons.

''Dick wasn't prepared to do the job,'' Wendell explained. ''I thought like others did that if he took over, then McMaster would really be in charge again. I didn't want that and neither did any of our people.''

Denied control of Local 299 since he was booted out as chief executive officer in 1970, McMaster had become obsessed with regaining power in Detroit. His push since then to regain his former position had been rivaled only by Hoffa's attempt to recapture the IBT presidency.

"Jimmy Hoffa and Rolland McMaster were two very tough, very strong men," Robert Holmes says. "They became friends and later enemies for that reason. After Hoffa was murdered, McMaster openly started coming to the union hall with his army—McHenry and that crew—behind him. They were determined to elect Dick Fitzsimmons president of the local; or they were ready to make sure that it would be thrown into trusteeship. McMaster knew that [Frank] Fitzsimmons would appoint one of his friends as its trustee."

Deadlocked with three votes for Fitzsimmons and three votes for Wendell, the local executive board was faced with yet another dilemma. And again the spotlight shifted to the man who wanted no part of it: Dave Johnson. Hoping he wouldn't be forced to break the tie, Johnson lobbied hard with Grayhek and Roxburgh, trying to get them to back Wendell. But the Fitzsimmons bloc remained intact, and the responsibility for breaking the deadlock fell into Johnson's lap.

"I knew that if I swung the election to Otto, then all the violence would start up again," Johnson says. "And if that happened, Frank Fitzsimmons would have his excuse to impose the trusteeship. So I decided to back Bob Lins as a compromise candidate."

A fifty-year-old trucker with a disarming Gary Cooper voice and manner (his CB handle was "Straight Arrow"), Lins was nominated in a letter Johnson sent to the executive board on May 25, 1976. Wendell immediately withdrew from the election and threw his support behind Lins.

Though the board now stood four to three for Lins, the situation was far from resolved.

Protesting Johnson's action, Rolland McMaster's men, led by McHenry, picketed Local 299, claiming that the executive board election had been illegally conducted. To appease McMaster and Dick Fitzsimmons—both clamoring for trusteeship—Holmes called a meeting of Detroit's joint council, which imposed a temporary trusteeship over the affairs of Local 299.

"I tried to take no sides in this continuing Hoffa-Fitzsimmons battle that was going on," Holmes says. "I was responsible for the smooth operation of Teamster affairs in this state—and that included a smooth transition of power in Local 299. Considering that McMaster was directly involved, I had to support the idea of trusteeship in order to avert further violence.''

''Now that's a murdering deal,'' McMaster insists. ''I had no hand in any violence. The system works, and I use the system. I went directly to Frank Fitzsimmons and told him what our problems were. And he set up a meeting with the general executive board and the Local 299 executive board.''

Because the IBT convention was going on in Las Vegas at the time, the June 17 meeting took place there. It was held without Johnson and Wendell, who refused to attend and simply sent in their proxy votes. Lins still had a majority, but he was not named as Johnson's official successor. Instead, Fitzsimmons wrote to the membership on June 24 to announce that

> during the course of this meeting, Brothers Roxburgh, [Dick] Fitzsimmons, Grayhek, Lins, and Riddle, a majority of the Local Union Executive Board, formally requested, in writing, that Local 299 be placed in Trusteeship as soon as possible ''because of the inability to resolve amongst the Board the conflicts that in our opinion would ultimately destroy our great Local Union. We agree that this action should be taken at this time in order to protect the interests of our members . . . '' It is feared that any further deterioration in the situation may result in the reoccurrence of violence and bombings.

Bob Lins disagrees with Fitzsimmons' report that the five board members voted for trusteeship. ''What we wanted was for Big Brother [the IBT] to send in an arbitrator and tell us who was right and wrong. I wanted the presidency of 299 and I was determined to run the union, not family affairs.''

''While all this was going on,'' Johnson adds, ''rumors had already been reaching Detroit that the man Fitz was going to name as trustee was Neil Dalton—and he was an out-and-out McMaster man.''

A Teamster leader in Saginaw, Michigan, Dalton had worked with McMaster on the IBT's iron and steel negotiating and grievance committees. He had also been a member of the ''advisory committee'' to McMaster's 1972–1974 task force.

As Johnson saw the situation: ''It was like this: if we didn't vote for young Fitzsimmons, then the election was no good. And we were in store for trusteeship with someone Fitz and McMaster could control.''

"That's not true," Richard Fitzsimmons counters. "The decision to consider placing the local into trusteeship was made long before the retirement of Dave Johnson. My contention in challenging the election was that the international union had already taken the stand that it was going to make the final decision as to who was going to run Local 299 . . . And even if McMaster would have been brought in—either himself or through someone else—that was a decision for the IBT general president or the membership to make, not the local executive board."

The June meeting failed to produce a resolution to the problem, and so did the subsequent intervention of IBT vice president Harold Gibbons. Frank Fitzsimmons called another meeting for July 7, in Detroit, to hear arguments for and against the imposition of a Local 299 trusteeship. But there was an office workers' strike against the Teamster locals and the Teamsters refused to cross the picket line, which was heavily manned by McMaster's goons. The hearings were postponed to mid-August. In the meantime Local 299's official headquarters became room 106 in the Holiday Inn on Trumbull Avenue, a few blocks from the union hall.

With strong membership support behind him, Dave Johnson attended the August hearings to insist that there was no reason for Local 299 to be placed in trusteeship. By the end of the three-day session Frank Fitzsimmons had begun back-peddling.

"The three-person panel, after hearing all the arguments, told Fitzsimmons that there were no grounds for putting the local into trusteeship," Johnson explains. "Anyway, Otto Wendell had already held several meetings with a Detroit attorney. Otto had given him several depositions about what was really going on in the local, the trouble and the politics caused by McMaster and Dick Fitzsimmons. Had Fitz thrown the local into trusteeship, there would have been one good court battle. And Fitz didn't want a lot of that stuff coming out."

Lins was finally president of Local 299, but McMaster did not accept defeat quietly. A few months later he led a battle to sever the steel haulers from Local 299. Bob Lins, not wanting a major fight with McMaster, allowed them to set up their own local, Local 124, and lent it $25,000. Already the new local was sanctioned by Frank Fitzsimmons and the IBT general executive board. Ralph Proctor, a former Local 299 business agent and long-time McMaster associate, was in charge as IBT trustee, and Dick Fitzsimmons, as an IBT general organizer, was next in command.

One of the reasons Fitzsimmons and McMaster had fought Local 299's executive board so hard was that Johnson had to some extent supported the rebel Teamsters during and after negotiations for the 1976 National Master Freight Agreement.

Fitzsimmons had begun the bargaining in January by asking for an increase of $1.50 an hour with no cost-of-living increases—which was completely unacceptable to the rebels. PROD and TDC actively protested. With PROD's publication in its newsletter of a legal analysis of the contract proposals and an insert entitled, ''To Strike or Not to Strike: Your Rights and Responsibilities,'' and TDC's picketing of Teamster headquarters in Washington combined with demonstrations around the country, Fitzsimmons began to get cold feet.

In early March the rebel leaders met secretly in Cleveland to plan a national wildcat strike. Whether Fitzsimmons got word of that or not, he responded to the growing dissension among the membership by demanding an increase of $2.50 an hour.

The union came under public pressure, too, when in late March Brian Ross, a correspondent from Cleveland's WKYC-TV, broadcast a five-part series, ''The Teamsters,'' on NBC Nightly News. An Emmy and DuPont Award winner for a similar telecast in Cleveland the year before, Ross portrayed the IBT with unsparing accuracy. Charging that Ross and NBC had ''cleverly staged . . . an attempt to interfere with the . . . master freight negotiations,'' the angry union leaders filed a complaint with the Federal Communications Commission for the network's alleged ''distortions, halftruths, and out-and-out lies.'' NBC stood behind Ross and his work, and the FCC dismissed the complaint.

''Fitzsimmons knew that the momentum had turned against him,'' says Ken Paff, TDC's official spokesman. ''He knew what he was doing when he asked for the $2.50 per hour increase in pay; management would never accept it, and that gave him grounds to call a strike himself. That was the only way he could undercut us. He knew that we were ready to wildcat and had the support to pull it off.''

At midnight on March 31, the expiration date of the three-year contract, Fitzsimmons slowed the rebels' momentum and shocked the country by calling a nationwide strike—the first in the union's history. The strike lasted for two and a half days, ending with a settlement of $1.65 an hour plus the cost-of-living increases the dissidents had insisted upon.

''Was the 1976 Teamster strike contrived? You bet it was!'' says an IBT official. ''It was the best stage-managed strike in the history of this nation. We knew that wildcats in 1967 and 1970 had lasted for months because of the actions of a handful of rebels. In 1976, however, we faced a problem we had never faced before: namely, the rank and file was actually listening to groups like PROD . . . and TDC. So to avert a strike that could last for several months, with all that went with it—the economic losses and the violence—everyone around the bargaining table just winked at each other and suffered through a more acceptable three-day strike. We thought the rebels would be appeased and we'd never hear from them again.''

The IBT's gamble paid off. Although TDC tried to prolong the strike with isolated wildcatting, only its Detroit chapter could muster the strength to remain shut down. The reason for the success in Detroit was twofold. First, Local 299 president Dave Johnson placed minimal pressure on the dissidents to end the strike; and second, the Detroit TDC was led by a big, brooding dock steward, Pete Camarata, a man of strength and a member of Local 299.

Camarata was a former member of the Hoffa/Johnson-supported Action for Concerned Teamsters, a local dissident group that grew out of the organization that planned testimonial dinners for Hoffa. When TDC was formed in August 1975, ACT decided not to affiliate and gradually evolved into an underground organization, Action Rank-and-File. After repeated efforts by McMaster's men to infiltrate the group, ARF closed its membership, accepting new affiliates only after they were recommended by two members.

Deciding that he had graduated from college fraternity politics, Camarata and other former ACT and ARF members joined TDC in November 1975 and helped organize a membership drive in Detroit.

Already respected by local union officials and the rank and file, Camarata led the wildcat strike in Detroit after the IBT's brief and ''staged'' strike.

''Dave Johnson was friendly with us and didn't step into the strike,'' Camarata explains. ''So, really, there wasn't any leadership in Detroit which could counter us.

''Certainly we were happy with the money concessions the union had received for us during their final bargaining session. But, especially in Detroit, we were concerned about the noneconomic issues, the grievance procedure and the hospitalization plan. These were our biggest problems.''

Communicating via their CB radios, Camarata and his supporters kept the trucking industry in Detroit shut down for nearly five days.

They went back to work only when it became obvious that their demands would not be met and that the rest of the country was not ready to follow their lead.

When the rebels decided to wildcat, Camarata had been compelled by union law to resign his post as a shop steward: union representatives cannot participate in unauthorized strikes. In retaliation for the strike his employer used Camarata's resignation as an indication that he had quit his job as well. But for Dave Johnson, the company's action might well have brought on another wildcat strike. Johnson stepped into the picture on Camarata's behalf, ordering his business agents to persuade the company to reverse its decision on the rebel. "And after that I called Pete's boss and repeated that I wanted him put back to work. He had been a good Hoffa supporter and was trying to help the membership. I didn't want him hurt in any way."

That summer, when Local 299 was in danger of being put in trusteeship, Camarata led a rank-and-file demonstration at the union hall in support of Johnson's insistence on local autonomy and against IBT intervention in Local 299's affairs.

After the wildcat strike eight TDC leaders were elected to Local 299's twenty-one-member delegation to the IBT convention, to be held in Las Vegas June 14–17. And as a result of Johnson's and Wendell's decisions not to attend, two other dissidents, elected as alternates, became delegates.

And so it happened that the only reformers at the 1976 convention were from the home local of both Jimmy Hoffa and Frank Fitzsimmons—and that they made up nearly half of the 299 delegation.

On May 28, two weeks before the convention, PROD was in the headlines with a searing report on the IBT. "Teamster Democracy and Financial Responsibility? A Financial and Structural Analysis," the result of a ten-month study by John Sikorski, was published to explain to the Teamster rank and file "how and why the Teamsters Union worked the way it did, just who ran it, and how their dues money was spent," according to Arthur Fox.

Based upon public information—newspaper clippings, the IBT constitution, local and regional by-laws, and especially the local unions' own annual reports filed with the Department of Labor—PROD's indictment pointed out that union government

does not flow uphill from the rank-and-file to their top officials. Rather, the IBT leaders derive their sweeping authority from the Union's constitution and various by-laws which the rank-and-file are virtually unable to touch.

As a result, the rank-and-file and their relatively few honest officials are captives of the Union's top brass.[5]

Through its examination of Labor Department reports, PROD had learned that during 1974

> seventeen Teamster officials were reported by the Union to have received more than $100,000. A dozen topped $120,000 while several approached the $200,000 mark," according to Fox. "All told, at least 147 Teamster officials took in more than $40,000 during 1974, according to the Union's own reported information. By way of contrast, I. W. Abel, head of the nation's second-largest union, was the object of scorching criticism by reformers in the Steelworkers Union for hauling in $75,000 in 1974. Leonard Woodcock of the UAW received only $62,500, while Floyd Smith, head of the million-member IAM, received only 46,500 that year. No official in the UMW makes as much as $40,000.[6]

Speaking for his union associates, Jackie Presser responded, "We will go along with the philosophy of private business, which is, basically: if you have a demanding executive job with major responsibilities, you should be appropriately rewarded for performance."[7]

The timing of the PROD report was bad news for the Teamsters Union. The IBT was being disrupted by its own membership at the same time the government was investigating, among other things, the Hoffa disappearance and corruption in the union's pension, and health and welfare funds. On June 5, nine days before the IBT convention opened, the Senate Permanent Investigations Subcommittee reported that organized crime had infiltrated several Teamster locals via a bogus mob-controlled life insurance plan.

"It isn't easy to find a truckdriver or freight loader who will say a good word about the leadership of President Frank E. Fitzsimmons," Jon Kwitny wrote in the *Wall Street Journal*. "And yet the Fitzsimmons slate is considered a shoo-in for reelection at the teamster convention in Las Vegas in June."[8]

Knowing that Kwitny was right but still hoping to make a respectable showing, leaders of the TDC met in June to change its name to Teamsters for a Democratic Union, and to map strategy for its delegates from Local 299. Since they would be the lone reform advocates at the convention, the burden of articulating the rebels' concerns was entirely theirs. Meanwhile, Arthur Fox drafted five constitutional amendments for presentation at the convention.

The proposals requested a ceiling on the salaries of union officials;

mandatory expulsion for convicted extortionists; that the union provide each member with a copy of its constitution; direct rank-and-file
election of the IBT president and general executive board; and separate
ratification by those affected of contract addenda applying only to particular groups of members. In short, the rebels were asking for rules
consistent with those of most American labor organizations.

On the opening day of the convention, Fitzsimmons gave his own
opinion of the union reform movement—one that was shared by most
of the 2254 delegates. ''Yes, we have had setbacks; we'll have them in
the future, possibly,'' Fitzsimmons shouted into the microphone.
''But for those who would say that it's time to reform this organization, that it is time that the officers quit selling out the membership of
their union, I say to them: Go to Hell!''

Amidst delegates' cheers of support for Fitzsimmons the convention
loudly voted down the rebels' resolutions and gave its officers a 25 percent pay increase while, incredibly enough, raising the monthly membership dues by 33 percent.

Saving his strongest wrath for Arthur Fox and PROD, Fitzsimmons
asked in his report to the delegates:

> Who in the hell appointed them to act as the Teamster conscience . . . This
> self-styled saviour of the Teamsters, Arthur Fox, Esquire—he is a lawyer,
> you know—really never worked at a craft which entitled him to a Teamster
> or any other trade union membership. He got out of school, went to work
> for the Labor Department [sic], then went to work for Ralph Nader. Ralph
> Nader—you know his background. He became a success because he said
> everything was unsafe.

Without responding to the charges in the PROD report—which
were derived primarily from the union's own reports—Fitzsimmons
wrapped up his attack on the rebels by saying: ''And I promise you, as
long as I have a drop of breath in my body, no damned communist
group is ever going to infiltrate this union!''

The delegates jumped to their feet and exploded into an ovation. The
ten rebel delegates from Local 299 sat quietly in their seats.

But redbaiting the dissidents wasn't enough. One had to be made an
example of. On June 16, the day Jimmy Hoffa had hoped to complete
his successful comeback, Frank Fitzsimmons was reelected president.
Because he was unopposed, Fitzsimmons was listed in the record as
receiving the unanimous vote of all 2254 delegates—though most of

the Local 299 rebels abstained. After the election of the sixteen vice presidents, the three trustees, and the general secretary-treasurer—all by acclamation—the third day of the IBT convention ended.

Pete Camarata left the convention center, alone at first. Then several colleagues in the rebel army joined him and walked him to his car behind the building. Had it not been for the small crowd surrounding him, Camarata would have been killed right then.

The rest of the story is told by an associate of Robert Tillman, who was one of the gunmen. Sitting in a car parked nearby were Tillman and three men, all members of Local 5 in Baton Rouge, who had been "hired to ambush and murder the dissident leader." They had been brought to Las Vegas for the single purpose of killing Camarata. Although they were not elected delegates, their expenses were picked up by Chuck O'Brien, who supplied each of them with a .38 automatic. Tillman says he is not certain who had ordered O'Brien to handle the murder contract.

According to a witness, O'Brien handed Tillman the revolver, and "Chuck was wiping his fingerprints off the gun when I walked in. He handed it to Tillman and said, 'Go do it.'

"I then asked Tillman what O'Brien wanted him to do, and he told me that he and three other men were supposed to kill Camarata."

Because of the number of people with Camarata on the evening he was supposed to be killed, the hired assassins balked and simply left the area. Unaware of what had happened, Camarata attended the final plenary session of the convention the next day and immediately began to upset Fitzsimmons again by asking for clarification about the results of the election for IBT general president. When Fitzsimmons told him he had been unanimously elected even though there were abstentions, Camarata barked into a floor microphone, "I have to say right now for an old friend of mine—that you haven't seen for almost a year now—that he wouldn't like it if there wasn't at least one dissenting vote at this convention. And I would like to go on record now to say that you have it."

Steaming with anger, Fitzsimmons shouted back that the vote would stand as recorded the previous day.

At the end of the session the IBT general executive board announced that it was inviting all delegates to a cocktail party at the Aladdin Hotel after the convention adjourned. Camarata defiantly attended the party, along with two other dissidents.

"We were walking around, talking to whoever would talk to us, when some guy tried to take a slug at me," Camarata says. "A sergeant-at-arms during the convention, whom I had kind of become friendly with, rushed over and told the guy not to start anything. But then everyone in the place seemed to be concerned for our safety. One delegate from Cleveland came up to us and asked if we wanted to leave; he said he'd protect us on our way out. I told them we didn't need it."

At the urging of his associates, Bob Combs and Steve Kindred, Camarata started toward the door with them. There they were quickly surrounded by several bruisers. "One of them stopped me and said he wanted to shake my hand," says Camarata. "We started talking while Combs and Kindred went on ahead. Then, just as I turned around and went out the door, I got it."

Tillman and his three friends from Baton Rouge raced up behind Camarata and knocked him unconscious, and after the union reformer fell to the pavement his assailants began kicking him in the head. Tillman had the gun tucked inside his boot but did not draw it.

Hearing the commotion, Kindred whirled and saw his colleague being beaten: "I ran over and drop kicked one of the guys who was beating Pete up," Kindred remembers. "Just then one of the IBT security squad came running out of the hotel and started kicking me too. That's when I dislocated my shoulder." Combs also darted into the brawl, but Tillman grabbed him before he could do any damage.

Frank Fitzsimmons, who was watching the fray with two of his assistants, sent his bodyguard, an ex-football player and a member of Detroit's Local 337, into the action. Swinging at Combs, the ex-jock cracked Tillman with a hard right hook and bloodied his mouth. After swearing at Fitzsimmons' bodyguard, Tillman and his associates fled, with two local hotel security guards in hot pursuit. Tillman ducked alone into an alley, crouched, and pulled out his revolver, resting it on his arm and ready to open fire. Then, second guessing himself, Tillman stuffed the gun back into his boot before the guards saw it. The guards grabbed Tillman and took him to the hotel security office. In the confusion somebody found a wheelchair for Camarata, and he, Combs, and Kindred went into the same office. As they drew the attention of the guards and the lone Las Vegas police officer called to the scene, Tillman took the revolver out of his boot and shoved it inside the sofa he was sitting on. He claims that he later told O'Brien how he had disposed of the gun.

Camarata says that "the man from Louisiana" (Camarata never

learned his name) claimed to the police officer that Camarata had started the fight. Other witnesses insisted that Tillman and his chums were the aggressors and that Frank Fitzsimmons could verify it. One of Presser's men drew the policeman aside, and after their conversation the officer decided not to press charges against anyone. He tore up his police report in front of everyone in the room, and suggested that they all leave town immediately.

"We asked for protection but never got it," Camarata says. "We were just told to get out while we still could."

The assault in front of the Aladdin capped a week of despair for the union reform movement. Perhaps it was foreshadowed by the keynote speech four days earlier by Secretary of Labor William J. Usery, who praised Fitzsimmons and the IBT general executive board as "outstanding representatives for the rank-and-file . . . Let me assure you [the convention delegates] that even though I don't have a Teamster card, I belong to this club because I believe in it."

At the time of Usery's remarks the Labor Department was considering criminal prosecutions against the sixteen trustees of the IBT's $1.4 billion Central States Pension Fund. All sixteen trustees were later forced to resign and the pension fund's fiduciary responsibility was temporarily given to other insurance companies. The sixteen trustees were immediately replaced by their individual heirs apparent, who still maintained considerable influence over the fund's administration, but the Labor Department nevertheless considered the procedures "reform measures."

One of the few mentions of Jimmy Hoffa's name at the convention had come on opening day, when the delegates passed a resolution expressing their "deepest sorrow and regret" at his disappearance. Anthony Provenzano supported the measure. His grief, however, was probably for his own problems.

Ever since he had been implicated in Hoffa's murder by government investigators—who didn't yet have the evidence to indict him for the crime—Provenzano had been the target of one of the most intensive investigations in FBI and Strike Force history. The resulting information had led to Provenzano's eventual conviction for extortion, and within a week after the convention he was to be charged with ordering the kidnapping and murder of the union rebel Anthony Castellito in 1961. He would be convicted two years later and sent to jail for life. Also in June 1976 Tony Giacalone was convicted of tax fraud and sentenced to ten years in prison. Salvatore Briguglio, Provenzano's union associate and the man named by the government as Hoffa's actual killer, was also indicted for Castellito's murder but he never came to trial. Twenty-two months later, standing outside a New York restaurant, he was approached by two men who knocked him to the sidewalk and pumped five bullets into his head and a sixth into his chest.

A month before he was murdered Briguglio reflected upon his embattled career. "I've got no regrets," he said, "except for getting involved in this whole mess with the government. If they want you, you're theirs . . . I have no aspirations any more; I've gone as far as I can go in this union. There's nothing left."

When he heard of Briguglio's murder, Chuck O'Brien probably worried a little more. Thought to be the only person who could finger Hoffa's killers without directly incriminating himself, he too was being muscled by the government. Soon after the convention he was indicted, convicted, and sentenced to a year in prison for labor extortion. Upping the ante even higher for his testimony, the government later convicted him for filing a fraudulent bank loan application. O'Brien remained free, still an IBT general organizer while he appealed both sentences. Similar pressure fell on Gabe Briguglio and Tom Andretta.

A sergeant-at-arms at the convention, Frank Sheeran supported the Hoffa hearts-and-flowers resolution. But because he was a suspected witness to the Hoffa murder, the ax fell on him too. Two years later he was charged with tax fraud because of a leased car which he had claimed as a business expense. The government believes this was the same car Sheeran used to drive Russell Bufalino into Detroit on the day Hoffa disappeared—and it may also have been the car used to pick up Hoffa's killers at the airport.

Russell Bufalino was also in trouble with the law. Within three months after the convention he was indicted for a New York extortion scheme. A year later he was convicted and received a four-year sentence, which he appealed.

Up to mid-1978, only Rolland McMaster had escaped prosecution. The Strike Force unit in Pittsburgh, which was studying his activities while he was head of the 1972–74 organizing task force, was disbanded by the Justice Department before any indictments were handed down.

Looking back over the years, however, McMaster has become pessimistic. "Right now the Teamsters Union is a powerful organization and a good organization," he says. "There may have been some poor judgments in some of the investments of our pension fund, but we're being chopped up because we took a definite position, supporting certain political people. Every time this happens, we get chopped up. I've watched us for some forty years now. At one time we were the bosses here in Detroit and Michigan; and, truthfully, we got a lot of governors elected. We put in prosecutors, judges, and everyone else. Our world was going good.

"Then Dave Beck got mixed up with Eisenhower, so the Democrats started chopping us up because we were too ignorant to get along with them.

"You can't believe what's happened to us. And now we're getting chopped up again. It's just like an FBI agent told me. He said, 'Mac, until we get to the bottom of the Watergate thing, the Nixon deal, and Hoffa's disappearance, we're going to hurt everybody.' "

Perhaps McMaster is right. For the first time since the Kennedy Administration union reformers are beginning to believe that the government is actually on their side. Encouraged by the Justice Department's dedication to cleaning up the IBT through litigation, the Teamster rebels are gaining an increasing understanding of themselves and their potential. Their small victories are becoming larger and more significant. Fundamental institutional changes in the structure of their union may be years away, but dissident groups are finding their support and membership rolls growing daily. Every time a rank-and-filer loses a grievance because his company has a sweetheart contract with the union, or a retiree can't get his benefits because his pension fund has been depleted by the underworld, the reform movement has a chance to pick up another crusader. And that means more job security and physical protection for other rebels.

Progress is being made, but there is still a great need for a "clean sweep." Many of those with the interests of the rank and file at heart hope the rebels will decide—as The Voice and DUOC did in the 1960s and FASH did in the 1970s—that decertification from the IBT is the best answer to their problems, at least in certain corrupt locals. However, establishing a new union or affiliating with another one is as complicated as it is dangerous. It will demand the sacrifice of seniority and of claims to whatever pension money is left, and it will undoubtedly bring on more broken heads and broken lives. To the underworld the Teamsters Union still represents billions of dollars in rank-and-file money, and the union, which is still under criminal control, will fight hard to preserve itself. Reform has been tried by a lot of good people for many years, but Jimmy Hoffa's "uncontrollable monster" is not susceptible to meaningful reform from within.

Today, as frustrated rebels analyze their limited options, the mob continues to flourish. Through both its quasi-legitimate and wholly illicit enterprises, organized crime—even by the most conservative government estimates—nets ten times more money annually than Exxon, the largest corporation in the United States.[9] Although the Teamster investigations have spilled over to shake the underworld's subculture, there is little chance of neutralizing its power without the full commitment and cooperation of the executive, legislative, and judicial branches of all levels of government.

This is certainly nothing new. The Kefauver Committee tried to warn us back in the early 1950s; Robert Kennedy was a latter-day prophet who put words into action and government programs. But after President Kennedy was assassinated, the general public was distracted from the problem. Years of war, domestic strife, and Richard Nixon left the country less surprised, less outraged, by gangland activities. Mobsters became civil libertarians, delivering their discourses on the horrors of government-authorized buggings and wiretaps. Hollywood exploited the situation; Christ figure Don Vito Corleone died for our sins and won an Academy Award.

Ironically, the impetus for union reform and the concern about organized crime that developed in the late 1970s was the disappearance of Jimmy Hoffa.

So then: Why did the mob, in the person of one of its most powerful chieftains, Russell Bufalino, order the killing of Jimmy Hoffa—as the government believes? What did Hoffa know or what was he going to do that made his elimination necessary?

Was it because, as many have theorized, Hoffa meant to recapture power in the Teamsters Union and wreak havoc on the order imposed by the mob—an ambition that seemed highly unlikely to be fulfilled, given Hoffa's estrangement from the centers of power?

Or is an answer to be found in the consistent cast of characters that threaded its way through Hoffa's life—and through fifteen years of American political violence? The men implicated in his murder were the same men whose names have appeared over and over again in the plots to kill Castro and Kennedy: Trafficante, Bufalino, Marcello, and Provenzano. There is therefore considerable reason to believe that Hoffa was removed for reasons more complicated than mere ambition —especially if his murder is seen in the context of the murder of Sam Giancana a month earlier and of John Rosselli thirteen months later.

Both were mobsters; both had been intimately involved with the Castro plots; both were summoned to testify before Congress on their roles in the plots.

Ironically enough, attorney William Bufalino, when I talked with him on October 25, 1976, may have inadvertently pointed a finger in the right direction. He was attempting to suggest that the mob had nothing to do with Hoffa's murder, preferring to shift the blame onto the government, but he put it this way: ''Tell the FBI to look into the CIA. And tell the CIA to look into the FBI. *Then* you'll have the answer [to the Hoffa case].'' And he added that it was his belief that Hoffa's murder was related to those of Giancana and Rosselli.

''We've got this horrendous maze of information about what is probably the most sensitive and ominous thing we ever dredged up on the Church Committee: the CIA's use of some of the nation's most dangerous Mafia leaders to plot the assassination of Fidel Castro,'' says a senator who is on the Senate Select Committee investigating alleged assassination plots against foreign leaders. ''This mysterious area of organized crime and intelligence activity was deliberately concealed from the Warren Commission.''

A congressman serving on the House Select Committee investigating the assassination of President John F. Kennedy says, ''The greatest difficulty will remain [in] conceiving of someone or some group who could have pulled it off and gotten away with it for so long, if in fact Oswald did not do it alone . . . It's a monstrous question: not just who the hell could have done such a thing, but who the hell could have had the power, and, beyond that, the ability to do it and not get caught . . . Who, if anyone, in the early sixties had that capability?''

A senior Justice Department official sums it up: ''What you're talking about when you speak of a purported Kennedy conspiracy—beyond someone with both an absolutely murderous and consuming rage toward President Kennedy's being in the White House, and a strong conviction that the government could be effectively altered through killing JFK—is a conspirator or conspirators who would have had an enormous ability (and no doubt considerable past experience) in not just evading but, more important, short-circuiting the standard investigative resources of the federal government . . . You'd be talking about someone who knew Washington—Washington power, politics—awfully well; someone with money . . . and, of course, someone with some underlings who were awfully damn disciplined. Someone who thought his most threatening enemies had to be killed . . . ''

Welcome back, Jimmy Hoffa.

Reference Notes

CHAPTER 2

Rebel Hoffa

1. According to authorities on the subject of organized crime, many underworld leaders wanted to stop the mob wars because these wars brought public attention to their enterprises, which conflicted with the primary purpose of making money. The actual date of the commission's formation is generally placed in 1934, after two meetings, attended by the nation's top mobsters, in New York and Kansas City. Al Capone's former boss, John Torrio, was one of the key figures in the transition to the ''Americanized'' version of the mob.

2. ABC News Close-up, ''Hoffa,'' November 30, 1974.

3. James R. Hoffa (as told to Donald I. Rogers), *The Trials of Jimmy Hoffa* (Chicago: Henry Regnery Co., 1970), p. 160.

4. Frank Cormier and William J. Eaton, *Reuther* (Englewood Cliffs, N.J.: Prentice-Hall, 1970), p. 107.

5. *Ibid.*, p. 85.

6. ABC News Close-Up, *op. cit.*

7. Farrell Dobbs, *Teamster Politics* (New York: Monad Press, 1975), p. 243.

8. *Ibid.*, pp. 247–248.

9. ABC News Close-up, *op. cit.*

CHAPTER 3

The Oppressed Become the Oppressors

1. *Detroit Free Press*, September 5, 1941.

2. *Ibid*.

3. *Ibid.*, September 13, 1941.

4. McClellan Committee Hearings, p. 13638.

5. Rodney Campbell, *The Luciano Project* (New York: McGraw Hill, 1977), p. 180.

6. The two women were on the payroll for eight months, receiving $6000 for no work.

7. Peter Maas, *The Valachi Papers* (New York: Bantam Books, 1972), pp. 174–175.

8. James R. Hoffa (as told to Oscar Fraley), *Hoffa: The Real Story* (New York: Stein and Day, 1975), p. 118.

9. McClellan Committee, Report No. 621, pp. 153–155.

10. McClellan Committee Hearings, p. 13127.

11. McClellan Committee, Report No. 621, p. 286.

12. Kefauver Hearings, Second Interim Report, p. 4.

13. *Ibid.*

14. Investigation of Racketeering in the Detroit Area, Joint Subcommittee Report, 1954, pp. 2, 4.

15. *Ibid.*, pp. 5–6.

16. McClellan Committee, Report No. 621, pp. 89–93.

17. Investigation of Welfare Funds and Racketeering, Report of a Special Subcommittee to the Committee on Education and Labor, 1954, p. 6.

18. *Ibid.*, p. 7.

19. *Ibid.*, p. 5.

CHAPTER 4

Stacked Decks and Dirty Deals

1. McClellan Committee, Report No. 1417, p. 241.

2. *Ibid.*, pp. 224–227.

3. *Ibid.*, p. 244.

4. *Ibid.*, pp. 244–245.

5. *Ibid.*, p. 247.

6. McClellan Committee Hearings, pp. 5356–5358.

7. *Ibid.*, p. 15957.

8. *Ibid.*, pp. 15971–15974.

9. McClellan Committee, Report No. 621, pp. 54–56.

10. Robert F. Kennedy, *The Enemy Within* (New York: Popular Library, 1960), p. 48.

11. James R. Hoffa (as told to Oscar Fraley) *Hoffa: The Real Story* (New York: Stein and Day, 1975), pp. 94–95.

12. Kennedy, *op. cit.*, p. 62.

13. According to Walter Sheridan in *The Fall and Rise of Jimmy Hoffa* (New York: Saturday Review Press, 1972, pp. 33–34), "Halfway through the trial a Negro newspaper, featuring a front page pro-Hoffa article and a picture of Hoffa's Negro defense attorney, Martha Jefferson, was delivered to the homes of the black jurors [of whom there were eight]. When the matter was brought to the attention of Judge Burnita Matthews, she was outraged and immediately locked up the jury. Then, near the end of the trial, on the day Hoffa took the witness stand, Joe Louis, the former heavyweight champion, walked into the courtroom and put his arm around Hoffa in the presence of the jurors. His appearance had been arranged by Barney Baker (a Central Conference organizer from Washington, D.C.) and Paul Dorfman."

14. Walter Sheridan, *The Fall and Rise of Jimmy Hoffa* (New York: Saturday Review Press, 1972), p. 204.

15. McClellan Committee, Report No. 1417, p. 167.

16. McClellan Committee Hearings, p. 5252.

17. McClellan Committee, Report No. 1139, p. 684.

CHAPTER 5
The Enemy Within

1. McClellan Committee Hearings, p. 5288.
2. *Ibid.*, pp. 5355–5356.
3. *Ibid.*, p. 5358.
4. *Ibid.*, pp. 5579–5604.
5. McClellan Committee, Interim Report No. 1417, 85th Congress, 2nd Session, p. 254, 450.
6. James R. Hoffa (as told to Oscar Fraley), *Hoffa: The Real Story* (New York: Stein and Day, 1975), p. 145.
7. James R. Hoffa (as told to Donald I. Rogers), *The Trials of Jimmy Hoffa* (Chicago: Henry Regnery Co., 1970), p. 160.
8. McClellan Committee Hearings, p. 11213–11214.
9. McClellan Committee, Report No. 1139, p. 487–488.
10. *Ibid.*, p. 509.
11. McClellan Committee Hearings, pp. 13486–13487.
12. *Ibid.*, p. 17469.
13. *Ibid.*, p. 17619.
14. McClellan Committee, Report No. 621, pp. 23–25.
15. *Ibid.*, p. 110.
16. Victor S. Navasky, *Kennedy Justice* (New York: Atheneum, 1971), p. 44
17. McClellan Committee, Report No. 1139, p. 717.
18. McClellan Committee Hearings, p. 19437.
19. *Ibid.*, p. 15953.
20. *Ibid.*, pp. 19786–19787.
21. *Ibid.*, p. 19789.
22. *Ibid.*, pp. 16112–16113.
23. *Ibid.*, pp. 17847–17848.
24. McClellan Committee, Report No. 621, p. 206.
25. Hoffa (as told to Rogers), *op. cit.*, p. 165.
26. McClellan Committee, Report No. 1139, pp. 724–725.
27. Robert F. Kennedy, *The Enemy Within* (New York: Popular Library, 1960), p. 159.

CHAPTER 6
The Making of Two Presidents and One Angel

1. Mickey Cohen (as told to John Peer Nugent), *Mickey Cohen: In My Own Words* (Englewood Cliffs: Prentice-Hall, 1975), p. 233.
2. Vincent Teresa (with Thomas C. Renner), *My Life in the Mafia* (Garden City, N.Y.: Doubleday, 1973), p. 308.
3. Walter Sheridan, *The Fall and Rise of Jimmy Hoffa* (New York: Saturday Review Press, 1972), pp. 141–142.
4. *The International Teamster*, September 1960.
5. James R. Hoffa (as told to Oscar Fraley), *Hoffa: The Real Story* (New York: Stein and Day, 1975), pp. 149–150.
6. Victor S. Navasky, *Kennedy Justice* (New York: Atheneum, 1971), p. 394.

7. Clark R. Mollenhoff, *Tentacles of Power: The Story of Jimmy Hoffa* (Cleveland: World Publishing Co., 1965), p. 343.

8. The indictment was handed down in June 1976. Provenzano was convicted and sentenced to life imprisonment in June 1978.

CHAPTER 7

Teaming Up Against Castro

1. Hank Messick, *Lansky* (New York: G. P. Putnam's Sons, 1971), p. 210.

2. McClellan Committee Hearings, p. 7416.

3. Ralph and Esther James, *Hoffa and the Teamsters* (Princeton, N.J.: D. Van Nostrand and Company, Inc., 1965), pp. 62–63; quoted in Victor S. Navasky's *Kennedy Justice* (New York: Atheneum, 1971), p. 410.

4. William Scott Malone, ''The Secret Life of Jack Ruby,'' *New Times*, January 23, 1978, p. 48.

5. McClellan Committee, Report No. 621, p. 14.

6. ''Alleged Assassination Plots Involving Foreign Leaders,'' Report No. 94–465, p. 92 (hereafter referred to as Church Committee Report).

7. *Ibid.*, p. 93.

8. Howard Kohn, ''The Hughes-Nixon-Lansky Connection: The Secret Alliances of the CIA from World War II to Watergate,'' *Rolling Stone*, May 20, 1976.

9. Church Committee, Report No. 94–465, p. 110.

10. *Ibid.*, p. 72.

11. *Ibid.*

12. The Siragusa story was first reported in Jack Anderson's column on January 4, 1978. Mr. Siragusa provided further details for this book.

13. Church Committee, Report No. 94–465, p. 74.

14. *Ibid.*

15. *Ibid.*, p. 75.

16. *Time*, June 9, 1975.

17. *Ibid.*

18. *Ibid.*

19. Charles Crimaldi (as told to John Kidner), *Crimaldi: Contract Killer* (Washington, D.C.: Acropolis Books Ltd., 1976), p. 218.

20. Church Committee, Report No. 94–465, p. 97.

21. *Ibid.*, p. 77.

22. *Ibid.*, p. 79.

23. *Ibid.*, p. 120.

24. Kenneth P. O'Donnell and David F. Powers, *Johnny, We Hardly Knew Ye* (New York: Simon and Schuster, 1973), p. 312.

25. Haynes Johnson, *The Bay of Pigs* (New York: W. W. Norton, 1964), p. 76.

26. Theodore C. Sorenson, *Kennedy* (New York: Bantam Books, 1966), p. 335.

27. Church Committee, Report No. 94–465, p. 126.

28. *Ibid.*, p. 128.

29. *Papers of the Presidents*, John F. Kennedy (1961), p. 724.

30. Church Committee, Report No. 94-465, p. 139.

31. *Ibid.*, pp. 139–148.

32. *Ibid.*, p. 102.

33. *Ibid.*, p. 130.

34. *Ibid.*

35. *Ibid.*

36. *Ibid.*, pp. 131–132.

37. *Ibid.*, p. 133.

38. *Ibid.*

39. *Ibid.*, p. 132.

40. *Ibid.*, p. 133.

41. Judith Exner (as told to Ovid Demaris), *Judith Exner: My Story* (New York: Grove Press, Inc., 1977), p. 165. Further on in the book she described rendezvous with Kennedy after he became President. She named three of Kennedy's personal assistants who she said knew of the affair. All of them denied it.

42. Interview with Jimmy Hoffa by Jerry Stanecki, *Playboy*, December 1975.

43. U.S. Senate Committee on Government Operations, "Organized Crime and Illicit Traffic in Narcotics," hearings, p. 94.

44. Ed Reid, *The Grim Reapers* (Chicago: Henry Regnery Company, 1969), pp. 158–159.

45. *Ibid.*

46. George Crile III, "The Mafia, the CIA, and Castro," *Washington Post,* May 16, 1976. When asked during the research for this book *who* was making the arrangements, Aleman replied that Trafficante had "made it clear" that it was Hoffa.

CHAPTER 8
Coincidence or Conspiracy?

1. Walter Sheridan, *The Fall and Rise of Jimmy Hoffa* (New York: Saturday Review Press, 1972), p. 224.

2. James R. Hoffa (as told to Oscar Fraley), *Hoffa: The Real Story* (New York: Stein and Day, 1975), p. 157.

3. *New York Times*, November 20, 1962.

4. CBS interview with Hoffa, January 28, 1963; quoted in Victor Navasky's *Kennedy Justice* (New York: Atheneum, 1971), p. 430.

5. Navasky, *op. cit.*, p. 431.

6. Sheridan, *op. cit.*, p. 282.

7. On June 22, 1962, Partin was indicted for misuse of $1659 from Baton Rouge Local 5 funds. On September 25 he was charged with kidnaping; the charge grew out of a family quarrel involving the children of a divorced union friend whose wife had refused him visitation privileges. The kidnaping charge was dismissed as groundless, and the charge of embezzlement was also dropped later on. Obviously these legal problems had something to do with Partin's decision to step forward, but as Walter Sheridan points out, "all his information was reliable and was corroborated by an overwhelming amount of evidence."

8. Benjamin C. Bradlee, *Conversations with Kennedy* (New York: W. W. Norton, 1975), p. 131.

9. *Life*, May 15, 1964.

10. Senate Committee on Government Operations, Organized Crime and Illicit Traffic in Narcotics, Hearings, pp. 6–7.

11. *Life*, May 15, 1964.

12. Warren Commission Report, Exhibit 1268.

13. FBI interview with Paul Dorfman, December 18, 1963. Perhaps the strongest implication of a relationship between Hoffa and Ruby came in a personal conversation I had with Hoffa's son, James P. Hoffa, in Detroit on December 27, 1977. His law partner, Murray Chodak, was also

present. "I think my dad knew Jack Ruby, but from what I understand, he (Ruby) was the kind of guy everybody knew. So what?" Young Hoffa could not recall any specific information on which he based his opinion. In briefly discussing the possibility that his father might have been involved in President Kennedy's assassination, Hoffa said, "It doesn't make any sense. . . If my dad had decided to kill Kennedy, he would have gotten a gun, walked right up to him, and blew his brains out."

14. McClellan Committee, Report No. 621, p. 597.

15. *Ibid.*

16. Warren Commission Report, Exhibit 1184.

17. *Ibid.*, Exhibit 1202.

18. *Ibid.*, vol. 14, p. 444.

19. *Ibid.*

20. *Ibid.*, vol. 23, pp. 158–160.

21. CIA Memorandum of November 28, 1963, Document 206–83.

22. Sheridan, *op. cit.*, p. 138.

23. Robert F. Kennedy, *The Enemy Within* (New York: Popular Library, 1960), pp. 92–93. Baker also worked with Rolland McMaster and David Yaras in setting up Local 320 in Miami.

24. Sheridan, *op. cit.*, p. 292.

25. Warren Commission Report, Exhibit 2302.

26. Bell Telephone records in New Orleans, September 24, 1963; call from David W. Ferrie (524-0147) to Chicago, Illinois, 312 WH 4-4970. Amount, $3.85.

27. Peter Noyes, *Legacy of Doubt* (New York: Pinnacle Books, 1973), pp. 80–82.

28. Interview with Jimmy Hoffa by Abe Peck, *Gallery*, October 1973.

29. FBI interview with Leopoldo Ramos Ducos, December 2, 1963.

30. McClellan Committee Hearings, p. 15949.

31. Warren Commission Report, Exhibit 2980.

32. *Ibid.*

33. Warren Commission Report, vol. 5, p. 200.

34. *Ibid.*

35. Milton Viorst (with Michael Ewing), "The Mafia, the CIA and the Kennedy Assassination," *Washingtonian*, November 1975.

36. *The Official Warren Commission Report on the Assassination of President John F. Kennedy* (Garden City, N.Y.: Doubleday, 1964), p. 801.

37. *Ibid.*, pp. 785, 790.

38. Sheridan, *op. cit.*, p. 356. The question of whether or not the exceedingly hardbitten Chavez was capable of being involved in a Teamster plot to assassinate either John or Robert Kennedy became moot several years later. In February 1967 the FBI and the Justice Department received reliable reports that Chavez had recently been discussing killing Robert Kennedy, and on March 1, 1967, Chavez arrived in Washington with two of his men. Packing pistols, the three men went to the old Continental Hotel in downtown Washington. The D.C. Police Department began around-the-clock surveillance of their movements, with outside coordination from Jim McShane, then head of U.S. marshals. Police protection was also arranged for Senator Kennedy's home in Virginia.

Frank Mankiewicz, who was then Kennedy's press secretary, recalls the FBI's providing various photographs of Chavez and his men, to enable quick recognition if they came near the Senator or his Washington office: "We were looking for them. The Chavez assassination threat was regarded as very serious by those around Kennedy." But Mankiewicz says Kennedy viewed the matter in a characteristically fatalistic manner. "It was clear that Bob didn't want to talk about it."

The murder plan came to an end as quickly and impulsively as it had begun. As Sheridan and the FBI learned shortly thereafter, Jimmy Hoffa dressed down his high-strung subordinate and took away Chavez' pistol. "Give me that goddamn gun," he said. "The last thing we need is another investigation."

Several months later Chavez was mysteriously shot to death by one of his own Teamster body-guards. Tom Kennelly, who worked under Robert Kennedy on the McClellan Committee and later in the Justice Department, says, "His bodyguard just pulled out a gun and nailed him one day during an apparent argument. No one seemed to know what it was about, though."

Walter Sheridan was the first to report this murder plot against Robert Kennedy, in *The Fall and Rise of Jimmy Hoffa*, pp. 406–408.

CHAPTER 9
Mob Wars and Paper-Napkin Contracts

1. Clark R. Mollenhoff, *Tentacles of Power: The Story of Jimmy Hoffa* (Cleveland: World Publishing, 1965), p. 379.

2. ABC News Close-Up, "Hoffa," November 30, 1974.

3. Walter Sheridan, *The Fall and Rise of Jimmy Hoffa* (New York: Saturday Review Press, 1972), p. 390.

4. Church Committee, Report No. 94-465, p. 79.

5. Clark R. Mollenhoff, *Strike Force: Organized Crime and the Government* (Englewood Cliffs, N.J.: Prentice-Hall, 1972), p. 12.

6. *The Detroit News,* August 1, 1976.

7. Lester Velie, *Desperate Bargain: Why Jimmy Hoffa Had to Die* (New York: Reader's Digest Press, 1977), p. 73.

8. *The Detroit News*, August 1, 1976. The plot to kidnap Hoffa proposed by Anthony Zerilli and uncovered by the FBI apparently never went past the talking stage. Vincent Piersante writes the matter off as "just another ploy for the mob to extort money." Nevertheless, the episode was indicative of the loss of prestige Hoffa suffered with the local underworld because of the way he dealt with his wife's affair with Cimini.

9. Interview with Jimmy Hoffa by Jerry Stanecki, *Playboy,* December 1975.

10. Mollenhoff, *op. cit.*, p. 155.

11. *Playboy,* December 1975.

12. *Detroit News,* August 1, 1976.

13. Vincent Teresa (with Thomas C. Renner), *My Life in the Mafia* (Garden City, N.Y.: Doubleday, 1973), p. 4. Joseph Bonanno had disappeared from 1964 to 1966 in the midst of threats of mob reprisals and government prosecutions. Although staged to appear as a kidnap-ing, Ralph Salerno told me that Bonanno had been spotted after he had vanished and "was ob-viously moving independently. there didn't appear to be any restrictions on his movements." Theoretically, it was during this period of time that Bonanno formed his southern alliance with Marcello and Trafficante.

PART 2

CHAPTER 10
The 1967 Revolt

1. Soon after the strike ended, a private entrepreneur tried to capitalize on Kusley's "fame" among truckers. The man had formed an enterprise called the Truck Owners and Operators National Association and asked Kusley's permission to attend the next meeting of the protest committee. On November 4, 1967, the businessman told the committee about the deals he could get them for trucking equipment through his quasi-cooperative. Suspicious of the idea and of the man's reputation, the committee, including Kusley, voted down the proposal.

The story was later told by Kusley's enemies that he had been working with the TOONA enterprise for personal gain. Although the story was untrue, Kusley had lost his forum to defend himself. Since 1967 hundreds of steel haulers have believed the false story that Kusley sold them out. The evidence shows that this was not the case.

CHAPTER 11
Rebellion in Detroit

1. *Detroit Free Press,* January 20, 1962.
2. *Detroit Free Press,* September 30, 1969.

CHAPTER 12
Tremors and Explosions—
and a Week in the Life of a Steel Hauler

1. *Detroit News,* April 17, 1970.

CHAPTER 13
Averting the North-South Mob War

1. See William Turner and Jon Christian, *The Assassination of Robert F. Kennedy: A Searching Look at the Conspiracy and Cover-up* (New York: Random House, 1978).

2. Vincent Teresa (with Thomas C. Renner), *My Life in the Mafia* (Garden City, N.Y.: Doubleday, 1973), p. 4.

3. *Ibid.,* p. 307.

4. *Life,* September 15, 1966.

5. Clark R. Mollenhoff, *Game Plan for Disaster* (New York: W. W. Norton, 1976), p. 45.

6. *Ibid.,* p. 47.

7. Lester Velie, *Desperate Bargain: Why Jimmy Hoffa Had to Die* (New York: Reader's Digest Press, 1977), p. 135.

8. *Oakland Tribune,* September 21–28, 1969.

9. Mobster John Rosselli had interested Hughes' advisers in purchasing the Desert Inn, which was owned by Morris Dalitz. Hughes rented the top floor of the hotel from Thanksgiving 1966 to the end of the year. However, during the New Year's weekend, Dalitz, who was still the owner, wanted to rent Hughes's accommodations to the high-rolling customers who usually flocked to the casino at that time of year. Knowing that Dalitz wanted Hughes out, Robert Maheu called Washington attorney Edward Morgan and asked him to get in touch with Jimmy Hoffa. After this was done, Hoffa called Dalitz, asking as a "personal favor" that Hughes be allowed to stay. Dalitz later said that he was willing to do this for his "old friend" Jimmy Hoffa.

During my interview with Maheu he told me, "All Hoffa did was on the New Year's weekend . . . he got [Hughes] to stay [at the Desert Inn]. They wanted to put him out. Ed Morgan talked to Hoffa, and then Hoffa talked to Moe Dalitz. And they let him [Hughes] stay the weekend."

Hughes purchased the Desert Inn in March 1967. Morgan received a $150,000 finder's fee and gave $50,000 of it to Rosselli.

10. Deposition of Michael Lewis Boano, United States Steel Corporation, et al., vs. Fraternal Association of Steel Haulers a/k/a Fraternal Association of Special Haulers, et al., in the United States District Court for the Western District of Pennsylvania (Pittsburgh), Civil Action No. 70-418.

CHAPTER 14
"Free Hoffa!"

1. On the basis of U.S. District Judge L. Clure Morton's earlier ruling that Fitzsimmons did not have the constitutional authority to place Don Vestal's Local 327 in trusteeship, Vestal claimed, in this second suit, that Fitzsimmons did not have the power to convene an IBT convention.

2. James R. Hoffa (as told to Oscar Fraley), *Hoffa: The Real Story* (New York: Stein and Day, 1975). p. 213.

3. To comply with Judge Green's ruling, the IBT constitution committee asked that the delegates pass a resolution insisting that specific constitutional changes for membership ratification be preceeded by a petition demanding that right signed by 10 percent of the union's two million members. Within seconds of the passage of that resolution, the delegates passed another, to appeal Green's decision and to revoke any language referring to a rank-and-file constitutional referendum.

4. *Wall Street Journal*, July 22, 1975.

5. *Washington Post*, December 2, 1973.

6. *Detroit News*, December 24, 1971.

7. *Detroit News*, January 13, 1975.

8. *Detroit News*, December 24, 1971.

CHAPTER 15
The McMaster Task Force and the Nixon Plumbers

1. Ralph Nader and Kate Blackwell, *You and Your Pension* (New York: Grossman Publishers, 1973), p. 41.

2. Walter Sheridan, *The Fall and Rise of Jimmy Hoffa* (New York: Saturday Review Press, 1972), pp. xvi-xvii.

3. Jeff Gerth, "Richard M. Nixon and Organized Crime," *Penthouse*, July 1974. The Illinois Legislative Commission quoted a federal investigator as saying the case against Richard Fitzsimmons was dropped because of the "love affair" between Fitzsimmons and the White House.

4. *Seattle Post-Intelligencer*, May 28, 1972.

5. Jack Anderson syndicated column, May 3, 1973.

6. *Newsday*, January 16, 1975.

7. *Local 299 News*, October 1972.

8. ABC News Close-up, "Hoffa," November 30, 1974.

9. Senate Select Committee on Presidential Campaign Activities (Watergate Committee), Hearings, vol. 3, pp. 982, 983.

10. White House Transcripts, March 21, 1973 (10:12–11:15 A.M.).

11. *Manchester Union Leader,* April 27, 1973.

12. *Washington Post,* June 7, 1974.

13. *Time,* August 8, 1977.

14. *Ibid.*

CHAPTER 16

Rebel Hoffa and the 1974 Shutdown

1. Immediately after the strike ended, fourteen owner-operator groups, including FASH, formed the National Independent Truckers' Unity Committee and chose Hill as its national chairman.

2. *Overdrive,* March 1974.

3. *Detroit Free Press,* February 6, 1974.

4. I uncovered the story of the McMaster task force in August 1975. Three months later I was hired by the *Detroit Free Press* to complete the investigation. While with the *Free Press* I worked with staff reporters Jo Thomas and Ralph Orr. Our story was published June 20, 1976. Frank Fitzsimmons, through his attorney, was told of our findings before publication. He took no disciplinary action against McMaster then or after the story was published.

5. *Detroit Free Press,* April 18, 1977. The series ran April 10-12 and 14-17, 1974.

CHAPTER 17

The Blank Check

1. *Los Angeles Times,* February 16, 1974.

2. *Detroit News,* February 24, 1974.

3. ABC News Close-up, ''Hoffa,'' November 30, 1974.

4. *Cleveland Plain Dealer,* June 16, 1974.

5. *Detroit News,* June 13, 1974.

6. *Overdrive,* July 1974.

7. *Detroit News,* May 4, 1974.

8. Jeremiah O'Leary, *Washington Star,* December 5, 1976. The special investigator whom O'Leary interviewed was Russell L. Bintliff; the man who ordered him to investigate was Colonel Henry H. Tufts, then the CIC commander.

9. *Detroit News,* September 11, 1974.

10. *Overdrive,* April 1975.

11. The Employee Retirement Income Security Act (Pension Reform Act) became law on September 2, 1974, with prevention of depredations against the Teamster pension funds as one of its prime objects. According to the Senate Permanent Investigations Subcommittee, ''The law is designed to require adequate public disclosure of the administrative and financial affairs of employee pensions and welfare plans; establish minimum standards of fiduciary conduct for trustees, administrators, and others dealing with plans; provide for appropriate remedies, sanctions, and ready access to the federal courts; establish standards for vesting and funding; and provide for adequacy of plan assets by insuring unfounded portions of promised benefits.''

12. *Wall Street Journal,* July 24, 1975.

13. *Detroit News,* January 9, 1975.

14. *Detroit News,* January 11, 1975.

CHAPTER 18
Living by the Sword

1. James R. Hoffa (as told to Oscar Fraley), *Hoffa: The Real Story* (New York: Stein and Day, 1975), pp. 217-218.

2. *Ibid.*, p. 15.

3. In April 1972, during a meeting of the IBT general executive board, Frank Fitzsimmons presented his son, Ostrer, and others connected with the insurance plan, and allowed them to make their pitch for the international union's business.

4. *Playboy*, December 1975.

5. Hoffa (as told to Fraley), *op. cit.*, p. 236.

6. Charles Crimaldi (as told to John Kidner), *Crimaldi: Contract Killer* (Washington, D.C.: Acropolis Books Ltd., 1976), p. 217.

CHAPTER 19
The Real Hoffa Legacy

1. *Detroit News,* August 1, 1975.

2. James R. Hoffa (as told to Oscar Fraley), *Hoffa: The Real Story* (New York: Stein and Day, 1975), p. 15.

3. John Kidner, *Crimaldi: Contract Killer* (Washington, D.C.: Acropolis Books Ltd., 1976), p. 218. Crimaldi also told Kidner that John Rosselli's death was the work of the same top mob people who ordered the death of Giancana and Hoffa. Rosselli's dismembered body was found stuffed in a 55-gallon oil drum, floating in a river in Florida, on August 22, 1976. He was last seen on a boat owned by an associate of Santos Trafficante.

4. PROD press release, May 27, 1976.

5. *Ibid.*

6. Teamster advertisement, *Cleveland Plain Dealer,* July 5, 1976.

7. *Wall Street Journal*, January 20, 1976.

8. IBT Convention Proceedings, 1976.

9. *Time* magazine, May 16, 1977, p. 33.

Index